RECONSTRUCTIONS OF EARLY CHRISTIAN DOCUMENTS

Reconstructions of
EARLY CHRISTIAN DOCUMENTS

BY

HERBERT JAMES BARDSLEY

VOL. I

LONDON
SOCIETY FOR PROMOTING
CHRISTIAN KNOWLEDGE
NORTHUMBERLAND AVENUE, W.C. 2
1935

PRINTED IN GREAT BRITAIN BY THE EDINBURGH PRESS, EDINBURGH

CONTENTS

CHAPTER XI

DOCUMENTS AND ABBREVIATIONS

§ 1. It has been necessary to invent a system of abbreviation for references.

1. Gospels are abbreviated thus : EvH (Hebrews), EvvC (Coptic), EvN (Nicodemus), EvP (Peter), etc.

2. In the case of an Acts (A), martyrdom (M), or apocalypse (Ap), the final letter or letters describe the disciple, the penultimate the nature of the work, the initial the language or editor. Sometimes, however, only two of these definitions are given. Thus MPP, MPol =the martyrdoms of Peter and Paul and of Polycarp. AhnApP =the Aknim fragment of Apoc-Pet. EApP =the Ethiopic recension. CMystJ =the Coptic Mysteries of John. CBRB = the Coptic Book of the Resurrection attributed to Bartholomew. SHJ =the Syriac History of John. RobEvvC = Robinson's Coptic Gospels. EP and EPl =the Ethiopic narratives of Peter and Paul. VP =the Vercellensian Acts of Peter. LM and LT =the Acts and martyrdoms of Matthew and Thomas in Lewis's translation of the Arabic. DAdd =the Syriac Doctrine of Addai. Proch =the Prochorus Acts of John. KP =the Preaching of Peter.

3. When a lost document is postulated Q is always used. Thus QPJ and QThec are the documents which underlie Protev.Jac and the various recensions of the story of Thecla.

4. In the case of the Clementines with Waitz I describe the Recognitions, the Homilies and their source as R, H and HR. His KII is described as QC because we shall conclude that the Ebionite Preachings of Peter were part of an early recension of the Romance which survives in the Mardin recension (M) and EP. The anti-Marcionite recension of KII which was used by HR is described as QHR. When citing the Gospels I have sometimes indicated my

view of the origin of a passage by prefixing a letter, *e.g.*
LLk. v. 8.

AA. Acts of Andrew. In one or two places LeuciusA
made slight use of QP. Bonnet, I. 1 f. J, 337. Cf.
James, Apoc. Anec., II. xxix.

AAM. Acts of Andrew and Matthias. It derives from a
lost Acts in common with MM. Walker, 348 f. Abbreviated in J, 453 f. Bonnet, i. 65.

AAPl. Acts of Andrew and Paul. J, 473.

ABarn. The Acts of Barnabas. Bonnet, II. 292. Translated
by Walker (293).

Abd. Abdiæ Apostolica Historia.

AJ. The Acts of John. LeuciusJ used QPl, QP and
Papias. The work was used by Heg. Bonnet, I. 151.
J, 228. Some lost portions survive in edited forms,
e.g. in Proch., 3 f.

AknApP. The Greek fragment of the Apocalypse of Peter.
J, 507.

AnaphPilB. Tischendorf, Evangelia Apocrypha, 420.
Abbreviated in J, 153.

APA. Acts of Peter and Andrew. Bonnet, I. 117. Walker,
368 f. Abbreviated in J, 458 f.

APh. Acts of Philip. Heg. Bonnet, II. 1 f. Abbreviated
in J, 439 f. Tisch. and Walker, 301 f., give 107–end,
6–29, from the Paris MS. 109–144.

APl. A late and orthodox Acts of Paul, which is in places
based on the Leucian Acts. Heg. The Greek of the
Thecla section and the martyrdom is printed in Lipsius,
i. 235. J, 270.

APP. Acts of Peter and Paul, Lipsius, 178. Walker, 256.

ApPl. The apocalypse of Paul is translated from the Latin
recension in J, 254. For information, see James Texts
and Studies, ii. 1.

ArmCall. The Acts of Callistratus translated from the
Armenian by F. C. Conybeare in his Monuments of
Early Christianity (p. 289).

ArmThec. Conybeare, 61.

ArmPhoc. The Acts of Phocas Conybeare, 103.

AscIs ed. Charles. Burkitt (Schweich Lectures, 45) against Charles holds that the whole work is Christian. In our view virtually the whole of it derives from KP.

AT. Acts of Thomas. Bonnet, II. 99. The Syriac is translated by W. Wright in his Apocryphal Acts of Apostles, ii. 146 f. Tisch. and Walker, 389 f. have 1–38, 42–61 and an abbreviated martyrdom.

AThadd. The various Thaddæan Acts seem to derive from a lost QThadd. Lipsius, 273.

ATim. See Lips., iii. 372 f.

ATit. The Greek Acts of Titus are printed by James in JTS, vi. 549 f.

AXanth. The Acts of Xanthippus and Polyxena. See James Apoc. Anec., ii. 43 f.

Bonnet. Maximilian Ac. App. Apocr., ii. Lipsiae, 1903.

CApPl. The Coptic recension of ApocPl is occasionally used in J, 526 f.

CBRB. The Coptic Book of the Resurrection by Bartholomew. Translated by E. A. W. Budge in Coptic Apocrypha (London, 1913), 179 f. Abbreviated in J, 181.

CEncJB. The John of the Coptic Encomium of John Baptist (Copt. Apocr.), 342 f., was originally the apostle.

CerM. The edition of M used by the followers of Cerinthus, whether M or a recension of M.

CHom. Coptic Homilies. E. A. W. Budge. British Museum.

ClemBps. The Clementine Bishops list is throughout based on Heg. See § 7, iv.

CMiscT. Coptic Miscellaneous Texts translated by E. A. W. Budge (British Museum).

CMystJ. The Mysteries of John (Copt. Apocr., 241 f.), an apocalypse of heretical origin.

CurSCeph. Translated from the Syriac by Cureton in Ancient Syrian Documents, 35 f.

DAdd. The Doctrine of Addai, translated by George Phillips. London, 1876. Cf. Burkitt Early E. Christ., 17 f.

The Dormitios are summarised in J, 194 f.

EApP. The Ethiopic Apocalypse of Peter is translated into English in J, 510 f.

Easton. A Commentary on Luke, by Burton Scott Easton. Edinburgh: T. & T. Clark, 1926.

Elkesai. The Book of Elkesai, which Alcibiades based on J.

II. Enoch. The Slavonic Enoch. Ed. Charles.

EpApp. The Epistle of the Apostles is translated in J, 485 f. It is largely based on EvXII.

EpClem. The epistle of Clement to James. It contains some matter which derives through QC from QP.

EP and EPl are Acts of Peter and Paul which are only found in the Ethiopic Contendings of the Apostles, translated by E. A. W. Budge. London, 1901. They derive in common from QEPP, a lost Acts.

Epiph. Hom. Portions of Homilies of Epiphanius, translated from the Armenian by Franko in ZNTW, vii. 318 f.

EusThadd. The Thaddæus fragment found in H.E., I. xiii., is based on QThadd.

EvB. The Gospel of Bartholomew is translated in J, 166 f.

EvEb. The fragments of the Gospel of the Ebionites are translated in J, 8 f.

EvH. Our numeration of the fragments of the Gospel of the Hebrews gives their order in J, where 2–10 are on p. 2, 11–16 on p. 3, 17–22 on p. 4, 23–32 on p. 5, 33–36 on p. 6, 37–51 on p. 7. On our view the peculiarities of the Gospel are due to a process of glossation (Schmidke).

EvInf. The Arabic Gospel of the Infancy. Tischendorf, 177; Walker, 125.

EvM. The apocryphal Gospel of Matthew is based on QPJ. Tischendorf, 50; Walker, 16 f. Summarised in J, 70 f.

EvN. The Acts of Pilate attributed to Nicodemus. Tischendorf, 203; J, 94 f.; Walker (100 f.).

EvP. The Gospel of Peter is translated in J, 90. It is based on EvXII. It is well annotated by H. B. Swete.

EvT. The Gospel of Thomas is a recension of the Leucian gospel of Thomas. Tischendorf, 134; Walker, 78; J, 49 and 14.

EvvC. Coptic gospel fragments translated in J, 147. They are composite.

EvXII. The companion volume of QP. It was in the form of a letter and attributed to the twelve.

FrankoAP. Translated from the Slavonic by Franko in ZNTW, iii. 315 f. Probably composite.

FrankoClem. The Slavonic of this Acts is translated by Franko in ZNTW, iii. 146 f.

H. The Clementine Homilies abbreviated HR.

Heg. Hegesippus.

HegMJas. HE, II. xxiii.

Hennecke. Commentaries on the NT Apocrypha, edited by Edgar Hennecke. Vol. ii. Tübingen, 1914.

HEvXII. The Gospel of the Twelve Apostles together with the Apocalypses of each. Translated by J. Rendel Harris. Cambridge, 1900. Based on QP and QPl.

HistJos. The history of Joseph the Carpenter (Tischendorf, 115; Walker, 62. Robinson, Coptic Gospels, 130).

HistPatr. The Arabic History of the Patriarchs of Alexandria is translated in Patrologia Orientalis, Vol. I. The writer used Heg and Origen.

HR, the source common to R and H, was a drastic revision of QHR.

J. The Steps of James. See §§ 13, 26.

J followed by a numeral. The Apocryphal New Testament. M. R. James : Oxford, 1924.

HR. The source common to H and the Clementine Recognitions, and usually regarded as the Grundschrift.

JamesAT. The Greek recension of LT printed in James Apoc. Anec., ii. 28.

JerBps. The list of the bishops of Jerusalem is discussed by Zahn in Forsch, vi. 221 and by Turner in JTS, I.

KP. The Preaching of Peter. The fragments are best studied in das Ker. Pet. by von Dobschutz. Leipzig, 1893. They are found in J, 16 f.

L. These Acts are translated from the Arabic by Agnes Smith Lewis in Horae Semiticae, IV. They are all influenced by Heg. This is most clearly seen if LJas, 144 f. is compared with HE, II. xxiii. Cf. Lawlor, 4 f.

Lagarde DAdd (Reliquiae JEA. Leipzig, 1856).

Lawlor. Eusebiana, by H. J. Lawlor. Oxford, 1912.

Lips. i.–iv. Die Apocryphen Apostelgeschichten. Schewet-schke Braunsenweig, by R. A. Lipsius.

Lipsius. Acta Apostoloreum Apocrypha' edd R. A. Lipsius. M. Bonnet. Lipsiae, 1891.

M. Except in discussions of the Clementines M is the source of Matt reconstructed by Streeter (230).

M. The Mardin recension of the Clementine Romance, printed in the Bulletin of the John Rylands Library, Manchester IV. 59. It derives from QC independently of HR.

McNeile. Commentary on Matthew, by Alan Hugh Mac-Neile. Macmillan, 1915.

MirKh. The legend of Khonai derives ultimately from Heg. See Ramsay, Ch. Rom. Emp. 464.

MM. The Martyrdom of Matthew which derives from the source of AAM is printed in Bonnet, i. 217. Walker 373 f.

MPl, the conclusion of APl, is printed in Lipsius, 103.

MPP. The Martyrdom of Peter and Paul is printed in Lipsius, 118; Walker, 260 f. (deduct 21 from the numeration). Discussed by Schmiedel in Enc. Bib., 4612 f.

NZos. The narrative of Zosimus is printed by James in Apocr. Anec. i. 86,.

Oxyrrh Pap (sayings) are translated in J, 25 f. Some of them derive from QPl.

Photius. See § 22.

PJ. Protevangelium Jacobi is translated in J, 39. It is based on QPJ and is composite. Tischendorf, 1; Walker, 1. For Arabic, see STrans.

Proch. The Prochorus Acts of John are printed by Zahn in Acta Johannis. They are in some sections based on AJ.

PsCyprian. See § 23.

PsPhilo. Translated by James (S.P.C.K.). See H. Thackeray, S. Paul and Cont. Jewish Thought, 204 f.

QC. The eight books of the Ebionite Romance and source of QHR.

QEPP is the lost source of EP and EPl.

QHR.   The antiMarcionite recension of QC in ten books. The source of HR.

QIrJos.   A lost source which referred to Irenæus and Josephus. Josephus must be Heg, and some work of Hippolytus who used both writers must have been used by the citator.

QP is an Acts which we reconstruct and identify with the Leucian Acts of Peter.

QPJ (the source of PJ and some Coptic matter) is the ancient Book of James.

QPl is an Acts which we reconstruct and identify with the Leucian Acts of Paul.

QPV.   The source of the two recensions of AJ, 1–17.

QThec.   The source of the existing recensions of Thecla, *i.e.* the story of Thecla.

QVitAnd.   The sources of the Life of Andrew collected in Lips., i. 557 f.   Heg.

R.   The Clementine Recognitions derive not only like H from HR but also from QHR the source of HR.

RobEvvC.   Coptic Apocryphal Gospels by Forbes Robinson. Cambridge Texts and Studies, Vol. IV.

RSteph.   A centoistic martyrdom in bad disorder and influenced by Acts.   It is abbreviated in J, 564.   Franko published it in ZNTW vii. 151.

SachauApP.   Z. f. Wiss. Thed., 1893, 471 f.

SchmidtEvvC.   Some Coptic fragments which deprave EvT were deciphered by Schmidt and are printed by Hennicke in NT Apokryphen, i. 42.

SHJ.   The Syriac History of John occurs in Wright, Apocr. Acts, 1 f.

SHPh.   The history of Philip occurs in Wright, 69 f.   Heg.

SObsBVM.   See J, 224.

SolokoffAP.   See Lips., ii.

STrans.   The Syriac Transitus BVM is an important document and is abbreviated in J, 219.   It is translated by Agnes Smith Lewis in Studia Sinaitica XI and contains PJ.   Clay, Cambridge, 1902.

Streeter (Burnett Hillman).   Unless otherwise stated The Four Gospels.   Macmillan, 1924.

B

Taylor.　Behind the Third Gospel, by　Vincent Taylor.
　　Oxford, 1926.

Tischendorf.　Constantin Evangela Apocry.　Lipsiae, 1853.

TransPh.　The Translation of Philip is printed by James in
　　Apocr. Anec., i. 161.

Vardan.　The references are to the Solutions which I read
　　in a French translation by M. Prudhomme, published
　　in Paris, ? 1850.　My reference numbers are defaced,
　　and there seems to be no copy of the work in England.
　　It is very short.

VitPol.　The Greek of the Pionian Life of Polycarp is
　　annotated and printed by Lightfoot in Ap. Fath., II. ii.
　　It is based on Heg.　Corson has a discussion in ZNTW
　　and Streeter in Prim. Ch. 265.

VP.　The Vercellensian Acts of Peter are printed in Lips., 45
　　and translated in J, 300 f.　Discussed by Schmiedel in
　　Enc. Bib., 4611.　Heg.

Walker.　The Ante-Nicene Christian Library, Vol. XVI.
　　A. Walker.　Apocr. Gospels, &c.　Edinburgh, 1870.

Wright (William).　The (Syriac) Apocryphal Acts of
　　Apostles.　London, 1871.

CHAPTER I

INTRODUCTION

§ 2. It is generally held that, with the possible exception of the story of Thecla, the Christian apocrypha contain no matter and present no problems which concern the historian of the apostolic age, and that they are a vast rubbish-heap which began to accumulate a generation or two after the close of that period and which it would be useless for him to examine. Yet on the surface of our documents there are many facts which suggest doubts as to the justice of this view. Whence derive the allusions to Hyrcanus, Pompey, Archelaus, Agrippa, the procurators Marcellus, Tiberius Alexander, Albinus and the recall of Pilate ? What is the source of the accurate topographical allusions and the explanation of hundreds of parallels which connect documents which at first sight seem to have nothing to do with each other ? What is the significance of the indications that the earliest of the extant Acts, AJ, is secondary and composite ? Again, there is much Ascension matter. How is it that it is hardly influenced by the NT ? Moreover, when it is brought together it becomes at once clear that it represents a narrative in which the apostles assembled in Gethsemane, and Christ discoursed with Peter, James, John and Andrew (cf. Mk. xiii. 3), that when they were come together (Ac. i. 6) Christ imparted the Spirit by inflation and that He ascended *after* He was encompassed by the cloud (cf. the West. variant at Ac. i. 9). Later in the day the apostles and others with them in their ecstasy spake in the tongues which they had been hearing in the streets of Jerusalem : Greek, Latin, and the two dialects of Aramaic. What is the value of this tradition, and how are we to account for it ? Probably most scholars are unaware of its existence and of many other splinters and fragments which are scattered over some sixty documents like coins and pieces of broken pottery in the surface soil of the mounds which conceal a buried city.

§ 3. When we turn to the Fathers our curiosity is again stimulated by the very little that they have to tell us. The most important name in connection with the Acta is that of Leucius, whom later notices represent as an important heresiarch, and who according to Jerome and Epiphanius was a contemporary of S. John. Photius ascribes to him an incident which was used by Basilides, and an Acts of Paul which cannot be the extant Acts of Paul. PsCyprian describes a Preaching of Paul, and Origen attributes to Acts of Paul *Domine quo vadis?* These notices also cannot refer to APl. Schmidt, it is true, says that the knowledge of Photius was superficial (*Die Alten Petrusakten*, 69), and James doubts the very existence of the Acts described by psCyprian, questions the accuracy of Origen and does not so much as mention the fact that Epiphanius and Jerome agree in making the writer a contemporary of S. John. But it is not a satisfactory situation that the two greatest living authorities on our subject should feel themselves compelled to scout almost all the patristic evidence there is. Clearly then some attempt should be made to excavate the rubbish-heap; but no one who knows anything about the NT apocrypha will suppose that the task will be an easy one.

§ 4. It will be one of our difficulties that we shall not be able to follow the normal procedure and prove first one point and then another advancing from positions generally accepted to the probanda, from the known to the unknown, from the easier to the more difficult problems. The situation may best be described by an illustration. Let us suppose that political motives led an artist to recast an historical picture, a second acting from somewhat different motives to combine the scheme and ideas of these two pictures and a third to combine the original picture with matter from the second misrepresentation of it. We will also suppose that the four pictures were converted into jigsaw puzzles which were to some extent mixed, that two-thirds of the fragments were lost and that the remainder were used as the centoists used lines of Homer in new combinations, and that they suffered in the process. In such a case a reconstructor of the original pictures would probably first draw such parts of them as he had reconstructed and then justify his procedure in detail. Our task will be both easier and more complex than that just described, but the illustration describes the plan of the book. The group of hypotheses in which the processes of comparison have resulted must be stated at the outset and their validity assumed.

The group of interrelated hypotheses now to be stated accounts for a multitude of related facts which occur in contexts which are for the most part formless and chaotic. An analysis which was based on a study of some of the narratives which contain them results in a record of the development of the earliest Christological controversies. Moreover, while the large and difficult literature with which we are concerned presents many problems which will remain unsolved, there is no group of parallel passages which has not supplied verifications of the fundamental positions which are now to be stated. It may be added that, if in the working out of a theory based on a great mass of difficult data it has not seemed worth while to use continually such phrases as " probably," " almost certainly," or " in the writer's judgment," on the other hand it is probable that many of the statements which will be made are more secure than they will seem to be, and that no reference or citation has been adduced without a previous study of the context in which it occurs and regard to the methods of the writer. Many comparisons of contexts have been made of which nothing will be said.

§ 5. The following canons of apocryphal criticism will be assumed.

1. The first canon is of great importance and may be stated without any qualification. *No apocryphist whose work either survives or underlies any existing document was capable of inventing a statement purporting to be historical*

which would possess any vraisemblance for a modern scholar. This canon, for instance, excludes the hypothesis that the Ascension matter described above is from the pen of an apocryphist.

2. *The fundamental depravations of the primary apocryphal Acts, the Preaching of Peter, were due to doctrinal motives which can be determined.* They were the work of the Ebionite J and Leucius. The latter introduced much matter into the apocryphal tradition, but it is middrash and easily detected. There was much invention in his narratives of Christ, but in practice this fact does not reduce the value of our canon. The earliest apocryphists did not write to satisfy curiosity as to the lives of Christ and His apostles.

3. All or almost all the contexts which we shall use show clear traces of the influence of a source. In such contexts the following canon holds good : *The secondary apocryphists hardly ever invent ; they quarry, pervert and retessellate.* Their method is well described by Tertullian in a sentence cited by Zahn : *Quis tam otiosus stilo ut materias habens fingat ?* (The exceptions are usually obvious, *e.g.* the one or two stories introduced by a later editor in EPl.)

4. *The interrelations of the extant apocrypha are the relations of the sources of Hegesippus.* Heg's sources can be determined, and the argument from elimination used with complete security. One or two exceptions, *e.g.* the influence of STrans on DAdd and that of AT on LT, are negligible.

§ 6. On the other hand the following difficulties confront us.

1. *There are no or hardly any traces of large sections of the primary Acts.*

2. *Ancient matter sometimes survives in a form so depraved that it is hardly possible to use it.*

3. *No summary of any primary Acts or any section of a primary Act survives, and the data for the reconstruction of the sequences of incidents are very rare.* On the other hand

the sequences of KP were largely those of Acts, and the complications which arise from the possibility of the direct influence of Acts fewer than might have been expected. Leucian matter occasionally shows a knowledge of Acts, but there is not a particle of evidence which suggests that Acts influenced either the Preaching of Peter (KP) or the Steps of James (J).

It was not until much of this work was in type that my views of the origins of EvT and EvXII became quite clear. I now hold that they were companion volumes to QPl and QP. Much gospel matter is described by these symbols. It is still more unfortunate that I did not discover until the last moment that Streeter's Ebionite gospel M was probably identical with the Cerinthian Matthew and certainly a source of our Mk and the fountainhead of the apocrypha.

I have been urged to write prolegomena to the documents which will be used, but, even if I were much better equipped for the task than I am, I should hesitate to do so not only from a reluctance to increase the size of my book but also from a fear lest discussion should be side-tracked into debates about the things which matter least. The reasonableness of this position may be shewn by another illustration of the nature of our task. If a thousand years hence our gospels had been lost and a writer of that age endeavoured to reconstruct them from the remains of the sermons of the last four centuries he would not be concerned with the preachers, their dates, and other matters which would interest church historians, but only with the way in which these preachers were likely to have used the lost documents which he was reconstructing. Possibly at an advanced stage of the discussion some extension of the enquiry might be desirable, but to write prolegomena to most of the sermons would be useless.

It follows that the apocrypha except for the advanced student must be regarded as a single book, and one written in a way which is quite unique. As a rule the reader would do well to pay little attention to the question what document is being cited. But there are some provisos.

i. Our maxim does not apply in the case of writers who do not quarry from a variety of sources. (*a*) ApP and EvP come under this head. Almost the whole of AscIs is based on KP. Almost the whole of EpiphHom follows Heg closely. There is hardly any retesselation in the Clementines. (*b*) The L group is important if only because EP and EPl belong to it. EP, 466–491 preserves for the most part Heg's wording and order. (*c*) I know very little about the history of CBRB and the fragments which I call EvvC and RobEvvC, but most of the matter thus described derives from EvT.

ii. AJ and the Clementines must be distinguished from all other Acts because AJ is earlier than Heg, and Heg's influence on R and H is not great.

iii. The reader who wishes to form an independent judgment of the evidence might do well to study with the help of the index the contexts of which most use has been made. I may add that he will do well to read the first paragraph in § 1.

§ 7. In view of the central place which Heg will occupy in the investigations presented both in this volume and the next, I must state at the outset the main positions at which I have arrived with respect to his work.

i. The hypothesis of the influence of Heg on the Acta originated in the observation that certain recurrences of incidents suggest that the writers of the Acta derived from the primary Acts through a volume of extracts.

ii. The Apocrypha contain topographical and geographical allusions which cannot be due to the secondary writers. The only instances which occur to me in which they used their personal knowledge are an allusion to the ordination of Palut by Serapion of Antioch and a few proper names (*e.g.* in the Acts of Thomas (AT)). On the other hand the author of KP (psMark) collected traditions, and Leucius occasionally used his personal knowledge, but the knowledge of Asia and Asian events shewn by the author of AJ (LeuciusJ) is due to his use of Papias. To return, the matter referred to suggests that the secondary writers used a work whose author had travelled from

Jerusalem, (*a*) through Bethgubrin and Azotus to Alexandria, (*b*) through Samaria and Paneas to Damascus, (*c*) along the Syrian coast, across Asia to Corinth, Puteoli and Rome.

iii. The writer of the source was a chronologist and was much interested in the names of rulers. The names of the procurators of Judæa derive from him, and he used Josephus. He was acquainted with ordinations by S. Mark at Alexandria (LMk, 149) and in a context in which he sent the evangelist to that city he said that Evodius the son of Lendæus was ordained at Antioch (EP 509). Sub FrankoClem, 149 (*ZNTW*, iii.) he referred to the ordinations of Linus and Ignatius. He held that S. Peter was twenty-five years bishop of Rome and suffered under Nero who reigned thirteen years (CurSCeph 40, DAdd 50). We shall find a contact with the fictitious list of the bishops of Jerusalem.

iv. The Clementine Bishops list (ClemBps), a passage which is of great importance and which in the next volume will be shewn to be based throughout on Heg (Ap. Const., vii. 46), gives the four ordinations mentioned above and shews a knowledge of three early Acts one of which only survives in the named fragments of Heg.

v. Epiphanius (whose use of Heg in c. Hær. has been well discussed by Lawlor) in his Homilies uses protevangelical matter which we shall attribute to KP. In connection with it he refers to Jewish chroniclers and uses matter which occurs in an Acts based on Heg's Martyrdom of James. He says that Ephratah in " our ancestral tongue " means Fruitbearing (§ 142).

vi. In some half-dozen passages Heg is cited by the other form of his name, Josephus (§ 171).

vii. The use of Heg in LJas is undoubtedly independent of HE, II. xxiii. LJas occurs in our largest and most important group of documents. Cf. Lips., Apocr. Ap., iii. 253.

viii. Heg's narratives of the Desposyni prove that he used an apocryphal Acts. He described the position of the tomb of James, mentioned the Antinioean games and Antinoopolis (HE, IV. viii.). When he arrived at Rome he compiled the " succession " of the Roman bishops and he tells us that *in every succession and in every city that which the Law and the Prophets and the Lord preach is faithfully followed* (HE, IV. xxii.). We infer that he made investigations in the cities through which he journeyed similar to those which he made at Rome. The title of his work (*Hypomnemata*) accords with our view of its contents. Like the Latin *commentarii* the word was applied to collections of the raw materials of history.

ix. It is in favour of the hypothesis that the existing Acta derive from a writer who excerpted from the earlier Acts and not from those Acts themselves, that if we except the Clementines and AJ. works which are not based on Heg, no existing Acts reproduces, perverts or abbreviates stretches of earlier narratives which are of any length, the story of Thecla excepted.

x. The evidence of one of our Acts (EP) indicates that Heg in a series of excerpts from the primary Acts brought the apostles from Jerusalem to Rome. This evidence when combined with that which is supplied by ClemBps, with that of the matter in Iren., I. and III. and Tert., de Præscr. which we shall attribute to Heg and with the fact that the Martyrdom of James occurred in Hypomn., V. suggests that in Books I. and II. Heg brought the apostles to Rome and narrated the Neronian persecution, that in III. he described the earliest heresies and stated when and by whom they were first taught at Rome. The climax of the work was at the close of III, at which point Heg narrated how Polycarp answered Valentinus and Marcion at Rome. If the death of S. John had seemed to Papias to close the apostolic era, the Martyrdom of Polycarp seemed to Heg to close the subapostolic. Hypomn., IV. dealt with Asia and the heresies of Cerinthus and the Nicolaitans, V. with the Desposyni, matters connected with Christ's origin and the history of the church of Jerusalem.

xi. Our reconstructions of Heg tally with the account of his work given by Jerome who elsewhere shews a knowledge of it : *Heg, who was not far removed from the times of the apostles, narrated the history of the church from the Passion to his own times. Collecting matter which would be of service to his readers from all quarters he wrote five books in a simple style* (de Vir. Ill., 22). It will be shewn below that Heg preserved Leucian narratives of the Passion.

xii. Eusebius who made more use of Heg than he acknowledged, mentioned his simple style, a phrase which Jerome remembered, and probably regarded him as being, like Papias, too credulous. Now it may be conceded that Eusebius, whose style was the worst possible, had more capacity for writing scientific history than Heg, but, if we are right, Heg was what the writer who belittled him was not, in a very true sense, a scientific historian. He saw that something more than an appeal to the documents was needed for the confutation of the Gnostics; he did a new thing and investigated the successions and traditions of the more important churches. He also set forth in excerpts the discrepant data and compared them, discussing the chronological problems which they presented and using in one case data provided by Josephus. His mistakes were due to the fact that he adopted absurd harmonisations where harmonisation was impossible and not to any failures in his tireless industry and in his determination to base his position on an accurate examination of the whole of the evidence. Eusebius evaded the problems stated by Heg, but happily accepted the absurd Martyrdom of James and the impossible story of the conversion of Abgar by Thaddæus. These documents had the merit of raising no obvious difficulties.

xiii. It is hardly possible to exaggerate the influence of Heg on later Christian literature. With the probable exception of the recension of the Acts of Thecla which underlies the existing narratives there is no Acts which is later than Heg which is not influenced by him and probably almost all are quarried from him. Other apocryphal matter also for the most part derives from him.

§ 8. The following table gives the apocryphal Acts which were used by Heg and their sources and their approximate dates :

1. The Preaching of Peter (KP : A.D. ? 80–90) :
   derived from the sources of I Acts, a Cæsarean manual,
   M and oral tradition, was directed against the Jews.

2. The Steps of James (J : c. A.D. 100):
   derived from KP, tradition, was directed against S. Paul,
   S. John and the apostolic discipline.

3. The Preaching of Paul (QPl : A.D. 101–103):
   derived from M, KP, J : Jn., Acts, tradition was directed
   against Cerinthus and the apostolic discipline.

4. The Acts of Peter (QP : A.D. c. 102–104):
   derived from KP, QPl, was directed against Leucius.

5. The Ebionite Romance (QC : A.D. ? 115–150).
   derived from J, QP, Papias, was directed against S. Paul
   and Papias :

6. The Acts of John (AJ : A.D. ? 115–? 155):
   derived from Papias, QPl and QP.

7. The Acts of the Desposyni (QDesp : A.D. ? 130–? 160):
   derived from QPl and traditions.

§ 9. Our reconstructions of the primary Acts may now
be summarised.

I. Matter which derives from the Preaching of Peter
(KP) presents parallels with every part of I. Acts.
Christ ascended at Pentecost after imparting the Spirit.
There was much pre-Ascension discourse. The apostles
were caught up into heaven, and at a eucharist which was
celebrated at the Holy Sepulchre Peter narrated their
experiences, which were written by John Mark. In a
parallel with Ac. iv. 6 Jonathan (John), Eleazar and Phinees
were mentioned. Stephen, who had become a deacon in
the third year, debated at the sixth passover with Saul and
the seven sects of the Jews on the related subjects of the
triplex munus and the virgin birth and was brought before
Pilate. The narrative had contacts with the Markan Passion.
At Samaria Simon wept and later at Cæsarea opposed
Peter. Peter established the evangelistic work of Philip not
only in that city but also at Lydda and Azotus, at which
city Mark was with him. At Joppa he stayed at the house
of Tabitha. At Cæsarea he was accompanied not only by

John (Mark) but also by Æneas, his wife, Mark's mother, Tabitha the daughter of Tobias the son of Tobias, a Jew of rank who lived at Cæsarea and whose house became his head-quarters, the daughters of Gamaliel and Nicodemus and other women, and by six " apostles " of the church of Jerusalem, Zacharias Zacchæus, Joseph Justus Barsabas, Judas Julianus Barsabas, Benjamin Alexander, Reuben Rufus and Ananias Antonius the son of Saphira. When the seven arrived at the prætorium a sentry announced them and Theophilus, whom KP identified with Pilate's successor Marcellus, ran out to welcome them. Peter healed his " lad " and in a long sermon based an attack on idolatry on the early chapters of Genesis. Adducing many prophetic testimonies he narrated Christ's career and the rejection at Jerusalem of Him who was Lord of all. There were thirty baptisms. The populace was evangelised and there were other baptisms. Peter stayed three months and ordained Theophilus and his son Cornelius who was a *frumentarius*. At the ordination he preached a long didactic sermon which was probably based upon a primitive manual. Peter left a gospel and a manual for the use of the newly founded church, returned for the seventh passover and reported what God had wrought.

§ 10. After the twelfth passover Peter evangelised the towns of the Syrian coast as far as Laodicea but failed to reach Antioch. The publicani had made trouble at Cæsarea, and a long and touching narrative of the Martyrdom of James closed with his execution in the *agora*. Matthew was murdered by being secretly thrown into the sea. Leading Cæsarean Christians had pleaded that James might be exiled and warned the disciples at Jerusalem that Peter's arrest was contemplated. He was persuaded to fly, but in a vision heard Christ say: " I go to Jerusalem to be crucified." He returned and was arrested. It was his friends at court, we may conjecture, who arranged his escape, and he ultimately reached Antioch. Barnabas and Saul evangelised in Cyprus or Galatia. In the KP narrative of the council which underlies Didasc (xxiv.) Paul took no part in the actual proceedings of the council.

The parallels of this matter with Acts are due to the fact that, like S. Luke, the writer (psMark) used a Markan Acts of Peter (I Ac. Mc.) and a Markan Acts of Barnabas.

§ 11. Our analysis will compel us to attribute to KP not a little matter which cannot have occurred in the course of the narrative just summarised. We infer that it occurred in a long introduction which narrated the historical setting of the apostolic preaching and some of the main points in the career of the Jesus whom Peter preached. The writer was much interested in the contacts of Christianity with the Roman Empire. There were allusions therefore to Pompey, Hyrcanus and Augustus and a passage of some length which spoke of the services of Theophilus to the empire. The Neronian persecution was narrated and also the fall of Jerusalem, which event was treated as the penalty for the Crucifixion and was the climax of the introduction. The Virgin Birth was narrated at length, the Crucifixion and the visible emergence of Christ from the tomb. Mark, the writer, introduced himself as the son of Aristobulus and as connected with Peter and the cousin of Barnabas, who was a disciple of Gamaliel. He cited a letter of Peter which underlies 2 Pet., i. 13–16 and which bade him write the work.

PsMark wrote after the fall of Jerusalem and the publication of the First Gospel, but before the date of I. Clem. and probably before the excommunication of Christians from the synagogue as *minim*. It reflected the controversies of the period in its violent antiJudaism. The writer's theology was mythological and influenced by the Tiamat legend. The miraculous nativity was part of the deception of the devil. The Incarnation was a paradox : God suffered. The writer supported his positions by fabricated prophetic testimonies. The work was one of some ability and written in a rhetorical style.

§ 12. The fragments of KP cited by Clement of Alexandria are printed in J, 16 f. The following matter is sufficient for our purpose and to give an idea of the subjects of the fragments.

Fragm. 2. . . . *One God . . . the invisible who seest all, the uncontainable who containest all* . . . Note the oxymora.

Fragm. 3. *Do not worship after the manner of the Greeks . . . cats and dogs . . .*

Fragm. 4. *. . . nor as the Jews who suppose that they alone know God.* Polemic follows.

Fragm. 5. *. . . A new covenant . . . Worship God in a new way, as a third race, Christians.*

Fragm. 6. *. . . If any of Israel will repent . . . his sins shall be forgiven him. After twelve years go out into the inhabited earth.*

Fragm. 7. *I chose out you twelve evangelising that there is one God, to declare what shall be, that they which have heard and believed may be saved and that they which have not believed . . . not having any defence.*

Fragm. 9. *. . . We found in the prophets . . . His coming and death and cross and the rest of the torments which the Jews inflicted on Him and His resurrection before Jerusalem was judged* (so rightly v. Dobsch.) *as all these were written— what he must needs suffer and the future after Him.*

Fragm. 10. *. . . We know that God in very deed ordained them, and we say nothing without* (*citing a prophetic*) *scripture.*

§ 13. II. The Steps of James (J : cf. § 24) probably began with an introduction, in the course of which was narrated the attempt of Saul, " the Tarsian " and a gentile, to marry the high priest's daughter. It contained a letter of James. Christ in the main narrative appeared to James on Olivet, gave him a copy of the true law without the interpolations which ordained sacrifice, and appointed him bishop of Jerusalem and head of the whole Church. James sent to Cæsarea his brother Judas who ordained there Zacchæus and eleven other Jews who had accompanied him. Judas went to the East and wrote to James a letter in which he described the ideal life of the nine and a half tribes. He returned for the seventh passover. The discourses of James, which were written by his deacon Ananias, had exercised great influence. At the seventh passover he debated like Stephen with the seven sects and had almost persuaded Caiaphas and the people to be baptised, but the

" Tarsian " ruined everything. He murdered James, pursued Judas (who succeeded James) to Antioch, there worshipped in a heathen temple and persuaded the magistrates to persecute. He followed Judas to Rome and appeared against him before Nero with the result that Judas suffered Peter's death.

J was used by Leucius, psClement and Alcibiades, and was perhaps written c. A.D. 100, and I attribute it to Cerinthus.

§ 14. III. The Asian elder who wrote the Acts of Paul attributed the work to Leucius Dionysius Cornelius. The companion gospel (EvT) replied to the Cerinthian and was attributed to Judas Barnabas Matthias (Matthew), Thomas, who was spiritually Christ's twin-brother. The gospel expanded and altered in the interest of docetism the evangelical element in KP. Not only Pilate but also Gamaliel wrote motived fictions. The question asked by Simon in VP, 23, *Deus nascitur ? crucifigitur ?* was answered with an emphatic, No. But if the paradoxical Christology of KP was obviously impossible, KP supplied the answer to the problem which it raised. If Christ assumed the form of the angels when descending through the heavens and deceived Satan He could assume merely the semblance of humanity and deceive the twelve. His nativity was heavenly, and His mother Mary the angel of the Spirit. When the Jews supposed that He was dying on the cross He ascended with His apostles from Olivet. He returned to the cross, cheated Satan, cursed Judas, smashed hell, and then accompanied by His mother-angel revealed these mysteries to the women at the sepulchre.

§ 15. The narrative of QPl probably began with the arrival of Theophilus at Cæsarea before the non-Passion. Christ accompanied by His mother appeared to John upon Olivet and gave him a mystical book in which was written the secret of the heavenly nativity. After Pentecost, in a narrative based on J, Judas founded the church of Cæsarea. Judas as in J ordained Zacchæus and eleven other elders. Theophilus was recalled to Rome and, on his return at the end of the fifth year, enraged by the encratism which they had taught his wife, attempted to burn the apostles. Judas went to the east. Later John was transported thither and saw an apocalypse. He was transported back to Cæsarea where he spent the last four months of the first septennium. The seven sons of Theophilus were ordained deacons, and the apostle returned to Jerusalem. Judas had baptized Cornelius by the name Theodore or Theodas which was said to have been the Greek for his own name, Matthias.

James, whose preaching as in J had been recorded, was as in J killed, but not by Saul. The apostles discussed the discipline which should be taught the nations, and Christ supported the Nicolaitan position advocated by Paul. John and Judas were transported to Antioch, and a Nicolaitan narrative followed. John and Judas journeyed with Leucius to Cyprus and Iconium. Here they met Paul, who had converted Thecla. Paul taught Leucius his mysteries and rebaptized him, giving him his own name and making him his disciple. There was Hierapolis matter in which Philip and John played a part. At Ephesus, when Paul was thrown to the lions Thecla's lioness licked his feet. It confessed its faith and was baptized. John and Judas arrived at Rome followed by Paul, Leucius and Titus and then by Peter. Simon, who took the place of the Saul of J, stirred up mischief, and a statue was erected to him as " the new god." Paul was beheaded. The incident *Domine quo vadis?* was moved to Rome, and in an haggadic narrative Peter was crucified head downwards. The suffering which Christ had predicted for John would occur in the last days to which John would survive.

§ 16. Leucius used not only KP and J but also the Gospels, Acts and the Pastoral epistles, a narrative of Thecla, traditions of S. John and the Lycus valley and a version of the *pericope adulteræ*. His date preceded A.D. 104, the date which Heg gave for S. John's death. Ignatius (A.D. 105) and Papias directed their polemic against him, and his work much influenced the earliest heresies. He had very marked peculiarities. He could be eloquent, but he was verbose and repeated himself. His narratives were

c

often absurd, and it was perhaps with a view to investing them with vraisemblance that he inserted as many names as possible.

The work of Leucius will be described as QPl and the Leucian Acts of Peter as QP, the terms which I used when I had discovered the documents but had not identified them. The identifications will be assumed, and the symbols will remind the reader that the assumptions are *probanda*. These terms for a similar reason will be often applied to EvT and EvXII. I shall describe the writers who used Leucius and adopted his pseudonym as LeuciusJ, etc.

§ 17. IV. The fact that the Leucian Acts of Peter was little more than a compilation makes it at once more difficult and less important to restore it. The narrative followed that of QPl up to the seventh passover. The seventh year of KP in QP became the eighth, but Peter went to Cæsarea to refound a church which had been corrupted by Simon. After the eighth passover Peter made a journey to Rome which was suggested by that which in QPl Judas made after the seventh. After the twelfth as in KP he evangelised the Syrian seaboard. A narrative of the Herodian persecution followed which was based on KP but influenced by QPl.

Against Leucius LeuciusP asserted the authority of the twelve and the historicity of the credal facts. The Lord's mother became a woman, and her ascension became her assumption after her death, the Good Friday apocalypse being moved to the evening of Easterday. There is a conflict of evidence as to the date of the Assumption, but nothing of importance seems to depend on it. Until the last moment I held that the Assumption was immediately after the seventh passover. It has not seemed worth while to disturb the type. LeuciusP attributed his gospel to the twelve.

It is probable that, owing to the fact that it was directed against Leucius and contained much of the matter which his readers found attractive, QP exercised much influence during the subapostolic age. Unfortunately Heg preferred

it to KP.   For us its value consists in the fact that it preserved KP and QPl in a form which was not adulterated
from other sources.   Probably LeuciusP wrote his work as
an antidote to QPl immediately after the publication of that
work.   The fact that he gave S. John the first place in his
list of the apostles suggests that he wrote in Asia.

V. A word must be said about the Clementines.   The
position which will be adopted is based upon that of
Waitz but varies at three important points.   (i.) The eight
books which Waitz attributes to the Ebionite Preaching
were part of an Acts of Peter which already included the
romance (QC).   The lost source of R and H (HR) was in
no sense the Grundschrift.   (ii.) R derived from the anti-
Marcionite redaction of QC (QHR) as well as from HR.
(iii.) It will be argued that HR was also influenced by Heg.
To understand the romance it must be remembered that,
except in the matter relating to Theophilus and Cornelius
which HR introduced into QHR, the narrative after the
first book never leaves Cæsarea.

§ 19.   I will now illustrate what has been said as to the
methods of most apocryphists and the way in which their
works should be used by discussing one of the more interesting L Acts, LLk.

LLk, 152 opens with the statement that when the disciples
had divided the cities of the world (most of the L Acts
begin with the story of the lots) Peter's lot was Rome,
and that Titus came thither from Galilee (Galatia) and Luke
from Antioch.   This association of Titus and Luke with
Peter at Rome occurs also in EP, 519.   In QPl they accompanied Paul from Galatia (§ 264).

S. Luke is " the scribe of Peter " because Heg identified
him with LeuciusP.   It is unnecessary to alter the text of
the Muratorian, a fragment which derives from Heg through
Hippolytus.   Heg stated that in a separate book (*semote*)
Luke narrated *the martyrdom of Peter and the journey of
Paul to Spain*.   We shall discuss other evidence which shews
that Heg had the Spanish journey, and the almost certain

allusion to it in I Clem. 5 is likely with much else in the
epistle to derive from KP.

Heg also identified S. Luke with Lucius of Cyrene (§ 175,
5, 14), and " Cyrenius " became by one of the many
corruptions of the text of Heg, Carinus. The connection
of S. Luke with Antioch occurs in the old Latin *argumentum*
and elsewhere and illustrates the influence of Heg on
patristic. When Jerome describes Luke *as a physician of
Antioch* as his *own writings prove* he is probably influenced
by an illusion of Heg to Ac. xiii. 1 (*de Vir. Ill.*, 7).

For the statement that Luke built churches cf. LSim., 118
and § 172.3 for the allusion to monasteries. For the ascription
of praise to God in 154.4 cf. LJas, 144.36 and EP, 524.1.

In 153 an illustrious Jew named Isaac has been associated
with Gamaliel and others. I cannot reconstruct the incident,
but the names are from QPl (§ 315, J). The fall of the
idols and the rent clothes are also interpolated into LJasZ, 33.

§ 20. The most interesting matter in LLk, its use of the
martyrdom of James the son of Zebedee, begins in 153.21.
The tradition of the (two) captains occurs in LBart, 78 and
Abd, iv. 5. I will abbreviate the James matter which follows.
The apostle told the congregation that Herod had ordered
his arrest and intended to put him to death, adding " God's
will be done." He was put in prison until the next day
and never ceased from singing praises (AT, 106 f., LPP,
186.36). He was accused of sedition (LJasZ, 36.18, LBart,
78.31). (Leading Cæsarean Christians) pleaded that the
capital sentence should be reduced to one of exile (LBart, 77,
AT, 164). In LLk, 155.31 Herod commanded that he should
be beheaded. The martyr was taken to the seashore where
was the *agora* (MM, 18). He said, I entreat you . . . that ye
wait for me a little that I may pray unto God. 156. And
when he had finished his prayer, one of the officers . . . knelt
on the ground and said to him : Forgive me . . . I have
sinned against thee. . . . They finished their course together.

The conclusion occurs in *HE* II., ix. where it is cited
from Clem. *Hytyp.*, vii. In *HE* II., i. 4 the same book is
cited for a statement that there were two Jameses, one of

whom was thrown down from a pinnacle of the temple and beaten by a fuller's club, and the other beheaded. The former martyrdom was taken by Clement from Heg, and the latter presumably is taken from the same source.

§ 21. We will now examine the splinters which are interspersed among the fragments of the noble story which Heg derived from KP.

In 153.22 Luke meets an old fisherman who turns out to be Theophilus. The tradition, which is important, will be discussed in § 192.

155.15. Luke's right hand is cut off because he wrote his gospel with it. The incident is suggested by an haggadic incident told in QPl of Mark (§ 332).

155.23 f. The proscription of the household of the vizier by the emperor (Nero) must be from Heg's account of the Neronian persecution (§ 194a).

156.2. " Father Peter " is from QP. Cf. Proch 6.6.

156.4. The centurion's blind eye is from QPl, where it occurred in a travesty of Jn. xx. The centurion who accompanied Pilate (§ 137) was healed when his eye touched the linens in which Jesus had been wrapped. The incident is also used in AT, 170.

The body of Luke is thrown ashore after being put in a sack. The incident was originally told of Matthew and survives also in ABarn, 23, MM, 24, LBart, 78.

In the Arabic the body is thrown up on an island. In the Greek (*JTS*, X. 53) the island is Proconesus. It is not in the least probable that our writer would have heard of Proconesus, an island in the Propontis, if he had not found it mentioned in Heg. The Propontis washes the western shore of Bithynia, and the Latin argumentum which states that S. Luke was an Antiochene also says that he died in Bithynia.

We have accounted for all the matter in LLk which is not obviously editorial.

§ 22. The following passages provide us with some very valuable information:

Photius (*Bibl.*, 114) writes of Leucius thus : " The
language is irregular and strange, for the author employs
constructions and modes of expression which are sometimes
well chosen but most frequently are vulgar and commonplace. He shews no trace of the uniform and simple
language (of the NT). He abounds in follies and contra-
dictions, for he states that there is an evil God of the Jews,
whose servant Simon the magician was different from Christ
whom he calls good, and he jumbles and confuses everything, calling Him now Father and now Son. He declares
that Christ was never truly incarnate but only in appearance,
that He appeared to His disciples now as a youth, now as
an old man, now as a child, of varying height and even of
such a stature that His head reached unto heaven. He
also invents many and preposterous tales about the Cross,
saying that Christ was not crucified, but that another took
His place and that He laughed at His crucifiers for that
reason. He rejects lawful marriage, and regards all begetting
as evil and the work of the Evil One. He narrates in his
folly works of demons, and tells of absurd and childish
resurrections of men, oxen and other animals. The Icono-
clasts believe that in the Acts of John he declares himself
opposed to images. In short, this book contains a thousand
things which are puerile, incredible, absurd, false, extrava-
gant, inconsistent, impious and godless. If any one were
to call it the fountain and mother of all heresy he would
not be far wrong " (Milligans's trans.).

§ 23. PsCypr *de Rebapt.*, c. 17 : *Est autem adulterini
hujus, immo internecini baptismatis, si qui alius auctor, tum
etiam quidam ab eisdem ipsius hæreticis propter hunc eundem
errorem confictus liber, qui inscribitur Pauli prædicatio, in
quo libro contra omnes scripturas et de peccato proprio con-
fitentem invenies Christum . . . ad accipendum Johannis
baptisma pæne invitum a matre sua Maria compulsum, item
cum baptizaretur, ignem super aquam esse visum . . ., et post
tanta tempora Petrum et Paulum post conlationem evangelii
in Hierusalem et mutuam cogitationem et altercationem et
rerum agendarum dispositionem postremo in Urbe quasi tunc*

primum invicem sibi esse cognitos et quædam alia hujuscemodi absurde ac turpiter conficta, quæ omnia in illum librum invenies congesta.

§ 24. Epiph. *Haer.* xxx. 16. " They put forward certain steps and discourses in the Steps of James representing his expositions as being directed against the temple and the sacrifices and the fire on the altar and much else that is full of empty sound. They shamelessly accuse Paul with forged discourses fabricated out of the malice and error of their false apostles, calling him what he claimed to be . . . a Tarsian but asserting that he was of Greek descent . . . the son of a Greek mother and a Greek father, and that he went up to Jerusalem and stayed there some time and desired to marry the daughter of the priest and for this reason became a proselyte and was circumcised, and that when he was refused he was enraged and wrote against circumcision and the sabbath and the law."

§ 25. The arrangement of my matter has raised difficult problems of great complexity. Originally the main purpose of this volume was to determine the relations of the sources of Heg, but owing to the nature of my materials and the fact that they contain evidence subversive of positions which are widely held it has been practically necessary to include in this volume much more discussion of NT problems than I had originally intended. I will now state what I believe to be the necessary reactions of the new data on the study of the NT. [My later views as to the Gospels are stated in § 89a.]

I. (i) (a) PsMark, who had visited Cæsarea, said that Mark accompanied Peter thither and wrote his Gospel there. Heg rightly accepted this tradition. (b) The Markan apocalypse was written about the date of the outbreak of the Herodian persecution, and was incorporated into Mk soon afterwards. The scribe, who wrote for western readers, did a little editing in the neighbouring chapters. (c) The lost end of Mk survives in the long ending, Matt, Lk, Jn and the apocrypha.

(ii) Mk and the Acts of Peter overlapped, and the latter work was well summarised by Mk. xvi. 20. It began with the Ascension and narrated the fulfilment of the prophecy of Joel cited by Peter at the first Pentecost. After the first arrest the prayer of iv. 23–31 was answered in 33, v. 12 f. There is a small hiatus at v. 41 in which we must place vi. 7a. The narrative made a fresh start with Stephen (vi. 8). His trial and martyrdom were assimilated to the Markan Passion (vi. 12–vii. 58a) and were followed by viii. 1bc. The narrative of the evangelisation of Samaria and Judæa culminated in the baptism of Roman officials at Cæsarea whither Peter had been accompanied by Mark and also by Alexander and Rufus who visited the church for which Mark wrote (Mk. xv. 21). The scheme of this Acts will be described in the next chapter.

(iii) The Acts of Barnabas began with the connection of its hero with Mary the mother of Mark and with the fact that he had sat with Saul at the feet of Gamaliel. Barnabas was a leader in the charitable work of the church (Ac. iv. 32–34, 36; ii. 43–46 is editorial). Ananias and Sapphira were contrasted. Stephen disputed in the synagogue of the Cilicians and Cyrenians and was arrested (9–11). His speech was recorded (xiii. 16–23, 32 f.). The persecutor (vii. 58b, viii. 1a, 3) was converted and introduced by his friend Barnabas to the disciples. The refugees preached in Syria and Cyprus, and the disciples sent Barnabas to Antioch. Peter journeyed to Syria after the twelfth passover but did not succeed in reaching Antioch, for when he was at Laodicea persecution broke out at Cæsarea. He returned to Jerusalem. He fled but saw Christ in the dream, *Domine, quo vadis?* and returned. After his escape he went to Antioch. About that date Barnabas and Saul were sent on a mission of relief to the churches gathered from the fellaheen of Judæa. After an absence of some years they returned to Jerusalem with Mark who had accompanied Peter in his journeyings through western Judæa and whose knowledge had been of service. Mark accompanied them later in a missionary journey in his account of which he made large use of the Cæsarea section of I Ac. Mc., using for instance the Cæsarea sermon in xiii. 24–31.

The Judaisers had attacked the positions vindicated in I Ac. Mc. Like that work II Ac. Mc. was a constructive apologia, had for its hero a leader with whom Mark was connected and narrated the foundation of an important church in the affairs of which he had played a part. The work mentioned his mother's name and also that of her servant. Like I Ac. Mc. it was written immediately after the events narrated. S. Mark's outlook, however, was very different in his later work. The only healings recorded were those in Galatia in a context in which he Cæsareanised. There are no *glossolaliai*, but the Spirit acts in the corporate life of the church (v. 3, xiii. 2, xv. 28). If in I Ac. Mc. Christ co-operated with the disciples, in II Ac. Mc. He suffered with them (ix. 4, *Domine, quo vadis?*). The work was written on the morrow of the Herodian persecution.

The primitive testimonies which Dr Rendel Harris has been reconstructing derive from the Markan Acts.

§ 26. II. PsMark in a second Cæsarea sermon used a manual which the church of Cæsarea attributed to S. Peter. It may have been a document of great importance, but unhappily very little of it can be reconstructed.

III. (i) The Pericope Adulteræ confirms the arguments for the identification of L with protoLuke. The parallels of L with Mk and Jn are due to the fact that all three Gospels derive from a primitive memoir (X) which was also used by Leucius and LeuciusP. Heg rightly dated Lk A.D. 47.

(ii) New evidence supports the early date for Acts and confirms the position that S. Luke endeavoured to shew that Paul was another Peter.

IV. (i) The evidence of his Asian contemporary Leucius proves that John of Ephesus was the apostle. The incompetent author of the Fourth Gospel used disordered fragments and scraps which contained S. John's midrashim and the passages of X on which he commented. In two papers S. John corrected Mk.

(ii) S. John wrote his epistles during a journey through

the churches, memories of which underlie Rev. ii., iii.
and AJ.   He was probably accompanied by Ariston whose
preaching may have influenced Rev.

V. KP influenced Rev and II Pet.

It is obvious that some of the positions just stated will
not be, and indeed ought not to be, very readily accepted.
On the other hand they ought not to be ruled out of court
ex limine. If the apocrypha deprave an uncanonical tradition
of Christian origins, which derives through works which are
earlier than the latest books of the NT from the sources
of the earliest, it is no more than might be expected that
our results would at points clash with positions which are
widely accepted but are based on scanty and difficult
data and are no more than more or less plausible working
hypotheses.

CHAPTER II

The Conclusion, Sources and Recensions of S. Mark's Gospel

§ 27. We will examine four documents which allude to the Appearance to the Eleven.

I. In by far the larger part of their discussions of the long ending of Mk (LEMk) scholars have been occupied with the proof that it was not the work of S. Mark, and the question what was the compiler's main source has received very inadequate attention.

That LEMk is early is shewn by some familiar evidence. Taylor has argued that there are indications of its influence on Hermas (Hermas ... 57 f.), and there is a close parallel in Just. Apol. i. 45, *His apostles went forth everywhere and preached.* Moreover there is other evidence of this character. But the relation of these passages to LEMk may be indirect. Irenæus, however, goes further and actually attributes LEMk. 19 to S. Mark. Further, the Eçmiadzin codex attributes the ending to the elder Ariston; but this attribution cannot be pressed. It is probably due to the fact that a scribe knew that the story of the poison cup of Barsabas to which the compiler alludes was derived by Papias from Ariston. It is a fairly safe inference from the evidence that the compiler wrote in Asia a little later than Papias.

The date and place are important. In the first half of the second century Asia was seething with the controversies which had originated in the attacks of Cerinthus and Leucius on the authority of the apostles. Now the compiler was orthodox, yet we find in LEMk exactly what we should not expect to find, an incrimination of the eleven for their unbelief which is more severe than anything which can be found elsewhere. The compiler would not have included LEMk. 11–14 unless he had found that passage in a very authoritative document. It is at any rate very improbable that an orthodox writer would have written LEMk. 11 f. after the Neronian persecution, and the noble simplicity of the last two verses has a primitive ring. There is a presumption then that LEMk was placed at the end of Mk because it was based on Mk and deemed to be Mk.

§ 28. We will examine LEMk verse by verse. It will be convenient that here as elsewhere I should assume my conclusions.

10. *Report*. The women delivered the messages of the angel and Christ. The word occurred in Mk *sub* Matt. xxviii. 8, 10, Lk. xxiv. 10, and in KP *sub* the short ending (SEMk: § 64) the women "announce."

Mourned and wept occurred in KP *sub* EvP, 27, EpApp, 10 (the transference is editorial), AJ, 97, EvvC, 1 and Cyr. Catech. xiii. 25. I do not think that psMark is at all likely to have introduced the phrase. Add SchmidtEvvC, 1.

11. *Disbelieved* is an important contact with Mk which varied from X in exaggerating the unbelief of the eleven. The word was possibly suggested by the occurrence of *unbelieving* in X *sub* Jn. xx. 27. The verb occurs in 16. It is used of the apostles in the parallel with our passage in Lk. xxiv. 11 where *for joy* is certainly an editorial ingenuity. All the instances of the noun and verb in the Gospels are Markan.

12. *Two of them*. Mk was parallel with LLk. xxiv. 13.

Into the country. Cf. xv. 21.

In another form is an inference from the failure to recognise Jesus and resembles *transformed* (ix. 2).

14. *The eleven* like " disbelieved " occurs in Lk. xxiv. 9 and also in 33, in Matt. xxviii. 16, and in two other Markan passages, Ac. i. 26, ii. 14.

Sat at meat is a contact with MkLk. xxiv. 42.

15. *Go* occurs in the parallel at Matt. xxviii. 19, *all the world* in xiv. 9, *preach the gospel* in i. 14, xiii. 10 (from I Ac. Mc.), xiv. 9. Apart from "creation" the whole phrase almost certainly derives from Mk.

16. There is an allusion to baptism in the parallel passage in Matt. xxvi. 19.

18. The evidence for *lay hands on* is Matt. 4 instances, Mk. 6, Lk. 1, I Ac. Mc. 4. The occurrences in II Ac. Mc. passages are ix. 17 (sight, Holy Ghost), xiii. 3 (commission). In xiv. 3 and xxviii. 8 S. Luke represents Paul as another Peter. In xix. 6 he may be suspected of editing in order to provide a parallel with viii. 7. In KP Peter laid his hands on the sick at Cæsarea.

The sick. The instances are Mk. vi. 5, 13, Matt. xiv. 14.

§ 29. The two last verses, read with the two that precede them, connect with the scheme of Mk and I Ac. Mc. In iii. 3 f. the mission with a view to which the twelve were chosen is described under two heads, preaching and the casting out of demons. These two modes of action had been attributed to Christ in i. 39 and illustrated in the preceding passage and in the same terms. The mission contemplated in iii. is described in vi. 12 f. and in the same terms. The twofold activity of Christ was shared by the apostles. Now according to xvi. 18 f. this twofold activity of Christ and the apostles was continued after the Ascension as a co-operation. Moreover the description of Mk in I Ac. Mc. *sub* Ac. i. 1 as a record of all that Jesus *began to do and to teach* corresponds not only with the heading of Mk (*the beginning of the gospel-preaching*) but also with what is in our view the last verse, for it implies Christ's continued activity and His co-operation. As the one verse looks forward, so the other looks back and describes Mk in its own terms. Moreover an examination of the sections of Acts which derive from I Ac. Mc. shews that this Acts narrated the fulfilment of LEMk. 17–18 and was an expansion of 20. We learn from Ac. ii. that Mk derived the word *signs* from Joel whom Peter cites as predicting the *signs and wonders* which his hearers had seen and which Jesus (who had been approved by God by His mighty works, signs and wonders) had poured forth (22, 33). In iii. Peter heals and preaches, and the two activities are connected (iv. 10). In iv. 24 f. the disciples pray that they may preach boldly *while thou stretchest forth thy hand to heal* and are again filled with the Holy Ghost. The prayer is answered in 33 and v. 12 f. In v. 32 the Holy Ghost is said to witness.

The preaching of Stephen which led to his arrest was introduced with the statement that he *worked wonders and signs*.

At the beginning of the next narrative of aggressive activity signs and wonders confirm the preaching of Philip (viii. 6, 13). Later Peter laid his hands on the Samaritans, and they received the Holy Ghost, and inasmuch as Simon saw that the Holy Ghost was given we infer that there were glossolaliai. Peter said to Æneas, *Jesus Christ healeth thee*, and the healing confirmed the word (ix. 34 f.), as did the raising of Tabitha (42). In KP Peter at Cæsarea used the imposition of hands for healing, and in Acts, as Christ had promised, those who believed spake with tongues.

Our examination of LEMk has confirmed our conjecture that the obvious solution of the problem of LEMk is the true one and that the compiler made Mk view the basis of his narrative.

§ 30. II. The short ending of Mk (SEMk) derives from KP (§ 64), and when our reconstructions of KP are completed the reader will not doubt that the writer of KP claimed to be Mark. Now SEMk cannot derive from LEMk, but it agrees with it in stating that the women announced and this in spite of Mk. xvi. 7 where they are said to have said nothing to anyone. It would appear that the source of SEMk like LEMk stated that Christ commissioned the apostles to preach to the nations and that they preached everywhere (*from the east unto the west He sent forth the message*).

§ 31. III. Ignatius, in whose letters we shall find several other traces of KP, writes: *After that He rose ... when He came to Peter and his company, He said, Lay hold and handle me, and see that I am not an incorporeal demon. And straitway they touched Him and believed. ... And after His resurrection He ate and drank with them* (Sm, 3).

Jerome says that the logion occurred in EvH (EvH, 18, 30), and inasmuch as EvH, as Schmidke has shewn, is the result of the glossation of Matt, we may safely accept the statement of Origen that the saying occurred in the Teaching of Peter. Moreover the whole of our matter has parallels in apocrypha which derive from KP and Ignatius agrees with SEMk in *Peter and his company*.

That KP derived from Mk is suggested by the Markan *straitway*, by the fact that the statement that they straitway believed suggests an earlier parallel of KP with the unbelief for which in LEMk Christ upbraids them and by the fact that *Peter and his company* is likely to have been suggested by Mk. xvi. 7, *his disciples and Peter*.

§ 32. IV. When we compare Lk. xxiv. 36 f. with Ignatius the canonical narrative is seen to be both closely related and inferior. They derive therefore from a common source which can only be Mk. We note the following points: (i) The statement that Christ ate and drank with His disciples is an almost unconscious variation from the tradition, which underlies Ac. x. 41 and which is illustrated in LLk. xxiv. 30 and Jn. xxi. 12, that the disciples ate and drank with Christ. S. Luke substituted for the all but primitive phrase of KP the statement that Christ asked for food and ate broiled fish. (ii) The statement that Christ calmed the fears of the disciples by saying that He was not an incorporeal demon is much nearer the primitive tradition than the Lukan saying in which Christ argues that He cannot be a spirit because He has flesh and bones. (iii) In both Lk and Ignatius Christ bids the apostles feel Him and this implies a subsequent statement that they did so. If we are dealing with fiction the point cannot be gainsaid; if with history, we are confirmed by 1 Jn. i. 1, *that which our hands felt*. It follows that S. Luke has edited his source so as to throw the emphasis on the eating, and the inference is confirmed by the words which follow, *he did eat before them*. S. Luke was probably actuated by two motives. (*a*) His interest was in the fact that his source seemed to imply that Christ's body was what it had been before He suffered. (*b*) He wished to spare the apostles and omit the incident of the unbelief which the handling brought to an end. He moved therefore S. Mark's allusion to the unbelief into a participial clause and connected it with the statement of X *sub* Jn. xx. 20 that *the disciples were glad* in the clever phrase *while they disbelieved for joy.* (iv) We compare A. KP *sub* Ign, EpApp, 11 (EvXII), EvH, 16 (M) *He came.* B. Lk. *He stood in their midst.* C. Jn. xx. 19, *He came and stood in their midst.* In view of the fact that the three phrases must be independent we can only account for the parallelism of AB with C by the hypothesis that A and B abbreviate Mk and that Mk was based on X *sub* C.

We have laid our foundation. If SEMk and Ignatius derive in common from KP, two positions which will be confirmed as we proceed, and KP and Lk derive from Mk, the case for the Markan origin of LEMk is strengthened, for two of its incidents, the report of the women and the appearance to the eleven, occurred in Mk. We have also two most important clues. (i) We must assume that LEMk preserves the framework of the lost end of Mk and that its strangest feature, its hostility to the eleven, is Markan. (ii) We have found indications that Mk, Lk and Jn derive from a common source X. The evidence for X will be much clearer in a later chapter and in the next volume than in the present enquiry, for most unhappily S. Mark made very little use of X at the close of his work.

§ 33. We will now examine the evidence for the sequel to the visit of the women to the sepulchre.

A. In LEMk. 11 under the influence of Jn. xx. only Mary is mentioned. She " reports," and the disciples disbelieve her.

B. In SEMk the women announce (ἐξήγγειλαν).

C. Just as S. Luke used both L and Mk in his account of the visit of the women to the tomb, so he combines L with Mk in his statement of their subsequent action (xxiv. 9 f.): *they reported* (the Markan word is used though the Markan incident of the message is omitted). The women speak (not only of the angel but) *all these things* (Jesus had appeared as He does in Matt) *to the eleven* (the phrase of Matt and LEMk) *and to all the rest* (cf. I Ac. Mc. *ap* Ac.

i. 14); *and they disbelieved* (as in LEMk. 11). *And they were M. Magd. and Joanna and M. of Jas* (the eccentric list is a sign of disturbance): *And the other women with them* (the confusion may be due to the fact that in L Mary Magdalene remained at the tomb (§ 39 f.) and Joanna was said to have returned with other women: in the previous phrase Lk adds the two Maries from Mk) *told* (in L they had not been sent) *these things* (cf. LLk. xxiv. 23) *unto the apostles* (the word is never a designation in Mk: there are perhaps four LLk instances: in Lk. xxii. 14 the word is editorial) . . . *as idle talk*. The confusion is due to the fact that S. Luke combines his two sources.

D. In Jn Mary with other women (" we ") runs (Matt) to Peter and John (editorial).

§ 34. E. Matthew abbreviates.

(i) At the outset we observe that the women *run* as in D to report as in ABC. It is not true that the evidence for the continued use of Mk stops at the same point as the MSS. The evidence that the women reported in Mk could not be stronger.

(ii) If the women reported in Mk something must have happened to allay the panic which according to Mk was the cause of their disobedient silence. The explanation, which is the only possible one, is given in Matt where Jesus meets them. The whole of Matt. xxviii. 9–10 so far as language goes may be Markan (Allen). Further, the narrative of the eleven was probably similar to that of the women. Presumably they disbelieved and their disbelief was brought to an end by the appearance of Christ which is implied by Matt. xxviii. 16 where Christ is said to have appointed the mountain and an appearance in Jerusalem is implied. The evidence could not cohere better than it does.

(iii) Any doubt that Matt derives from Mk will be removed when we examine the evidence as to the women in the light of our hypothesis that LEMk derives from Mk and Jn and Mk in common from X.

§ 35. If we omit from Lk and Jn all the matter which has parallels with Mk it becomes clear that the narrative which

D

followed was the story of the sacred body. S. Mark however introduced at this point a secondary hero and diverted attention to him and the stone. Moreover there is likely to be something fundamentally wrong with the narrative. If we add the events recorded in LLk. xxiii. 55–56 to those related in Mk there is not time for everything.

Why should Pilate have sent a centurion to enquire whether Jesus was dead? He could grant the body before death. In any case Joseph's word was enough. The incident is an ill-motived triviality. Our suspicion is confirmed by the following parallels:

Mk. *Because it was the Preparation.*	Joseph a councillor goes to Pilate.	Pilate sends a centurion to Calvary.
Jn. *Because it was the Preparation.*	His fellow-councillors go to Pilate.	Pilate's soldiers come to Calvary.

§ 35*a*. It would appear that the centurion of Mk was originally in command of the soldiers of Jn and that Joseph accompanied the other members of the sanhedrin. The arrangements for the burial would naturally be discussed when they asked for the *crucifragium*, and we may conjecture that the complaint about the title was made at the same time. Our hypothesis accounts for the unexplained "their" in a splinter of L, *he had not consented unto their counsel and deed* (LLk). In Jn. xix. 31–37 the editor almost obviously preserves one of his papers in its original form. 31 is the necessary introduction to what follows and in X may have occurred at an earlier point.

§ 36. On our view Mk, Lk and Jn derive their narratives of the Crucifixion from X, Lk and Jn being also influenced by Mk.

We will compare the following parallels:

Mk. 27. *They crucify with him two thieves . . . the other on the left.*	LLk. 33. *And there they crucified him and with him two thieves* MkLk . . . *and the other on the left.*	Jn. 18. *Where they crucified him and with him two others on this side and on that and Jesus in the midst.*

Lk and Jn agree against Mk in placing the passage at the beginning of the narrative, in "where," "there" and in "him and with him." Their order is the probable order of the story of an eyewitness. Jn agrees with Mk in the emphasis on the fact that Christ was between the two thieves and in stating the incident of the lots immediately after the crucifying.

If we omit the taunts, which are themselves open to criticism, the Mk Crucifixion is strangely brief and reads like a clumsy abbreviation. This is best seen by a comparison of verses 34–38 with Jn. 18 f., 23 f. That Jn itself only preserves a few fragments is suggested by *these things the soldiers did*. Other people did other things, *i.e.* taunted. Mk's few verses contain a sure indication of editorial activity in the use of a source. 25 repeats *they crucified*, the purpose of the repetition being to state that it was the third hour. Now this statement has two contacts. On the one hand it connects with S. Mark's introduction of the unhistorical incident of the three hours' darkness over all the land at the sixth hour and on the other hand with his variation from the superior evidence of Lk and Jn in the Trial by night. S. Mark has moved the allusion to the sixth hour (Lk and Jn agree in "*about* the sixth hour") from the Crucifying to the Darkness. On this view Christ died within about four hours. The discussion is continued in § 91*d*.

The taunt about Christ's kingship is likely to have been originally in some way connected with the title. In Mk it is spoken by the priests, in Lk by the soldiers, in Jn. xix. 14 by Pilate. This verse is one of the many misplaced splinters scattered about Jn. "About the sixth hour" connects the taunt with Calvary, "it was the Preparation" with the visit of the priests to Pilate. They would naturally go to Calvary before they made their visit. Lk. gives the connection of the taunt with the title, but the incident is editorial and composite. In Mk the taunts are unconvincing. That of the passers-by is more likely to have been suggested by the title than by the evidence of the false witnesses which they had not heard. On the other hand the priests, who were annoyed by the title, are more likely to have said, Aha! thou temple builder. There are three problems, the probable transposition of taunts in Mk, the fact that in Lk and Lk alone the soldiers taunt and the misplaced taunt of Pilate in Jn. xix. 14. The solution is that in X as in Lk the soldiers taunted but used the taunt which Jn attributes to Pilate and addressed it to the priests as they passed. Hence the fact that in Mk the priests use it themselves, their own taunt being attributed to other passers-by. Naturally they mentioned the matter to Pilate.

§ 36a. All our problems seem to be solved by the following reconstruction of X.

Jn. . . . 18. *where they crucified him . . . Jesus in the midst. And Pilate wrote . . . King of the Jews. This title therefore read many . . . for the place was nigh to the city. . . .* 14, LLk. *Now it was about the sixth hour,* 14, 31 *and because it was the Preparation, that the bodies might not remain . . . (they said, Let us) ask Pilate that their legs may be broken. (And they came unto Calvary.)* Mk. *And as they passed by they mocked with one another, saying, Aha! thou that . . . buildest the temple. . . .* LLk. *And the soldiers said* Jn. 14 *unto them, Behold the king of the Jews. (Then went they and said unto Pilate, Write another title).* 21. *Write not King. . . .* LLk. *And one of them, Joseph by name, being a good and righteous man who had not consented to their counsel and deed asked for the body of Jesus.* Mk. *And Pilate granted it, and Joseph bought a linen cloth.* Jn. 23. *The soldiers therefore when they had crucified Jesus, took his garments. . . .*

There are some points at which our reconstruction is uncertain, but they do not affect the preceding discussion, and it results in a chronology which tallies with that at which we arrived on independent grounds and in a plausible arrangement of the narratives of X. That Gospel completed its narrative of the priests and Pilate, and there followed a continuous account of what took place on Calvary. The story of the sacred body was not interrupted by an incident of which Joseph was the hero.

We conclude that Mk, LLk and Jn derive in common from X and that there is a fundamental disturbance in Mk which is due to the introduction of the Three Hours' Darkness and the story of Joseph and the stone.

One of the later perversions may be mentioned at this point, for it connects with the story of the women which we are about to examine, and by itself it goes far to shew that S. Mark was using a written source. The words of xiv. 28 *I will go before you into Galilee* on the one hand prepare for the story of disobedience and on the other have no connection with the context which runs quite smoothly when they are removed.

§ 36*b*. We will resume the reconstruction of X.

Jn. *Then came the soldiers and brake the legs . . . pierced his side.* LLk. *And Joseph took down the body of Jesus and wrapped it round* Jn. *with linens. Now in the place where he was crucified there was a garden; and in the garden*

Jn.	LLk.
a new tomb	a tomb hewn in stone
wherein was never man yet laid.	where was never man yet laid.
There then because of the Preparation	And it was the day of Preparation,
	and the Sabbath drew on
(*for the tomb was nigh at hand*) *they laid Jesus*	

LLk. *And all his acquaintances and the women that followed with them from Galilee stood afar off, seeing these things. And they followed.*

At the close of our reconstruction we notice three points : (i) It is clear that Jn and Lk are in literary relation and that Jn is not secondary. (ii) LLk. 50–52 is misplaced under the influence of Mk. It is probable that X completed the narrative of what took place on Calvary and of those who were not disciples, the scoffers, the man who gave the vinegar, the centurion, the multitudes, Joseph, before he began his narratives of the disciples. (iii) The repetition of *the women which followed with him from Galilee* is on S. Luke's manner when he is returning to a source which he has deserted. *E.g.* we compare Ac. vii. 57 f., *and they stoned Stephen* (II Ac. Mc. *the witnesses . . . Saul*). *And they stoned Stephen.* The repetition is evidence for the con-

tinuity of 49 with 55*b* and therefore for the misplacement
of the visit of Joseph in Mk.

§ 37. S. Mark treated the X narrative of the women
in the same way as he treated the X Emmaus narrative.
He abbreviated it into an inaccurate introduction to the
statement that the eleven disbelieved witnesses. But
S. Mark had a second motive. He desired in his allusions
to the empty tomb to use all the resources of his literary art
so as to fill his readers with awe in the presence of the
supernatural. But he was no Shakespeare. He began by
suggesting that the angel had rolled away the stone in order
to get into the tomb or that Jesus had rolled it away in
order to get out of it. For this reason he says that Joseph
rolled to the stone and that the women discussed who
should roll it away and that *looking up they see that the stone
is rolled back: for it was exceeding great.* They all crowd
through the door, which according to Lk. xxiv. 12 and Jn.
xx. 5 they must have stooped to pass, into the narrow space,
find an angel sitting there and learn from him and not
from their eyes that the body was not there. He begins
his composite harangue by telling them not to be astonished.
They hear him to the end, go out, and then fly panicstricken.

The absurd incidents of the entrance and the exit suggest
that S. Mark was not writing his melodrama freely but
blundering in his use of a source.

§ 38. We now return to the point at which we desisted
from our reconstruction of X.

LLk *followed and beheld his tomb   and how his body was laid.*
Mk *beheld   where he   was laid.*

We observe that LLk illustrates the exactitude of X in its
allusions to the position of the body, the movements of Mary
and the positions of the angels. The women did not only
notice where but also how the body was laid. Mk here
and later abbreviates.

According to LLk. xxiv. 1 the women went to the tomb
at deep dawn (22. *at dawn*). With this agrees Jn. xx. 1,

early while it was yet dark, but the phrasing shews the influence of Mk. xvi. 1, *exceeding early when the sun was up*. For the explanation of "when the sun was up," see § 91.10. S. Mark began by copying X.

The angels are described thus:

Mk. *A young man sitting on the right side clad in a white robe.*	Lk. *Two men in dazzling apparel. 23. a vision of angels.*	Jn. *Two angels in white sitting the one at the head the other at the feet, where the body of Jesus had lain.*

(i) Jn and LLk vary together in stating that there were two angels. In both Mk and Jn the angels are robed in white and their positions are defined.

(ii) In LLk the women notice how the body of Jesus was laid. Mk and Jn agree in stating the precise position of the angel or angels, and the precise statement of the position of the angels in terms of the position of the body, which we find in Jn, connects with the fact that in LLk the women remembered the position of the body. Mary Magdalene connected the position of the angels with the position of the body.

§ 39. The narrative of X must have run as follows : Mary Magdalene, whose name is significantly in the first place in Mk. xv. 40, 47, xvi. 1, LLk. viii. 3, Lk. xxiv. 10, arrived first at the tomb. She stooped and said, They have taken away the Lord, and I do not see where they have laid Him (Jn). She advanced (Mk) and then experienced a vision and audition, and said, Angels say He lives (LLk. xxiv. 23). Joanna and the other women ran (Mk *sub* Matt and Jn) to the disciples. Mary remained at the tomb and saw Jesus. She returned to the disciples.

S. Mark treated the X narrative of the women much in the same way as the Emmaus narrative. He abbreviated it into an introduction to the appearance to the eleven, telescoping the return of Mary into that of the other women and accentuating the unbelief of the eleven, who disobeyed the twice repeated command to go to Galilee.

Our reconstructed X underlies Mk.

(*a*) The well-motived entrance and exit of Mary account for the absurd parallels in Mk.

(*b*) In the angel's speech *he is risen* paraphrases *he lives* (LLk. xxiv. 23). *He is not here* is suggested by *they have taken away the Lord* (Jn). *Behold the place where they laid him* is probably suggested by *I know not where they have laid him. That he goeth before you* . . . is schematic, as is *his disciples and Peter. Go tell* is from X (*v. infr.*). The absurd sentence in which the angel tells the women whom they were seeking is based on Mary's answer to Christ's question, *whom seekest thou?* She replied: Mk. *Jesus I seek*, and then remembering that the name was common added, *the Nazarene whom they crucified.* Jn. *Sir, if thou hast borne him hence.* . . .

The parallels continue:

Matt. *They came*	*and took hold of his feet*	*and worshipped him.*
Jn. (variant). Mary *ran forward* from the tomb to Jesus	*Touch me not,*	*for I am not ascended;*

         Jn.   *but go unto my brethren and say* . . .
         Matt. *Go tell my brethren.*
         Mk.   *Go tell his disciples.*

The wide diffusion of the variant at Jn. xx. 17 shews that it is early. We shall also attribute to X the interpolations at v. 4 and vii. 53. The sentence, *touch me not, for I am not ascended* is meaningless. The words *for I am not ascended* incorporate into the narrative S. John's comment on the statement of X *sub* Matt that Mary worshipped Christ: "worship was not due to the Lord until He ascended."

We conclude that Mk and Matt derive from the source of Jn and that Matt derives through Mk.

§ 40. Lk. xxiv. must be studied as a whole. Its two most important features are the absence of any allusion to an appearance to the women and S. Luke's editorial activity. The former fact is probably due to a motive which we shall conclude much influences Lk. xix.–xxii. his reluctance to decide between discrepant narratives of Mk and L. If

in several passages in our chapter he decides against Mk it
is in order to spare the eleven. On the other hand a decision
in favour of Mk is due to a statement of that Gospel that
Jesus ate with the disciples. I attribute one long passage
and five splinters to Mk. The five or six transpositions are
important, and in most cases the motive is S. Luke's desire
to use L matter which he regarded as of value. When the
passages are collected it is clear that they need to be accounted
for and that our hypothesis accounts for them.

A. Lk. v. 8. *Depart from me, for I am a sinful man,
O Lord* is from the appearance to Peter (§§ 55, 84, 86).

B. Lk. xxiv. 3. *Why seek ye the living among the dead?*
Mary Magdalene deprecated the second visit to the tomb.

C. 7. *The Son of man must be delivered up and delivered
into the hands of sinful* men is from the L narrative of the
appearance to the eleven (§ 56). The words *and be crucified,
and the third day rise again* like the similar passages in ix. 22
and xxiv. 46 are influenced by Mk.

D. 25. *O foolish men* . . . is from Christ's rebuke of the
eleven in L.

E. 41b–42. *Anything to eat . . . broiled fish* is suggested
by X *sub* Jn. xxi. 5 f.

F. 44b–45 is probably suggested by the similar passage
in the Emmaus narrative (26 f.).

My analysis is as follows: 1–2, L; 3, Mk (*they entered*),
L edited; 4–5a, ed, L, Gen. xviii. 2, Mk (*affrighted*); 5b
transposed; 6a Mk; 6b, ed; 7 transposed; 8 ed; 9–11, Mk
and L; 13–19, L; 20ab, ed; 20c–24, L; 25 is transposed;
26–32, L; 33–34, L edited; 35, L; 36–48, Mk, but 39a is
edited, an omission follows, *for joy* is from L, 41b–42 is
transposed and from L, 43 is ed, 44–45 is transposed from
L; 49–52, L (ἕως ed); 53, ed. In xxiv. as in xxii.–xxiii.
S. Luke inserted matter from Mk into a narrative based on L.

§ 41. We now return to the movements of the women.
The two disciples who later in the day went to Emmaus
are likely to have been on their way to the temple and to
have spent only a short time with the eleven. Before they
went on their way Joanna had reported that an angel said,

He lives and " certain " had confirmed her report as to the grave. The silence of Lk suggests that this second party had not seen Mary and that she had not returned when the two disciples left the eleven. The difficulty presented by these facts seems to be solved by the simple hypothesis that her first thought had been for the Lord's mother; but another solution of the problem is far more probable.

The same motive which led S. Luke to omit both the L and the Mk narratives of the appearance to Mary may have led him to edit out an allusion of the Emmaus disciples to it.

They say: *Yea and beside all this, it is now the third day. . . . Moreover certain women of our company amazed us having been early at the tomb; and when they found not his body, they came, saying, that they had also seen a vision of angels, which said that he was alive. And certain . . . went to the tomb, and found it even as the women had said: but him they saw not.*

This passage implies the discussion of evidence for the Resurrection which Lk omits. (*a*) The emphatic allusion to the third day implies that someone, presumably S. John, had cited one of Christ's sayings about the third day (cf. Jn. xx. 8 f.). (*b*) The Crucifixion had been followed by a second disappointment, the account of which is introduced by the emphatic phrase "moreover besides all this," and which was connected with the fact that it was now the third day. (*c*) In the phrase *but him they saw not* "him" is very emphatic and connects with the previous allusion to the third day. The paraphrase, "the grave was as the women said, but the body they saw not" is nonsense. The Emmaus disciples are disappointed by the fact that while, as the women said, the grave was empty the living Jesus had not been seen. S. Luke was acquainted with a fact which shewed that they hoped or might be supposed to have hoped that Jesus would be seen by the second party that visited the garden. In other words, S. Luke was acquainted with the appearance to Mary Magdalene.

§ 42. Inasmuch as I am about to argue that S. John was convinced by the position of the linens that Christ had risen

I observe that while the allusion to the third day coheres
well with the fact that a few days before He had said, . . . *in
three days I will raise it up* and with the statement, when He
was raised His disciples remembered *that he spake thus*
(Jn. ii. 18 f.), S. John's conviction does not account for
him they saw not. The apostle had no ground for anticipating
that Christ would be seen.

Our reconstruction is supported by a fragment of positive
evidence. The Lukan angel says, *why seek ye the living
among the dead?* S. Luke never composed editorial matter
of this kind, and we shall find independent grounds for
attributing the words to X (§ 76). We conjecture then that
Mary arrived almost immediately after the other women,
and when it was proposed to examine the grave indignantly
said that the risen Lord would not be found in it. When
the second party returned they confirmed Joanna's report
about the grave but not Mary's statement that she had seen
Jesus in the garden. *Him they saw not.*

§ 43. We may now continue our reconstruction of X
thus: Lk. *And the women which had come with him out of
Galilee, followed after and beheld the tomb and how his body
was laid. And they returned and prepared spices and oint-
ments. And on the sabbath they rested according to the
commandment. But on the first day of the week at early dawn
they came unto the tomb, bringing the spices which they had
prepared. And they found the stone rolled away from the tomb.*
Jn. *And Mary stooped and looked into the tomb and said,
They have taken away the Lord, and I know not where they
have laid him.* Mk. *And she entered* Jn. *and beholdeth two
angels in white sitting* Mk. *on the right side,* Jn. *one at the
head, and one at the feet, where the body of Jesus had lain,*
Lk. *and they said unto her, He lives. And Joanna and the
other women* Matt, Jn. *ran* Lk. *and told these things unto the
disciples, and their words appeared unto them as idle talk.*
Mk. *And Mary came forth from the tomb,* Jn. *and was
standing without the tomb weeping. And Jesus said unto her,
Woman why weepest thou? whom seekest thou? And she
turned herself back and beheld him standing, and knew not*

that it was Jesus. And supposing him to be the gardener she saith unto him, Mk. *Jesus I seek, the Nazarene whom they crucified.* Jn. *Sir, if thou hast borne him hence, tell me where thou hast laid him, and I will take him away. Jesus saith unto her, Mary. She turneth herself and saith, Rabboni.* Gloss. *And she ran forward* Matt. *and took hold of his feet and worshipped him.* Jn. *Jesus saith unto her, Do not stay holding me, but* Matt, Mk, Jn. *go tell my brethren.*

Mk, Jn. *Mary M. goeth and telleth the disciples that she had seen the Lord and how he had said these things unto her. (And they said unto her, We will go to the tomb and seek him.)* Lk. *She saith unto them, Why seek ye the living among the dead? And certain of them* (Gloss) *arose and ran to the tomb, and* (?) *Peter stooped down and saw the linens only, and* (?) *he departed wondering to his quarters,* Lk. *and the others returned to the disciples and said, We found the tomb even as they said, but him we saw not.*

§ 44. Before I give my reasons for holding that the gloss at Lk. xxiv. 12 derives from Mk I will analyse Jn. xx. 1–18. The passage consists of (A) S. John's correction of the Mk narrative of Peter's visit to the tomb (*i.e.* the gloss), (B) splinters from the setting of this narrative which are due (*a*) to the writer of the paper and (*b*) to the author of the Gospel, (C) the X narrative of the visit of the women, (D) a midrash on X (17). The two papers were in the wrong order and X was discrepant with the Mk abbreviation. The editor's main purpose was to produce a narrative which would run smoothly and not obviously contradict Mk. His main editorial changes are the following: (*a*) In Mk Mary Magdalene ran with the other women to the apostles (Matt. xxviii. 8). They do so in Jn, but the other women only survive in Mary's " we." (*b*) In X Mary remained at the tomb after the other women had gone to the apostles and then followed them. In Jn owing to the order of the papers the apostles are Peter and John, who are in the garden, and she remains after Peter and John have left it. (*c*) The discourse is retesselated. The angels ask Christ's question, Why weepest thou? and Mary replies with words which in Jn she also addresses to the apostles and in X she addressed to the other women.

§ 45. The gloss at Lk. xxiv. 12 finds a place in the following reconstruction of Mk: . . . *Tell his disciples and Peter. . . . They said nothing to anyone, for they were afraid* (cf. Mk. iv. 41) *with a great fear.* (Matt) *And Jesus met them saying, Hail. And they came and took hold of his feet. Then said he unto them, Fear not: go tell my brethren that they depart unto Galilee, and there shall they see me.* (Lk) *And they ran and reported all these things to the eleven and to all the rest. And they disbelieved them.* (Gloss) *But Peter arose and ran unto the tomb; and stooping and looking in, he seeth the linens alone; and he departed to his home, wondering what had come to pass.* (Jn) *For as yet he knew not the scriptures that he must rise from the dead.* The appearance to Peter followed [in protoMk. The Ebionite reviser, whose activities I shall describe, would be likely to omit it].

LEMk. *And he was seen in another form by two of the disciples as they walked on their way into the country. And they returned and told it unto the rest. Neither believed they them.*

And as they sat at meat (KP) *Jesus came* (MLk) *and stood in the midst.* . . .

The derivation of the gloss at Lk. xxiv. 12 appears as follows:

1. The sources of the other glosses at the end of Lk are 1 Cor. xi. 29, (?) L or X, Mk. xiv. 72, L or X, (??) Mk. xvi. 19, Jn. xx. 19, 20. I Ac. Mc. or KP (*borne up, i.e.* in or on a cloud), either L or the end of Mk (§ 83). This list shews that the glossator used ancient and valuable documents with which he did not tamper, that he certainly used Mk and, probably, the end of Mk.

2. Peter like the man with a sponge in Mk. xv. 36 and the women *ran.* The statistics for *arose and* followed by a verb of motion are Matt 2 (= Mk), Mk 4, Lk 7 (3 edit.), I Acts, I Ac. Mc. 5, II Ac. Mc. 1, II Acts 2 (Markan passages). *Stooped*: like Mary in X *sub* Jn. xx. 11. For the emphatic *alone* at the end of the sentence cf. Mk. ix. 2. 8. *Alone* was

corrected by S. John who substitutes emphatically " lying."
What had happened occurs only here, in Mk. v. 14 and the
MkLk parallel.

§ 46. 3. The gloss makes some very striking contacts.

(i) It throws unexpected light on the phrase of the Markan
angel *his disciples and Peter* and on the whole of the lost
end of Mk. In LLk. xxiv. 23 others besides Peter go to
the tomb and the statement is confirmed by Jn. xx. 2 f.
We must conclude that the end of Mk exalted Peter.

(ii) In the gloss Peter does not return to the eleven but
goes to his quarters. He leaves the tomb wondering, for as
yet he knew not the scriptures. The passage seems to be
clearly leading up to the narrative of the appearance to him.
Now this conjecture coheres with the evidence of LLk.
xxiv. 34 [1] where the Emmaus disciples are greeted with the
words, *the Lord is risen indeed and hath appeared unto Simon.*

(iii) S. John corrected and supplemented the statements
of the gloss.

§ 47. The writer of the paper which underlies Jn. xx. 2 f.
probably adopted a procedure which he used elsewhere and
embodied S. John's comments in the text on which he
commented. This expanded Mk the editor inserted in
its Markan setting. We note traces of Mk (i) in the word
"run" (1) (§ 33), (ii) in the return of Mary with the other
women ("we"). (iii) In 3 the editor writes a sentence
which is suggested by Mk:

Jn.   *Peter went forth* (sing) *and the other disciple and*
Gloss. *Peter arose*   *and*

they were coming to the tomb.
     ran   *to the tomb.*

The use of the singular verb is in accordance with the
editor's usage when the first subject is primary and the
second additional.[2]   In our passage the singular is used

---

[1] LEMk. 13 shows that Mk is not the source. I can find no motive
for two minor editings at this point. (*a*) *The eleven* refers back to
MLk. xxiv. 9. (*b*) For *saying* cf. Ac. vii. 59. Evidence for the position
that X narrated the appearance to Peter will be adduced below.

[2] Abbott *Johannine Grammar* 2418 f. where the instances are i. 35,
45, ii. 12, iii. 22, iv. 53, xviii. 1, 15.

because John was not mentioned in the source.   There is
a good parallel in xviii. 15, *there followed* (sing) *Jesus Simon
Peter* (Mk. xiv. 54) *and another disciple*.   The whole phrase is
a weak paraphrase of *arose and ran* and is due to the avoidance
of *ran* because it occurred in the expanded phrase of the
paper *they were running both together*.

(iv) The narrative of the paper ended with S. John's word
believed, that of the gloss with *wondered*.   The editor carelessly treated them as equivalents and added a phrase from
Mk which adheres well to *wondered* but makes an absurd
adhesion with *believed*:

Gloss.	*Wondering at that which had come to pass*	*he departed to his quarters,*	*for as yet he believed not the scriptures.*
Jn.	*Believed,*	*for as yet they knew not the scriptures.*	*So the disciples departed to their quarters.*

Forgetfulness of Christ's testimony teaching explains the
wonder of Peter but not the belief of John.

§ 48. S. John's corrections of Mk are as follows:

Jn.   *They ran both together, and the other disciple did*
Gloss. *Peter ran*
outrun Peter and came first to the tomb; and stooping and
                                        to the tomb; and stooping and

looking in he seeth lying the linens.
looking in he seeth the linens by themselves.

Jn continues: *yet entered he not in. Peter ... following ...
entered; and he beholdeth the linens lying, and the napkin, that
was upon his head, not lying with the linens but wrapped round
into one place. Then entered ... the disciple which came first
to the tomb and he saw and believed.*

We may comment as follows:

1. The word *lying* occurs three times and in the first
instance is as emphatic as possible. S. John said that the
point was not that the linens were *alone* but that they were
lying. *Wrapped round into one place* is as bad Greek as

it is bad English. Realising their importance the scribe took down S. John's precise words. The apostle's Greek vocabulary was very limited and he borrowed *wrapped round* from X *sub* LLk. xxiii. 53, explaining his meaning by a motion of his hand. We may paraphrase *in a wrapped round shape confined into one place*. The linens were lying, that is, lying flat, and in this respect unlike the napkin which was annular and separated from the linens in its place and not in two places, that is, in its original position on the raised part of the ledge where the head had rested and not spreading into the rest of the shelf or falling over the side. *That was about his head* helped to explain that *wrapped round* meant *annular*. The allusion to the head helped to explain what was meant by *into one place*.

2. The processes of S. John's thought were connected with his movements, which are stated therefore with precision. He ran with Peter and outran him. He stooped and looked in. Something checked him. Peter passed him. Peter saw *lying the linens* (it must have been this fact that checked John: it is stated in connection with Peter because John was correcting Mk) and the napkin. John entered and saw what he had not seen before, *i.e.* the carefully described napkin. What he had not seen before completed the process of conviction. The napkin was in the shadow round the corner of the rock wall. The linens lay flat along the ledge. There was a space where the neck had been. The turban retained its shape and its place on the raised part of the ledge where the head had rested. The body had passed into space. I have followed Latham (Risen Master 35) whose views were suggested by the vesture of a corpse which he himself had seen. No other view of S. John's words seems to me to do justice to the passage, but my main point is concerned not with the details, important though they are, but with the fact that it was what he saw when he entered the tomb that brought conviction.

§ 49. 3. An earlier visitor to the tomb had almost had the same experience as S. John and like the apostle described her movements with precision. When she arrived at the

tomb she stooped and looked in (Jn).   She entered and came
out (Mk).   She remained standing, turned herself back,
turned (Jn) and ran forward (gloss).   When she first looked
in she said, *they have taken away the Lord, and I don't see
where they have laid him*.   Like John she saw the linens,
but the significance of the fact that they were lying escaped
her.   When she entered her mind like John's received a
suggestion.   The idea that Christ was risen came to her in
an emotional flash.   She had an audition and a vision.   For
her the world was crowded with good and evil spirits.   The
linens and the napkin catching the dawning light and
speaking God's message became two angels sitting one at
the head, the other at the feet, where the body of Jesus had
lain (Jn) on the right side of the grave (Mk).   The angels
said, He lives (LLk).   We now understand why when Mary
told her story to the writer of X she was careful to say that
when she brought the spices she saw *how the body of Jesus
was laid*.   We also observe that the two angels and their
positions correspond with the linens and the napkin and
their positions with the position of the body.

4. It is obvious but important to observe that by the lake
as at the sepulchre John was the first to see and Peter the
first to act (Jn. xxi. 7).

5. S. Mark's narrative of S. Peter's visit to the tomb, as
far as it goes, gives the impression of accuracy, and it
probably abbreviates X.   The order of the incidents in L
was parallel with that of Mk, which work narrated the
visit of the women which occasioned the apostle's, the
allusion to the Emmaus disciples and the appearance to
Peter.

§ 50. That S. Mark made Christ appear to the eleven at
Jerusalem appears from three independent arguments.

(i) In § 32 we observed that while the KP narrative
of the appearance was related to that recorded in Lk it did
not derive from Lk but was superior in its report of the first
saying of Christ, in *they touched him*, in the retention of the
Markan *straitway*, in *they believed* and in *he ate and drank*

E

with them. KP was attributed to S. Mark, and we shall discuss evidence which shews that the writer used the end of Mk.

(ii) Lk. xxiv. 1–9 is a much edited passage in which S. Luke is influenced by Mk but draws most of his materials from L. In § 33 we concluded that its statement of the report of the women derives both from Mk and from L. The L Emmaus narrative follows, and then the appearance to the eleven which is told in a style which can only be contrasted. At the outset there is a contact with Mk. Just as the women are amazed, tremble, are astonished and disobey, so the eleven are terrified, affrighted and unbelieving.

(iii) Matthew, whose continued use of Mk has been proved, implies an appearance at Jerusalem.

§ 51. We will now notice some points at which S. Luke has edited Mk.

(i) *While they still disbelieved for joy.* That S. Luke is editing a statement of Mk that the apostles *still disbelieved* is shewn not only by the occurrence of that phrase in a recension of EvXII, which we shall discuss, but also by the fact that it follows the logion and in KP the unbelief continued until the touching, an incident which Lk omits. S. Luke has " spared " the eleven by omitting the touching and the unbelief which the touching ended and by throwing the emphasis on the fact that Christ ate before them, an incident which clearly much impressed him. The disbelief is thrown into a participial phrase, and with it there is cleverly combined the gladness of the disciples which S. Luke found in the XL parallel with Jn. xx. 20.

(ii) In the words which follow S. Luke uses XL substituting for the *ate and drank with* of Mk matter from the appearance by the lake.

Lk. *Have ye any meat?*	*They gave him a piece of broiled fish.*
Jn. *Have ye τι προσφάγιον :*	*A fire of coals. Bring of the fish.*

(iii) Christ is not likely to have repeated the testimony teaching which He gives in Lk. ix. 22, 44, and we shall conclude that in Mk He gave new teaching. Lk telescopes the two passages and spares the eleven by omitting a sentence in which Christ blamed the eleven for not remembering His earlier teaching.

§ 52. Jn. xx. 19–29 is based on a paper which preserved the X narrative of the appearance to Thomas and which was edited as follows. (*a*) It was introduced by an abbreviated narrative of the appearance to the other disciples. (*b*) Into this paper at 21 the editor interpolated a scrap which contained two Ascension midrashim (§§ 78 f.). (*c*) Knowing that 21–23 was a separate incident he inserted *peace be unto you* from 19. (*d*) Just as in order to make his narrative read plausibly he introduced allusions to feasts in the first part of the Gospel, so when he repeated the introduction in 26 he wrote without any justification *after eight days*. (*e*) In 26 he copied his paper more carefully than in 19 and preserved "within." This word survives *in situ* in EvXII (§ 54). (*f*) The paper itself contained the midrash *and my God* (§§ 34, 354, 357).

We have observed that the agreement of Jn with our reconstructed Mk shews that the sentence *he came and stood in the midst* occurred in X. Like *my brethren* (Jn. xx. 17) the salutation *peace be unto you* (*i.e.* "good evening") discloses the profundity of meaning that is implicit in the commonest words of ordinary speech. The vraisemblance in both cases is very impressive. *My brethren* occurs in Matt. xxv. 40 but nowhere in conversation.

Jn then states that Jesus shewed His hands and His side and that the disciples *rejoiced when they saw the Lord*. But they saw Him before He spoke and shewed His hands. Either the writer of the paper abbreviated or the evangelist copied carelessly. Clearly X must have run: *they were glad when they saw that it was the Lord*. Their previous doubt has been omitted. Moreover the shewing was presumably accompanied by words. Jn then is parallel with MLk, *see my hands and my feet*. At this point must be placed the phrase preserved by S. Luke, *still disbelieved*. We require therefore they *touched him* which we find in Ign. and in 1 Jn. i. 1.

Our view that Jn and Mk derived from a common source is confirmed by the fact that the curious use of *see* in the phrase of Mk *sub* MLk and KP, *feel me and see* has a precise parallel in Jn, *reach hither thy finger and see my hands*. Further, our reconstructed *saw that it was the Lord* refers back to the phrase of Lk, *see . . . that it is I myself*.

§ 53. We can fill up one of the lacunæ in our reconstruction of X from Mk. vi. In 48 f. S. Mark works up a miracle which he supposed he had found in X *sub* Jn. vi. 17 f. The situation as he conceived it was similar to that described in the X narrative of the Appearance. The kind of thing which he would have written if he had invented the sequel to his supposed miracle has been already illustrated. We cannot then doubt that S. Mark borrows when he writes: *they supposed that it was a phantom, for they all saw him and were troubled. But he straitway spake unto them, Be of good cheer* (edit. for " peace be unto you "). *It is I: be not afraid. Phantom* is parallel with MLk *spirit*. We shall conclude that the word probably occurred in our Mk narrative.

§ 54. I will now print a narrative which occurs in EPApp, 11, and beyond any doubt derives like much else in the work from EvXII. LeuciusP, I shall argue, used not only KP and QPl but also X. His motive is clear. He was defending the authority of the twelve against the attacks on it made by Cerinthus and Leucius and wished to write a narrative more favourable than S. Mark's. In 10 the allusions to Jn are editorial and are presumably so in 11. But EvXII had matter at this point for the names occurred in QP (§ 95). The parallels shew that *mourned and wept* is transferred from the apostles.

I will print in italics the matter which I ascribe to X and Mk and place in square brackets that which I ascribe to KP. I will add matter from Ignatius and from the Syriac Testament of the Lord (STest) or I Bk. Clem. (Lagarde RJEA, 80).

A. Thither went three women, Mary . . . of Martha, Mary Magdalene . . . and (?) Martha. . . . 10. B. as they (*mourned and wept. . . .*)   11. C. Then said the Lord unto Mary and her sisters: Let us go unto them.   And He *came* and found us *within* ("sitting veiled" or "fishing" Eth.) and called us out; D. *but we thought it was a phantom and believed not that it was the Lord.*   E. *Then said he unto us: Come, fear not.   I am* your Master, even *he*, F. Peter, whom thou deniedst.   G. And we came unto Him, doubting in our hearts whether it were He.   H. *Then said he unto us: Wherefore doubt ye still and are unbelieving?*   J. (*I am he that spake unto you of* my flesh and *my death and my resurrection* [Ign. (feel me.)] EpApp. Peter, put thy finger. . . . Thomas, put thy finger. . . . Andrew, look on my feet. . . . L. [for it is written in the prophet, *A phantom* of a devil maketh no foot print on the earth.   M. 12. *And we touched him*] N. that we might learn of a truth whether He were risen in the flesh; O. [*and we fell on our faces and worshipped him, confessing our sin*].

§ 55. We may comment on the ancient matter in this passage thus.   B. That *mourned and wept* occurred in EvXII is shewn by EvP, 27.   That this phrase occurred in Mk is shewn by the agreement of LEMk and QPl *sub* SchmidtEvvC, 1 and AJ, 97.   Cf. Cyr. Cat. xiii. 25.   The incident is not in line with the motivisation of S. Mark's editing (§ 51, iii) and probably derives from X, in which work Mary wept. C. For "came" cf. § 31.   *Within* is placed as in X (§ 52). D. *Phantom* derives from X *sub* Mk. vi., but *phantom of a demon* (KP *sub* L) shews that the word occurred in our Mk context.   *Believed not that it was* the Lord was picked up in X *sub* Jn by *Were glad when they saw that it was the Lord*. E. *Fear not; I . . . am he* is from X *sub* Mk. vi. and cannot derive from Mk, nor would S. Luke have omitted the words. In Mk Christ "upbraided."   G may paraphrase an incident in which some of the eleven moved towards Christ.   He had appeared to Peter, and John was already convinced.   H. *Wherefore doubt ye still?* is parallel with Lk *while they still disbelieved?*   S. Luke is editing and *still disbelieved* may be misplaced.   J is superior to MLk in making Christ refer back to testimony teaching which had been already given. The use of KP may begin at this point.   The testimony

(L) is from KP (§ 93 (2)). O is transferred from the Appearance to Peter (§ 84).

(*a*) EvXII also survives in STestDom: *we remained trembling in much fear . . . . Why did your heart thus fall? and why were ye struck exceedingly with amazement?* (*b*) O may also influence CBRB, 213. (*c*) I shall attribute to X the close of the Appearance, *he took bread . . .* (§ 91).

§ 56. I now print my reconstruction of X, anticipating some further discussion. I will also add in a parallel column a narrative which we shall attribute to X and which seems to somewhat resemble the narrative of Thomas in style.

Jn. xx. 19. *When it was evening on that day and the disciples* 26 EpApp C. *were within*, Jn. *the doors being shut for fear of the rulers.* § 32. *Jesus came and stood in the midst and said, Peace be unto you.* Mk. vi., EpApp D. *But they supposed that it was a phantom, for they all saw him and were troubled,* EpApp D. *and believed not that it was the Lord.* Mk. vi. *And he spake with them and said,* Mk, MLk, EpApp EJ. *It is I;* Mk, EpApp F. *be not afraid.* Lk, EpApp G (?). *And they came to him,* H. *still disbelieving.* LLk. *And he said unto them, Foolish fellows and slow of heart to believe.* LLk, Mk *sub* EpApp J. *Remember how I spake unto you when I was yet with you that* KP. *the Son of man* LLk *must needs be delivered into the hands of men and* (cf. LLk)(?) *enter into his glory.* MLk, KP. *Feel me and see that it is I myself.* Jn. *And when he had said this, he shewed them his hands and his (feet).* KP *sub* Ign, EpApp (M), 1 Jn. i. 1. *And they touched him.* Jn. *Then were the disciples glad when they saw that it was the Lord.* EvH (§ 91*h*). *And taking bread he blessed and brake it and gave it to them.*

But Thomas was not with them when Jesus came. And the other disciples said unto him, We have seen the Lord. But he said unto them, Except I shall see in his hands the print of the nails, and put my finger into the print of the nails I will not

Lk. vii. *She began to wet his feet with her tears, and wiped them with the hair of her head, and kissed his feet, and anointed them with ointment.*

Then Jesus cometh again and saith unto Thomas, Reach hither thy finger and see my hands; and reach hither thy hand and put it in my side, and be not faithless but believing.

Thomas saith unto him, My Lord. Jesus saith unto him, Because thou hast seen me thou hast believed; blessed are they that have not seen, and yet have believed.

Jesus saith unto Simon, Seest thou this woman? . . . Thou gavest me no water for my feet; but she hath wetted my feet with her tears, and wiped them with her hair. Thou gavest me no kiss: but she hath not ceased to kiss my feet.

Wherefore I say unto thee, Her sins which are many are forgiven; because she loved much: but to whom little is forgiven, the same loveth little.

With *my Lord* compare Mary's *Rabboni*. *And my God* is or is based on S. John's comment.

§ 57. Mk may be reconstructed from LEMk, MLk, the glossator of Lk and the writers who used KP as follows: (LEMk) *And when they were sitting at meat* (Ign) *Jesus came* (Lk) *and stood in the midst of them. And they were terrified and affrighted and supposed that they beheld a spirit.* (LEMk) *And he upbraided them for their unbelief and hardness of heart* (Lk) (cf. STest) *and he said unto them, Why are ye troubled? and wherefore do reasonings arise in your heart?* (44) *These are my words which I spake unto you when I was yet with you that* (J, QPl) *the Son of Man* (Lk, EpApp) *must needs suffer and rise again from the dead on the third day.* (Ign, Lk) *And he said unto them, See my hands and my feet, that it is I myself* (Ign, EvH) *and not a bodiless demon.* (Ign) *And straitway* (Ign, EpApp, STest) *they touched him.* (EpApp, STest). *And they fell on their faces* (EpApp, gloss (Lk), Matt) *and worshipped him* (EpApp) *confessing their sin.*

§ 58. Apart from the appearance to Peter four incidents remain.

(i) The statement that Christ ate and drank with the eleven was, as has been already said, a modification of S. Peter's words *we ate and drank with him.* It will be shewn that S. Mark not only transferred this phrase from the

Cæsarea sermon but also the preAscension testimony
teaching which underlies MLk xxiv. 47–48.

(ii) It will be convenient to postpone our discussion of
the appearance by the lake to our second volume. The
incident has no bearing on our reconstruction of the end of
Mk and a discussion would involve an examination of
Lk. v. and xxii. This decision involves the postponement of
the discussion of the saying *I will go before you into Galilee.*
Inasmuch as the saying was at any rate edited by S. Mark
and according to our reconstruction disobeyed by the
eleven the argument of the present chapter is not affected.

(iii) The appearance on the mountain was no more than
a sequel to the saying of Mk. xiv. 28.

(iv) The Ascension will be briefly discussed.

§ 59. Something must now be said about the methods
of the three synoptists.

(i) Matthew, as might be expected, preserves in his last
chapter the two Markan incidents which narrated the
ultimate obedience of the women and the eleven. But it
is to be observed that his candour compelled him to admit
that the faith of the eleven was not flawless. He added
therefore *and they worshipped him, but some doubted.* The
doubt like the worship (EpApp, O) is moved from Jerusalem. The discourse in Matt. xxviii. 18–20 is the impressive
paraphrase of preAscension sayings with which Matthew
winds up. In I Ac. Mc. Christ ascended from Olivet, and
there was probably an allusion to Olivet in the curious
lacuna which follows LEMk, 14. That Matthew did not
regard his concluding discourse as continuous with the
preceding narrative is shewn by the words *and Jesus came to
them saying.* In much the same way the second *peace be
unto you* in Jn. xx. 21 shews that the narrative makes a
fresh start.

(ii) We have already analysed Lk. xxiv. For the
appearance to the eleven S. Luke chose Mk because of his
interest in the matter which followed, *i.e.* the fact that Christ
ate and gave testimony teaching about His preaching to
the Gentiles, but he corrects Mk from L and abbreviates

the narrative into an introduction to the eating and the teaching. In v. 8 he had already corrected Mk *sub* EpApp, O by rightly assigning the prostration and confession to S. Peter. He preferred the close of L to the close of Mk. He was not contemplating a second volume when he wrote and did not copy S. Mark's very attractive last verse. I shall argue that his last verse is likely to have been the conclusion of X.

§ 60. (iii) S. Mark in the concluding section of his Gospel was actuated by four motives, and they did not include a desire to record the facts known about the self-manifestations of the risen Lord, A. the desire to represent the circumstances connected with the Resurrection as no less awe-inspiring than the events which had occurred at the time of the Crucifixion, B. the desire to exalt S. Peter and (C) to belittle the other apostles. D. Mk prepared the way for I Ac. Mc. [I now attribute A and C to "JMark."]

There is something to be said in defence of the programmatic matter at the end of Mk. The scheme which underlies Mk and I Ac. Mc. was a good one and probably reflected the thought of S. Peter who at any rate believed that the activities of his which S. Mark narrated were in accordance with the promises and "commandments" of Christ. We may wish that the concluding logia had been less in S. Mark's phrasing, but he meant no more than is implied in the conviction which we have attributed to the apostle.

We may summarise the end of Mk and its motivisation thus: (*a*) AC. The stone, the angel and his message; (*b*) C. the appearance to the women and their report; (*c*) B. Peter's visit to the tomb; (*d*) B (?), the appearance to Peter; (*e*) C. the Emmaus narrative; (*f*) C. the appearance to the eleven; (*g*) *they went unto the mountain where Jesus had appointed them*; (*h*) D. *he ate with them many days* and the testimony teaching; (*j*) D. preAscension teaching; (*k*) D. the Ascension and the summary of I Ac. Mc.

A survey of the incidents which we have attributed to the end of Mk suggests that nothing of importance has been omitted. There was nothing in the X narrative of the appearance by the lake which was to S. Mark's purpose, and the unbelief of Thomas was included in that of the eleven.

It remains that (i) we should examine the passages which refer to the testimony teaching in Galilee, (ii) reconstruct the close of EvXII, (iii) reconstruct the Markan passage which followed the eating, and examine the section of I Ac. Mc. which overlapped Mk, (iv) and the appearance to S. Peter. We will then examine two objections to our reconstruction. A word or two must also be said about 1 Cor. xv. 1 f.

§ 61. We will return to the subject of the reference of Jesus to His earlier testimony teaching about the destiny of the Son of man and also comment briefly on the Emmaus narrative.

We have discovered that S. Luke sometimes transferred matter which he did not wish to use *in situ*. He must have done so in the passages which assume that the women and the Emmaus disciples had heard testimony teaching which they are not said and are not likely to have heard and which made the hearts of the two disciples burn as if they had heard it for the first time. Moreover there are two contacts with the eleven. (i) In LLk. xxiv. 6 *remember how he spake that the Son of man must be delivered up into the hands of . . . men* picks up the variation of LLk. ix. 44 from the parallel in Mk. ix. 31, *let these sayings sink into your ears . . . The Son of man* has dropped out of EpAppJ but survives in the J and QPl depravations of KP (§§ 69, 92). (ii) *O foolish men and slow of heart to believe in all that the prophets* . . . is likely to have suggested the words of LEMk. 14, *he upbraided them for their unbelief and hardness of heart,* a phrase which our reconstruction shews is likely to have preceded Christ's reference to His earlier testimony teaching. On the other hand S. Luke transferred from 27 in the reverse direction. *Moses . . . (44)* and, probably, also *then opened he their mind . . . (45).*

§ 62. Another instance of editing in the Emmaus narrative may be conjectured. In 20 the two disciples speak of *the things concerning Jesus . . . which was a prophet . . . and how (the chief priests and*) *our rulers* (*delivered him up to be condemned to death and*) *crucified him.* S. Luke uses a phrase suggested by XL, for in LLk. ix. 44, xxiv. 7 the Son of man will be delivered into men's hands, but he applies it to the delivering of Jesus over to Pilate. He also combines the fuller tradition that Pilate was responsible for the Crucifixion with the primitive phrase which he found in XL and which was used by S. Peter (Ac. x. 39), *they crucified him.* The bracketed words therefore are editorial as is the similar sentence in Ac. xiii. 27 f. Another instance of primitive phrasing is, *behoved it not . . . the Christ . . . to enter into his glory?* A writer who was influenced by the earliest preaching would have written *ascend* or *be taken up.* The word *Christ* confirms our view that the disciples had not heard the testimony teaching about the Son of man. Jesus speaks as an unknown companion.

The XL Emmaus narrative may have run thus: . . . 19. *The things concerning Jesus of Nazareth, which was a prophet mighty in deed and word before God and all the people: and our rulers crucified him. . . . Then opened he their mind that they might understand the scriptures, and beginning from Moses he interpreted to them the things concerning himself. . . . And they returned to Jerusalem, and the disciples said to them, The Lord is risen indeed and hath appeared unto Simon. And they rehearsed the things that happened in the way, and how he was known unto them in the breaking of bread. Now the day was drawing to a close, and the disciples were within the doors being shut for fear of the Jews. And as Cleopas and the other disciple said these things Jesus came and stood in the midst. . . .*

§ 63. The following passages illustrate the influence of the section of Mk which followed the Appearance to the Eleven on KP and that of KP on later writers.

We have noted the parallelism of the KP narrative of the Appearance with S. Luke's. In KP6 and 7 the parallelism is continued. As in Lk the preaching is to be first to the Jews and then to the gentiles. PsMark paraphrases as S. Luke does in Ac. i. 8 but borrows " go ye " from Mk sub LEMk. 15, Matt. xxviii. 19. KP6 like Lk refers to the preaching of the remission of sins in Christ's name: *If any of Israel will repent . . . through my name his sins will be forgiven. After twelve years go ye out.* The passage which follows, KP7, contains a probable echo of Mk. sub LEMk. 16, *that they which have . . . believed may be saved.*

Our context of KP influenced EvXII as follows:

At the end of the EvXII narrative of the appearance to the eleven Christ commissioned them to preach in the four quarters of the world, and this phrase influenced a parallel with LEMk. 20.

(i) A. EpApp omits the commission *in situ*, but in 30 Christ says, *go ye and preach* (cf. LEMk. 15) *unto the twelve tribes of Israel and also unto the heathen* (text *tribes . . . heathen . . . land of Israel*) *from the east unto the west and from the south unto the north, and many shall believe.* The twelve tribes are from QPl (cf. LJasZ, 35) and probably, ultimately, from the Cerinthian Matthew. We observe the parallel with MLk. xxiv. 47, *unto all the nations beginning at Jerusalem.*

B. HEvXII, 27. *Go and evangelise the four quarters of the world.*

C. In R. iv. 4 *north and south* are added to a citation of Matt. viii. 11.

D. Cf. also EApP, 513.

(ii) The following passages preserve the conclusion of EvXII. It will be observed that it was based on the last verse of Mk.

E. In the codex Bruce of Pist. Soph. we find: *They went forth three by three to the four points of heaven; they preached the gospel of the kingdom to the whole world, the Christ being active with them in the words of confirmation and in signs and wonders which accompanied them* (LEMk. 20). *And thus was known the kingdom of God to the whole land* (*earth*) *and to all the world of Israel* (cf. A), *and this kingdom* (*preaching*) *is a testimony* (Mk. vi. 11, xiii. 9, EvEb, 1) *for all the nations which are from the east even unto the west.* The phrase *gospel of the kingdom* occurs in QPl *ap* SchmidtEvvC, 1, and is probably another contact with the Cerinthian Matthew.

F. In HEvXII, 27 B is followed by *And we carried out the preaching from the ends of the earth unto the ends of the same*.

G. AT, 27. *His heralds do preach in the four quarters of the world*.

§ 64. It is probable that the EvXII parallel with LEMk. 20 was influenced by the KP parallel with that verse and the close of our section of KP used in the short ending of Mk. This ending runs: *And they reported all things which were commanded concisely to Peter and his company. And after these things Jesus also himself appeared to them, and from the east even unto the west he sent forth the holy and incorruptible message of eternal salvation*. Here *reported* is a contact with our reconstruction of Mk in a phrase which is strongly connected with KP by its parallel with Ignatius, *Peter and his company*. *Eternal*[1] is another contact and the phrase *east unto west* is connected with KP by its probable influence on EvXII and the parallels in EpClem, 1 and I Clem, 5.

§ 65. Other contacts of our section of KP with LEMk will be found in § 378. In a context of AscIs, which like most of the work is certainly based on KP and which describes the sending forth of the twelve disciples, there are some contacts with MLk. xxiv. 47, LEMk. 16, 17, 18: *they will teach all the nations . . . those who believe will be saved . . . and many who believe will speak through the Holy Spirit. And many signs and wonders will be wrought* (iii. 17 f.).

The influence of Mk occurs also in Proch, 32, 2 f.: *He appeared to us the twelve apostles and ate with us and drank with us fleshliwise. And he commanded us as spiritual men to go into all the world and teach and baptize. He that believeth on him shall be saved, but he that disbelieveth shall be condemned*. A comparison with SHJ, 16 shews that both writers substituted other matter for the sermon of AJ which like that in AJ, 88 f. is likely to have been much influenced by QPl. Here as elsewhere Prochorus is influenced by Heg. The influence of KP is shewn by the parallel with Ign. Sm. 3 (§ 29).

---

[1] Compare *eternal kingdom* (II Pet. i. 11; Arist, 16; H. x. 25; MPol, 20), *eternal king* (MPol, 21; AT, 139; MPl, 2; APh, 11), *eternal oil* (I Clem, 18).

§ 66. In Mk the recognition of Christ was followed by
the statement that *he ate and drank with* the disciples (Ign)
and this statement by testimony teaching that *remission of
sins must be preached unto all the nations beginning from
Jerusalem.* Two problems arise. (1) At what point in Lk
does the use of Mk end and that of L begin? (2) Did
Christ as in Lk eat with the eleven at His first appearance
or did the phrase refer, as we shall find it did in the Cæsarea
sermon, to an intercourse which lasted for *many days*?

1. We must assign 49 to L for the following reasons :
(i) 48 comes within the scope of the heading in 47, but 49
does not. (ii) The words *I am sending forth the promise of
my Father* is not testimony teaching but a saying which
implies an earlier interpretation of Joel. We shall conclude
that 47–48 derive from the Cæsarea sermon, but 49 cannot
do so. (iii) We shall conclude that in I Ac. Mc. Christ
ascended at Pentecost after breathing upon the disciples
and saying, Receive ye the Holy Ghost, and was then taken
up and sat down at the right hand of God. On this view the
MarcoPetrine tradition restated in terms derived from
theological reflection the simple matter of fact X tradition
in which Jesus said that He was fulfilling the promise of Joel
and then or shortly afterwards disappeared. Similarly *tarry
in Jerusalem until ye be endued with power from on high* is
parallel with *preached to all the nations beginning at Jerusalem.*
The apostles were to remain at Jerusalem until they were
endued with power for their larger task. They would leave
the nest when strength came to their wings. The command
to tarry in Jerusalem explains the remarkable fact that the
apostles did not return to Galilee after Pentecost. We
conclude that 47–48 is from Mk and 49–52 from L.

§ 67. 2. We noticed above that *he ate and drank with*
(Ign) coheres with LEMk. 14 *as they sat at meat*, and this
fact when combined with Lk. xxiv. 42 suggests that in Mk
Christ ate and then taught on the evening of Easterday.
On the other hand S. Luke is editing Mk with a view to
shewing that it was the eating that produced conviction and
does so in terms of the Appearance by the Lake. Further,
the teaching given in 47–48 must have been preAscension

teaching. At His first appearance Christ's purpose was to convince His disciples that He had risen. Their minds were not prepared for further instruction. That S. Luke has telescoped his matter is also shewn (*a*) by the fact that, probably *per incuriam*, he alone makes Christ ascend on the evening of Easterday and (*b*) by the fact that " ate and drank with " almost certainly derives from the Cæsarea sermon and that in the original form of that sermon the phrase referred to the " many days " which followed the appearance to the eleven. We conclude that it is probable that Mk after narrating the appearance in Jerusalem and the return to Galilee deserted X and made the close of the sermon an introduction to a short Ascension narrative. We shall conclude that the Ascension was narrated at greater length at the beginning of I Ac. Mc.

[The evidence for the conclusion of the Appearance is collected on p. 147. It shows that the statement that Christ ate and drank with the eleven was almost certainly introduced into Mk by an Ebionite reviser who derived the incident from M but borrowed his phrase from EMk.]

Our conclusion is confirmed by Ac. i. After the Markan introduction (1–2) if we substitute *many* for *forty* 3–4*a* is parallel with our suggested end of Mk: *he presented himself alive by many proofs* (being seen, heard and touched), *being seen of them many days and speaking the things concerning the kingdom of God and eating with them* (συναλιζόμενος). The sermon supports the translation (68). The words which follow in Acts are a chaos of splinters. When S. Luke altered the Markan chronology and divided the fifty days he retained the Markan phrase *many days* in *not many days*.

§ 68. Our discussion of the Cæsarea sermon (it has been already stated that much of the Antioch sermon derives from it) must be postponed. Our reconstruction of the close will be as follows: Ac. x. *whom they slew hanging him upon a tree*. xiii. *And when they had fulfilled all things that were written of him*, EvP, 17 (cf. Barn. v. 11) *and accomplished their sins upon their heads*, xiii., EvP, 21, *they took him down from the tree*, xiii., AThadd, 6 *and laid him in a tomb*. x. *Him*

God raised up the third day . . . made manifest . . . unto wit-nesses that were chosen before of God, even to us who did eat and drink with him, gloss, SHJ, 16. *and we conversed with him,* xiii., AThadd, 6, AscIs xi. 21 (" remain days ") *many days.* x. 42, xiii. 46a. *And he charged us to preach unto the people.* xiii. *Seeing then that they thrust it from them we turn to the gentiles. For so hath the Lord commanded us: I have set thee for a light of the gentiles, that thou shouldest be for my salvation unto the uttermost part of the earth* (Is. xlix. 6). x. *This Jesus is he who is ordained of God to be the judge of quick and dead. To him bear all the prophets witness that through his name,* x., xiii., SHJ, *every one that believeth on him shall receive remission of sin.*

§ 69. If this restoration of the close of the Markan sermon is accepted our view that Mk *sub* MLk. xxiv. 47–48 derives from S. Peter is confirmed. We will discuss the context.

(i) In Mk Jesus upbraided the eleven for forgetting His testimony teaching about His passion and resurrection. S. Luke telescoped his statement that Christ repeated it into fragments of the testimony teaching which according to S. Peter and in Mk Christ gave during the "many days."

(ii) In Ac. x. 43 Peter refers to *all the prophets.* Clement in the Latin fragment of an abbreviation of the Hypyposeis writes: *Mark wrote when Peter was preaching publicly at Rome in the presence of certain imperial knights and adducing many testimonies to Christ.* It will be shewn below that the preaching referred to was that to Marcellus at Cæsarea. Our passage proves that in KP the apostle either cited (cf. KP, 9, 10) or was said to have cited many testimonies.

(iii) It is probable that when applying testimonies to Himself Jesus always spoke of Himself as the Son of man and that the disciples never used that expression. Ac. xxvi. 23 and 1 Cor. xv. 3 supply instances of the latter usage. It follows that the phrase *the Christ* is evidence that Mk *sub* MkLk. xxiv. 46 derives from the testimony teaching at second hand through S. Peter.

The use of " Son of man " in I Ac. Mc. *sub* Ac. vii. 59 and HE, II. xxiii. 13 is not a real exception to this rule.

S. Luke edited out the antiJudaic matter both in Ac. vii. and Ac. x. and assimilated the martyrdom to the L Passion. S. Mark in order to shew that the Jews had crucified again the Son of God assimilated it to the Mk Passion. Stephen, speaking like Christ (Mk. xv. 34), his last word with *a loud voice*, said Ac. vii. *I see* Heg *the Son of man sitting at the right hand of power and coming on the clouds of heaven* (in judgment). S. Mark meant, if he did not write, *as he said he would* (Mk. xv. 62). S. Peter at Cæsarea may have been influenced by Stephen if as is almost certainly the case the following passage derives from James-Stephen: *the temple shall be destroyed . . . and the gospel shall be preached to the gentiles for a testimony against you* (Ac. xiii. 51) *that your unbelief may be judged by their faith* (R. i. 64).

§ 70. (iv) MLk states that Christ taught from testimonies *that repentance and remission of sins should be preached in his name unto all the nations, beginning* (ἀρξάμενοι) *from Jerusalem. Ye are witnesses of these things.* Matt. xxviii. 19 provides a contact with LEMk. 15 in *go ye* and contacts with MLk in *all the nations* and *in the name of*. We shall conclude below that the Markan apocalypse is based on I Ac. Mc. *sub* Ac. i. and is an interpolation. It has a contact with LEMk. 15 *the gospel . . . preached* and contacts with MLk in *must* and *all the nations* (Mk. xiii. 10). *Ye are . . . witnesses* occurs in Ac. i. 8. See also § 63 *ad init.*

If on the one hand the evidence just stated confirms our attribution of our passage to Mk, S. Luke on the other hand has edited. An examination of the passages in which he abbreviates shews that he endeavours to use the phraseology of his source, that his syntax suffers and that he sometimes inserts ill-chosen words. There is no better illustration than Ac. x. 34–43 where we meet again with the ungrammatical *beginning* (37) and *asseverate* (42) is the wrong word. In MLk *beginning* is ungrammatical and editorial and, as is shewn by its loose reference, *of these things* is also editorial. If S. Luke has edited and may abbreviate, on the other hand it is improbable that in Mk our context was a long one.

F

§ 71. (v) The discussion which follows confirms our view that our matter derives from the Cæsarea sermon.

(a) We gather from Ac. xxvi. 21 that S. Paul's argument from the prophets was a long one, for Festus tells him that his great learning had made him mad, and the apostle on the other hand thought that he ought to have convinced Agrippa. His epistles shew that he made much use of the Markan testimonies, and it is probable that S. Paul when pleading before Festus would use some of those which had been used by S. Peter when he was preaching in the same pretorium to Marcellus. S. Luke was probably present and, inasmuch as in Ac. ix.–xxviii. it was one of his principal aims to represent S. Paul as another Peter, it is probable that xxvi. conceals a reference to I Ac. Mc. *sub* Ac. x. Now at 23 he writes an untranslatable sentence which, as Harris (i. 9: cf. ii. 77) argues, states three testimony headings: *does the Christ suffer? and does he first by the resurrection proclaim light to the people and to the gentiles?* The phrasing shews that the headings are influenced by Is. xlix. 6.

Our attribution of the testimony is confirmed by Irenæus who in his Demonstratio, a work full of primitive testimonies, uses this passage for another purpose and then comments: *He is Lord of all, the Saviour of them that believe both Jews and Greeks* (50). *Lord of all* occurs in the sermon as also *them that believe* and in the same connection of thought.

We now observe that Is. xlix. 5 f. is a servant passage and the passage in the OT which Christ *sub* Lk. xxiv. 47 would be most likely to cite for the position that both Jews and gentiles were to be evangelised and that in Ac. i. 8 after the citation *Ye are my witnesses* (Is. xliii. 10) and the programmatic words *in Jerusalem, all Judæa, Samaria*, there follows a splinter from our testimony, *unto the uttermost part of the earth*. Again, in Ac. xiii. 47, where the source is almost certainly the Cæsarea sermon, it is introduced with the words *the Lord commanded us saying*. We conclude that S. Mark attributed the use of the testimony to Christ on the authority of S. Peter.

§ 72. (b) The phrase from Is. xliii. 10 also was probably

attributed to the risen Christ in MLk and Ac. i. on the authority of S. Peter.   In Ac. x. 39 we read *we are witnesses of all things* . . ., and in 41 *witnesses chosen before of God.* The latter phrase is very obscure and is likely to abbreviate a statement that the disciples were chosen in accordance with a testimony in order that they might witness.   At any rate this is the meaning of Aristides who writes in a passage which has links with KP, *and He had twelve disciples in order that a certain dispensation of His* (*i.e.* a passage which He had inspired a prophet to utter) *might be fulfilled* (Syr. II). Aristides is full of KP, and I shall shew that the KP Cæsarea sermon, with which Aristides has one or two contacts, stated the call of the twelve.

§ 73. (*c*) The phrase *to every one that believeth*, which occurred at the end of S. Peter's sermon, is a variant from the LXX translation of Is. xxviii. 16, a passage which S. Paul cites from the LXX in an epistle which is full of early testimony matter (Rom. ix. 33 : Harris ii. 12 f.).   In x. 4 and 11 he uses S. Peter's variant and makes two clear allusions to the sermon : *for there is no distinction between Jew and Greek, for the same Lord is Lord of all*, two phrases which occurred in I Ac. Mc. *sub* Ac. x. 36, xi. 12 and xv. 9 (as used in II Ac. Mc.).   That Is. xxviii. 16 was cited in a Markan Acts is shewn by its occurrence in VP, 24, a context which contains other primitive testimonies, and by Rendel Harris whose arguments are wholly independent of our reconstruction.

§ 74. The saying *I am sending forth the promise of my Father*, which immediately follows *ye are witnesses* . . . does not come under the head of the announced testimony topics and is connected with Pentecost.   It has the ring of an authentic saying, and we have attributed it to L.   This assignment is confirmed by the very noteworthy phrase *my Father* (cf. ii. 49, xxii. 29).   Even the phrase *the Father* is only used in the NT by Christ, passages which distinguish the Father from the Son or the Spirit excepted.   The present tense perhaps suggests that the words were spoken very shortly before the giving of the Spirit.   We may compare the fine editorial saying with which, probably paraphrasing LEMk. 20, Matthew concludes his Gospel, *Lo I am with you always even unto the consummation of the age.* The saying implies an earlier exposition of Joel as also does Ac. i. 5 (§ 76).

It will be observed that on our view two sources which were almost contemporary with the events attributed to the risen Christ the interpretation of specified testimonies.

§ 75. Like Jn. xx. 1–18 Ac. i. is based on materials of the highest value, and like the editor of Jn S. Luke has produced a narrative which is of hardly any service to the historian until it has been subjected to analysis and criticism. After an introduction (1–2) which follows I Ac. Mc. closely Christ is said to have presented Himself alive to the apostles, a statement which on our view refers to the first appearance to them. The overlapping of Mk in I Ac. Mc. *sub* Acts continued. *Being seen of them forty days and speaking . . . and eating with them* is based on a parallel with the passage of Mk in which Jesus during a period which lasted many days ate and spake with the disciples and (at the close) gave them testimony teaching on the subject of their mission. The charge *not to depart from Jerusalem* is also Markan. To this command S. Luke makes an addition, *but to wait for the promise of the Father which ye heard from me.* S. Luke's misinterpretation of the command to tarry and his combination of it with Christ's allusion to Joel not only wrecks his grammar but results in a chronology which is wholly inconsistent with the Markan and which in 3 had led him to substitute forty days for *many days.* It is obvious to observe that inasmuch as the apostles had come up to Jerusalem to keep the feast, a fact which was implied both in Mk and L, the injunction was pointless. Indeed if they had remained in Jerusalem for forty days it would have been hardly less so. Not only Mk and Matt but also Lk. xxiv. 41 f. (§ 51), Jn. xxi. 1 and, possibly, I Cor. xv. 6 testify to the return to Galilee.

§ 76. The next saying is schematic and refers back to Mk. i. 8 where John says, *he shall baptize with the Holy Ghost*. This saying is picked up in LEMk where the apostles will baptize and those who believe will speak with tongues. Inasmuch as according to LEMk. 20 and Ac. i. 1 f. Christ after His ascension co-operated with the disciples we should expect that in Acts the Baptist's " He " would become " ye " and that we should read in 5 *John indeed baptized with water but ye shall baptize with the Holy Ghost*; and this is what we find in one of a series of western variants which preserve I Ac. Mc. S. Luke wrote, *ye shall be baptized not many days hence*. S. Luke has again altered his source to suit his chronology. Once more, at Cæsarea Peter obeyed the command to baptize the gentiles and as Christ had promised they had spoken with tongues. We may be sure then that just as the close of Mk refers back to i. 8 so the close of I Ac. Mc. referred back to our passage. Now in Ac. xi. 16 in a sentence which derives from I Ac. Mc. *sub* x. 47 Peter remembers the saying. But clearly Peter's remembrance of the fact that Christ had promised that he (Peter) should be baptized is pointless. The sense requires *ye shall baptize*. S. Luke has again altered his source.

§ 77. In 6 the apostles come together though they have not separated. In 8 Christ's last words are not as they are in LLk. xxiv. 50 a benediction but two testimony splinters *plus* programmatic editing.

After the conclusion of the Ascension narrative we learn that Christ ascended from Olivet. The apostles return to the upper chamber and we are then told their names, the first quaternion being separately copulated (cf. Mk. xiii, 3). The first act of church government and organisation would naturally follow the events of Ac. ii. and precede the inception of the witnessing. We are confirmed in our surmise by the introductory phrase *in those days* and still more by the words *unto the day in which he was taken up*. The incident closed a period of some length which followed Pentecost. ii. 1–42 hangs in the air. There is nothing to account for the glossolaliai which, as S. Peter himself said,

(x. 47) resembled those at Cæsarea. ii. 43–47 is composite
and editorial.

§ 78. If the first two chapters of Acts resemble a geological
formation which has been thrown into confusion by a
volcanic upheaval, there is a parallel narrative which though
extremely brief derives from a source of the highest value
and is as far as it goes intelligible. In LLk. xxiv. 49 f.
Christ says that He is about to fulfil the promise of Joel
and bids the disciples make Jerusalem the scene of their
labours until God endued them with strength. In L He
then led them forth by the Bethany road (§ 382 (ii)) and disappeared in the act of blessing them. The apostles evidently
regarded the event as a climax but not as a departure, for
it occasioned the great joy with which they returned to
Jerusalem. That joy connects on the one hand with the
words *I am sending forth the promise* and on the other with
the tongues. If this was the event which in the language
of the first preaching was the Assumption and if Christ
imparted the Spirit on Olivet the narrative is quite inconsistent with that of Ac. i. but entirely in accordance with
the evidence of the rest of the NT, where apart from
S. Peter's natural allusion to the glossolaliai which we find
in Ac. x. 47 there is no allusion to the events recorded in
Ac. ii.
    Our reconstruction receives a striking confirmation from
a misplaced fragment in Jn. In xx. 22 Christ breathes upon
the apostles, saying, Receive ye the Holy Ghost. The
contextual sayings are S. John's midrashim on the commission given at the Ascension. In Jn then as in LLk the
Spirit was given by the ascending Christ.

§ 79. We will now use a fourth group of fragments which
occur in the Markan apocalypse and in the apocrypha. The
uncanonical evidence is plentiful, but only a few passages
can be cited and discussion must be postponed.
    The apostles returned to Jerusalem for the feast of
Pentecost, bivouacking as at the passover in Gethsemane.
There they received preAscension teaching on which S. John

commented in midrashim preserved in Jn. xiv.–xvi. 30, 33.
At the dawn of Pentecost Christ said, *Arise, let us go hence*
(Jn. xiv. 31, I Ac. Mc., ApP, 4) and led them a sabbath
day's journey (Ac. i. 12: cf. LLk. xxiii. 54) towards Bethany
(LLk. xxiv. 50). For a short time Christ was alone with the
first quaternion of the apostles (Mk. xiii. 3, EP, 467) who
asked Him about the last things in a conversation which
survives in Mk. xiii. 22, 32, Ac. i. 6, 7 and the variant. The
other apostles then arrived (EP, 467, Ac. i. 6*a*) and Christ
spoke final words (LEMk, 19) of benediction and commission (LLk. xxiv. 51, Matt. xxviii. 20*b*). The saying
Receive ye the Holy Ghost (Jn, EP, 467) immediately preceded
the Ascension.

§ 80. The Markan terminology shews that in primitive
thought the event which took place on Olivet was compared
to the action of the Spirit at the creation and to the departures
of Moses and Elijah. They had spoken to Christ about
their departures, and had been mentioned in the teaching
given at Cæsarea Philippi which provided materials for a
dream which a week later like that at Joppa and *Domine, quo
vadis?* revealed to Peter his deeper mind (LLk. ix. 31,
Mk. ix. 2). On Olivet the two prophets (Ac. i. 10, EApP,
510) seemed to speak again. The initiation of the Session
of Jesus as Lord and Christ at the right hand of God
(LEMk. 19) and of the perpetual presence (Matt. xxviii. 20)
and the donation of the Spirit and all that the Ascended had
received (Ps. lxviii. 18: cf. Harris ii. 39, Robinson on
Eph. iv. 8) were one event. The previous teaching to some
extent enabled the disciples to understand what had happened, and as they descended Olivet they were filled with
a great joy which later became an ecstasy in which they
spoke in the tongues of the pilgrims, in the two dialects of
Aramaic, in Greek and in the Latin of the Spanish Jews
(EP, 476, HEvXII, 29). S. Luke paraphrased I Ac. Mc.
in a fine passage which was in part his *Te Deum* for the
spread of the Gospel at the date at which he wrote. A little
less than a generation later psMark introduced into his
narrative of the Ascension the statement that the apostles

remained praying upon Olivet on the place where His chariot had rested (EP, 475). The practice of praying on the site of the Ascension on the Day of Pentecost, which is mentioned by S. Silvia of Acquitaine, was ascribed to the apostles not very long after the fall of Jerusalem. The rite preserved the primitive tradition of the date of the Ascension. For the Easter rite see § 164 (D).

§ 81. Our reconstruction both on its historical and its theological side is coherent and intelligible. It is independent of Acts, but it finds places for S. Luke's medley of fragments. The disturbing force which wrecked his narrative was, to use Harnack's phrase, his " love of a good miracle." It is comparatively a small point that by making the Ascension precede the reception into a cloud he converted a dogma into a wonder. His fundamental blunder was that he regarded the glossolaliai not as the sign of the gift of the Spirit but as the gift itself and supposed that the words *tarry . . . ye shall be endued* meant, " wait until ye shall speak with tongues."

Under the influence of this misapprehension he edited as follows. (*a*) He inserted an interval of *not many days* between the Ascension and Pentecost. (*b*) He changed *ye shall baptize* into *ye shall be baptized*. (*c*) If they occurred in I Ac. Mc. he omitted the words *I am sending forth* and he certainly omitted much other matter, both narrative and discourse. In particular he omitted the words, *receive ye the Holy Ghost* and substituted two fragments of testimonies (Ac. i. 8). (*d*) In order to fill up the chronological gap which he had created, he moved into it the election of Matthias, relying perhaps on the words *and in those days* and (*e*) he inserted the list of the eleven. (*f*) His list of tongues helped to give a unique and permanent importance to the narrative of the tongues as also perhaps his omission of an explicit reference to the fact that many others besides the apostles spoke with them (EP, 476). (*g*) He substituted 44–47 for the passage which he had transposed.

§ 82. The net result of these changes was that by

separating them he concealed the real meaning both of the Ascension and the events which followed.

A Markan passage which in a terminology of profound significance narrated an event which was the fulfilment of the OT, the climax of the Ministry and the fountainhead of the activities of the Catholic Church and of a river of benediction which still flows became the incoherent story of a levitation followed by an ecstasy. That this has not been more widely perceived is due to the fact that there has been read into Ac. i. and ii. 1–21 what is not there.

It is possible that S. Luke misinterpreted the saying, *Tarry in the city* . . . when he wrote his Gospel. But he evaded the rejection of the chronology of I Ac. Mc. just as, so we shall find, he evaded the chronological problems raised by Mk and L in xix.–xxii. The result was that *per incuriam* he made Christ ascend on the evening of Easterday.

§ 83. We will now return to the conclusion of the EpApp narrative of the first appearance to the eleven, *we fell on our faces and worshipped Him, confessing our sin* (§ 46 (O)). That the incident occurred in EvXII is shewn by the parallel in STestDom. That it occurred in Mk is shewn (i) by the fact that neither psMark nor LeuciusP would have been in the least likely to have invented it; (ii) that the worship is placed in other contexts by Matthew and the glossator of Lk; (iii) that the incident of the confession agrees with the motivisation of the end of Mk; and that (iv) its ultimate source was presumably the prostration and confession of Peter in X *sub* LLk. v. 8.

That the worship recorded in Matt. xxviii. 17 is transferred is shewn by the statement that some of the apostles doubted. Matthew who "spared" them cannot have invented the incident, and the appearance was merely the sequel to Mk. xiv. 28, the allusion to the mountain being suggested by such incidents as those recorded in iii. 13, vi. 46. The sentence in Matt is transferred from Jerusalem and Matthew has spared the eleven by converting the statement of Mk that Jesus upbraided them for their unbelief into

a statement that some doubted and by omitting the confession which accompanied the worship. The glossator of
Lk could not insert the incident of the worship *in situ* and
made the best possible use of it by placing it at LLk. xxiv. 52.

§ 84. In Lk. v. 8 the incident like that of the broiled fish in
xxiv. 42 is clearly transposed. S. Luke's motive is clear.
He is converting into a miracle an XL narrative of a large
catch of fish which preceded S. Peter's call and which the
editor of Jn worked into the X narrative of the appearance
by the lake. The resemblance of LLk. v. 8 to EpApp,
sec. O is too close to be accidental.

It is impossible to assign S. Peter's confession to any point
before the Passion, and it is likely to have followed his
denial and his tears. It must derive from the XL narrative
of the appearance to him, a conclusion which tallies with
its occurrence in S. Mark's narrative of the appearance to
the eleven. That L narrated the appearance is shewn by
LLk. xxiv. 34.

§ 85. In LLk. v. 8 and in this passage only S. Luke
describes the apostle as Simon Peter, and the only other
passage in the synoptists in which he is so described is
Matt. xvi. 16: *Simon Peter answered him, Thou art the
Christ, the Son of the living God.* Now it is at any rate a
remarkable coincidence that Turner, who held that Matthew's
copy of Mk ended at xvi. 8, argued that Matt. xvi. 8 f. derives
from the Mk appearance to the apostle (*Theology*, 1926, 70 f.).
He points out that in Mk. i. 1 the Gospel is described as
the good news of Jesus the Christ, the Son of God and that
in viii. 29 Peter uses the first of these two designations of
Jesus but not the second, that this omission cannot be
accidental and that the Sonship becomes the subject of
Christ's teaching. The title of Mk postulates a later confession resembling that which we find in Matt, and the
narrative of Matt has to be accounted for. We have confirmed Turner's argument by the important contact with
Lk. v. 8, by our proof that Matthew used the end of Mk,
by our illustrations of the fact that Mk was based on a
carefully thought-out scheme.

[The appendix to the chapter throws new light on the

incident. It will there be shewn that Matthew used a
deuteroQ which contained matter which did not occur in
Q. See § 91.1.]

§ 86. We now turn to a prose poem which from the first
verse to the last is built up out of large and small fragments
which have been gathered from all quarters. In Rev. iv.
Christ is in heaven, and we shall trace the influence of the
KP Ascension apocalypse upon this and other contexts.
In the preceding chapters we may suspect the influence of
preAscension discourse in the warnings against false apostles,
false prophets (Rev. ii. 2, 20; cf. 1 Cor. xi. 19; 2 Cor. xi. 13;
Ac. xx. 20; ApP, 1; EApP, 511; Tryph. 35, 51, 82;
Mk. xiii. 22). Now the opening narrative is probably based
on the X narrative of the appearance to Peter. The writer
dates the appearance of Christ on the Lord's day and
continues:

(i) 10 f. *I heard behind me a . . . voice. I turned to see the*
     voice. . . . I saw . . . one like unto a son of man.
     Cf. Jn. xx. 14. *She turned herself back and beholdeth*
     Jesus standing.
(ii) 17. *And when I saw him I fell at his feet as one dead.*
     And he laid his right hand upon me.
     In X *sub* Matt. xxviii., Jn. xx. 17, Mary took hold of
     Jesus' feet and worshipped Him.
     Lk. v. 8, 11. *Simon Peter fell at Jesus' knees.*
(iii) *Fear not; I am . . .*
     X *sub* Mk. vi. 50. *It is I; be not afraid.*
(iv) 18. *the Living one ; and I was dead.*
     LLk. xxiv. 5. *Why seek ye the living one among the dead.*
(v) *I have the keys of death and of hell.*

By far the best interpretation of Matt. xvi. 18 is McNeile's,
" the gates of hell will not prevail against the church by
keeping its Messiah imprisoned." On our view Christ
said, " The gates of hell have not prevailed." With the
slight alteration which we should expect in the writer, this
is precisely what Christ says in Rev.

In estimating the significance of these parallels it must
be remembered that early Christian writers had not the

smallest capacity for inventing narrative. It is certain that the writer of Rev. would be likely to use the narratives of the risen Christ, and the impressiveness of his narrative is a proof that he did so.

§ 87. A word must be said on the subject of S. Paul's allusions to the Resurrection in 1 Cor. xv. He writes: 3. *I delivered unto you first of all that which I also received, how that Christ died for our sins according to the scriptures; and that he was buried; and that he hath been raised on the third day according to the scriptures; 5. and that he appeared to Cephas; then to the twelve; then to above five hundred. . . . 7. then he appeared to James; then to all the apostles.*

S. Paul is using a document. He reminds the Corinthians of the instruction which they had received, and he was handing on what he himself had received. That he is citing is shewn by the irrelevant *he was buried* and by the awkward phrase *on the third day he hath been raised*. S. Paul's point was that Christ had been raised, but the point of the document was that Christ rose on the third day. Probably the source had $\dot{a}\nu\acute{e}\sigma\tau\eta$. S. Paul uses $\dot{e}\gamma\epsilon\iota\rho\epsilon\iota\nu$ in twenty-five places, but in 1 Thess. iv. 14 where we observe the introductory phrase *if we believe that* we find $\dot{a}\nu\acute{e}\sigma\tau\eta$. S. Paul only uses the word elsewhere in a citation (Eph. v. 14).

The statement that Christ rose on the third day according to the scriptures suggests the influence of S. Mark (cf. Mk. viii. 31, ix. 31), but the list of the appearances which follows is presumably from the same source and is unlikely to be from Mk. On the other hand, in so far as there are contacts, the list is in agreement with our reconstruction of X and Mk. There is the same order Cephas, the twelve, all the apostles (the Ascension). The appearance to James in EvH is a mere perversion and has no connection with that mentioned by S. Paul. The apostle mentions the appearances which happened to interest him most. There is no ground at all for supposing that the list is intended to be as full as possible.

A possible source for S. Paul's two passages is the manual which there are grounds for conjecturing was used at an

early date at Cæsarea and was attributed like Mk to S. Peter.
It may have been drawn up by S. Mark and used in other
gentile churches.

§ 88. It remains that I should deal with two difficulties,
the fact that I attribute to an excellent Gospel an end which
is unworthy of it and that it does not survive in the MSS.

It would be an overstatement, but one which would
not be seriously misleading, to say that the Gospels are what
they are in spite of the evangelists and because of the
excellence of the sources which they used. Such a statement
would be entirely true of Jn, to some extent true of Matt
and Lk, and it may be more true of Mk than it is possible
to shew. It is enough for my purpose that I have already
shewn that the faults which are so conspicuous in the end
which I attribute to Mk are present in our Mk. The Gospel
begins to deteriorate at the beginning of its narrative of the
Crucifixion, and if it is pardonable that in vi. 45 f. S. Mark
misunderstands the incident which is better preserved in
Jn. vi. 15 f., his attribution of hardness of heart to the
disciples is a mere invention and inexcusable. Again it is
pardonable that S. Mark misunderstood the saying *I will go
before you into Galilee*, but he was not justified in making,
as the evidence shews he did, his rewriting of that saying
fundamental in his account of the closing events and still
less in basing upon it the close of his Gospel a story
of disobedience and unbelief.

.   .   .   .   .

THE DEPRAVATION OF MK

§ 89. My first attempt to deal with the problems raised in
the last paragraph postulated the position that S. Luke
conceals the seriousness of the controversies which divided
the primitive community. The Hellenisers were led by
Stephen, Philip, Barnabas and his sister-in-law Mary the
mother of Mark, whose husband Aristobulus was according
to KP a Cyrenian and who was connected with Peter by

marriage (Hist. Patr. i. 131). With this section the apostle
was largely in agreement. On the other hand a conservative body of opinion was led by the brethren of the
Lord. We shall find that Joseph and Judas accompanied
Peter to Cæsarea (§ 341a) and that his other four companions were the Cyrenians Alexander and Rufus Ananias,
who had been in contact with Paul and Zacchæus. It is
practically certain then that the brethren condemned
Peter's converse with uncircumcised gentiles (Ac. x. 45,
xi. 2). The later claims of the Judaisers had real contacts
with the views of James. I hold that the brethren were
apostles, and, inasmuch as Mk was written at the moment
when this controversy was at its height, I reluctantly concluded that the youthful Mark had heard a distorted account
of what was happening at Jerusalem and made a foolish
attack on the eleven as a body.

I had already printed in § 343 an argument that the
Markan Apocalypse and the Withering of the Fig-tree
were interpolated by a gentile who was influenced by
Streeter's Judaistic source of Matt, but I did not suspect
that the attacks on the eleven were Ebionite until it occurred
to me that the seven crates in the doublet narrative of the
Feeding (Mk. viii. 8) were originally filled not by apostles
but by deacons and recalled the fact that APh, 94 supports
the conjecture and connects the variation with QPl. Further,
the historical statements scattered over patristic writers can
seldom be ignored with impunity. Now we shall find
reason to think that Epiphanius's account of Cerinthus
derives through Hippolytus from Heg. The statement then
of Haer. xxviii. 2 that Cerinthus opposed Peter on his
return from Cæsarea is evidence that Heg held that the
Ebionite heresy originated at that date and that he regarded
Cerinthus as an exponent of the position of M. My book
was almost through the Press, but I resolved to delay publication and to examine the problems raised by Streeter's
important discovery.

§ 89a. I will now summarise the positions as to the
history of the Gospels which I intend to defend.

(i) X was written shortly after the Ascension and became

the basis of protoMk (pMk), L (pLk), to some extent of
M and of S. John's discourse. Either X or pMk was used
by LeuciusP (§§ 46, 86). It is probable that the copy of
X used at Ephesus had been glossed from S. John's
midrashim.

(ii) Soon after S. Matthew wrote the Logia for the use
of converts at Jerusalem.

(iii) S. Mark wrote at Cæsarea in A.D. 37. PMk contained
no discourse of any length.

(iv) Q was written soon after and was based on the Logia.

(v) After another very short interval S. Luke in pLk
combined at Antioch Q with X. I assign the Pericope
Adulteræ to pLk.

(vi) Much of M was midrash based in part on Jewish
traditions, but the writer, who called himself Matthew,
made large use of the Logia and in his abbreviated narrative
of the Ministry used X. He greatly exalted John, with
whose disciples he had been in contact, and began his work
with a narrative of Zacharias. He stated that the government of the church had been committed by Christ to James,
to whom He privately explained his sayings and parables
in an Ebionite sense. He denounced the hierarchy and
fabricated a long series of marvels, e.g. the two Walkings
on the Water, the Coin in the Fish's Mouth, the Withering
of the Fig-tree and the Descent of the Angel of the Sepulchre.
At the close in an Ascension narrative which was based on
X *sub* EP, 466 Christ spoke to James the nucleus of the
Markan Apocalypse. This apocalypse dates M *c.* A.D.
39.

(vii) In reply to M an editor of Q wrote simple explanations of sayings and parables which M had misinterpreted.
DeuteroQ was used at Antioch by GMark (iv. 10–20, 33 f.,
vii. 17–23) and by Matthew (xiii. 36–43, 49–51). In Matt
and Mk the James of M became Peter or the disciples. It
is possible that deuteroQ contained narrative and is a factor
in the problem of the Birth narratives.

(viii) At the outbreak of the Herodian persecution a
Judaiser (JMark) introduced much M matter into pMk
and made room for it by omitting six sections. He attacked

the eleven and edited the M Apocalypse, again urging a flight to the mountain.

(ix) A second reviser of Mk (GMark), whose ignorance of Jewish customs (§§ 90g, 343a (ii)) proves him to have been a gentile, omitted most of the M matter inserted into JMk as for instance the Sermon on the Mount, which occurred in the hiatus which precedes viii. 1–2. He substituted, e.g. in vii. 7–23, for the exegesis of M that of deuteroQ and reintroduced into Mk the beginning and conclusion, two voyages, the journey from Gerasa to Nazareth and the Mission of the twelve, misplacing the last two sections. He edited the apocalypse, moved it to its present position and substituted for James the four apostles.

(x) PMk had been written for Theophilus, who was puzzled by the controversy and the editings. S. Luke writing in A.D. 47 at Antioch (§ 372 f.) abbreviated pLk and introduced into that work a large part of GMk, omitting almost all the M matter which GMark had allowed to remain.

(xi) Matthew combined as much of M as was possible with GMk and also used deuteroQ.

(xii) S. John commented on X, and his comments were used not only in Jn but also in Rev and QPl.

(xiii) PMk survived in Egypt. Complete copies of GMk were used by S. Luke, Matthew, psMark, the editor of Jn, LeuciusP and the compiler of LEMk. All our MSS of Mk derive from a copy from which the pages which contained the attack on the eleven had been removed.

(xiv) This last fact may be accounted for by the conjecture that soon after S. John's death Gaius of Pergamum and other Asian bishops collected as a canon of the apostolic doctrine the works known to have been written by apostles and their disciples Mark and Luke. Hence the disappearance of X and pLk. The latter was written before S. Luke became acquainted with S. Paul. The former was not improbably written by a woman. The Logia of S. Matthew was identified with our Matt.

(xv) Inasmuch as Cerinthus may have edited M I call the recension of M which he and Leucius used CerM.

(xvi) Leucius based EvT on CerM using also KP, Jn and S. John's midrashim. He identified his Judas Thomas with Matthias and the Matthew of CerM.

(xvii) EvH was our Matt glossed from KP, CerM and QPl (EvT).

To sum up, the main task of the critic of the Gospels is to reconstruct X and the Logia. (i) X was used by S. Mark, by S. Luke in pLk, by M, by S. John and by the writers of his midrashim. M was used by JMark, by the author of Lk. i.–ii., by deuteroQ, by Matthew, psMark, Cerinthus and Leucius. (ii) The Logia was used by M and Q. Q was used by S. Luke and deuteroQ. DeuteroQ was used by GMark and Matthew.

§ 90. There are two important indications of the motives which must have actuated Christ during the period recorded in Mk. iii.–viii. In iii. 6 we learn that Herod had decided to destroy Him, and in iii. 13 He appoints the twelve. But the sequence of events cannot be related to these outstanding events and is a mere chaos. With this fact we must connect S. Luke's important omissions and the statement of the elder of Papias that Mark did not write in order. We shall find that S. Luke's editing is often influenced by the discrepancies of L with GMk.

We will now follow a little further the clues just mentioned. (i) JMk. vi. 14 f. is among the less trustworthy passages inserted from M. We may safely follow Josephus when he tells us that Herod killed John because he feared his popularity with the people (Ant. XVIII. v. 2). It is probable that John's death soon followed his arrest and that Herod about the same time plotted with the hierarchy against the new prophet whom he would regard as John's follower and likely to become as dangerous. However this may be, the journey to Phœnicia was presumably a flight from Herod. (ii) But the flight can have been no mere flight. Christ on his way to Phœnicia showed that He had meditated on the histories of Elijah and Elisha (LLk. iv. 25 f.), and there were even more important precedents, His allusions to which were recorded in the X narrative of

G

the appointment of the twelve. At God's bidding shortly before his death Moses appointed Joshua as his successor in the shepherding of Israel (Numb. xxvii. 17, MMatt. ix. 36), and he had already associated with himself seventy elders of whom it was promised, *I will take of the spirit which is upon thee and put it upon them* (Numb. xi. 16, LLk. x. 1). It was in anticipation of His death that Christ appointed the twelve.

The following scheme of the Ministry results from the positions just stated and from our analysis of the documents. When co-operation with John was no longer advisable Christ left Ænon and worked in Upper Galilee and then at Capernaum. Herod's alliance with the hierarchy compelled Him, with an increased body of disciples, to retire to Decapolis. He then journeyed through Samaria (Jn. iv.) and Nazareth to Phœnicia. During this period He taught and trained the twelve, and He exulted when not long before His return to the lake they reported the success of their first mission. It proved that His work could be entrusted to unlearned men, to "babes." Soon after His return crowds had collected from all south Syria, and among them were Phœnicians (Mk. iii. 7*b*–8). He healed and fed them, and when they tried to make Him king, after solitary prayer among the hills He resolved on a retirement to the neighbourhood of Cæsarea Philippi, and there in expositions of the prophets He disclosed to the twelve His deepest thoughts. Part of what He said survives in the record of a dream of S. Peter's which like that at Joppa and *Domine quo vadis?* reveals what had been in the apostle's mind during the preceding days. We learn that Christ had spoken of the things which He had learnt from Moses and Elijah as to His departure and of the part which the disciples would play in the rebuilding of the tabernacle of David (Amos ix. 11).

The discussion which follows will be at several points clearer if the reader bears in mind that the following sequence of events is assigned to X: the plot against Christ (Mk. iii. 6), the controversies with scribes from Jerusalem about Beelzebub and Meats, a flight to Gerasa, Nazareth and

Phœnicia, the call of the twelve, the healing of the crowds gathered from all South Syria (iii. 7 f.), the resumption of these healings near Christ's house (iii. 19b), a voyage across the lake (vi. 32), resumed healings (MMatt. xiv. 4, LLk. ix. 11), the Feeding. After the Crossing JMark under the influence of M interpolated the Call of the twelve, the Sermon on the Mount and a parable discourse (JMk. vi. 34; iv. 1).

§ 90a. That our section of Mk (iii.–viii.) is in disorder is obvious. That this is due to the fact that it is composite is suggested by the presence of a doublet, the two narratives of the Feeding. The antecedent probability that the Four Thousand is not an isolated fragment but from a second gospel tallies with the following facts :

(i) An examination of the Feedings suggests that they derive from a common source. In all the narratives Christ takes, breaks (Jn omits), blesses and gives, and there are important contacts of Jn with the Four Thousand.

(ii) Just as the Four Thousand is a doublet of the Five Thousand so the Stilling of the Tempest and the Walking on the Water are likely to be doublets of vi. 32 and 45, and to have preceded and followed the Four Thousand.

(iii) There are two incidents in which the *onus probandi* is on those who deny that Mk and Matt derive from a common source. (*a*) In Matt. xiv. the narrative of the Walking on the Water (James's) is one of a series of marvellous stories in Matt which are not in the least likely to be editorial. Moreover Matthew would not have invented *O thou of little faith*, and these words are likely to be from the same pen as *have ye not yet faith?* in the Stilling of the Tempest. (*b*) In the SyroPhœnician Mk. vii. 14 f. omits Matt. xv. 23–4, a passage which is or might be regarded as Judaistic. I may add that the reading of SyrS *I have not been sent save after the flock which hath strayed from the house of Israel* is precisely the position of Cerinthus in J and CerM. His sect obeyed the Law, and the hierarchy were heretics. It is noteworthy that this is the only passage in Mk in which Christ is addressed as Lord.

(iv) Our section of Mk contains two attacks on the twelve. (*a*) *They understood not concerning the loaves, but their heart was hardened* (vi. 52); (*b*) *have ye your heart hardened* (viii. 16–21). Both passages are editorial. Both deal with the subject of the loaves in the same way and are presumably from the pen of the editor who introduced into pMk the doublet of the Five Thousand and attacked the eleven at the close of the Gospel.

§ 90*b*. We will now examine the data bearing on the plot of the Pharisees and the Herodians against Christ. We shall find that the internal evidence of the contexts of Y and Z shews their derivation from M.

A. In ii. 6, 16, 24 Christ is in conflict with local scribes as to the observance of the sabbath.

B. In iii. 6 the Pharisees go out (of the synagogue) and straitway take counsel with the Herodians how they may destroy Christ.

C. iii. 22–30. The Beelzebub controversy with scribes who have come from Jerusalem.

Y. vi. 16. *Herod, when he heard thereof* (the current rumours) *said, John whom I beheaded is risen from the dead*.

Z. vii. 1 ff. *Scribes . . . from Jerusalem. . . . Hear me and understand. . . . Nothing from without defileth*.

The sequence AB is a very improbable explanation of Christ's withdrawal from Capernaum. A consultation of the local Pharisees and Herodians would not have involved Him in any great danger. Moreover the matter recorded in ii. 1–iii. 5 leads one to expect that the hierarchy would be suspicious and hostile, but it is not probable that even the healing on the sabbath would lead them to take the extreme step of an alliance with Herod for the destruction of the new Prophet. If, however, Mk is composite and in disorder the solution of our problem is clear. The order of events was A, B, Y, C, Z, iii. 7*a*. The local Pharisees and Herodians reported to the hierarchy and Herod. The former sent to Capernaum the scribes mentioned in C and Z, and Herod concluded that Jesus was as dangerous a popular leader as John. After consultation the alliance was arranged. C followed the arrival of the scribes from Jerusalem, but Christ, who saw what was happening, was undaunted. In Z He explicitly and emphatically challenged the whole existing system. But His hour was not yet come, and He fled.

Our discussion has shewn that Mk is composite and that its disorder is due to revisions. We have also noticed two passages in which Matt is parallel with Mk but probably independent. One of these occurs in Streeter's M, and the other in a series of strange and marvellous stories which occur in Matt and have no parallels except in several passages of Mk which on our view are influenced by M. The principle of economy in the postulation of documents leads us to assign all this matter to M.

§ 90c. We will now examine some cohesions, contacts and indications of misplacement.

(i) Mk. iii. 7 reads smoothly, but 7b cannot have originally followed 7a. Christ is in flight from Herod, but He only goes a mile or two out of Capernaum and then invites arrest by healing crowds which have gathered from all south Syria and which have gathered too early in the narrative.

(ii) iv. 41–v. 1 also reads easily, but the sequence is quite impossible. Christ starts on a long voyage in the evening and encounters bad weather. No daylight is left for v. 14–19, where the whole countryside collects after a healing which must have occupied some time.

(iii) On the other hand v. 1–vi. 6 makes a perfect adhesion with iii. 7a. After the coalition of the hierarchy with Herod Christ fled to Decapolis and paid a short visit to Nazareth. Moreover, if this was the order of pMk, inasmuch as the Mission of the twelve can have occurred neither before the Flight nor after the Feeding, it follows that the result of our analysis agrees with the date to which on independent grounds we assigned the Mission.

(iv) The obvious conjecture that the single verse which narrates the return from the Mission (vi. 31) was originally continuous with vi. 13 may be confirmed. (a) The intervening passage contains a pair of doublets (14–16) and a

narrative of John's death which resembles nothing else
in Mk and which presumably was derived by M from one
of the disciples of John by whom he is said to have been
buried.   Herod's oath is another contact with M (§ 91c).
(b) Apart from an argument which must be postponed that
LLk. x. 1–20 derives from the source of Mk. iii., vi. and
Matt. ix., x. that passage is connected with the Mission of
the twelve by its allusion to the seventy (Numb. xi. 16) and
the use of discourse elsewhere addressed to the twelve.
Here we are concerned with the fact that in LLk the Call,
the Mission and the Return are continuous.   (c) In Matt. x.
the appointment is followed by a charge which contains
matter from M and in which Christ instructs the twelve as
to their activities after the Ascension.   This perversion is
likely to be M's substitute for the Mission.   Matt has no
parallel with Mk. vi. 31.

(v) If the fragments which narrate the Mission of the
twelve are misplaced, it follows that they were reinserted by
GMark.   Obviously if JMark abbreviated pMk in order to
find room for his M matter there is no section of pMk that
an opponent of the eleven would be more likely to omit.
Moreover, he may have substituted (cf. vi. 34) the Judaising
narrative of M *sub* Matt. x.   Similarly the reinserted narrative
of the flight to Nazareth may take the place of an objection-
able section of JMk which preceded JMk. vii. 24 and which
perverted the sermon at Nazareth in which Christ spoke of
the examples of Elijah and Elisha (LLk. iv. 24–27).

(vi) The position that the Beelzebub controversy (iii. 22–
29) is interpolated has been advocated by others and is
confirmed by the fact that the scribes from Jerusalem take
part in it.   We place it with the fateful controversy about
meats after iii. 6.   In pMk iii. 19*b* was continuous with 12.
The main narrative tells us that Christ came home and that
the crowd gathered again.   He and the twelve had no time
in which to eat.   This incident recalls 9 where owing to the
thronging crowd Christ uses a dinghy.   The cause was
presumably the same.   He had resumed His work of healing.
Owing to the abbreviation of the introduction the Beelzebub
matter refers not to the healings which suggested its insertion

but to those by the lake. Christ's friends think Him mad, for in or near the boat He was safe and now He is courting arrest. After the interpolation, as our writers often do, JMark repeated his source at the point at which he left it but more fully. With a view to Christ's saying about His relations GMark used a phrase of pMk, "His mother and His brethren." The crowd is sitting round Him, each little group waiting for the summons to bring its sick to Him.

(vii) We find inserted into the narrative of the Mission (vi. 6b–13, 30) a composite block which consists of two doublets (14–15, 16) and the parenthetical and transposed (§ 90h) Death of John. Each doublet states that when Herod heard he said that Jesus was John risen, *i.e.* that He was another John and must be similarly treated. In spite of the fact that the preceding context only speaks of healings worked by the twelve the first doublet connects Herod's saying with Christ's miracles. Presumably "Herod heard" refers to the report made by his followers when they plotted with the Pharisees (iii. 6) and preceded the arrival of the scribes from Jerusalem (23). Now vi. 14 coheres well with pMk. iii. 22 thus: *And Herod heard and said, John . . . is risen . . ., and therefore do these powers work in him. Others said . . . Elijah . . . others . . . a prophet. But the scribes which came down from Jerusalem said, He hath Beelzebub. . . .* The attribution of the second doublet to M tallies with the fact that there is no trace of an M narrative of the Capernaum ministry (hence the omission of Herod's allusion to Christ's miracles) and that the scribes from Jerusalem appear in the next M incident (vii. 1).

(viii) The Stilling of the Tempest (iv. 35 f.) contains two important words, "rebuked" and "be muzzled," which are taken from an exorcism (i. 25) and which convert an historical incident into a marvel. It must be from M and presumably a doublet of the voyage of vi. 32.

M's method of composition in the Tempest has several parallels. (*a*) The Tempest itself is used in Peter's Walking on the Water (Matt. xiv. 31 f.). (*b*) The blind man of Bethsaida (viii. 22 f.) is influenced by the X Healing of the

Deaf-Mute (vii. 29–37). (*c*) M *sub* EvH, 33 is influenced by X *sub* Jn. ii. 12. (*d*) See also §§ 53 and 91*h*. M's method suggests that he has probably inserted the incident of the storm from another voyage. Alternatively, GMark has omitted it in vi. 32.

(ix) We will now examine the following sequence: (*a*) GMk Healings at the lake and (*b*) in Capernaum, (*c*) the M voyage, (*d*) the reinserted voyage. The reader will note the cohesions of the fragments of the pMk incidents with each other and the doublet. The contacts of the M and pMk voyages are obviously evidence for X. This is also true of the coherence of the M voyage with the preceding healings. That they derive from pMk is antecedently probable and appears from the vividness of the narratives which have hardly suffered from the attrition which we find in some M narratives (*e.g.* the dinghy of 9 became in M *sub* iv. 1 a boat).

GMk

A. PMk. iii. 7*b*. The healings.
B. 19*b*. *He cometh home. And the multitude cometh together again,*

D. *so that they could not so much as eat bread.*

JMk

M. MMk. iv. 35. *And on that day when even was come,*
N. *He saith unto them, Let us go over to the other side.*

O. 36. *And leaving the multitude they took him . . . with them in the boat.*
P. *And other boats went with them.*
   The Feeding.

GMk

C. vi. 31*b*. *And (for) many were coming and going*
D. *and they had no leisure so much as to eat bread.*

E. 31*a*. *He saith unto them, Come ye yourselves (apart to a desert place) and rest a while.*
F. *And they went away in a boat (to a desert place apart).*

G. vi. 47. *When even was come.*

(*a*) (*a*) The important narratives of two consecutive days close with two incidents introduced by the phrase "when even was come" (MQ). That this was in the manner of X is shewn by a comparison with Mk. xi. 19 (RV mistranslates) where this phrase follows the Cleansing and xiv. 17 where it precedes the Supper.

(b) The multitude of M (O) is that of Mk (B). Christ again leaves them, and we shall find that they will again follow Him. M coheres with Mk. (α) GMk in C completes the picture drawn in iii. 34 where the crowd sits round Christ. They come with their sick to Him, and then go. (β) M in N unexpectedly records a commonplace logion in the *oratio recta*. E shews that this is another case of attrition. (γ) O = E − F. (δ) C and D in vi. pick up the pMk story of the healings at Capernaum and repeat its close (just as iii. 31 repeats in part 21). We shall conclude that when the same crowd reassembled the healings were resumed before the Feeding as they were afterwards (vi. 55).

The bracketed words in E and F indicate that GMark is editing. We shall conclude that 34 is editorial. 33 is rewritten and ill written. *They saw them going*. "They" refers awkwardly to the crowd which comes together in iii. 20 and vi. 31. *And many knew them*. All must have known them. *And they ran together on foot from all the cities and outwent them*. The parallels shew that GMark means that the crowd at Capernaum outwent Christ. And this is confirmed by *on foot*, the antithetical phrase to which is almost certainly that of P, *other boats went with them*. Who then were the people from all the cities? The crowd who made for the point for which the boats were making and arrived before Christ cannot have brought with them others from all cities. It would appear that GMark is clumsily referring to the description of the crown which in GMk. iii. 7b–8 has collected from all south Syria.

(x) There are many indications that X preserved a fisherman's story. This is especially the case in Jn. xxi. 1 f. Now in 8 we read of a dinghy which was towed behind the fishing boat. Presumably this is the dinghy which waits on Christ in Mk. iii. 9. Now inasmuch as the crowd was very large (those who followed Christ to the other side were about five thousand in number) and it included contingents from the other side of Jordan, there must have been a little fleet of boats collected where He healed. Many of these accompanied Christ (iv. 36). After the Feeding Christ sent the disciples across the lake with the boat and went up into the hills (vi. 45). The sequel is told in Jn. vi. 22, a verse which is a confused editorial abbreviation of X which the commentators do not really explain. It tells us (*a*) that *on the morrow the multitude which stood* (? remained) *on the other side of the sea saw that there was none other dinghy save one, and that Jesus entered not with his disciples into the boat* and (*b*) that they embarked in dinghies which came from Tiberias. But these dinghies could only have embarked a few of the five thousand, and why did not the crowd go away the previous evening? and did they expect to go home in dinghies? Probably X stated that the multitude saw the disciples embark as they did in X *sub* Mk. vi. 33 but without Christ. A few followed Him into the hills. When they returned to the shore they found all the boats gone except a dinghy. On the morrow some fishermen from Tiberias lent them their dinghies. Using X, M made the whole crowd stay until the next day for a second discourse (JMk. viii. 2) and, combining the dinghy of Jn with that used by Christ in Mk. iii., made Him preach the parable discourse from it (JMk. iv. 1). S. Luke used Mk. iv. 1 in Lk. v. 1.

(xi) There are four narratives of the departure after the Feeding to be considered. Matt. xiv. follows Mk. vi.

We shall discuss the parallels presented by the narratives on p. 107. Here we observe that in *b* and *c* B is parallel with C and in *a* with A.

A and B(*b*) are the juncture of the M Voyage with the pMk Feeding. In X and pMk "when evening was come" occurred before "he constrained" and was one of three notes of time, the first being "when it was late" (35) and the third "about the fourth watch" (48). When GMark reinserted 31–45 he omitted the phrase because he found it (misplaced) in B(*b*). B (*e*) and D make Christ enter the boat immediately after the Feeding because the walking on the Water had been already narrated.

A (pMk)	B (M)	C (X)
Mk. vi. 45. *And strait-way he constrained his disciples to enter into a boat,*	(*b*) vi. 47*a*. *And when even was come*	Jn. vi. 16. *And when evening came his disciples went down to the sea, and they entered into a boat.*
while he himself sendeth the multi-tude away.	(*a*) viii. 9. *And he sent them away.*	
	(*c*) vi. 47. *The boat was in the midst of the sea . . . about the fourth watch.*	*and were going over the sea.*
	(*d*) 51. *He went up into the boat*	
	(*e*) viii. 10. *And strait-way he entered the boat . . . Dalman-utha.*	

D (M)
Matt. xv. 39. *And he entered the boat . . . Magadan.*

Our view that the narrative of Jn is related to but inde-pendent of that of MJMk is confirmed when we read on. 17 seems to be rewritten. *When they had rowed twenty-five or thirty furlongs* is not in the manner of the editor and is in the manner of X. 19*b*–20 reproduces precisely the words of Mk when the editor would be most likely to remember. 21 is strikingly different from the close of the JMk narrative and cannot be editorial. Jn does not relate a miracle. Jesus was walking "by the sea," the phrase of xxi. 1, and the disciples not knowing that they were almost at Bethsaida offered to take Him on board. "By the sea" suggested to M "on the sea." Christ's refusal of the offer suggested "would have passed by them."

§ 90*d*. We have completed our examination of the con-tacts of the disordered incidents of Mk. iii. 7–viii. 26, and we have drawn some inferences from them. Before we enlarge our enquiry as to the influence of M we will submit

our results to eight tests. (i) Does our analysis account for
the variations in the narratives of the Feeding? (ii) Little
has been said about the narrative of John's death. Does it
derive from M? and what was its original context? (iii)
Does our analysis enable us to solve the problems which
arise in connection with Christ's voyages? (iv) Does it confirm the view that S. Luke preferred pLk to Mk? (v) Does
it make contacts with X matter in Jn. i.–v.? (vi) Does
it solve the problems raised by Mk. vii. 1–23? (vii) Do
the incidents which we have attributed to JMk seem to
form elements in a coherent whole and can we account for
JMark's procedure? (viii) Can we account for the procedure
of GMark?

1. It is obvious that an argument which postulates X is
vitally concerned with the five narratives of the Feeding.
If most of the evidence derives from M, it is good evidence.
M used X, and the Logia, and the motives and methods
of his perversions can be determined. We are in the
first place concerned with the parallels on the following
page.

§ 90*e*. Each of the Gospels supplies the table with matter
which confirms our main conclusions.

(i) The following comments may be made on the evidence
which derives from the M narrative of the Feeding : (*a*) The
superiority of Matt. ix. 36 to Mk. vi. 34, a key position, is
certain. (α) In X Numb. xxvii. was used in connection with
the call of the twelve. (β) The other allusions to Christ's
compassion (Mk. i. 41, ix. 22, LLk. vi. 13, x. 33) confirm
the antecedent probability that it led Him to heal. This
motive connects with the call of the twelve, for Christ sent
them to heal (Mk. vi. 7) and exulted when they reported their
success (Mk. vi. 30, L *sub* Lk. x. 17, 21). The common
derivation of these passages from X will be argued in the
next volume. (*b*) Mk in an M context is influenced by the
M Sermon (§ 91.6), which in M (as the Table shews) like the
allusion to teaching in JMk. vi. 14 preceded the Feeding.
The phrase "they glorified the God of Israel" (cf. ii. 20 f.,
ix. 33, x. 23, xv. 24) confirms the derivation of Matt.

	From M						Neither from M nor Mk		
	Matt. iv.–v.	ix.–x.	xiv.	xv.	Mk. vi.	viii.	vi.	Lk. ix.	Jn. vi.
A. Syrian crowds healed	24	..	..	..	..	..	..	..	1
B. They followed Christ	..	..	13	..	..	..	33	11	2
C. to the mountain	1	(..)	..	29	..	..	..	..	3
D. He was seated	1	..	..	29	..	..	..	..	3
E. The disciples came or were called	18 1	36	..	32	(35)	..	..	..	*with them*
F. He beheld the crowds	1	36	..	..	..	..	..	..	5
G. His compassion	..	36	..	..	34	2	..	..	..
H. The healings resumed	..	35	14	30	..	..	..	11	*suggested*
J. He taught	1	5	..	..	34	*three days*	..	..	•

xv. 30–31 from M. If then we ignore the interpolated Call and Sermon M stated the Healings of the Syrian crowds, then the crossing of the lake, then the resumption of the healings, then the Feeding. Now according to our reconstruction pMk after the Healings of the Syrian crowds stated their resumption at the house, then the crossing, then the Feeding. At the point where on our view pMk stated the second resumption of the Healings (vi. 34) we find the incident of the teaching interpolated from JMk. The two sequences were originally the same.

(ii) I shall maximise the influence of L on S. Luke when he is using Mk. His statement in ix. 11 that Christ healed is an instance, for it agrees with the M evidence.

(iii) Jn. vi. is in agreement with M and our previous reconstruction in its statement that the multitude followed Christ to the other side of the lake because they saw the signs that He did. This agreement is the more important as the influence of X on our context of Jn is very clear. Much of the Jn Feeding authenticates itself. I shall argue that with one explicable exception the preceding non-Jerusalem passages are in the order of X. The subsequent attempt to make Christ king explains the solitary prayer of Mk. vi. 46 and the retirement to Cæsarea Philippi. The narrative of the voyage is related to but independent of the Walking on the Water.

The table emphasises the significance of the support which Jn gives to our main conclusion. The following parallel like the contacts of the two voyages illustrates the common dependence of M and Jn on X.

Matt. xv. 20. *And going into the mountain he sat there.*

Jn. vi. 3. *And Jesus went up into the mountain and there sat with his disciples.*

Streeter (413), who holds that Matt does not influence Jn, is so impressed with this parallel that he cleverly alters the text of Mk in order to explain it away. But the other evidence shews that the parallel is part of a large problem and that Matt derives not from Mk but from M.

§ 90*f*. We now turn to the subject of the variations in

the narratives of the Feeding. Our problem is to detect
the editorial influence of M, and with that end in view to
detect the influence of GMk on Jn. The most important
clue is the fact that the narratives shew that in its original
form the tradition stated that Christ observed the practice
which He observed at the Last Supper, Emmaus, by the
Lake and also on our view (§ 91, 12) when He appeared to
the eleven. He took the loaves, blessed, brake and gave.
These passages shew that it is extremely improbable that He
blessed the fish or employed the agency of the disciples.

In Mk. viii. the five loaves and two fishes become seven
loaves. Now in view of Col. ii. 22 (cf. Rom. xiv. 2) and the
rejection of flesh food by the Essenes and Cerinthus we must
assign this variation to M who had in view the kind of
community meal and food law which he advocated for the
use of the church of Jerusalem. This hypothesis also explains the seven crates. M made the point of his midrash
clear by introducing seven servers. It is also possible that
after the death of S. Stephen and the departure of Philip
the diaconate had become the stronghold of the reactionaries
and M desired to exalt their office. We will return to this
conjecture. GMark reintroduced the "few fish" and, not
knowing that the blessing of the bread was a grace for the
whole of a Jewish meal, made it a separate incident, writing
"blessed" (contrast "gave thanks" in 7 and Jn) and substituting disciples for deacons (6).

The Jn narrative of the Feeding is as valuable as its
context. The conversation with Philip and Andrew
authenticates itself as also "much grass" and, above all, the
fact that Christ does not use the agency of the apostles.
Jn varies with JMk. viii. against Mk. vi. in assigning the
initiative to Christ, "gave thanks," ἀναπεσεῖν and χορτάσαι
(26); with JMk, Matt and Lk in prefixing "about" to the
number of the crowds and with Lk in connecting the number
with the command to make them sit down. (M seems to
have understood the phrase "about five thousand" to mean
"less than five thousand.") When Christ spoke to Philip
(Jn. vi. 5) He assumed that the crowds had taken food with
them when they left home in the morning, but thought that

they were overwrought and that it was time for them to have a meal. He also desired to offer what hospitality he could. Philip pointed out that owing to the size of the crowd they could not do what they had done on some other occasions. Did Christ then work a miracle? To put the question with more precision our Gospels imply that Christ fed the crowds with the food which He actually took into His own hands: did He do so in X? The reply is clear. Christ followed His customary usage. He said grace for the whole multitude, breaking the five loaves and giving them and the fishes to those who sat near Him. The incident of the distribution of these loaves among the whole multitude was due to M's introduction of the seven deacons (JMk. viii. 6), and the similar distribution of the fishes to GMark's extension of the incident. The editor of Jn under the influence of the Markan narratives and contemporary exegesis emphasised the miraculous nature of the Feeding by inserting 6, "as much as they would" and 14 and also by writing in 26, *ye seek me because ye saw signs*, a sentence which was suggested by the words of the paper which he used in 2, *followed him because they saw the signs which he did*.

§ 90g. The M incident of the deacons survives in the Acta. One of the aims of Leucius was to exalt the order of deaconesses (§ 264). As M may have desired to exalt the diaconate, so Leucius attributed the institution of the order of deaconesses to Christ by identifying them with the women who minister to Him in Lk. viii. 2, making them seven and bringing them to the Sepulchre (§ 315 A). Now in APh, 94 one of the seven, Mariamne, is said to have prepared the bread and salt at the breaking of bread and another, her sister Martha, to have ministered to the multitudes. As often Leucius was adapting CerM to his own purposes. APh shews that CerM introduced deacons into its narrative of the Feeding. For the use of bread and salt in the Ebionite sacred meal and the rejection of flesh food see § 251.

§ 90h. 2. The narrative of the death of John raises the problem of the beginning of M. My reconstruction will be incomplete.

I started with two positions. (i) The fact that the first evangelist called himself Matthew suggests that it was his chief purpose to combine with Mk as much of M as possible and to controvert some of the rest. (ii) The narrative of the death and burial of John seemed likely to have been the conclusion of a long account of him, which unduly exalted him.

Two fragments of evidence fit into this scheme. (*a*) The story that Jesus came to John's baptism with His mother and His brethren undoubtedly occurred in CerM and EvT (EvH, 33, § 23); and it would be in accordance with M's methods thus to use the statement of X that Jesus went to Capernaum with His mother and His brethren (Jn. ii. 12). (*b*) Matt. iii. 14–5 is deuteroQ's correction of M matter which unduly exalted John. The fact that the return to Nazareth occurred in the omitted section of M accounts for the omission of it in Matt. Jesus returned to Nazara in X *sub* Mk. i. 9 (Nazareth) and LLk. iv. 16 (Nazara). Matt. iv. 13 provides the only other instance of the name.

If M narrated John's death and burial we may be sure that he invented a narrative of his birth. This story survives as follows: (i) Lk. i.–ii. confutes the undue exaltation of John and the position that Jesus became the Son of God at His baptism (EvEb, Tryph, 88, D at Lk. iii. 22) or some similar position: He was the Son of God by the origin and constitution of His personality. The parallelism of the narratives enforces the contrast. Now the antecedent probability that the story of Zacharias is the story of M seems to be established by the parallelism of the three following passages: (*a*) Lk. i. 15, where John will drink no wine or strong drink, is based on Jg. xiii. 4 f. and postulates a tradition that he was a Nazarite (Easton). (*b*) Matt. ii. 33 cites Jg. xiii. 7 for the fact that Jesus was a Nazarene. Clearly M cited it for his statement that Jesus was a Nazarite. (*c*) Cerinthus described James as a Nazarite (HE, II. xxiii. 5: I shall ascribe the whole context to J). (ii) PJ xxii. 3–xxiv. seems to me to continue the M story of Zacharias. In this passage he is said to have been killed because he did not disclose the hiding-place of Elizabeth.

H

PsMark used this passage in a narrative of the Virgin (§ 143). (iii) In the KP context used in § 140 C Zacharias is the son of Barek (Epiph. Hom. 321), as is John the apostle in APh, 129. It follows that M must be the source of "son of Barachias" in Matt. xxiii. 35 (Lk. xi. 51 omits).

§ 90*j*. The motivisation of Lk. i.–ii. is certain. The elaborate parallelism of the two nativities inculcates the position that while John was called from the womb to be a prophet Jesus by an act of God and by the very constitution of His personality was God's son. Like Matt. iii. 14–5 this position is likely to be directed against an undue exaltation of John doubtless in M, a clumsy use of which gospel is the most probable explanation of the following facts. (i) We are not told why Elizabeth hid herself in the hill country (Lk. i. 24, 39). (ii) The incident of the naming of John is awkwardly told. John, who in 20 is dumb is deaf in 62. How did Elizabeth know what the name was to be? If she had been told why does Zacharias write it? Why are the neighbours surprised? It was not customary to give a boy his father's name. We may suspect that in a source the angel appeared to both John's parents as in Matt and Lk he appears to Joseph and Mary. (iii) The conversation of John with the angel was not long enough to account for the surprise of the people at his tarrying.

We may find some clues to the solution of these problems in the narrative of Judges which on our view influenced M and in Matt. i.–ii., a passage which is parallel with Lk. i.–ii in stating that Christ was born of a virgin in Bethlehem, in motivisation ("God with us") and its agreement with the narrative of John in the bestowal of the name by the announcing angel. (i) We may infer from the fact that the angel appeared to Manoah's wife first that it was from the angel that Elizabeth heard that her son was to be named John. (ii) The appearance of the angel to Joseph and the Flight from Herod explain the hiding of Elizabeth in the mountain. Under the influence of the Tiamat myth Elizabeth fled before the birth of John. Joseph plays the part of Zacharias. (iii) According to Josephus Herod killed John because he feared lest he should become king. For the same reason another Herod tried to kill John as soon as he was born. (iv) It is clear from Matt. iii. 14 that M unduly exalted John. Its writer may have been one of the group of fanatical followers of the Baptist who roused Herod's fears and have held that John like Hyrcanus (§ 139) had been endowed with the *triplex munus*. This would explain why in Lk. i. 67 a priest prophesies and agrees with the fact that in M *sub* Matt. xxiii. 35 the prophet of Zech. i. 1 is identified with the priest of 2 Chron. xxiv. 20 f. (v) Did then Herod, foiled in his attempt to kill the infant John, repeat the crime of Joash? The hypothesis is in accordance with the motivisation of M and accounts for the fact that Zacharias in Lk remains in the temple while the people wait. Further, we may conjecture that the son of Barachias whose blood would be required *sub* Matt. xxiii. was not the victim of Joash but his descendant. The passage on this view is parallel with Matt. xxvii. 25. The blood of John's father like Christ's was on the hated hierarchy, and the rending of the veil portended the coming vengeance.

§ 90k. The narrative which we have reconstructed survives at the close of PJ and was used by psMark in his prot-evangelical narratives.

(i) According to the fragment preserved in xxii. 3 f. Elizabeth, knowing that Herod sought for John, went to the hill country and in order to hide John said, O mountain of God, receive a mother with a child. The incident must derive from the myth or the source which underlies Rev. xii. 4, 6, 16. With the bright light which shines about Elizabeth and John when the angel of the Lord is with them we compare the light on Jordan in M *sub* EvEb and QPl (§ 23) and Lk. ii. 1 f. We may at any rate plausibly con-jecture that the angel bade Zacharias as he bade Joseph take the mother and her child to a place of safety. PsMark, whose protevangelical narratives we shall reconstruct in § 139 f., used this John matter *sub* PJ. xvii. 4, where Joseph desires to hide Mary's shame and finds a cave.

(ii) PJ also confirms our conjecture that in M Herod murdered Zacharias. According to 23 Zacharias was killed by Herod's officers in the temple because he refused to disclose Elizabeth's hiding-place, a statement which confirms our conjecture that he had accompanied her to the mountain. At the hour of the salutation he did not meet the priests when they stood waiting. PJ again explains the difficulties suggested by Lk.

That PJ derives from M is also shewn by the fact that another version of the story occurred in KP. According to Origen (de la Rue, iv. 845) Zacharias was killed because he allowed Mary to go to the dais reserved for virgins. No other source than KP is possible. Mary goes to the dais in EpiphHom in a context which is based on Heg and contains other matter from KP (§ 143) and in which Zacharias, who in EpiphHom, 321 is the son of Barek, is chief priest. The incident of the dais is one of a series of protevangelical narratives which derive from KP. Like M psMark directed his polemic against the hierarchy, and his tendency to misapply his sources in the fictions by which he supported the doctrine of the virgin birth is illustrated by the fact that he made a topic of the preaching of Stephen (*e.g.* *sub* RSteph, 162 f.).

The position that psMark used M is confirmed by the fact that, as we shall find, both writers narrated the visible emergence of Christ from the Sepulchre and the rising of the sleepers. While it was startling to conclude that the NT apocrypha have a continuous history from *c.* A.D. 39, I had already concluded that KP was influenced by matter in our Matt which I now attribute to M and by Jewish matter for the origin of which I could not account. My fundamental positions as to the relations of J and QPl to KP are not affected by this new factor in my scheme, but there are several passages in the next chapter which may require revision in the light of the fact that M and not KP was the earliest apocryphon. The new problems seem to be very intricate and to require much consideration.

§ 90*l*. The Temptation and the events which followed it are so closely connected with the ministry of the Baptist that we will deal with them at this point.

(i) That Matthew derived his narrative of the Temptation from M is suggested by its variations from QLk, and the conjecture is confirmed by the fact that apart from Rev. xi. 2, xxi. 2, xxii. 19 the only occurrence of "the holy city" (Matt. iv. 5) is in Matt. xxvii. 53 (§ 91.8).

(ii) We will now return to Mk at i. 13*b*: *he was with the wild beasts and angels ministered unto him. Now after that John was delivered up...* This is probably GMark's abbreviation of JMk. The next chapter will prove the interest of Cerinthus in angels, and his interest in the religion of wild animals underlies the matter collected in § 265). On p. 123 we shall confirm the view that "after John was delivered up" is GMark's substitute for the JMk narrative of John. Further, our hypothesis accounts for the hiatus which follows the notice of the preaching in Galilee. (*a*) There is no Mk parallel with the statements of Matt. iv. 13 and Lk. iv. 31 that Christ came from upper Galilee to Capernaum. In i. 16 the allusion to the lake is too vague. (*b*) The narrative of Christ's ministry at Capernaum begins with the statement that when walking along the shore of the lake He saw fishing in a boat a man who is known neither to Him nor the reader and bade him follow Him (i. 16). The incident is explained in Jn. i. 40 f.

S. Luke confirms our view of the history of Mk. i. 14*a* by inserting an abbreviation of Mk. vi. 17–29 at iii. 19. Ac. xiii. 25 dates the Baptism "at the end of John's course" (Lake on Ac. ii. 1). When Lk differs from the chronology of Mk he avoids explicit contradiction (§ 346).

We conclude that GMark for doctrinal reasons substituted i. 1–12 for the parallel in JMk. He then in 12–14*a* abbreviated JMk, making the erroneous assumption that the concluding narrative which narrated John's death was in its chronological position. Unhappily he did not reinsert the section of pMk which was parallel with Jn. i. 35–51, iii. 22–iv. 3, but contented himself with copying JMk. i. 14*b*–iii. 7*a*.

§ 90*m*. 3. We will now apply our analysis to the problem of Christ's voyages.

(i) The Feeding was in a desert place (vi. 31) and therefore *on the other side* (JMk. iv. 35, Jn. vi. 1). The statement of

Mk. vi. 45 that after the Feeding Christ sent His disciples *across to Bethsaida* need not be pressed. "Across" need not mean "to the west side."

(ii) The Bethsaida of Mk. vi. 45 was the fishing village of that name, where was S. Peter's home, and not Bethsaida Julias. Christ walked alone across the hills (46) and met His disciples at Bethsaida (Jn. vi. 20). The completion of the voyage is stated in Mk. vi. 53 where he arrives and heals in Gennesaret. MMatt. xv. 39 defines the place as Magadan which was in the extreme south of Gennesaret and *in the parts of Dalmanutha* (JMk. viii. 10). The two latter passages omit the Walking on the Water which had been already narrated. JMark may have inserted " across " in 45.

(iii) Our reconstruction is inconsistent with Jn. vi. 58, where the crowds have found Christ at Capernaum. The statement may merely represent the editor's misinterpretation of an abbreviated introduction to the paper which he was using. Further, this paper contained a statement which he reproduces confusedly thus: *They came to Capernaum seeking Jesus. When they found him on the other side....* The phrasing suggests that, as we might have conjectured, the crowds expected to find Christ at Capernaum; but that they may have found Him somewhere else. He was avoiding arrest, and Capernaum was some little distance from the shore. We observe that after an encounter with some Pharisees He recrossed the lake to Bethsaida (viii. 11, 22).

(iv) Presumably the encounter with the Pharisees only hastened Christ's departure. In the next pMk passage (viii. 27) He is at Cæsarea Philippi. Inasmuch as vii. 1– viii. 26 derives from MJMk and Bethsaida (viii. 22) was on the way thither M was probably again parallel with pMk.

(v) S. Luke's statement that the Feeding took place at Bethsaida raises the problem of the Long Omission. Streeter (175) solves it by assuming a lacuna beginning at Mk. vi. 47 and ending at viii. 27a. But on our view the omission is accounted for by the fact that it begins and ends with M incidents and contains matter hopelessly discrepant with L, in which gospel Christ must have arrived at Cæsarea very shortly after the crossing to Gennesaret. Moreover S. Luke probably based his phrase "the village Bethsaida" (Streeter, 569) on Mk. viii. 26.

S. Luke had in some way to connect Mk. vi. 46–7 with viii. 26. He did his editing under the influence (a) of the view that the village Bethsaida was one of those mentioned in Mk. vi. 36 and very possibly was one of the group otherwise designated in viii. 27 and (b) of a statement of L that after His solitary prayer Christ met His disciples at Bethsaida, and spent much of the night there. He said that the Feeding was at Bethsaida because it was near that village, added in 17 "and lodge," made the disciples meet Christ after His solitary prayer and made the combination smoother by omitting "Cæsarea Philippi."

§ 90n. 4. My view of the situation which confronted S. Luke when he wrote the Third Gospel is in part determined by results reached in §§ 372 f., 382 f. He was writing at Antioch in A.D. 47 at the close of a period of acute controversy. Theophilus, for whom S. Mark had written pMk, had returned to the east five years before and was almost certainly stationed at Antioch, where he had access to all the gospels which had been written. Like many of the Antiochenes he was perplexed not only by the controversies but also by the variant presentations of Christ's career which they had elicited. A gentile, who may have been one of his colleagues, had revised JMk, but S. Luke felt that Christians who could only buy a single gospel needed one which added to GMk a large part of his own work and that in writing it he must keep in mind the problems as to the order of events which had been suggested in the first instance by M. Being a man of his time he was more competent and at greater pains to state in good Greek what needed to be done than to carry out his aims. It is only in xxii. 14–xxiv. that he really takes strong measures with the perversions of Mk.

It was in vi. 12–x. 24 that S. Luke was most perplexed by the problems arising from the glaring discrepancies of the order of GMk from that of X, pMk and pLk. Guidance as to the line which he followed may be found in the results of our examination of xix. 45–xxii. 2. In this section he

questions but in fact dissents from the chronology of Mk.
xi. 11–xiv. 9 in nine places. Now in six he merely omits
Markan matter, and in the other three he uses evasive phrases.
We must expect him therefore to take a similar line as to
the problems raised in our section and in particular with
respect to Christ's journeys and crossings of the lake. His
procedure tallies with our expectation. He omits all the
Markan journeys and all the crossings with the exception
of that narrated in viii. 22 f.,[1] and this he presumably preserves for the sake of the Stilling of the Tempest. On the
other hand he preserves two pLk journeys, that from Nazara
to Capernaum and the last journey through Samaria. GMk
has no parallel with the first, and S. Luke could not avoid
narrating the journey to Jerusalem. It is improbable that
he thought about the meaning of Mk. x. 1, but if he did
he would know that Theophilus would interpret "Judæa"
as including Samaria. Christ was a fugitive (Mk. ix. 30,
LLk. ix. 57, xiii. 22, 31 f., Jn. vii. 10, xi. 54 f.) and would
enter Pilate's territory at the nearest possible point. We
conclude that S. Luke's editing shews that the pLk journeys
and crossings were discrepant with those of GMk.

§ 900. Our conclusion is confirmed by three passages in
which S. Luke is unexpectedly more definite than Mk in his
allusions to Christ's movements.

(i) We have just attributed the placing of the Feeding at
Bethsaida to his comparison of GMk. vi. 24 f. with pLk.

(ii) He observed the hiatus which precedes Mk. i. 16,
and he is not only parallel with MMatt in making Christ
return to "Nazara" (the only two instances of that form
of the name) but also in stating the journey to Capernaum.
His procedure is instructive. He omitted Mk. i. 18–20,
altered "entered into Capernaum" into the noteworthy
accuracy "came down to C." and inserted the pLk Call
of the Four in the wrong place, prefacing it with a Markan
incident (Mk. iv. 1) which he omits in viii. 4.

(iii) Lk. viii. 28 adds to Mk. v. 1 the statement that the
country of the Gerasenes was over against Galilee. Why is

---

[1] The phrase of pMk. v. 21 preserved in viii. 37 is obviously
irrelevant.

S. Luke so precise? How did he know that Gerasa was not in Galilee? We will now use our reconstruction of pMk. In Mk. iii. 7 "to the sea" belongs to the narrative of the healings. PMk therefore ran: iii. 6 f. . . . *took counsel how they might destroy him.* The controversies with the scribes from Jerusalem. *Jesus with his disciples withdrew * * v. 1, and they came to the other side of the sea to the country of the Gerasenes.* Clearly we must insert "from Galilee." Christ was a fugitive from Herod and therefore from Galilee. If then pLk was parallel with our reconstruction of pMk we have accounted for "over against Galilee." If we continue our inquiry and compare Lk. vi. 11 f. with Mk. iii. 6 f. we find that precisely where the disorder of Mk begins S. Luke deserts Mk and begins a disorderly section consisting, with an exception which is hardly an exception, of fragments of pLk (vi. 12–viii. 3). In vi. 13–19 he uses Mk. iii. 7*b*–19 but he does so in order to lead up to the pLk sermon (20–49) and probably because in Q that sermon was preceded by the Call and Mission of the Twelve. For the last journey see also § 359.

§ 90*p*. 5. In §§ 349 f. I shall shew that all the Jerusalem matter in Jn. i.–vii. is misplaced. When it is removed the following Galilean incidents remain: A. Andrew and Simon; B. Philip and Nathanael; C. Cana; D. A short visit to Capernaum; E. Ænon; F. Samaria; G. Galilee; H. Cana; J. the Nobleman's Son; K. Healings; L. the Feeding; M. Bethsaida; N. Christ on the western shore; O. His secret journey to Jerusalem.

In this matter there is a repeated sequence, which becomes more impressive when it is examined:

B. i. 43. A decision to go to Galilee.	C. ii. 1. The marriage at Cana.	D. ii. 12. A short visit to Capernaum.
E. iv. 3. A journey to Galilee.	H. iv. 46. A visit to Cana.	J. iv. 47. The Nobleman's Son.

(i) In H nothing happens: why then is the incident recorded?
(ii) D and J are from the same Visit to Capernaum. (*a*) D cannot refer to the residence at Capernaum narrated in

Mk. i. 16–iii. 6, and in view of Christ's danger the visit which followed His return must have been very brief. Moreover in D Christ is with His family, with whom on our view He lived on His second visit (Mk. iii. 19, 31). On the other hand in Mk. i. 35–6 He sleeps at Simon's house. (*b*) In J Christ is descending from the hill country (49, 51) and the boy is at Capernaum.

If we rearrange Mk, identify B–C with E–H and connect J with D, and assume the derivation of both gospels from X we have an almost continuous narrative of Christ's mother and His brethren. This narrative confirms a later identification of the brethren with the sons of Cleopas and the apostles which we shall base on some new evidence. (i) In Mk. vi. 3 (an edited context) Christ's sisters are mentioned and the brethren are named. (ii) In C Christ, His disciples and His mother are at the marriage feast. (iii) In D His mother and brethren go with Him to Capernaum. (iv) In Mk. iii. 32 He is living with them there. (v) In Jn. vii. 2 the feast was originally the last passover, and the story of the signs, which were so prominent after the Flight is continued. His brethren desire Him to work them at Jerusalem. Christ does not go up with them in the caravan but secretly. This last incident adheres well to Mk. ix. 30, and the repetition of the teaching about the Passion was probably occasioned by the protest of the brethren. (vi) In Jn. xix. 25 His mother is at the cross with her sister Mary of Cleopas. (vii) In Ac. i. 24, a passage which I shall argue derives through I Ac. Mc. from the close of X, Christ's mother and brethren again form a group.

When we return to the beginning of Jn in order to find an explanation of its disorder we find another confirmation of the identity of E with B. Presumably Christ accompanied John from Bethany (AB) to Ænon (E) and the two prophets worked together until their disciples disputed. The journey which followed must have been that recorded in Mk. i. 14, but the editor was familiar with Mk and remembered that this verse (as edited by GMark) states that John was in prison. He therefore invented an earlier journey and used his papers twice. Our hypothesis explains the glaringly otiose statement of iii. 34 that John was not yet cast into prison. The point was in the editor's mind, and he preserved one of S. John's corrections of Mk. Unfortunately it is impossible to determine the lengths of the periods covered by Mk. i. 14–5 and i. 16–iii. 6, but the first period may have been much longer than the second. At any rate it is improbable that S. John's imprisonment was of long duration. The omission of papers parallel with Mk. i. 16–iii. 6 in Jn may be due to the editor's perplexities.

§ 90*q*. We can now return to our reconstruction of X. The usual route from Ænon to Galilee must have been along the east bank of the Jordan. Between Jn. iv. 3 and 4 we must place Mk. i. 14*b*–iii. 7*a*, v. 1–vi. 1*a*. The reason why it was necessary for Christ to go through Samaria (iv. 4) was that He was a fugitive in Decapolis (Mk. v. 20). He then went to Nazareth (Jn. iv. 43–5), where He was received gladly because His fellow-townsmen had heard of the miracles which He had worked at Capernaum (Mk. vi. 1–3*ab*, LLk. iv. 16–22). When He told them of His danger they turned against Him (Mk. 3*cb*, LLk. 23). The phrase of Jn "received him gladly, having seen (heard) all the things which he did at Jerusalem (Capernaum)" led up to S. Luke's "what we have heard done at Capernaum." In a discourse Christ compared His flight to Elijah's. The journey to the region where Elijah had been a fugitive and the Marriage at Cana followed. He returned to Capernaum, meeting the nobleman as He was going down into the city.

Just as the editor assigned papers which mentioned the feasts (*i.e.* the last passover) to a series of feasts, so he assigned A, B and C to consecutive days. Just as he numbered the Appearances so He numbered the signs in Galilee. When we restore his Galilean matter to its original order we find that it derives from an earlier gospel the order of which corresponded with that of our reconstructed pMk.

I have as yet said nothing about Christ's journey "A from the borders of Tyre through Sidon B. through the midst of the borders of Decapolis" (Mk. vii. 31). A journey through Decapolis cannot have immediately preceded the Feeding. Our problem therefore is to place the incident

of the Deaf-mute. The cited words are very awkward and
I suggest that the continuity of B with A like that of v. 1
with iv. 35 f. is the work of GMark. If we ask on what
occasion Christ can have journeyed from some distant place
through Decapolis to the Sea of Galilee our reconstruction
of X *sub* Jn. iii.–v. has provided an answer. We may conjecture that in JMk and M after the Death of John the
Ministry began with the sentence "now after that John was
delivered up Jesus came through the midst of the borders
of Decapolis to the Sea of Galilee. And they bring . . ."
In X Jesus returned from Aenon to Nazara through
Decapolis. It was probably the point of M that the
disciples of the two prophets held the same views about
purification (Jn. iii. 25) and that Jesus was John's successor.
(PsClement's doctrine of syzygies (Waitz, 131) and of the
inferiority of John was a modification of the position of
J and M.)

§ 90r. 6. There is no section of Mk which shews clearer
traces of the editing of sources than vii. 1–23. (*a*) It is
improbable that at a critical moment the scribes from Jerusalem condemned the disciples for a non-observance which
must have been customary throughout the masses of the Galilean population. (*b*) 3–4 is one of GMark's inaccurate explanations of Jewish customs (§ 342*a*). Note "*all* the Jews."
(*c*) The citation of Is. xxix. 13 may be authentic, but it
shews no trace of the Hebrew, the point of which is not
quite the same. Moreover in the words "nothing from
without defileth" Christ rejects not only the tradition but
the Mosaic law itself. (*d*) 9 repeats 8, a fact which suggests
that a section has dropped out after 8. (*e*) The difficulties
raised by Jewish scholars about the Corban passage may not
be quite insuperable but they are very real. (*f*) The multitude
has not been mentioned but Christ is said to have summoned
it again. (*g*) *Making all things clean* is an ungrammatical
splinter. (*h*) The fact that Christ expounds His parable
when he was entered into the house from the multitude suggests
that the setting of the exposition derives from the source
of iv. 11, where there is an esoteric explanation of the parable

of the Sower, and of iv. 34, where there is an allusion
to other expositions not preserved in Mk. Matt. xiii.
preserves the source of Mk. iv. and gives two omitted
parables and expositions. Now one of these, that of the
tares, is given like that of Mk. vii. 20 f. when Christ had left
the multitudes and entered the house. (*j*) Just as Matt. xiii.
shews an independent knowledge of the source of Mk. iv.,
so Matt. xv. 12–14 shews an independent knowledge of the
source of Mk. vii. In 15 Peter (James), and not the disciples,
questions Christ. We compare also xiii. 3 where the
apocalypse, which on our view derives ultimately from M,
is spoken privately.

The only matter in vii. 1–23 which is likely to be historical
is 14*b*–15 and 18*b*–19, to which we may add the allusion
of Matt. xv. 12 to the offence given to the Pharisees, and
with a query, the citation of Is.

Our argument for the influence of M on Mk may be
again confirmed by the apocrypha. We may compare the
fact that Christ in Mk and Matt gives esoteric teaching
when he had left the crowds and entered into the house
with the Clementine scheme, according to which Peter at
the evening meal gave esoteric explanations of the teaching
which he had given to the crowds (R. ii. 70, v. 35). His
previous ablutions connect the incident with J. One of
these expositions, that of the Sower (R. iv. 36) is certainly
from J and may be from M. Believers are graded, the first
step bringing forth thirty commands, the second sixty and
the third an hundred (§ 228). In view of the importance
which the Ebionites attached to the matter of food and the
fact that problems in connection with it arose at Cæsarea
M must have made some attempt to explain away Christ's
saying. The evidence which derives from J suggests that
in M Christ privately said that many disciples were not
expected to keep the whole law and that they and their
teachers were least in the kingdom of heaven, those who
kept the whole law being great (Matt. v. 17).

To attempt to reconstruct the positions of M would be
to multiply alternative hypotheses which would be almost
entirely uncontrolled by known facts. The data which we

have been examining prove the disturbing influence of an
unseen planet, but they do not enable us to make any
approach to a precise determination of its orbit. It is only
certain that deuteroQ *sub* Mk. vii. and Matt. xv. corrected
an esoteric misinterpretation of Christ's great saying which
the writer found in M.

In the next volume I shall argue that Mk. x. 35–45
contains matter which was misplaced by GMark. The Discussion about Divorce (2–12) is likely to have preceded the
Flight and seems to have had the same history as vii. 1–23.
Pharisees again engage Christ in controversy with hostile
intent. The crowds are again present to hear the discussion.
Christ again gives further teaching in the house, and just
as Matt. xv. is in part independent of Mk. vii., so the Matt
parallel with Mk. x. 2 f., as is pointed out by Streeter,
who conjectures the influence of M (259), is at several points
superior.

§ 90s. 7. To restore the order of JMk we must move
the Death of John to i. 14 and reconnect with the Four
Thousand some matter which GMark has connected with
the Five Thousand. Thus corrected after iii. 6 JMk ran
thus: vi. 16 Herod deems Jesus another John, vii. 1–23
(edited) "Nothing from without defileth," (?) a visit to
Nazareth, 24–26 a journey to Syrophœnicia, iv. 35–41 the
voyage from Capernaum, vi. 34 the Call of the Twelve and
the Sermon on the Mount, iv. 1–34 the Parables (edited),
viii. 1–9 the Feeding, vi. 47–52 the Walking on the Water
and arrival near Dalmanutha, 11–13 a controversy, 14–26 the
Forgotten Bread and the Blind Man of Bethsaida.

We must insert after the Return to the Lake the M Healing
of the Syrian Crowds, for this incident was necessary to
the understanding of the subsequent narrative and there are
probable traces of the incident in JMk. iv. 36. There is however no indication or probability that M and JMk narrated
the resumed healings in Christ's house (pMk. iii. 19). We
may also assume that JMark followed M in narrating healings
before the Feeding. I shall argue that the sequence, Call—
Sermon—Parables, is due to the influence of the Logia.

(i) In spite of its incompleteness but for the discourse this sequence is clearly historical. It begins with the plot of the local Pharisees and Herodians at Capernaum. Herod who according to Josephus killed John because he feared him regards Jesus as John's successor. Scribes from Jerusalem arrive, and Christ repudiates the law of Moses. He journeys beyond the boundaries of Palestine. There is then an hiatus which we have filled from Matt. iv. 24 f., where Christ heals the Syrian crowds. He crosses the lake and is out of Herod's reach. He feeds a great multitude and returns but not to Capernaum. He meets Pharisees and again seeks safety.

(ii) The narrative corresponds with the reconstruction of the history at which we arrived on other grounds, and there are no fewer than seven doublets or quasi-doublets with pMk matter: Herod and John, a controversy with scribes from Jerusalem, journeys to or towards Syrophœnicia, a return (explicit or implicit), a voyage, the Feeding, and embarkation and the return voyage, journeys to or towards Cæsarea Philippi.

§ 90*t*. 8. Before we examine in detail the procedure which GMark adopted in iii. 7–viii. 26 we may recall the fact that Matthew and S. Luke, as also even more markedly the editor of Jn, shew a surprising indifference to chronological considerations in the arrangement of their materials. S. Luke, holding that the claims of GMk were such that he must combine it with pLk, destroyed the framework of both Gospels.

Matthew inserted as much of M as possible into his recension of Mk but only allowed one or two traces of M's distinctive teaching to remain. GMark based his edition of Mk on JMk and completely eliminated all traces of JMark's Ebionism but not the attacks on the twelve either in iii.–viii. or xvi. He did not make any thorough or systematic attempt to make good all JMark's omissions of pMk, and he was as indifferent to chronology as the editor of Jn. His plan was (*a*) to reintroduce the pMk Feeding and, probably, to substitute the pMk for the MJMk Visit to

Nazareth, (*b*) to use later and after careful editing our section of JMk, (*c*) to produce a narrative which, like the composite narratives of Jn. xx., would run smoothly and to an uncritical reader seem plausible, (*d*) and to make his sequence of events somewhat resemble that of JMk. We must remember however that a writer writing on such lines as these was likely occasionally to be somewhat capricious.

Almost immediately after iii. 6 GMark found in JMk Judaistic narratives of the controversy about meats, the Syrophœnician and the Feeding. He resolved to postpone his editing of this section and to reintroduce from pMk the Beelzebub controversy, the Call and the Feeding but in his arrangement of events to follow the guidance of the section of JMk which he had just surveyed.

(i) iii. 7*b*–12. JMk narrated the healing of the Syrian crowds (Matt. iv. 24). GMark substituted the pMk narrative.

(ii) iii. 13–iv. 34. The order of JMk was the Crossing, the Call, Sermon, Parables. GMark followed this variation from X and pMk but omitted the crossing in order to keep Christ in Capernaum where occurred the healings resumed at the house and the Beelzebub controversy. It cannot be a mere coincidence that our Mk like M places the Call in the series of events which followed the healing of the Syrian crowds and that as in M it is not followed by the Mission but by discourse which we have concluded is influenced by M and which preserves JMark's introductory verse (iv. 1).

(iii) A voyage followed in JMk which GMark intended to use at vi. 45. He therefore inserted the voyage which he had omitted. The insertion of the Flight to Nazareth at this point may have been due to various motives. It adhered plausibly to the voyage. He may have wished to substitute the pMk narrative of the visit to Nazareth for that of JMk. He substituted the Flight to Nazareth for the Flight to Cæsarea Philippi which in JMk followed the teaching and a voyage. In pMk the Flight followed shortly after the Beelzebub controversy which he had just narrated.

(iv) vi. 6*b*–31. GMark had now to arrange for the introduction of the pMk Feeding, which was preceded by A.

the Healings by the Lake and at the House; B. "They had no leisure so much as to eat" (iii. 20, vi. 31); and by C. "Come ye yourselves apart ..." (vi. 31). He had two problems to solve. C arose out of A and B, and these incidents had been already narrated in ch. iii. He had to find another explanation of the fatigue of the twelve. He had also to complete his narrative of the Mission of the twelve which under the influence of JMk he had left unfinished. He arranged that these two problems should solve each other and that the Mission of the Twelve should be connected as it was in pMk with the narratives of the Flight. The Mission follows the Visit to Nazareth and the Return immediately precedes C. The apostles return weary with their journey, and the point is brought out by a repetition of B in 31. By inserting the matter about Herod and John before the return GMark gave the impression that important events had taken place during the absence of the twelve. When they returned from their prolonged journeyings the needed rest was impossible. GMark, as compilers often do, repeated (in 31) his source at the point at which he left it (iii. 28).

In vi. 34 GMark shews right feeling in his insertion of a beautiful sentence which occurred in the MJMk parallel with Matt. ix. 35 in X. GMark however could not preserve its MJMk connection and made Christ's compassion the motive of the teaching to which he refers under the influence of JMk. Similarly in viii. 2 he again edits JMark's reproduction of M *sub* Matt. ix. 36 and makes the compassion the motive of the Feeding.

In vi. 45–56 GMark combines his two sources and then returns to the beginning of our section of JMk. In vii. 1–23 he edits much and clumsily, again making substitutions from deuteroQ. He then omitted two Judaistic verses in the story of the Syrophœnician and misplaced the Healing of the Deaf Mute. He then rewrote the JMk narrative of the Feeding and in the narrative which followed inserted viii. 19. He had already used the Stilling of the Tempest and the Walking on the Water.

I

§ 91. I will now discuss some instances of M matter which occur elsewhere than in Mk. iii.–viii.

1. In X *sub* Jn. i. 42 Christ's ministry began on the day on which He discovered a man whom with kindly humour He could describe as a Cephas, one with whom and on whom He could begin to build. At this point we have noted an hiatus in Mk. In i. 16 Simon is assumed to be known both to Christ and to the reader and Christ to Simon. If then Matt. xvi. 16–18 is placed after the Resurrection, Christ referred to His first conversation and said that the apostle would be again His Cephas. This passage may have been reinserted by GMark, who reinserted the Markan matter in LEMk. 15–20. But this hypothesis does not account for 19, *I will give unto thee the keys of the kingdom of heaven, and whatsoever thou dost bind.* . . . This saying cannot in its present form be authentic, but it becomes intelligible when we remember that Cerinthus made James bishop of bishops (EpClem, 1), M made Christ give the keys to James because Peter had opened the door too wide at Cæsarea. I now suggest that deuteroQ not only expounded parables misinterpreted in M but also dealt with sayings and that in this case he merely substituted Peter for James as he did *sub* Matt. xv. 15. In this latter context deuteroQ corrected the food law which Christ had enjoined in private conversation with James (JMk. vii. 17 ff.). Our new hypothesis has the additional merit of accounting for the misplacement of the incident in Matt. xvi. Peter, who is similarly exalted in EP, 524 may have been originally James. For his intercessions compare those of James in HegMJas, 6.

§ 91*a*. Our critical position at this and several other points involves a discussion of the usage as to the names of S. Peter. The passages to be discussed stand out against the following statistical background. The instances of "Peter" are in Matt 20, Mk 17, Lk 17, Jn 16, Acts 50, I Cor and Gal "Peter" 1, "Cephas" 8, I Pet 1. Total 130.

(i) In the discourse of the sources of the NT the apostle was always either "Symeon" or "Simon." (*a*) The instances are Matt. xvi. 17, xvii. 25; (*b*) Mk. xiv. 37; (*c*)

LLk. xxii. 31, xxiv. 34. (*d*) In Jn. i. 42, xxi. 15 f. "Simon son of John" makes a very striking contact with Matt. xvi. 17 "Simon Bar-Jonah." (*e*) In Ac. x., xi. "Simon called Peter" distinguishes the apostle from the tanner. (*f*) Ac. xv. 14 "Symeon." (*g*) Only a complex hypothesis can account for the strangest of all our passages, the occurrence of "Symeon (the harder reading) Peter" in the KP letter underlying II Pet. i. 1 and EpClem (§ 244). The clue is to be found in the influence of *Domine quo vadis?* on the letter. Christ probably called the apostle Symeon in the source (II Ac. Mc.). PsMark was probably attempting vraisemblance. He added "Peter" to Symeon either for the sake of identifying him or because he was familiar with "Simon Peter." In the latter case he was almost certainly an Asian. The exceptions are instructive. S. Luke in MkLk. xxii. 34 interpolates "Peter," and in Ac. x. 13 writes "rise Peter." On the other hand the Didascalia parallel with Ac. xv. 7 f. (xxiv.) we find "rise Simon" though "Peter" occurs in the preceding narrative. The whole passage derives from II Ac. Mc. through KP. At xv. 14 "Simon" is substituted for "Symeon."

(ii) The abnormalities in narrative are as follows: A. "Simon" occurs in Mk. i. 16, 29 f. but is clearly Andrew's brother. B. In iii. 16 "whom he named Peter" follows "Simon." C. Matt. x. 2 and Lk. vi. 14 are influenced by B as is MkMatt. iv. 18. D. In Jn. i. 41 f. we read "Andrew, Simon Peter's brother . . . findeth his own brother Simon." E. "Simon Peter" occurs in Matt. xvi. 16 and LLk. v. 6. F. In every incident in Jn which mentions the apostle he is introduced as "Simon Peter." The 16 instances of "Peter" are for the sake of brevity.

(*a*) In D "Simon Peter" is obviously interpolated into a source in which the apostle was named Simon, and on our view the incident is presupposed in Mk. i. 16 (A). This view is confirmed by B. In Mk. iii. 16 the aorist is timeless, and the position that Jesus gave the names Peter and Boanerges when he commissioned the twelve is improbable and inconsistent with Jn. (*b*) The fact that in Mk the apostle is always "Peter" after iii. 16 raises three points. (*a*)

Matt. xvi. 16 can hardly derive from Mk. (β) If Mk. v. 37 originally preceded iii. 16 it is improbable that S. Mark wrote "Peter." On the other hand if he wrote "Simon" GMark would certainly write "Peter," the name familiar to himself and his readers. In ch. i. the change was unnecessary. (γ) The earliest instance of the fact that among the gentiles the apostle was always known as Peter is the usage in Mk. iv.–xvi. (c) "Simon Peter" must have originated at a time when and in a place where it was necessary to distinguish between Bar-Jonah and the Cananæan. Now in E Matt and LLk are independent of each other and must derive independently from X. It is improbable however that the usage of X accounts for the 21 instances of "Simon Peter" in Jn. They seem to shew that S. John habitually spoke of Simon Peter. He thought of him as Symeon, adding "Peter" and Græcising "Symeon" for the sake of others. This usage became that of the circle in which the Gospel originated.

§ 91*b*. 2. In Matt. xxi. 15 f. the priests condemn children who cried in the temple, Hosannah to the Son of David. McNeile points out that the incident is highly improbable and holds that the Hosannah of the children is an echo of that of the Entry. In the Aramaic source Christ had said that if the *banim* were silent the *ebanim* would shout. We have here our first indication of the influence of X, for in LLk. xix. 40 Christ says that if His disciples held their peace the stones would cry out, and immediately after uses the phrase *thy children* (44). Moreover, in Jn. xii. 12 f. the crowd comes from Jerusalem and many of them were probably in the phrase of Matt *children of Jerusalem*.

McNeile's note interested me for two reasons. (i) I had already concluded that the Baptist's epigram had sunk into Christ's mind and that it suggested the saying reported in Lk and perhaps connected itself with other thoughts about stones. (ii) I had not noticed the significance of Matt. xxi. 15 f. but had based a reconstruction similar to McNeile's on the following apocryphal passages to which he makes no allusion.

A. Harris (i. 46) cites from a Tract against the Moslems: *The children of Israel met Him with olive trees and palm branches, with their wives and children. The babes and sucklings adored Him saying, Hosannah to the Son of David: blessed is He who cometh king of Israel. The priests of the Jews said to the Christ: Hearest thou . . .? Doth not their saying exalt Thee when they adore Thee as God is adored? Then Christ said unto them, Out of the mouth of babes and sucklings thou hast foreordained thy praise? This is the eighth psalm.*

B. The Dialogue of Timothy and Aquila, 93 (Conybeare) (I italicise the parallels with A): "Bu when *the children of* the Hebrews *met Him* crying the *Hosannah* then encircled (C) Him the high *priests* and elders of the people saying, Hearest thou not what these witness against Thee? And Jesus said: Yea. It is written, *Out of the mouth. . . . Ib. 73. Because the children of* the Hebrews *met Him* with branches of *olives* saying the *Hosannah*, David saith in *the eighth psalm*."

C. Tryph, 103. Ps. xxii. 9 f. . . . *For on that night when the men of your people who were sent by the Pharisees and scribes, as their teaching bade them, surrounded* (B) *Him* (cf. LLk. xix. 39, Jn. xii. 19). . . . *Your teachers were the cause that their children went out into the Mount of Olives.*

D. EvN, i. *The children of the Hebrews held branches . . .* (saying) *Hossana membrone. . . .*

E. EvH, 23. *Osanna barrama.*

A and B derive from a common source and, as Harris conjectures, from a lost Gospel which underlies D and, we may add, C. That this lost Gospel was EvT is shewn by the following facts. (i) Justin is influenced by Leucius elsewhere.[1] (ii) The use of the incident to shew that Jesus was adored as God is distinctive of QPl. The same motive underlies the bowing of the standards in EvN, 1, where the source is undoubtedly QPl. (iii) The following phrases are very characteristic of QPl: *the priests of the Jews* (A), *your teachers* (C), the absurd *that night* (C).

[1] *E.g.* for *ploughs and yokes* (Tryph, 88) compare EvT, 13.

With the statement of B and C that the priests surrounded Jesus cf. X Jn. x. 23, *the Jews came round about him.*

The following parallels concern us:

	Mk. xi.	LLk. xix.	Jn	QPl	Matt. xxi. 15 f.
A.	..	37. multitude	12. crowd	..	..
B.	..	40. stones	..	children	children
C.	..	..	18. met him	met him	..
D.	8. branches	..	13. branches	branches of	..
E.	..	..	of palms	olives and palms	..
F.	10. kingdom	38. king	king of Israel	king of Israel	..
G.	of our father David	..	..	the son of David	the son of David
H.	..	39. Pharisees complain	19. Pharisees are per- turbed	the priests complain	the chief priests complain
J.	..	..	..	Ps. viii. 2	Ps. viii. 2

That our authorities derive from a common lost source must be deemed certain.

(i) The uncanonical evidence proves that a passage such as McNeile postulates occurred in an early Gospel.

(ii) Jn, LLk, QPl and Matt agree independently in H.

(iii) The crowd had cried, May he who dwells on high be glorified. When the Pharisees rebuked them Christ reminded them that according to Ps. viii. 2 he who set His glory above the heavens established strength out of the mouth of babes and sucklings. For Christ's use of the last phrase we may compare Matt. xi. 25 . . . *hide them from wise and understanding and didst reveal them unto babes.*

(iv) The agreement of Jn and QPl in C combines with Mk. x. 32 to explain Mk. xi. 9, *they that went before and they that followed after.* The Jerusalemites went in front: Christ's Galilean disciples followed behind.

We conclude with security that Matt and EvT derived in common from M and are confirmed in holding that M used X.

3. In the Mk narrative of the Anointing "certain," in Jn, Judas and in Matt the disciples criticise the woman. It is strange indeed that it should be Matthew who alone throws the blame on the disciples and, if he was acquainted with the X tradition, spares Judas. His use of M solves the problem.

§ 91*c*. 4. In an M context and the phrase, *the city of the great King* (Matt. v. 35) the designation of God has no parallel in the Gospels and can hardly be authentic. In J, which Acts we attribute to Cerinthus, it was given to the Son of God (§ 107 (ii)). That Matt. v. 35 derives from M is suggested by the fact that the Essenes condemned the taking of oaths and that M's statement that the murder of John was due to a tipsy oath illustrates their folly.

Streeter's view that the beginning of the Sermon on the Mount derives from M is confirmed by the fact that in QPl *sub* Ep, 7 and LBart, 76 Thomas preached an Encratite recension of the Matthæan beatitudes on his arrival at Cæsarea as *sub* Thec, 5 Paul did at Iconium. Presumably it derives from M through EvT and CerM and not from Matt.

5. In a context in which GMark has been active (§ 343*a*) one of a series of marvels which we attribute to M and which is composed in its manner, the Withering of the Fig-tree, is followed by a discourse which in 25 contains a clear allusion to MMatt. vi. 14 (Streeter, 251). But the enforcement of the duty of forgiveness seems to have no connection with the miracle or with the subsequent sayings about faith in God. The connection of thought is supplied by the following table of passages. It shews that the duty of forgiveness was in M taught in the saying which immediately preceded 23.

[TABLE

GMk. xi.	MMatt.	QLk.
	A. xviii. 15. *If thy brother sin against thee* 16–17. M has edited. 21. *Peter said . . . If my brother sin against me seven times. . . .*	X. xvii. 3. Variant wording Variant wording
	B. xvii. 21. *If thou hast faith as a grain of mustard seed*	Y. 5. *If ye have faith as a grain of mustard seed*
P. 23. *Whosoever shall say to* *this mountain* *be taken up* *and cast into the sea* *it shall happen*	C. *thou wilt say to* *this mountain* *depart hence* *and it will depart*	Z. *ye shall say to* *this sycamine* *be rooted up* *and planted in the sea* *and it shall certainly obey*
Q. 25. *And when ye stand praying* *forgive,* *if ye have aught against anyone,* *that your Father which is in heaven may forgive you your trespasses.*	D. vi. 5. *And when ye stand praying. . . .* *Instructions about prayer. The Lord's prayer.* 14. *For if ye forgive men their trespasses* (v. 23. . . . *rememberest that thy brother hath aught against thee.*) *your heavenly Father will also forgive you.*	

B and C are not *in situ* but substituted for Mk. ix. 29. XYZ shew that in the Logia BC followed A. PC shew that GMark had just read M *sub* ABC. He did not use A, but A suggested a section of the JMk Sermon on the Mount which like M *sub* ABC connected prayer and forgiveness. Matthew is shewn to have edited in C by the fact that P is more vigorous and a closer parallel to Z. P is more likely

to be original than Z and probably suggested 1 Cor. xiii. 2.
Z may combine S. Luke's recollections of Mk. xi. and a
lost saying about the fig-tree (Israel) which suggested the
miracle to M.

The occurrence of "your Father which is in heaven"
is by itself almost sufficient proof of the influence of M on
Mk. See § 343.

§ 91*d*. 6. Inasmuch as the rending of the veil and the
Three Hours' Darkness are marvels which portend the
punishment of the crucifiers, a theme which exercised much
influence on KP (cf. KP, 9), they are likely to derive from M.
Now in a passage which probably derives ultimately from J
(R. i. 41 : cf. 37) the veil is rent in lamentation for the
impending desolation. M wrote when it was expected that
Gaius would erect his statue in the temple.

Our attribution of this matter to M accounts for several
perversions in Mk. xv. (i) JMark pushed back the trial
to the preceding night in order to make room for the Three
Hours' Darkness. The meeting of the Sanhedrin in xv. 1
is a doublet and confirms our hypothesis. (ii) We can complete our criticism of 23–27 (§ 36). (*a*) "With him they
crucified two thieves" is based on S. Mark's reproduction
of the first sentence of the X Crucifixion. (*b*) In 26 under
the influence of the M Darkness JMark prefaced 27 with
"it was the third hour and they crucified him" and also
edited the subsequent narrative with a view to modifications
of the Visit to Pilate. (*c*) In 24 f. GMark reintroduced the
Lots, misplacing that incident and prefacing it with "and
they crucified him." Our analysis therefore accounts for
the three occurrences of "they crucified him." (iii) We
read in 39: *when the centurion saw that he so gave up the
ghost*. McNeile regards "so" as an unsolved difficulty.
On our view it abbreviates M *sub* Matt *when the centurion
. . . saw the earthquake and the things happening*. The
centurion's saying, *truly this man was the Son of God*, is
influenced by the same motive and must be attributed to
the same pen. In LLk it runs, *certainly this was a righteous
man*. S. Luke would not have weakened the testimony, and

S. Mark would not have heightened it. It follows that LLk and M derive independently from X.

7. Matt. xxvii. 52 f. *Many bodies of the saints which slept were raised; and coming forth out of their tombs after his resurrection they entered into the holy city and appeared unto many.*

(i) There is a presumption that the rising of the sleepers was consequent on Christ's and that the earthquake which accompanied the rolling away of the stone opened their graves. Matthew antedated the incident when he omitted the Emergence. KP must be both related and superior to Matt in making the sleepers rise with Christ (§ 98 (i)).

(ii) An interval during which Christ preached to the sleepers is implied by I Pet. iii. 20 where "disobedient" refers to the preaching of Noah, an incident which occurred in KP (I Clem. 7, 9, II Pet. ii. 5, Theoph. iii. 19). I Peter like I Clement may come between KP and Polycarp.

(iii) In the Gospels "the holy city" only occurs in Matt. iv. 5 where the variation from QLk proves derivation from M.

(iv) In EvT *sub* HEvXII, 30 the apostles went to the mountain on Good Friday. *Sub* EP, 476 John ("Peter") on the next day saw the dead on Olivet rejoicing in their graves.

(v) Christ rises from the sleepers in EvH, 16, a passage which I shall argue derives from M.

§ 91e. 8. Matthew derives from M when he makes the women come to the sepulchre " in the dawning towards" the first day of the week, *i.e.* late on the sabbath. (*a*) He would not have varied from Mk to this extent if he had not been following M. (*b*) Our hypothesis explains the following verbal contacts: "wound it up" (LLk. xxiii. 53), "dawning towards" (54), "beheld the tomb" (55), the fact that the women saw what was done (55), "new" (Jn. xix. 41). (*c*) In the preceding and subsequent narrative there is a vein of apologetic and polemical fiction such as we should expect in M: Pilate's wife, "I am innocent of his blood," the rending of the veil which portended the punishment of the Jews, the earthquake and rising of the sleepers, the second earthquake and the descent of the angel, the watch.

The following facts shew that in M the angel rolled away the stone, not to let the women in but to let Christ out. (*a*) In xxvii. 61 the women sit over against the tomb. If they so sat on the next day they would see Christ emerge. (*b*) Matthew alone says nothing about the spices. (*c*) The Visit of the Women is moved back and timed for something to happen between it and the following dawn. On the other hand the statement of X that the women "beheld the tomb" (LLk. xxiii. 55) is moved forward to their second visit and becomes "came to behold." They came not to anoint but to see Christ emerge. (*d*) The watch tell the chief priests, who were not expecting Christ to rise, all the things that happened at the tomb. The reply shews that they said that the body was no longer in the tomb. (*e*) The women depart from the tomb with fear and joy. If Matthew had been writing freely he would have postponed the joy of the women until they had seen Christ and went on their way to the eleven (11). (*f*) In AT, 168 f. LeuciusT has Christ in mind. Thomas is speared. The brethren bring linen and bury him. One of them steals the body. Thomas, like Christ, who in EvT ascended from the tomb, has received all that he was promised. Here we are concerned with the fact that he appears to men who sit and watch. AT derives from the source of EvH, 49 and EvP, 33, where the watch sit, and EvH, 29 where they sit over against a cave. They do so because in CerinthusM they were with the women who in Matt. xxvii. 61 sit over against the sepulchre. It follows that AT is evidence that in M they saw Christ emerge from it. (*g*) In CBRB, 190, RobEvvC, 51, HEvXII, 30 and EP, 477, four very depraved passages, there survives a Leucian tradition of a eucharist on the morrow. The eucharist perverts an X tradition, which underlies EvH, 16, that when Christ appeared to the eleven He blessed, brake and gave them bread. In EvT this was on the morrow of a message which Christ sent and which was parallel with Jn. xx. 17 but which immediately followed

His non-death (§ 102). This matter therefore is evidence for a sabbath Resurrection. The evidence is too difficult for brief discussion. Until I made the present inquiry these allusions to a morrow were entirely unintelligible. Cf. § 123.

The Matt tradition that Christ rose at the end of the sabbath makes an interesting contact with Cerinthus, who insisted on the observance of the sabbath (Philastr.). The Judaisers protested against a tendency which became marked between the dates of X and M for the observance of the Lord's day to oust that of the sabbath. The purpose of the perversion must have been to make the sabbath the Lord's day. Sunday therefore was the holy day of the primitive community.

For the Cerinthian doctrine of the Resurrection see Lips. d. Q. 119, DCB. i. 448b.

§ 91f. 9. In Mk. xvi. 1 "very early" is inconsistent with "when the sun was up." The former phrase agrees with LLk and Jn, and the latter can be best explained as due to GMark's misunderstanding of M's Jewish word "dawning towards." (a) In Matt the women seem to remain sitting after they went with Joseph to the tomb and are not said to have bought or prepared spices before the sabbath, as they do in LLk and as presumably they did in pMk. GMark harmonised by moving the incident to after the sabbath. (b) In Mk we have not been told that the stone was great, yet the women discuss the problem of its removal, and why did they not bring a man with them? The incident is not suggested by anything in the previous narrative and cannot have been suggested by any tradition. The inevitable conjecture that it is motived by a lost document is confirmed by the fact that the writer after saying that the women looked up (why did they not look up before?) goes back and says that the stone was very great. The lost document therefore is that used at an earlier point in Matt (xxvii. 60), where the stone is said to be great. It seems clear therefore that what I wrote in § 37, while pointing in the right direction, does not account for all the facts. Matthew does not write as if he were working on the story of Mk, and Mk is based on a source. Matt explains Mk, and Mk does not explain Matt.

A word may be added as to JMark's editing. In X and protoMk Christ appeared to one of the women at the tomb. This suggested to M that they should all see Him emerge and then rejoice. JMark compromised. As in M all the women saw Christ and rejoiced. On the other hand as in protoMk Christ's appearance is later than His emergence from the tomb. This procedure had the advantage of enabling the eleven to disobey both Christ and the angel.

S. Luke who almost always omits M matter uses the Mk story of Joseph but omits the statement that he rolled up the stone. The simple statement of LLk. xxiv. 2 that the women found the stone rolled away was read by M in X and worked up.

§ 91*g*. 10. We have not solved the following problems: (*a*) How did Pilate's wife know that Christ was a just man? If she had been told it in her dream she would have said so. (*b*) In Matt. xxviii. 11 the soldiers have no motive for going to the priests. (*c*) What suggested to JMark the misplacement of Joseph's visit to Pilate? (*d*) Pilate let all the world know that Jesus was innocent, had been told by the priests that Jesus foretold His resurrection, and permitted the sealing of the sepulchre. Did his part in the drama stop at this point? What followed the bribing of the soldiers?

The apocrypha solve these problems. (*a*) Pilate's wife knew that Christ was innocent because Joseph had already told Pilate that He was (EvP, 3). (*b*) The soldiers did not go to the priests who were already at the tomb with their servants (EvP, 38, EvH, 16). In Matt the soldiers go to Jerusalem because owing to the omission of the Emergence the priests are still there. (*c*) The priests went to the sepulchre after their visit to Pilate on the morrow of the Crucifixion (Matt. xxvii. 62) and therefore not long before the Emergence. JMark, who knew from pMk that Joseph was one of the elders who went to Pilate, converted their visit into a visit of Joseph and moved it to Friday because in pMk nothing happened on the sabbath. (*d*) Pilate reported

(§ 125) that his soldiers saw Jesus rise and that they said that they had been bribed to remain silent.

§ 91*h*. 11. EvH, 16, runs: *the Lord, when He had given the linen cloth to the servant of the high-priest, went unto James and appeared to him, for James had sworn that he would not eat bread from that hour wherein he had drunk the Lord's cup until he should see him again risen from among them that slept.* (Again after a little.) *Bring ye, saith the Lord, a table and bread.* (And immediately it is added.) *He took bread and blessed and brake and gave it unto James the Just and said, My brother eat bread, for the Son of man is risen from among the sleepers.*

Nicholson has collected some traces of this passage from Greg. Tur. Hist. Franc., i. 21, Abdias vi. 1 and Jac. de Vorag. Leg. Aur., lxvii. Abdias used Heg elsewhere. Jacobus gives Josephus as his authority. For other instances in which Heg is so cited, see § 171.

The derivation of Abdias from Heg (who was the source of many variants) is confirmed by the fact that Christ asks James to eat honey with Him and that this incident underlies a variant at Lk. xxiv. 43. That James is here substituted for the eleven is shewn by the fact that, just as in EpApp, 11 Christ goes from the tomb to the eleven, so in EvH he goes to James in whose house others are assembled (*bring ye*).

That EvH derived from M is shewn (i) by the exaltation of James. The presence of the high-priest's servant at the sepulchre and Christ's allusion to the sleepers cohere with our reconstructions of M in (8) and (11). (iii) In M and J John, Jesus and James were Nazarites (§ 90*h*). In EvEb John eats honey and not locusts. James, like the eldest sons of the tribes (LM, 101), was a priest (HE, II. xxiii. 6), and honey was the meat and drink of the tribes. Not only at the Feeding but also after the Resurrection Christ justified the Ebionite view of the community meal. (iv) Our passage illustrates M's practice of transposing splinters. Such splinters occur in our passage and make it important. (*a*) The servant of the high-priest is presumably Malchus. (*b*) "Linens" occurs in Mk and

Lk. xxiv. 12. (*c*) As in Mk *sub* KP (§ 69) Jesus speaks of Himself as the Son of man in connection with the Resurrection. (*d*) "The house of James" (R. i. 71) may have occurred or been implied in II Ac. Mc. *sub* Ac. xii. 5, 17. When M wrote the house of James was the headquarters of the Judaisers. The Hellenists probably met in the house of Mary the mother of Mark. (*e*) The most striking of the parallels with X matter is the concluding sentence. In the Feeding, the two narratives of the Last Supper and at Emmaus Christ takes, breaks, blesses and gives the bread. In Jn. xxi. 13 He takes and gives. In his Markan sermon S. Peter said that the apostles ate and drank with Christ many days, and in LEMk, 14 the apostles are at meat. We conclude with confidence that EvH preserved the concluding sentence of the X narrative of the Appearance to the Eleven.

The history of the tradition of the close of the Appearance to the Eleven may now be summarised. I bracket some doubtful words. It is probable that the tradition that Christ ate began with M.

X	He took, brake, blessed, gave.	..
The sermon	..	We ate and drank with him ... many days.
PMk	(He took, etc.)	They ate ... days
I Ac. Mc.	..	..
M	He took, etc. Honey.	..
JMk	As in M.	He ate and drank with them.
GMk	..	He ate and drank with them.
Lk	..	The broiled fish.
Acts	..	(Eating) with them.
KP	..	He ate and drank with them.
CerM	He took, etc. Honey.	..
EvT	A spiritualised eucharist.	..
EvXII	A eucharist.	..
EvH	He took, etc. Honey.	..

The oath of James in EvH may have been added by Cerinthus, who probably enjoined the oath of secrecy described in EpPet Adjur. Perhaps it was only light and frivolous swearing that was condemned in M.

We observe that our analysis of GMk had thrown light on the problem discussed in § 67. In PMN Christ ate and drank with the disciples many days. M added to X the statement that Christ ate the honey. In JMk, GMk and KP *sub* Ign. Sm. 3 Christ ate and drank.

On our view the series of documents, M, JMk and deuteroQ, reflects the controversies which followed S. Peter's converse with uncircumcised gentiles and preceded the apostolic council. M's exaltation of James, which to some extent survived in JMk, would have been pointless at a later date. M must have been written when James was regarded as an opponent of the Hellenisers, and JMk not much later. It follows that the case for the very early date of Mk, which is already printed and which rests on arguments which are wholly unconnected with the present discussion, has received a striking and wholly unexpected confirmation.

CHAPTER III

SOME DOCETIC NARRATIVES

I. *The Appearance to the Eleven*

The reader must remember that this chapter was printed
before I discovered the influence of M on KP and J. It is
probable that the discussion in several places should be more
complex, but the main results are not affected.

§ 92. The last chapter has justified me in inviting the
reader to undertake the very laborious task of investigating
the literary relations of the NT apocrypha with a view to
determining the relations of their lost sources. We will
begin our task with reconstructions of some of the docetic
narratives of QPl for the following reasons. (i) We shall
be able to continue our study of some of the Resurrection
matter which we have been considering. (ii) We shall find
clues which will help us to understand the perversions of
the historical narratives of KP. (iii) We shall be able to
use some documents which are known to be early. (iv) The
motivisation of the fragments which we shall use will usually
be very clear. We shall be able quite safely to assign to KP
all matter (*e.g.* the visible emergence of Christ from the
tomb), the motive of which is apologetic, to J all matter
which exalts James, to QPl all docetic perversions, and to
QP all matter which shews the influence both of KP and
QPl.

§ 93. We will now examine some passages in which
Leucius depraved the Appearance to the Eleven.

1. In ad Sm, 3 Ignatius was attacking an opponent
whom we shall identify with Leucius, but he occasionally
used him. He does so in the words, *as one with him in the flesh
though spiritually united to the Father*. They are based on

Jn. xiv. 10 or 20, *I am in the Father and the Father in me*, and Leucius was the only primary apocryphist who used Jn. This citation survives in a QP speech of Peter (VP, 20) just before *He ate and drank for our sakes* and in EpApp, 17.

2. AJ, 92. *When I felt Him . . . the substance was sometimes immaterial. . . . And if He were bidden . . . by some one of the Pharisees He would part His loaf among us* (a probable allusion to the Anointing). . . . *I desired to see the print of His feet whether it appeared upon earth, . . . and I never saw it.* This passage obviously preserves the docetic reply to the Appearance to the Eleven. It is denied that the act of feeling shewed the reality of the body and that Christ ate with the disciples. The distribution of the bread occurs in EvH. For allusions to Pharisees see § 315 G. The concluding words of AJ misuse a KP testimony which occurred in QP (EvXII) *sub* EpApp, 11 and CApol, 564, *a phantom of a demon maketh no footprint upon earth.* It was implied that Christ's footprints when He " came " could be seen. Leucius denied that they were seen. The passage is a long context which is throughout based on QPl and QP.

3. We shall conclude that Leucius spiritualised the eating and drinking in an apocalypse which was seen on Good Friday (§ 101 f.).

§ 94. 4. SchmidtEvvC have been edited, but the discourse is clearly Gnostic.

A. In fragment 3 the disciples and the seven women-disciples have gone (edit.: after the resurrection) to the mountain in Galilee. Christ appears not in His earlier form but in that of an angel of light (Matt. xxviii. 2 f.). (*a*) Leucius supposed that Galilee bordered on Jerusalem, that Olivet was in Galilee and that the sepulchre was on Olivet (§ 132). (*b*) The appearance to the eleven and the seven was parallel with CBRB, 187 f., where on other grounds we shall conclude Christ was originally the angel of the sepulchre and the women are joined by the apostles. The CBRB women are M. Magdalene (edit. M of James) whom Jesus delivered from the hand of Satan (Lk. viii. 2), Salome,

Salome the temptress, Mary who ministered unto them
(APh, 94), Martha her sister (edit. Susannah), (Joanna) who
refused Khousa's bed, Berenice the woman with the issue
and Leah the widow of Nain. If M. of James and Susannah,
are omitted, neither of whom is described, there are seven
women, a number which corresponds with that of Schmidt-
EvvC and which is due to the wish of Leucius to attribute
the foundation of the order of deaconesses to Christ. For
his exaltation of this order see § 264.

B. SchmidtEvvC, 1 is based on the matter which in
QPl followed the appearance at the tomb. This is shewn
by the fact that the apostles named are those named in the
QP narrative of the Appearance to the Eleven. Its derivation
from QPl is shewn by its exaltation of Mary (the sister of
Martha) and its depreciation of Peter and Andrew. In QP
Thomas and John whom Leucius exalted were present,
but in our passage only those apostles are mentioned who
were depreciated.

The Redeemer had appeared to the disciples and had
conversed with them, bidding them proclaim to the heathen
the Gospel of the Son of man. They were sorrowful and
mourned (a perversion of the KP parallel with LEMk. 10)
and said, If they have rejected Him (the phrase like Son of
man derives from KP *sub* EpApp, 11 J) will they not reject
us? Mary embraced them and said, His grace will go with
you. Levi rebuked the complaints of Peter.

LeuciusP used this passage in his narrative of the gathering
of the apostles for the seventh passover, an incident which
was used in AJ *sub* Proch, 3 f. and underlies LJas, 140.
The apostles lament their lots. Peter reminds them how
Christ *commanded us to go into all the inhabited earth* (a
slight variation from LEMk. 15 which was due to the
influence of KP, 6) *and to preach and to baptize* (almost the
phrase of EvXII as we reconstructed it from Proch, 32, 2).
In 5, 7 we find the QP phrase " father Peter " (EP, 469).
This phrase was suggested by Leucius who exalted
John. In the Templar MS. at Jn. vii. Christ says,
John shall be your father until he comes to me in Paradise
(Thilo, 880).

§ 95. The following table shews that the persons present were the same in QP as in QPl :

SchmidtEvvC, 1	..	..	Levi	..	Pet	And	Mary s of Martha
EpApp, 11	Thom	..	..	..	Pet	And	Mary s of Martha
EvP, 60	..	(? Matt)	Levi	..	Pet	And	..
I Bk. Clem.	Thom	Matt	..	John	..	..	..
Commod. A.	Thom	..	..	..	..	..	..
Apol, 564							
Didasc. xxi.	..	..	Levi	..	..	..	..

On the other hand as in KP Christ comes and the apostles handle Him.

Our reconstruction accounts for the close of EvP, a passage to which scholars have attached too much importance: *I Simon Peter and Andrew . . . took our nets and there were with us Levi the son of Alphaeus whom the Lord * * * (Mk. ii. 14: cf. Matt. ix. 9). In the Coptic recension of EpApp the apostles are sitting veiled when Christ appeared, but in the Ethiopic as in EvP they are fishing. Leucius who made large use of Jn was using Jn. xxi.

Possibly the story of the fishing devils (EvvC, 5 : cf. EvB, iv. 44) occurred in this context of EvT, but it was suggested by Mk. i. 17.

II. *The Two Angels of the Sepulchre*

§ 96. The main subject of this long section is the place of the two angels of the sepulchre in the scheme of Leucius. We will begin our enquiry with the EvP narrative of the watch. The numerous unexplained contacts of that Gospel are due to the fact that it is based throughout on QP (*i.e.* EvXII).

EvP, 31 f., runs: *Pilate gave them Petronius, the centurion, with soldiers to watch the sepulchre; and the elders and scribes came with them to the tomb. . . . 33. . . . and they pitched a tent there and kept watch. 34. . . . The soldiers kept guard two by two.* They see the angels descend and summon Petronius, who saw Christ emerge.

(i) This narrative must derive from an incident of KP, the purpose of which was to show that the Roman and

Jewish authorities heard from their representatives that
Christ emerged from the tomb. One result was the official
report which Pilate sent to the Emperor, in which he stated
that his soldiers saw the Resurrection (§ 125). KP also
said that crowds were at the sepulchre (EP, 477) and saw
Christ ascend (467). They had seen Joseph ascend Olivet
during the ordeal of water (Epiph. Hom. 329, §§ 135, 142).
All this is clearly manufactured evidence.

(ii) Our context also contains clear traces of QPl. (*a*)
" Petronius " is an instance of Leucius' habit of naming
the unnamed. He also named the Jewish watch and perhaps
also the Roman (§ 315 D). Moreover, we shall find that
the centurion played a part in some docetic narratives.
(*b*) EvP derives *two by two* from QPl *sub* AT, 169 f. (§ 91*e*),
where two men sit at the tomb of Thomas, who says,
" I have gone up and received all that I have promised."
In the source Christ referred to His ascension from the cross,
a docetic incident (§ 101 f.). The watch sits in EvH, 49.

§ 97. EvP continues : 36. *They saw two men descend from
heaven. . . . 37. Both of the young men entered the sepulchre. . . .
38. They waked up the centurion and the elders. 39. . . . they
saw three men come out of the sepulchre, and two of them
sustaining the other and the cross following after them. 40. . . .
Their heads reached unto heaven, but His who was led by
them overtopped the heavens. 41. And they heard a voice
. . . Hast thou preached unto them that sleep. And an answer
was heard, Yea.*

The M incidents of the visible emergence, the elders
and the sleepers (Matt. xvii. 52) are preserved in EvH,
16 (§ 98): *The Lord when He had given the linen cloth to
the servant of the high priest . . . risen from among the sleepers.*
On the other hand the curious incident of the emergence
of the cross is the QPl substitute for the M emergence of
Christ. Leucius, who allegorised the cross, made it emerge
at a later date from the tomb to heal Rufus (§ 137).

§ 98. (i) It is certain that the sleepers occurred in KP.
(i) Probably all fictitious testimonies which support orthodox

doctrines derive from KP, whose testimonies were much used by Justin. Now the preaching of Christ to the sleepers in Hades is supported by a testimony which occurs in Tryph. 72 and also in Iren. Dem. 78, III, xxii. 1. (ii) Ignatius writes: *Christ died in the sight of those in heaven, those on earth and those under the earth* (Trall, 9). (iii) The QPl parallel survives as follows: (*a*) In EvB, i. 6, we read: *The angels coming down from heaven and worshipping Thee.* 9. *I went down into Hades that I might bring up Adam and all that were with him.* 21. *The dead rising and worshipping Thee and going up into their sepulchres.* The phrase of EvB *going up* is due to the fact that Leucius placed the Crucifixion in Gethsemane (§ 132) and the graves on Olivet. Hence in EP, 477 (a QPl context), the dead are seen rejoicing in their graves when Peter ascends Olivet. (*b*) In AJ, 98 (an obviously docetic context), Christ shows John a cross of light (on which the sleepers had ascended: § 325) " and about the cross a great multitude . . . and in the cross another multitude " (J, 254). The incident was used in the martyrdom of Peter (LinusAP, 12).[1] The worship of the sleepers occurs in James of Serug (§ 124). For the influence of QPl on Ignatius at this point, see § 325 F. The descent into Hades and the ascent were the nearest approaches made by Leucius to the acceptance of Christ's death and Resurrection.

§ 99. The KP incident of the emergence from the sepulchre survives in Asc.Is. iii. 15. As in EvP the watch is mentioned. As in *k* at Mk. xvi. 3, an angel descends from heaven (Matt. xxviii. 5). There follows an incident which underlies EvP: the Beloved comes from the tomb sitting on the shoulders of Gabriel and Michael. Leucius, who denied the Resurrection, transferred this matter to the first and most important of the sleepers, *sub* EvB, i. 21 f., where Adam, who is of great stature, as he was in QPl *sub* CMystJ, 250, is borne up by the hands of angels.

---

[1] Ishodad (114), who may be deriving from Bar Salibi, says that the graves were opened and five hundred dead raised, and that some say that a few remained until Titus. The incident and Ishodad's number probably influence APh, 22 f. (cf. 138).

§ 100. Before we discuss an incident to which allusion has been already made, Christ's ascension from the cross, it may be observed that Christ's ascensions and descents were frequent in QPl, and hardly more than appearances and disappearances. Two instances may be given.

(i) The fact that the Acts of Paul narrated *Domine quo vadis?* (Origen: J, 297) explains the fact that Christ ascended at the close of the incident in QP (VP, 35).

(ii) In AJ, 90, there is a parody of the story of Gethsemane which obviously derives from QPl. Jesus takes Peter, James and his brother John into the mountain where He was wont to pray (Lk. xxii. 39). As he was praying John saw His shining feet and His head touching heaven. (So far from being in an agony He ascended for a moment in glory: we shall find in QPl Christ again ascending in this manner.) He then became a man of small stature (§ 22) and gave the apostle's beard a sharp twitch. " If this is a pleasantry," said John, " what would a buffet be "? Christ bade him not tempt Him who cannot be tempted.

§ 101. The primary apocalypses may be dated as follows: (i) In KP Christ ascended at the dawn of Pentecost after imparting the Spirit to the apostles who in the Spirit also ascended and beheld the unseen. (ii) In J, which work we shall attribute to Cerinthus, Christ left Jesus before He died and flew back to heaven (§ 115, iv.). The apocalypse was seen by Judas in the east at a later date. (iii) (*a*) In QPl Christ left the cross during the three hours' darkness, appeared to the apostles who were mourning on Olivet, and took them up with Him into heaven. (*b*) John saw the J eastern apocalypse shortly before the seventh passover. (iv) LeuciusP used KP and QPl as follows: (*a*) *Sub* EvP, 20, he said that Christ was taken up, but it is probable that this phrase hardly means more than "gave up the ghost" or "went to heaven," for in QP Christ emerged from the tomb, and the incident followed the Last Word. (*b*) LeuciusP moved the unorthodox ascension of QPl to Easter Day, and made Christ ascend with the eleven after His appearance to them. (*c*) The apostles saw the QPl eastern apocalypse.

We are here concerned with the apocalypse seen in QPl at the time of the Crucifixion.

[There is always a presumption that a late writer who uses primary apocryphal matter derived it from Heg, and if this matter derives from more than one Acts this presumption is very strong, and it is so in the case of the documents now to be examined.

A. The whole of EP and EPl will be shewn to be based on Heg and our section to derive from KP, QPl and QP. It contains a trace of one of Heg's harmonisations. At the close of a QP Ascension narrative, which must originally have been dated at Pentecost, the apostles for ten days return to the place on Olivet from which they had seen Christ ascend, James making an offering on the Sunday after the Ascension (475). The statement evidently preserves one of Heg's ingenious harmonisations. He reconciled the two dates by making the Ascension through the heavens last during the whole period. The statement that Christ was ten days ascending is actually made by a Clementine writer (Rév. de l'Or Chrét., xxii. (ii), 22 f.).

B. The chaotic narrative of HEvXII preserves a trace of the harmonisation in the week which precedes the prophesyings of the twelve (30). After this week the apostles speak the same tongues as in EP (28). These tongues were those of QP. That HEvXII also used QPl is shewn by the doublet in 30, where the apostles speak in the tongues of the holy fathers. The title we shall attribute to QP, and as in QP Christ ascends after appearing to the eleven (27 f.). We shall find one or two more splinters from QPl.

C. Like HEvXII CBRB is in obvious disorder. There are several Ascensions. The names of the women who come to the tomb are Leucian (§ 315 A), as are the docetic perversions of Jn and the cursing of Judas by Christ, the only parallel with the cursing Jesus of EvT. On the other hand the Ascension at Pentecost (193) and the list of the instruments of the Passion (205: cf. 213) must derive from either QP or KP. The stoning of Ananias of Bethlehem (J, 182) perverts a tradition preserved by Heg that Ananias was stoned at Bethgubrin.

We will begin our reconstruction of QPl with our most important document, CBRB. (i) In 179 the editor says that Christ was crucified and rose. He then begins the use of QPl, and says that the Saviour took with Him into heaven the soul of Ananias, who ate and drank with Him at His table in His kingdom. *Ananias* must be editorial, and the fact that Christ's ascension precedes the Descensus (179–187) due to the QPl narrative of Good Friday. To this narrative belong the hymns of the angels (195, 199). The matter about Adam and the patriarchs (199 f.) belongs to the section of QPl used in § 98, and must originally have followed the Descensus. (ii) In 202 Christ takes the apostles to Olivet, where they see *His body going up into the heavens, and His feet were firmly fixed upon the mountain with us. And we ourselves also went up with Him into the tabernacle of the Good Father*. Like the parallel in AJ, 90 this passage derives from QPl but probably through QP.]

§ 102. We will now combine our data. In HEvXII, 30, there is a parody of the three hours' darkness. On a Friday there is great light which lasts three hours, and a great voice is heard saying, " Blessed is the mystery of salvation." The apostles are then bidden go to the Holy Mountain (Olivet: cf. EP, 475 and EApP, 518, where it is the scene of the apocalypse). They will speak there in the tongues of the fathers (30). As in KP they were caught up in the Spirit, so in HEvXII they are bound by the Spirit. We then read: *Suddenly there were set before them tables full of good things*, and we compare the statement of CBRB that Ananias ate and drank with Christ at the table in His kingdom. The two works explain each other. CBRB gives us the meaning of the cryptic phrase of HEvXII, and HEvXII shews that we were right in our view that the editor of CBRB substituted Ananias for the apostles. Christ appeared to the eleven not to prove that He had risen, but to prove that He was not suffering on the cross, and they then ascended with him. The allusion to the tables was probably suggested by that which Jesus bade James prepare, and the phrase *ate and drank* occurred in KP (§ 25). The eating narrated in these two Acts was spiritualised, Lk. xxii. 30 being used.

Christ returned to the cross and after His non-death was embraced by Ananias (J, 182), laughed at Death in the sepulchre, smashed Hades, cursed Judas and, so we may infer, narrated these events to the holy women and to the apostles who had just descended Olivet. Our reconstruction of CBRB, 185 f. is confirmed by a misplaced splinter in HEvXII, 27, where Judas is said to have inherited death by strangling *according to the mystery which our Lord revealed to Symeon Cephas and to the holy women.* The editor disapproved of the cursing and substituted the canonical suicide. The Leucian holy women were at the sepulchre in QP *sub* EpApp, 9 f.

§ 103. Our section of QPl also underlies AJ, 97, where John is in a cave (the sepulchre) on Olivet, and Christ, whom the Jews suppose they are crucifying, appears to him. There is an allusion to the apocalypse in 88, where John says: *I can neither set forth nor write the things which I both saw and heard.*

The QP apocalypse seen after the appearance to the eleven underlies EpApp, 12. When the apostles have touched Christ He says: *Rise up* (cf. AknApP, 4, " let us go ") *and I will shew that which is above the heaven. . . . My Father hath given me power to take you up thither.* [In 13–50 there is some pre-Ascension discourse. In 51 Christ is borne up on a bright cloud, and the angels rejoice and sing as they do in the QP narrative of the Ascension at Pentecost (EP, 467 f.), where we note the absence of any allusion to the apocalypse which occurred at this point in KP.]

§ 104. I must now mention a fact which does not fit into our scheme. Basilides, who shews other traces of the influence of QPl, says that Christ made Simon of Cyrene die in His place while He stood by and derided the Jews (Iren. I. xxiv. 4). This is inconsistent with the CBRB embrace of Ananias (§ 132). Photius, however, also using the same passage of QPl only attributes to Leucius the statement that another was crucified in the place of Jesus while He stood by and derided. It is obvious to conjecture that in the Leucian burlesque Christ returned again to the cross, again exchanging forms with Simon. Basilides either misremembered the passage or went a step further. The derision is parallel with CBRB, 181, where Christ laughs when Death removes the napkin from His face.

§ 105. We will now return to the subject of the two angels of the sepulchre, who played a very important part in QP1. Some of the evidence occurs in the following edited passages of EP and EP1. [(a) 469, 28–474, 2, is a cento inserted in the QP narrative of the Ascension. (b) 477 f. follows a QP parallel with Acts ii., but the allusion to the souls (of the sleepers) rejoicing in the graves on Olivet connects the incident with the Crucifixion. (c) The journey of John to Antioch in 491 originally followed the seventh passover. (d) The transportation in 700 is misplaced. Our rearrangement of this matter will be justified below.] There are the following allusions to the angels:

A. In 469 "my Lord and my God" gives Peter (John) a book containing the rest of the knowledge, which had been written by His own hand, [and sends him to all cities, *i.e.* those mentioned in 479 (the allusion to Antioch is editorial). 477 f. continues the earlier cento.] The angel of the Lord bids Peter ascend Olivet and read the book. This angel the editor identifies with the angel of the sepulchre, his companion being Uriel. A voice from heaven says: *The cloud which covered me shall not leave thee until the day of my second coming.* "Peter" revealed the names of the two angels to his brethren, a sentence which proves that the identification of the second angel has been edited out.

B. In EP, 700, Raphael and Uriel, the two angels which used to appear to "Peter" and reveal to him hidden things, transport him on a cloud to Warikon.

C. In 491 the angel of the Lord who had often appeared to "Peter" transports the apostles to Antioch. (In QP1 John's journey was after the seventh passover.)

To these passages we may add the following:

D. In 489 the editor inserts a transportation in a QC narrative. There stands on the transporting cloud a young man whose face was ten times brighter than the sun.

E. In LT, 88, Christ appears to the apostle on a shining cloud, and in 9 He is a young man whose raiment shone like the sun.

This evidence shews that in QPl Christ was one of the two angels of the sepulchre and that the names Raphael and Uriel are editorial.

(i) A is in confusion because the editor converted the narrative of QPl into two incidents in order to conceal the fact that Christ (469) was the angel of the Lord (477). Hence it is that in the second incident His voice is heard from heaven. This cannot be original. Again, our hypothesis explains the fact that the apostle reveals the names of the two angels to the apostles. There is nothing to suggest that Leucius took any interest in the names of the angels.

(ii) The transportations by angels in B and C are the fulfilment of the promise (A) that the cloud which covered Christ will not leave Peter (John) until " my second coming."

(iii) The Christ of D and E is one of the angels of B and the angel of C.

(iv) If Christ was in QPl one of the two angels of the sepulchre, we have accounted for the narrative of QPl which made Him narrate the mystery of Judas to the women at the sepulchre, and it also becomes clear that the descriptions of Christ in D and E were suggested by Matt. xxviii. 3, where the angel who descends to the sepulchre has the appearance of lightning, and by Mk. xvi. 5, where He is a young man. We shall presently find that in the QP perversion of QPl Christ, like the angel of Matthew, sits on the stone.

§ 106. The identification of the second angel will involve a prolonged investigation.

EP, 469 f., a much-edited passage, connects the two angels with the donation of a mystical book to Peter (John). Now the ancient matter in this context must derive through QPl either from KP or J, and the incident is hardly more likely to have occurred in KP than in Acts. On the alternative hypothesis, derivation from J, it is easily accounted for. In QC Christ, the true prophet, who was identified first with Moses and then with Jesus, appointed James Bishop of Jerusalem, as the analogues shew, on Olivet, and gave him the righteous ordinances with which he governed the Church (R. i. 43; LJas, 140). In J and QC this law was the law as it was before it had been interpolated, *e.g.* by the commands enjoining sacrifices (§ 24). We conjecture then that in J the second Moses gave James on Olivet a new and authentic copy of the law.

Our conjecture is confirmed by the fact that in the much-edited sections of EP with which we are concerned, the writer who converted Leucius and John into Clement and Peter seems to have recognised a connection between the first book of the QC discourses, which dealt with the tradition of the law of Moses (R. iii. 75: Waitz) and the mystical book given to John, for he identifies them (EP, 470, 480, 520). It is obvious to conjecture that he was influenced by the fact that the Clementine discourse stated that Christ gave the law-book to James on Olivet. [The suggestion may have come from KP. In EP, 467 Heg's excerpt from the QP narrative of the Ascension begins with the statement that Christ had commanded Peter concerning the law. Now a long series of passages (cf. KP, fragm. 5), which will be adduced in the next volume, shew that in KP the Christian revelation was regarded as a new law, and they suggest that this law was said to have been promulgated on Olivet. [Ps. In Vol. II. I may revise this paragraph, but the argument will not be affected.]]

§ 107. Our reconstruction is confirmed by the accounts of the Book of Elkesai in Hipp. Ref. ix. 12 f.; Epiph. Haer. xix., xxx., liii.; and Orig. ap. HE, VI, xxxviii.

(i) Elkesai is undoubtedly closely related to QC, and if the relation is literary it must be due to the common use of J. It is unnecessary to repeat the parallels adduced by other writers. I will emphasise the fact that each work permitted disciples to dissemble their faith. Origen says that the Elkesaites did so, and Gamaliel does so with the approval of the apostles in R. i. 65. [I may add a reference to LagardeDAdd, 93, and the interesting fact that Epiphanius mentions an Elkesaite patriarch who claimed to be descended from Gamaliel (Haer. xxx. 4). The fact suggests that Gamaliel was a person of importance in Elkesai, and is evidence for the influence of J on both works. In § 130 it will be shewn on other grounds that Gamaliel played a conspicuous part in J. Further, Alcibiades said that Elkesai came from the Seres, and we shall conclude that in J Judas journeyed in that region, and it is not likely to be a mere coincidence that the Clementines describe the Seres (§ 249 A).]

(ii) Elkesai gave the Son of God the title the *Great King*. Now Christ is so designated in a passage which probably derives from J (NZos, 1: § 250 f.). The designation almost certainly derives from M (§ 90 (*l*) 5) through J.

(iii) The contacts with QPl are: (*a*) Both works taught rebaptism (§ 23). (*b*) QPl, like Elkesai, permitted the denial of the faith in times of persecution (§ 253). (*c*) In QPl *sub* CBRB, 182 and MPl, 3, Christ, as in Elkesai, is the Great King. (*d*) Both recorded the donation of a book from heaven. (*e*) Elkesai is parallel with our reconstruction of QPl *sub* EP, for it was given by an angel who was the Son of God, was ninety-six miles high and was accompanied by a female angel, who was the Holy Spirit. (*f*) Our hypothesis accounts for the height of the two angels in EvP, 46; for the peculiar ascension in CBRB, 202; and for the statement of Photius that Leucius made Christ's head sometimes reach heaven (cf. Herm. S. ix. 6).

(iv) Alcibiades said that his doctrine was found in a book which came from the east and which Elkesai preached in the third year of Trajan (Hipp. Ref. ix. 12). We must date then the publication of his source in A.D. 100. Now this was approximately the date of J, for Leucius replied to J, and QPl can be securely dated *c.* A.D. 103.

Elkesai has suggested the hypothesis that the second angel of the sepulchre was the Holy Spirit.

§ 108. From Alcibiades we pass to a long and somewhat digressive discussion of Cerinthus. We are about to attribute to him the authorship of J and a preface in his own name.

Gaius (HE, III. xxviii.) says that Cerinthus *by means of apocalypses purported to have been written by a great apostle foists marvellous tales ... shewn him by angels. ... After the resurrection the kingdom of Christ will be upon earth ... in Jerusalem ... a thousand years spent in wedding festivities.*

The problems raised by this passage and some others are solved if Cerinthus wrote J. There is an antecedent probability that so important an heretic would embody his views in writing.

§ 109. (i) Cerinthus rejected the apostolic letter and was an opponent of S. Paul and S. John. Who then was the apostle whom he recognised as great and who wrote eschatological predictions shewn by angels? Only one answer is possible. J exalted James and Judas the Lord's brethren, and we shall conclude that it identified the latter with the apostle Judas of James, that in J Christ spoke of the last things to Judas in the east, and that Judas wrote his experiences in the east. Again, in the NT and the apocryphal tradition which derives from KP it is Christ who answers questions about the last things. Now in J Christ was the angel who gave the law, and He was accompanied by another angel. Further Elkesai spoke of the presence of the Son of God and of another angel near the scene of the apocalypse. It follows that the angels of the Cerinthian apocalyptic are almost certainly the angels of J.

(ii) In a famous passage discussed in § 367 f. Papias mentioned among the delights of Paradise, " the splendours of the city ... the couches on which the guests will recline having been invited to the wedding " (Iren. V, xxxvi.) and the millennial vine (xxxiii.). No other apocalypse so closely resembles that attributed by Cerinthus to an apostle. Irenæus makes Judas the traitor question Christ. This however is a blunder, for in the apocrypha to ask eschatological questions is to play an honourable part. Our conjecture that it was Judas the Lord's brother to whom He spoke is confirmed by an independent report of Papias which occurs in a fragment of Hippolytus and does not designate Judas (Zahn Forsch. vi. 128).

(iii) In QPl it was (Judas) Thomas who questioned Christ about the vine (CBRB, 343). It is almost certain that Leucius derived all his matter about James and Judas from J.

(iv) The apocalyptic of Papias and Cerinthus is very closely related to some J matter which occurs in R. iv. 35 f. and is discussed in § 228 f. This context refers to the successors of James, *i.e.* to Judas.

(v) Hippolytus not only cited our passage of Papias but also in his Heads against Gaius (the work from which Epiphanius in Haer. li. derives his matter about Cerinthus and "Ebion") dealt with the work cited by Eusebius. Now the Heads against Gaius was also used by Philastrius, and that writer tells us that Cerinthus honoured the traitor Judas. Hippolytus cited Papias correctly, but influenced by Irenaeus he made Judas the traitor. The apostle of Cerinthus or Gaius must have been the apocryphal Judas or J. Now J cannot have been earlier than Cerinthus.

§§ 110–111. The statement of Alcibiades that Elkesai preached in Trajan iii. implies that J contained a dated preface and that someone who was not Elkesai taught the doctrines of J in A.D. 100. Now a preface to an apocryphon which was dated long after the time of the events narrated must have been signed by some heretic who stated in it how the apocryphon reached him. And an Ebionite who claimed in Trajan. iii. to have discovered a document containing a primitive revelation is likely to have been Cerinthus. Further, this hypothesis accounts for some facts which require explanation, some of which will be discussed in the next volume.

(*a*) There is clear evidence that Papias replied to an opponent, who can only be Cerinthus, and who asserted that the beginnings of the gospels were discrepant and who rejected Jn. When making this comparison Cerinthus naturally said that he preferred Mk, *i.e.* to the other three (Iren. iii. xi. 7). It may be added that his Mk may have been JMk.

Mk. x. 18, "why callest thou me good? There is none good but God only." Our hypothesis has the merit of accounting for the Leucian phrase, *the good Father* (CBRB, 202, EvH, 52), and for the statement of Photius that Leucius taught that the God of the Jews was evil and that His agent was Simon, who in KP was an apostle of the Jews, and for a QPl context in LJasZ, 35 which states that the tribes did not worship the one true God.]

§ 114. We can now, after a long parenthesis in our discussion, return to the two angels of the sepulchre, one of whom we have identified with Christ. Our reconstruction has shewn that Leucius based his incident of the donation of the book by Christ on a passage of J, in which the two angels were the Son of God and the Holy Spirit, who was a female angel. The inference that the Spirit was the second angel of QPl is confirmed by a passage which adds another point to our reconstruction.

Clement cites from the Alexandrian EvH the phrase "my mother the Holy Spirit" (EvH, 5). Now Leucius identified his EvT with the Hebrew Matthew and Clement attributes to EvH a saying which almost certainly occurred in QPl, "he that wonders shall reign and he that reigns shall rest." (*a*) This saying occurs in the Oxyrrhynchus Sayings of Jesus (J, 26), one of which is certainly Leucian (§ 266). (*b*) In AT, where there is much matter from QPl, we find the words, *they that worthily communicate rest and resting reign* (136). In the same context the Spirit is described as mother (133), and the underlying doctrine is Leucian (cf. 29, 39, 50).

The evidence then indicates that according to Leucius the Son of God was, to use S. John's phrase, *born of the Spirit* in heaven. Now this inference tallies with the evidence which proves that Leucius denied not only Christ's Resurrection, but also His Incarnation. (*a*) Just as we have reconstructed QPl narratives of the non-Passion and the non-Resurrection, so we shall reconstruct a narrative of the non-Nativity. (*b*) In our view Leucius was the Docetist against whom Ignatius directed his polemic, and who denied that Christ was born (Trall. 9, Sm. 1). (*c*) In what was originally a docetic narrative (CBRB, 195) the angels sing, *Glory to Thee undying One. Amen. . . . Glory to Thee who wast not born. Amen.*

§ 115. We might well conjecture that of all the theologians who ever lived Leucius would be the least inclined to honour the Lord's mother. Yet in QPl *sub* EP, 520, 473, and CBRB, 190, she was the depositary of divine secrets, was exalted to the highest heaven and was at a table set in that heaven, presumably that at which the apostles feasted. These facts suggest that in QPl she was both the angel of the Spirit and Mary. If "God" seemed to be Jesus and a man, His mother, the Spirit, could seem to be Mary and a woman. The actual evidence may now be stated. Inevitably it is fragmentary and sparse.

(i) In the scripture of a mediæval Bulgarian sect, the Bogomil Book of John (J 191), Mary is an angel sent by the Father, and the Lord entered her. The Bogomils held the conception through the ear (SHJ, 14 ; RobEvvC, 19), but if this event occurred in QPl it must have taken place in heaven. The influence of QPl on this sect (for whom see *Dict. Rel. and Eth.*) is confirmed by their exaltation of the Fourth Gospel.

(ii) We read in a discourse of Theodosius: *Wicked men will think concerning thee* (Mary) *that thou art a power which came down from heaven and that this dispensation took place in appearance* (RobEvvC, 109).

(iii) CMiscT, 637 (cf. a note in J, 8) attributes to an heretical monk the following citation from EvH : *The good Father* (§ 113 (vii)) *called a mighty power in the heavens and committed Christ to the care thereof. And the power came down into the world and was called Mary.* The monk had probably confused his mind by reading Heg. The seven months' gestation is inconsistent with the citation and from Papias (Chapman, *JTS*, ix. 45 f.). The monk had read some of our QPl matter, for he said, "After they had raised Him up on the cross the Father took Him up into heaven."

(iv) Our hypothesis is an element in the explanation of
EvP, 19, *My power, My power, thou hast forsaken me.*
(*a*) Cerinthus taught in J that Christ flew back to heaven
before Jesus died (Iren. I. xxvi. 1). (*b*) Leucius used the
incident twice. He derived from it the idea of the Good
Friday ascension and apocalypse, and he attributed to Christ
the words of EvP with the purpose of explaining away
Jn. xix. 27, where Mary leaves the cross. The saying
burlesqued Mk. xv. 34, and was also a reply to Cerinthus.
(*c*) Some evidence collected by Swete shews that LeuciusP
may have understood *My Power* to mean *My God.*

§ 116. If the Leucian doctrine of the heavenly Nativity
was influenced by J it was also influenced by KP.

(i) It is an extension of the doctrine of a heavenly
generation which psMark certainly taught. Lactantius in
a context, which is full of KP (and contains some Heg)
writes, *Jesus was both of God before the worlds, of men 600
years ago (Div. Inst. Epit.* 43, iv. 14 f.) and *twice born* (iv. 13).

(ii) Christ was sometimes in KP designated Spirit or
Angel (Harris, i. 19, 95 f., 101: for " Spirit," see § 113 (vi),
§ 100), and the two designations are combined in a fictitious
testimony which occurs in a context which I shall shew is
based in KP: *My beloved angel, the good spirit of sonship*
(RSteph, 162). This spirit, according to KP, took the form
of the angel Gabriel (EpApp, 14: cf. PJ, xiv. 1, *lest that
which is in her be the seed of an angel*). At the Incarnation
Gabriel became instellate and was the power from on high
which took the form of a star (RobEvvC, 237), *i.e.* the star
in the East. This instellation underlies Ign. *Eph.* 19, where
the star outshines all the stars and the constellations form
a chorus about it. They are Gabriel and the heavenly host
instellate. So Basilides said that the Magi gazed wistfully
at the star because Jesus was mentally conceived before the
generation of the stars (Hipp. Ref. vii. 27). The allusion
is to a KP testimony, "before the morning star I begat thee"
(Ps. cx. 3 LXX: cf. Harris, i. 14 f., 88). Perhaps in view
of *conceived*, we may go further and hold that Basilides was
thinking of the Leucian doctrine of the mother spirit.

§ 117. The KP doctrine of the instellation underlies the following passage which is shewn to be Leucian by the identification of Christ with the cross: *for it was not a star like all the stars, but it was a great star in the form of a wheel, its figure being like a cross, sending forth flashes of light; letters being written on the cross, This is Jesus the Son of God* (EvvC, 1). In another passage Leucius based a statement of his doctrine of the power Mary on a KP testimony which Stephen in RSteph, 163 ascribes to Nathan: *I saw a virgin with a child in her arms, and He was the Lord of the whole earth.* The Leucian adaptation occurs in the Cave of the Treasures: *the star was greater than all the stars; and there was a girl in the midst of the star holding a boy with a crown on His head* (Light., *Ign. Eph.* 19). A heavenly power identified with the Virgin of KP is instellate.

The Leucian doctrine of the heavenly Nativity influenced Pist. Soph. 13, where Christ says: *I found Mary whom they are wont to call My mother. I spake also unto her in the form of Gabriel* (cf. EpApp, 14), *and she turned herself also to the height unto me. I cast into her the first power.* Perhaps we may compare CBRB, 190: *Hail thou who didst receive in thyself seven æons in one composition.*

§ 118. There can be no doubt that Leucius and, to some extent, Cerinthus wrote in reaction from KP. In that work the writer's doctrine of the Virgin birth was the cornerstone of his doctrine of the Incarnation. Cerinthus denied both doctrines. The influence of KP on Leucius was still stronger. In KP *sub* RSteph, 161, Saul in controversy with Stephen said, *thou preachest that a crucified man is God.* In QP Stephen became Peter and Saul Simon, and in VP, 23, Simon asks, *Deus nascitur? crucifigitur?* Leucius felt that Saul's question was unanswerable. But if psMark's paradoxical Christology suggested the problem, his mythological presentation of it provided the answer. Ignatius sums it up in *Eph.* 19, *hidden from the prince of this world was the virginity of Mary and her child-bearing and likewise also the death of the Lord.* Irenæus, whose *Demonstratio* is based very largely on KP testimonies, says

that the word was not known during His descent, but that
when He ascended the powers saw Him (84). The deception
of the powers by the descending Son occurs in Asc.Is.
x. 8 f. In EpApp, 41, Christ becomes an angel among the
angels. If the devil and his angels were repeatedly deceived,
argued Leucius, why not the apostles?

[I will digress and observe that *Dem.* 84, is also shewn to
derive from KP by the fact that the use to which it puts
Ps. xxiv. 8, is parallel with EP, 468 and EApP, 519. Leucius
sub EvN, xxi. 3, transferred the incident to the ascent from
hell.]

§ 119. The evidence has shewn that in QPl Jesus was
the J angel Son of God, and that like the Christ of Cerinthus
He vanished from the cross, that shortly before His non-
death He ascended with His disciples, and that He was one
of the two angels of the sepulchre. It has also shewn that
in QPl the J angel of the Spirit became a docetic Mary.
The question now arises how in QPl the angel Mary returned
to heaven. The orthodox editors, who endeavoured to
prevent our knowing, almost but not quite succeeded.

(i) CBRB is in utter disorder. We have already discovered
one or two transpositions. Here we are concerned with the
story of Philogenes the gardener. Leucius was perverting
Jn, and in QPl the gardener must have spoken to Mary
Magdalene and not, as in CBRB, to the Lord's mother.
He told her what he had seen during the previous night.
The name Philogenes, the rewriting of John and the fact
that (the non-risen) Christ does not appear to Mary, are
sufficient proof that our matter derives from QPl. Philogenes
tells Mary that the Jews, whose subsequent activities will
be described below, brought the body to the tomb. (Joseph,
whom Leucius identified with the supposed husband of
Mary, in RobEvvC, 181 denies that he has done so.)
According to Philogenes thousands of angels were singing
hymns (those preserved in CBRB, 196 f.). The Saviour
addressed His mother in the language of the Godhead (it is
significant that it is assumed that she understood it). He
mounted on the chariot on which He was about to ascend.

An hiatus follows. Our conjecture that in QPl Mary was the second angel and ascended with Christ is supported by the fact that the women who were at the sepulchre are enumerated but the Lord's mother is not among them.

§ 120. (ii) We used above a cento which is interpolated into a QP Ascension narrative which narrates how Christ gave "Peter" (on Olivet) the mystical book which He had written. In EP, 477, this vein of matter is resumed; there is matter relating to the two angels; "Peter" reads the book and reveals their names to his brethren. In 520 the editor describes the book and confirms our whole reconstruction. It contained the mysteries which Paul revealed to Dionysius, a fact which much concerns our later reconstructions, and also *the mysteries which John the beloved had revealed (together with those) which our Lord . . . and our Lady, the mother of the Light* (473) *had revealed unto him.* The Clementiser here shews that his Peter was originally John, a fact which is confirmed by other passages which we shall discuss, and at the same time discloses the fact that Christ was one of the two angels of 477, and that the angel who was with Him was "the mother of the Light." The writer similarly discloses in 656 the fact that his Paul and Philip were originally the "Peter" and "Paul" of QEPP.

Even more important for our present purpose is an incident which occurs in 472, where the mother of the Light is in the highest heaven for three hours, which were presumably the three hours of light (HEvXII, 30) and the period during which Simon of Cyrene was on the cross. Throughout this section EP follows the order of Heg, and Mary's presence in heaven, which in EP precedes Pentecost, cannot have been preceded by her death.

§ 121. (iii) PsMelito (J, 210) and EvM (J, 72) agree in approving what Leucius wrote about the acts of the apostles and rejecting the doctrines which he attributed to them. Their agreement is doubtless due to the fact that they used Heg, from whom "Melito" probably derived his pseudonym. Here we are concerned with his claim that he derived from S. John the account of the departure of Mary which Leucius had corrupted with an evil pen.

We infer that the Leucian narrative was not a *Dormitio*, and that Leucius claimed to have received his narrative from the apostle. What, then, was the gross heresy which psMelito condemned? We have concluded that in QPl Christ left the cross during the three hours of light and ascended with His apostles. This apocalypse was based on that of KP, in which Peter was caught up through the heavens and in the seventh saw the Trinity and heard the worships (§ 157 A). We infer that in QPl John must have been caught up during the three hours and seen the Trinity, *i.e.* the Father, the Son, and His mother Mary, and heard the praises of the angels. Now in EP, 472 f., Peter (John) sees Mary in the tabernacle of light wherein is the Lord on His throne, and she sat down with Him for three hours. Peter also hears the praises of the angels.

§ 122. LeuciusP corrected the heresy of Leucius by making Mary a woman who was taken up to heaven after her death. He also used some of the details of the narrative of QPl. Christ and Mary again ascend from the sepulchre. The only important change is that Mary is a woman and her body is laid there.

(i) The narrative was twice used in AJ. (*a*) In AJ *sub* Proch, 4, 4, the apostles are gathered in Gethsemane, the QPl scene of the Crucifixion and burial, *after the death of the mother of us all*. (*b*) The *Dormitio* underlies the story of Drusilla. As in QP so in AJ, 72 f., the deceased woman is laid in the sepulchre. Christ appears and ascends. As in QP (RobEvvC, 51 f.), there is a eucharist. A sermon follows. When the door of the tomb is opened Christ is seen as a beautiful young man sitting by it (Matt. xxviii. 3; § 38).

§ 123. (ii) Many of the variations of the *Dormitios* are explained by the fact that they are quarried from Heg, to whom is due the fact that the sepulchre where S. Mary is laid is said to have been like Gethsemane in the valley of Jehoshaphat (RobEvvC, 41, 61 (Gk. 48), Mel. xvi. Joseph. i. 4; STrans, 51, "head of the valley"; CMiscT, 642). Like the Acta the *Dormitios* are much edited, and the narrative of QP is defaced and interpolated. Yet it is clear that the source derived from a perversion of the canonical visit of the women to the sepulchre which identified the angel with Christ.

(*a*) In all the *Dormitios* Mary is taken to the sepulchre which was originally Christ's. (*b*) Women, as in the Markan tradition, go to the sepulchre with the body in all the *Dormitios*. They are three in number in the Greek (4), psMel, 7; Jos. 5; STrans, 25. In RobEvvC, 59, they include Johanna and Salome. (*c*) In the last passage Christ, like the angel of Matthew, sits on a stone outside the door and converses as He does in AJ, 73. (*d*) As in CBRB and HEvXII the apostles were with the women, so in SObsBVM (J, 224) the apostles sit before the entrance to the tomb, and the same incident underlies STrans, 62. (*e*) The vital point which is common to most of the *Dormitios* is that Christ and Mary ascend from the sepulchre. (*e*) The sitting at the sepulchre derives from M through EvT (§ 91 *e*).

§ 124. Our QPl matter also influenced the QP narrative of the visit of the women to the sepulchre. [In AThadd, 6, Christ appears to His mother, the other women, Peter and John. We recall the fact that in CBRB, 187, the apostles are at the sepulchre with the women, and our conclusion that in QPl Mary, the Lord's mother, was only present as one of the angels. Connolly (*JTS*, 1907, 587) says that Ephraim and Jacob of Serug when using Tatian state that a Mary, who was not Mary Magdalene, spoke to Peter and John, and was addressed by one angel who was without the tomb, and that they identify her with the Virgin. Connolly calls attention to various contacts of his documents with EvP, and suggests that they are not necessarily due to the influence of that Gospel (589), and also mentions other contacts with our matter. For instance, Jacob says that the dead worshipped at the cross (585).]

III. *Pilate, Ananias, Gamaliel, and Joseph*

§ 125. The most important persons in this section will be Pilate, Ananias, and Gamaliel, and we will begin it by discussing them.

The letter of Pilate to the Emperor is connected with KP by its statement that Christ rose while the soldiers were watching (§ 96), and survives in MPP, 19, whence it wandered into some MSS. of EvN (J, 146). It is one of the best attempts at historical vraisemblance which is to be found in the apocrypha, and runs as follows: "There has recently happened an event which I myself laid bare. The Jews, through envy, have punished themselves and their posterity with fearful punishments. Their fathers announced that God would send them from heaven His holy One who would be called their king . . . by a virgin. This God of the Hebrews came when I was president in Judæa, and they saw Him enlighten the blind, cleanse lepers, heal paralytics, . . . and all the people of the Jews call Him the Son of God. The chief priests moved with envy . . . handed Him over to me, told one lie after another and said that He broke their law. I believed them, scourged Him and handed Him over to their will. They crucified Him, and set guards over His grave. But while my soldiers watched He rose on the third day. Such was their malice that they bribed the soldiers to say that His disciples stole His body. They took the money but could not keep silence, saying that they had seen Him rise. . . . These things I report. . . ."

That Heg is the source of MPP is indicated both by the fact that the Acts are composite and contain some ancient matter and also by the allusion to S. Paul's journey to "Spania" (§ 207 B). We shall conclude that Heg was occasionally used by Tertullian who, in Apol. 5, says that Tiberius has laid a report before the Senate. This incident occurs also in CurSimCeph, 38, where the source is certainly Heg. The report was presumably the letter preserved in MPP.

§ 126. In Apol. i. 48, Justin, who makes much use of KP, after citing Is. xxxv. 5, with an addition which may be due to KP ("and the dead shall rise and walk about"), appeals to the testimony of Pilate's Acts. An earlier appeal to those Acts (33 f.) follows a brief summary of Christ's career which, like the letter, emphasises the Virgin birth and the rejection, but gives one or two details of the Passion, *e.g.*

the uncanonical incidents of the nailing and the setting on the judgment-seat (EvP, 7), to which the letter makes no reference. Stanton, after a valuable discussion (*Gosp. Hist. Doc.* i. 102 f.), conjectures that Justin refers to an early Acts of Pilate for the existence of which there is no other evidence. It seems, however, to be very much more probable that Justin made his own summary and then remembered that the letter supported his main points. Moreover, no fiction could be more in the manner of KP, and Justin made large use of that work. Like the letter it was violently anti-Jewish, concerned with the contacts of Christianity with the Empire, and interested in the Virgin birth and testimonies to it (KP, 9), and it was one of its themes that the capture of Jerusalem was the penalty of the Crucifixion.

§ 127. Our position is established by the fact that Pilate reported to the Emperor both in QPl and QP. (i) In a fragment which will be shewn below to be based on QPl (RobEvvC, 177; J, 148, fragm. 5), Pilate writes a report. (ii) Pilate's report (Tisch. B) is certainly influenced by both QPl and KP and must be based on QP. The influence of QPl is shewn in § 136, and that of KP by the following parallel with a long account of the Crucifixion which occurs in a sermon of Athanasius of Rahote (CHom, 270), the whole of which will be shewn to be based on KP.

Anaph.—" The moon did not shine. . . . The stars made a lament about the Jews because of the abominable wickedness done by them."

Ath. Rah. " The whole creation was moved to wrath because of the abominable insolence of the Jews. . . . The moon hid itself, and the stars ceased to shine."

§ 128. Vardan, in his *Solutions*, speaks of a work by Ananias of Damascus which was called the *Discourses of James* and the *Discourses of Justus*, and the latter phrase occurs in an Armenian list printed by Zahn in Forsch. v. 117. These *Discourses* of James Justus were presumably those which he gave to Mariamne (Hipp. Ref. v. 7), and, if so, they were, like Mariamne, Leucian. There are other allusions to the literary activity of Ananias. He translated the Hebrew of Nicodemus (EvNProl), and an Arabic life of Pilate is attributed to him or to Annas (J, 152). He wrote for Abgar Christ's deeds in Jerusalem and met Christ in the house of Gamaliel (DAdd, 3). Doubtless he was the Ananias who embraced Him after His non-death and saw Him after His non-Resurrection. There is a presumption that the prominence of Ananias and his connection with James, derive from J, which Acts Leucius followed in his characterisation of James.

§ 129. In STrans, 16 f. an Anton or Danton gives a brief account of the death of James which derives from QPl (§ 182 (ii)). Inasmuch as he is described as the deacon of James, and in J the death of James followed his discussion with the seven sects (R. i. 69; HE, II. xxiii.) he presumably wrote the *Discourses*, playing Mark to the Peter of James. That Anton occurred in J is shewn not only by the fact that Leucius was using J, but also by the fact that the collocated names James Antonius occur in a QPl name-list (§ 315 B).

The evidence indicates that Ananias and Antonius were in QPl and J the same person. Our result may be confirmed. In STrans, Anton is a native of Jerusalem, and in R. iii. 68, a section of R which derives matter from KP, Ananias is the son of Sapphira and a companion of Peter at Cæsarea. In LPP, 175, he is "the apostle," *i.e.* of the Church at Jerusalem (§ 312), and is, as in Vardan, identified with Ananias of Damascus. Now these facts enable us to connect up the evidence. We shall find that the nomenclature of KP was very full. At Acts iv. 6, it gave the names more fully, *e.g.* John Jonathan (west. var.) and it gave both the Jewish and the Greek or Grecised names of Peter's six companions (*e.g.* Zachariah, Zacchæus, Reuben, Rufus). Clearly, then, Ananias is likely to have been named Antonius. Further, when J determined to supplant the Mark and Peter of our context of KP (Mark wrote at Cæsarea in this context), he selected Ananias as Mark's counterpart, in order to detach him from the Tarsian idolator, who in KP was presumably baptized by him, and make him the faithful scribe of the man whom Saul murdered.

§ 130. We have already attributed to J the doctrine which R. i. 65 connects with Gamaliel, that a Christian might dissemble his faith, and we have observed that an Elkesaite patriarch claimed descent from him. Again, in § 293, we shall securely attribute to J the warning which comes from his household in R. i. 71. We must infer then that, like Ananias, Gamaliel was one of the *dramatis personæ* of J. Further, the *Book of the Cock*, which is read in the Abyssinian rite on Maundy Thursday (J, 150), states that Saul plotted against Christ with Judas. J is perhaps the only writer in Christian history who would have invented this libel, and Gamaliel is the member of the Sanhedrin who is most likely to have divulged the incident.

§ 131. We will now examine, with the help of other documents, the *Acts of Pilate*, which Nicodemus wrote and which Ananias translated. EvN is composite, a fact which is undoubtedly due to the influence of Heg (§ 196 f.). [I know very little about the history of the Coptic matter, which I call EvvC, but it is composite, for while most of the matter is from QPl, there is a fragment of a Peter apocalypse in EvvC, 4. STrans is certainly based on Heg.]

1. The composite character of EvN, i. ii. is very clear. In KP the Jews said that Jesus was the son of Panther. This charge with two others underlies EvN, ii. 3 (§ 151). PsMark replied with fictitious proofs that Jesus was miraculously born of a Virgin. The reply of J to the Jews and to psMark was that He was the son of Joseph and Mary (Iren. I. xxvi; Epiph. *Haer.* li. 12). Leucius attributed the position of J to the Jews. In EvN, i. 1, they say to Pilate: *He is the son of Joseph the carpenter, begotten of Mary, and He saith that He is the Son of God and a king* (EvvC, 4, 5). Similarly in LJas, 145, a fragment of the QPl martyrdom of James is interpolated into that of QDesp, and we are told that *all the scribes and Pharisees desired that James would say that Jesus was the son of Joseph and he himself His brother.* We compare also AT, 143, *called the son of Mary the virgin, and termed the son of Joseph the carpenter,* and STrans, 23.

§ 132, 2. The influence of QPl on EvN is shewn in two topographical blunders. (i) Leucius confused the garden of Gethsemane with "Joseph's" (EvP, 24). Thus in EvN, ix. Christ is hanged in the garden in which He is taken. See also § 102. (ii) Leucius identified Olivet with the mountain of Matt. xxviii. 16. In CBRB, 198, the apostles are bidden to go at dawn on the morrow to Galilee. In EvN, xiii. f. the rulers are in session on Easter Day. In xiii. the watch (§ 96 f.) reports that they saw the angel roll away the stone and that Jesus was in Galilee. In xiv. a priest reports that he saw Jesus ascend. The border of Galilee was supposed to run near Jerusalem.

[§ 133, 3. In EvN, i. ii. there are two name-lists which derive from QPl and which are composed in the same way, a matter which will be discussed later. The first group are against Christ, the second for Him; but here there is editing. Our concern is with the fact that the first has ten names, the second twelve. This suggests that in EvN, i. two names have dropped out. Now in LagardeDAdd, 93 we find Nicodemus associated with Gamaliel, Annas, Caiaphas and Alexander, who head the list in EvN, i. and we may conjecture that he and Joseph, who is very prominent in EvN, supplied the two missing names. Nicodemus also plays an active part in EvvC, 4, a depraved passage. Carius, who presumably is Leucius Carinus, reports Christ's mighty works to Herod, saying that he ought to be made king. Annas and Caiaphas accuse Jesus before Carius. Joseph and Nicodemus oppose them as they do before Pilate in EvN, xii. 1. Herod casts them into prison as the Jews do in EvN. Clearly EvN and EvvC derive from a common source and Carius was originally Pilate.]

4. The following facts shew that the source from which EvN and EvvC derive in common was a Gospel written by Gamaliel. (a) In EvvC, 13 he writes in the first person. (b) The Arabic *Acts of Pilate* are attributed to Gamaliel and Ananias. (c) In EvN, v. Nicodemus using Gamaliel's speech says: *If the signs which He does are of God they will stand, but if they be of men they will come to nought* (cf. § 136, note).

§ 134, 5. The evidence shews that Leucius identified Joseph the carpenter with Joseph of Arimathea.

[(i) In QPl the priests charged Jesus with being the son of Joseph and Mary (§ 131). In STrans, 23 they call Him *that son of a carpenter who was born of thee* (*Mary*) *whom thou callest the Son of God. And we call Him a man ... knowing whose son He is, and how He was born and brought up amongst us* (this phrase is from KP: cf. the charge in AJ, 3). *We scourged and pierced Him. Joseph the senator buried Him.* (We shall find that the Jews made similar affirmations about the burial in QPl *sub* EvvC. In RobEvvC, 181, Joseph denies that he buried Jesus.) ... *The house where the Blessed One dwelt in Jerusalem had been bought by Joseph the carpenter from the household of Caleb the Sadducee, and it was near the house of Nicodemus.* Now Caleb, like his father Jephunneh (51), is editorial (the editor invented some other names). Who, then, was he? The answer is given in 39 where we read: *Caleb the Sadducee who was a believer in Christ ... and was afraid to make himself* (*i.e. his faith*) *known to his countrymen whispered to the governor.* Caleb can only be Gamaliel the Pharisee, who was a secret believer in QPl, and in EvN, v. Nicodemus (Gamaliel) like Caleb speaks to the governor. We will now compare the following data :

A. STrans Mary lived in the house of Joseph the carpenter which had been Caleb's (Gamaliel's).

B. In DAdd, 3 Jesus is in the house of Gamaliel.

C. In EvN, xv. 4, Joseph of Arimathea abides in the house of Nicodemus (Gamaliel).

It is clear that in QPl Mary, Joseph and Jesus stayed at the time of the Passion at the house of Gamaliel and that the Joseph of A is the Joseph of C. Two other points remain. (*a*) When Leucius said that the house of Gamaliel (where Jesus stayed) was near the house of Nicodemus, he probably had in mind Jn. iii. 1. (*b*) The purchase from the household of Caleb-Gamaliel is senseless, and is suggested by the fact, which the writer preserves in 25, that Gamaliel's daughter Neshra was a disciple. The editor's procedure shews what needs no proving, the fact that he found the tradition of

Neshra, Calletha and Tabitha in Heg. We shall conclude that in KP they accompanied Peter to Cæsarea.]

§ 135. (ii) In Epiph. *Hom.* 328 f., a context which will be shewn to be based upon a context of Heg which was based on KP, the priests at Nazareth send a letter to those at Jerusalem informing them of Mary's pregnancy. The latter write to Joseph who comes to Jerusalem. After drinking the water of ordeal he ascends Olivet, watched by a crowd (§ 96), returns radiant and is kissed by the priests. In EvN, xiv. 1, priests come from Nazareth, and in 3 they return. In xv. 2, the priests at Jerusalem send a letter to Joseph, who in 3 comes to Jerusalem. He kisses the priests. The people meet Joseph and were astonished at the sight of him, *i.e.* at his radiant face. Joseph the carpenter is again Joseph of Arimathea. [I may add another link between the protevangelical matter of KP and EvN. In PJ, which is based on our context of Heg, the priests complain that Joseph (the carpenter) has not appeared in the synagogue (xv. 1). In EvN, xii. 2, they ordain that men should appear in the synagogue.]

Our identification of the two Josephs is in a line with the fact that Leucius made other rulers the depositaries of the Docetic secret. Joseph the carpenter, who we shall find was a witness to the non-Nativity, was Joseph the senator who did not bury Jesus and was in contact with the ruler Nicodemus and the great Gamaliel. There was more excuse for this identification than for some other vagaries of Leucius. We shall find that in KP Joseph the carpenter was a priest and that Annas lived at Nazareth.

§ 136. We will now return to the subject of the common derivation of EvN and EvvC. Pilate in his letter spoke of Christ's miracles, and it would be in accordance with the scheme of KP that the healed should testify to them. At any rate they did so in QPl *sub* EvN, EvvC, Anaph. Pil. and STrans, 35. Berenice is from QPl (§ 315).

EvvC, 2. The servants   ..   ..
    at Cana testify.
              ..   EvN, vii. f. Bernice   Anaph.   Bernice
                        and others testify.   was healed.
RobEvvC, 175. Lazarus   ..   Lazarus was raised
    was healed on the   on the sabbath.
    sabbath.

In STrans, 35, those healed by Mary (Christ) testify
before Sabinus (Pilate).[1]

§ 137. In EvvC, 13, the fragment which contains Gamaliel s "I," we learn that Pilate remembered the saying
of Christ, *Great wonders shall happen in my tomb.* He
goes to the tomb with the centurion, who was blind with
one eye, an incident which must have occurred in Heg,
inasmuch as it is transferred to another centurion in LLk,
156, and influences AT, 170, where dust from the empty
tomb of Thomas heals Misdai's son. We have already used
this context (§ 96). In Mingana's fragments the centurion's
eye is healed when it touches the shroud. In the travesty
of Jn. xx., which follows, Pilate does not find the grave-
clothes. The Jews, who were present at the tomb as they
are in EvP, say that a body which had been found in a well
was that of Jesus. Joseph and Nicodemus say that the grave-
clothes are His, but that the body is the robber's. Pilate
remembers Christ's words, *The dead shall rise in my tomb.*
For the rest of the narrative we are indebted to the skill

---

[1] The parallels with another EvN incident are worth noting. (a) In
xii. 1, the Jews arrest Joseph and shut him up in a room which has neither
window nor door, and when it was opened he was not there (Acts v. 24).
Nicodemus suggests that Jesus (originally Joseph) had been taken up by
the Spirit. Joseph was then found at Arimathea. (b) In STrans, 33,
Mary is in her chamber . . . with the apostles. The Jews suggest that
the governor should send men to them to bring them (Acts v. 24). In 37
Mary and the apostles are transported. They try to burn the house of
Mary. (c) In EPl, 637, the persecutors try to burn the room. A captain
(Acts v. 24) is mentioned. He (Gamaliel) tries to restrain them saying,
"Be patient, keep thyself quiet for a little." They opened the door, and
the Spirit of God seized the apostles and brought them into the hall of
judgment to the two governors (Herod and Pilate). Probably the same
context of QPl ap. Heg was used in the same centoising way in EPl,
549–551.

of Mingana (John Rylands Library Bulletin, XII, 454). The body proved to be that of the robber, and at Pilate's command it was enshrouded in Christ's wrappings. The spiritual form of the robber appeared.

A sequel to the narrative of the robber occurs in RobEvvC, 183 f., and almost certainly derives from QIrJos, which is cited in 181, for the malice of the Jews who wished to hide the cross. This fact is definite evidence for derivation from Heg, and this hypothesis is confirmed by the fact that Heg knew of a Rufus who was the son of Cleopas (§ 284 S, § 285 (c)). This Rufus was carried to the sepulchre and healed by the figure of the cross which emerged from it. The incident is a Leucian parallel with the emergence of the cross in EvP, 39, and provides also another contact of QPl with KP.

§ 138. It is clear that the incident which underlies the following passage has little contact with the motivisation of either J nor QPl, but that, on the other hand, it agrees entirely with one of the chief motives of the only alternative source in its strong anti-Judaic tendency, and also with psMark's representation of Pilate's friendly attitude to Christ (§ 125 f.). Our reconstruction of KP accounts for Pilate's visit to the tomb in QPl and the QPl incidents of the emergence of the cross.

	VP, 17	DAdd	STrans	RSteph	
Prayer at the tomb stopped	..	12	21	..	
The instruments of the Passion hidden	VP	12	..	..	EP, 522; RobEvvC, 181
Pilate	Pompey	Herod	Sabinus	Pilate	..
Made the Jews reveal them	VP	11	43 f.	..	Later legends of the Invention
The Jews are scourged	VP	..	48	..	..
Pilate's wife and child healed	..	12	..	164	Later legends

The KP matter underlying these parallels seems to have
preserved some history. There is evidence that psMark
visited Jerusalem and found there rites which were regarded
as of apostolic origin (cf. § 172) and among them a rite
at the Holy Sepulchre (§ 163 f.). Legends, as our parallels
shew, had grown up which told of the hiding of the
instruments of the Passion in the tomb and of healings
worked by them. The sacred place of the Nazarenes became
the scene of rioting. Hence in QP *sub* STrans, 20, Mary
(in KP Peter and the apostles) was stoned when she went
there to pray morning and evening. In consequence of the
rioting the tolerant Hadrian at a later date made the place
hateful to both parties by building on the site a temple
of Venus to which there was an allusion in Heg *sub* VP, 17
(Eubola's idol).

We note an indication of the fact that KP was written
before the excommunication of the Nazarenes as *Minim*.
In STrans, 21 f., the priests prohibit prayers at the tomb
and say, *If thou wishest to pray enter the sabbath house.*
We have already noted the complaint made against Joseph
and the decree enjoining attendance at the synagogues (§ 135).

IV. *Protevangelica*

§ 139. The KP *Protevangelium* was motived as follows:
(i) psMark invented evidence to prove the Virgin birth and
disprove the Jewish slander that Jesus was born in fornication. (ii) The Tiamat myth influenced the narrative.
(iii) The doctrine of the *triplex munus* influenced the
accounts of Joseph and Mary and suggested a story that
Jesus was elected to the priesthood. Josephus says that
Hyrcanus, to whom psMark alluded (§ 141 VI), *was esteemed
of God worthy of those privileges, the government of the
nation, the dignity of the high priesthood, prophecy* (Ant.
xiii. x. 7). (iv) psMark had visited Jerusalem and used
haggadah, which he may have heard there, about the visit
of Melchizedek to the cave Qapara. (v) He connected his
narrative with the course of secular history. (vi) The
narrative of Mary's birth and life in the temple was obviously

based on 1 Sam. i. That chapter suggested to psMark the name Anna, and KP suggested to Leucius the name of his priest Samuel (§ 143 (c)).

The task of J was to implicitly refute the narrative of KP by writing an account of Christ's birth, in which He was the son of Joseph; but our section of KP influenced him elsewhere. In the account of the life of the ten tribes which we shall assign to him (§ 249 f.), the eldest sons were dedicated like Mary (psEvod; RobEvvC, 187) to the service of the temple at the age of three (LMatt. 101). James was similarly dedicated, and like Mary (Epiph. *Hom.* 321; PJ, xiii. 3), he interceded for his people in the Holy of Holies (Epiph. Haer. lxxviii. 7). We shall find that Leucius used our KP matter. I have detected no combinations of KP with QPl which are assignable to QP, a fact which will be explained in § 279 (iv), but EvP doubtless derived from QP its agreement with KP in the position that the brethren were the sons of Joseph (*sub* EvP: Orig. in Matt. t. x. 17).

§ 140. Before we discuss the matter which Epiph. *Hom.* and PJ derive from Heg, we will collect some instances of the direct influence of KP on early writers.

A. Ign. *Eph.* 18, . . . *by Mary of the seed of David.* 19. *And hidden from the prince of this world were the virginity of Mary and her child-bearing and likewise also the death of the Lord—three mysteries to be cried aloud. A star shone above all the stars; and its light was unutterable . . . amazement; and all the rest . . . formed themselves into a chorus . . . thence all things were perturbed.* (Cf. §§ 116 f., and PJ, xxi. 2.) There is a striking parallel with Ignatius in Asc.Is. x. 9 f., where Christ when descending through the heavens before the Incarnation takes the forms of their angels in order to deceive the princes and angels of the world (cf. EpApp, 14). The passage leads up to a series of parallels with PJ, which work has no obvious parallel with Ignatius or with the incident of the Bethlehemites in Asc.Is. xi. 12. KP was certainly influenced by Ignatius; Asc.Is. is based on KP, and EpApp on QP.

B. PsSolomon, who is influenced by KP elsewhere, writes: *the Virgin travailed and brought forth a son without incurring pain. . . . She had not sought a midwife* (Od. xix. 7 f.).

C. Justin has the following matter. (i) In Tryph. 52, Herod is of Ascalon. This statement is explained by the popular story, which is inconsistent with Jos. Ant. XIV. i. 3, and which is given at length by Julius Africanus, who probably derived it from Heg (HE, I. vii. 11). Epiph. *Hom.* 321, where the source is Heg, adds the statement that Augustus made Herod king. (ii) In Tryph. 100 Mary is of the race of David. Justin and Heg derive independently from KP. (iii) We compare:

Ap. i. 33, "the word over-shadowed the virgin."	PJ, xi. 2. "Thou shalt conceive of His word." Cf. Iren. *Dem.* 33.
"He shall save His people" is added to Lk. i. 31 f.	So PJ, xi. 2.
Tryph. 100. "She received faith and joy."	Or, Sib, viii. 467. "The damsel laughed." Epiph. *Hom.* 326, "filled with exultation and joy."
Tryph. 70, Mithras was born in a cave. Dan. iii. 24, is cited.	VP, 24. Dan. iii. 24, is cited.

§ 141. Much light is thrown on the *Protevangelica* by the Armenian *Homilies* of Epiphanius. Conybeare, who translated them, says that the Armenian scribe interpolated here and there, and adds the interesting fact that Epiphanius frequently appeals to traditions of the Jews and to Jewish rabbis. If we are right, matter from Heg may be recovered from the untranslated sections. It will be argued that the matter with which we are concerned derives from KP through that writer, but it is possible that Heg himself may have used legends current at Bethlehem. Some of them, however, certainly influenced KP. They provide us with an interesting illustration of *the tales and endless genealogies* which are condemned in 1 Tim. i. 4, *i.e.* of the rank growth of legends about the earliest heroes of their history which had grown up among the Jews (cf. Hort, *Jud. Christ.* 135 f.), and which is illustrated in the *Jubilees* and psPhilo. (The question now arises whether some of this matter did not occur in M.)

Too briefly summarised, our extracts from Epiph. *Hom.* run as follows: "318. God the Word took clay from Sion and water from the spring which ran down by the ravine of Gethsemeni, the Kedron, which Hezekiah and the prophet and others laid waste, for they were often straightened by the inroads of the gentiles, and they permitted a little to pass out which is now called Selowam, and is translated Sent. He also took fire from the sun and the holy wind . . . and so (319) framed man. . . . And He blessed him, bestowing on him the priesthood and kingship and the spirit of prophecy.

"II. . . . Melchi begat Sedek who, with Shem, brought the relics of Adam and Eve to Palestine. 320. They laid those of Eve in a cave near Qapara and the skull of Adam in Golgotha. Shem said to Sedek, My son thou wilt receive priesthood and kingship: thou shalt be gathered near the end of the world when the Maker Himself of Adam shall be born of a holy virgin upon the relics of Eve.

"321. III. In the reign of Antipatros of Ascalon, whom Augustus made king, Zacharias was chief priest, son of Barek. Joachim who was of the house of David and Anna besought the Lord for a child, and brought Mary to the temple when she was three years old. She was blessed by Simeon. . . . Elizabeth was sister of Anna. Mary prayed in the midst of the temple for Jews and gentiles and (322) lived an angelic life. Her mother was of the house of David and the daughters of Levi. Wherefore the virgin had priesthood and kingship.

"Zacharias and Simeon mustered the presbytery of the twelve tribes and after casting lots entrusted Mary to the keeping of Joseph who was of the house of David and a priest. He had a wife Marem the sister of Anna and by her four sons and three daughters. 323. Marem bore Jacob the less eight days after Mary's arrival. We have heard from some that Marem was dead. . . . 324. Marem was making the veil of the temple . . . and saw full opposite her the Lord God of Israel. . . .

"IV. 325. This was in the 5500th year and the day was Kyriake, because on that day God said, Let there be light (§ 290).

§ 142. "V. 326. When Mary visited Elizabeth she was filled with exultation and joy (PJ, xii. 2). She went up for the feast Zatik with Joseph, his two sons, Simon and Jesse, and his daughter Solome. 327. Mary returned and went to the garden of Joseph where she received the tidings (*JTS*, ix. 51; add *Haer*. li. 29).

"VI. 328. . . . Her pregnancy became visible. The priests who dwelt at Nazareth hated the just priest Joseph . . . and sent to Jerusalem Annas who was a scribe . . . and wrote to Zachariah, Simeon and Alexander who bade Joseph bring Mariam in haste. Joseph hastened to Jerusalem with Marem, Solome, his two sons and the Virgin who, entering the temple, went to the raised dais reserved for virgins. Hyrcanus and the other priests and elders took counsel. . . . The ordeal of water. . . . 329. The crowd followed, and others watched from the walls. Joseph went down and ascended Olivet, returning resplendent. Alexander and the other priests kissed him. Elizabeth received the babe Jacob.

"VII. Two months later they went from Nazareth to Bethlehem. Christ was born without pangs, a cloud of light overshadowing the cave.

"Melchizedek was on Thabor. 329. Angels bore him and set him down in the cave. He brought bread and wine and worshipped and laid his hands upon Him. And he bestowed on Him the kingship and priesthood which he had received from Him. . . . 330. The angels buried him near the tomb of Moses.

"VIII. 331. Why was Bethlehem called House of Ephrath? We consulted the earliest chroniclers and doctors of the Jews why Bethlehem was called the House of Bread. They told a story of a youth named Jose who in the time of Joshua married a gentile, found the bones of Eve (332) and made a manger in the cave. The woman's name was Ephrat. 'In the ancestral tongue by translation Ephrat is called Fruitbearing.' Joseph found a shepherd who was

related to him and named Isaac. They remained outside
the cave praying and saw the miraculous birth."

§ 143. The use of Heg is proved by the words: *This
and many things hard to understand we accurately learned
from doctors of the Jews and ancient chroniclers*, and by
the allusion to the meaning of Ephrat in *the ancestral tongue*.
Our conclusion tallies with the fact that some of the matter
is used in EvN (§ 135).

Apart from the fact that the motivisation of much of
the matter in these excerpts proves the influence of KP on
Heg, this influence may be shewn as follows:

[(i) In 328 the priests at Jerusalem are Simeon, Zachariah,
the son of Barek, to whom there is a misplaced allusion
in PJ, x. 2, and Hyrcanus. (*a*) The allusion to Hyrcanus,
like that to Herod of Ascalon (§ 140 C), was one of the links
by means of which the writer of KP connected his narrative
with secular history.[1] Hyrcanus is mentioned in QVitA,
575, and in Menol. Basil (Lips. ii. 7), where there is some
other matter which we shall attribute to KP. (*b*) According
to Orig. in Matt. tract. 25, Zacharias was slain for allowing
Mary to go to the dais mentioned by Epiphanius. This
must derive from the same source as her temple ministry.
See also p. 116. (*c*) In a QPl list (§ 310 (v)) we
find a companion of the apostles named Zacchæus
Zacharias. The absurd Zacchæus, therefore, of EvT, 7,
was probably the Zacharias of KP, for I am about to shew
that Leucius derived from KP the view that some of the
priests lived at Nazareth. The fact that Epiphanius makes
Zacharias a *chief* priest is evidence for derivation from
KP. Cf. § 90*k*.]

(ii) The crowd which saw the ordeal (328) is introduced
for the same reason as the crowds which visited the sepulchre
and saw the Ascension in KP (§§ 96, 152). The incident
occurred in Heg (§ 135). It may be added that the knowledge
of the topography of Jerusalem which is shewn is part of
the evidence which shews that the author of KP had visited

---

[1] The allusion to Pompey in VP, 17, probably derives from our KP
context.

Palestine. He probably heard the Melchizedek legend on the occasion of his visit.

§ 143a. (iii) That KP contained Melchizedek matter is shewn by the reply of Epiphanius to the Melchizedekians (*Haer*. lv.). We learn that the Samaritans identified Melchizedek with Shem (6), and that Jews said that he was a righteous man and a priest, but born in fornication, being the son of Hercules by Astaroth or Asteria (2, 7). This matter derives from KP.

(*a*) It will be argued that the debate with the seven sects of the Jews which underlies parts of R, i. 45–69 and HE, II. xxiii. 8, derives from KP. Inasmuch as it included the subject of the *triplex munus* (R, i. 45 f.), and the Samaritans were one of the sects, it underlies our context.

(*b*) The Jews, or some of them, admitted that Jesus was a good man, but denied that this fact proved the two points on which in KP the debate turned, *i.e.* that He was the son of a virgin and the legal heir of the *munus* of Joseph and His mother, for even Melchizedek was a bastard. Now this is precisely the position which Jews affirmed about Christ in a context which we shall attribute to KP (§ 151).

(*c*) The two name-lists in EvN, i. ii. are accounted for by the hypothesis that Leucius quarried them from KP, J and Acts. Our section of KP provided *Ze(cha)r(i)as*, *Asterius*, *Shem* (Semes), and *Dathaes* (some of the Jews compared Jesus with Dathan: cf. PJ, ix. 1). *Samuel* (§ 149) was suggested by the narrative of KP, which was influenced by 1 Sam. i. f.

(*d*) Our matter gives us an interesting glimpse into the controversies which, towards the end of the first century, preceded the expulsion of the Nazarenes from the synagogue as *minim*. That it derives from a writer who, like psMark, was concerned with those controversies, is shewn by the fact that the identification of Melchizedek with Shem occurs in the Targums of Jonathan and Jerusalem (Westcott, *Hebrews*, 202). This identification occurs in Jerome (Ep. lxiii.) who, like Epiphanius, was probably using Heg.

§ 144. (iv) EvT is directed against the Cerinthian position

that Jesus became the Son of God at His baptism. The following passages shew that Jesus, according to Leucius, made the sparrows at Nazareth in the same way as in KP He made the world.

EvT, 2 f. Jesus . . . gathered together the water that flowed into pools . . . and made soft clay, he fashioned thereof sparrows on the sabbath.	Epiph. *Hom.* 318. God the Word took clay from Sion and water . . . from the Kedron . . . Siloam.
The Jews departed (from Nazareth) and told their chief men. . . . But the son of Annas the scribe. . . .	328. The priests that dwelt at Nazareth . . . sent to Jerusalem as messenger, Annas the scribe.

The last parallel leads on to the incident of the ordeal and so connects with PJ, xvi. For "priests," see § 175, 12. As in the story of the ordeal, KP showed a knowledge of the topography of Jerusalem.

§ 145. We will now examine the complex problem of the narratives of the Nativity.

A. PJ, xviii. 1. *And he found a cave there and brought her into it, and set his sons by her. And he went forth and sought a midwife of the Hebrews in the country of Bethlehem.* (*Now I, Joseph, was walking, and I walked not . . .* (xix. 1). *I seek a midwife. . . . She said to me, Is she not thy wife? And I said to her. . . . She hath conception by the Holy Ghost.*) *And the midwife said unto him, Is this the truth? . . . 2. And they stood in the place of the cave; and behold a bright cloud.* The QP1 narrative of the non-Nativity follows. *And the midwife cried aloud and said. . . . 3. And the midwife went forth of the cave, and Salome met her. . . . And Salome said, If I make not trial I will not believe . . .* (xx. 1). *. . . . And Salome made trial.* Her hand was withered and healed. She was enjoined to keep silence.

B. PsMatt. 13. A beautiful boy appears. Joseph went forth and found two midwives, Zelome and Salome. When they arrived Mary had already brought forth. Zelome examined Mary and said that a virgin had brought forth. Salome doubted and her hand was withered. Salome went forth and began to tell the wonderful tidings. Many believed. The shepherds testified to the angels. 14. The ox and the ass worship.

C. RobEvvC, 196. After a parallel with PJ, xvii. 3, we read: *Joseph left her therein. It was the hour of evening. Joseph went forth seeking a woman that he might leave her with her. Now whilst Joseph was without the Virgin brought forth . . . and laid Him in a manger. Joseph found at dawn . . . Salome . . . a midwife. . . . She ran and came outside, and cried with a loud voice to all the borders of Bethlehem, Come ye and see this great wonder.*

D. In CMiscT, 631, Mary remains in the temple until she is fourteen as in Epiph. *Hom.* 322, and in psEvodius (EvvC, 187). In PJ, viii. 2, she is twelve. In 653 Joseph finds the midwife Salome. They see Christ in the manger. The ox and the ass worship.

E. RobEvvC, 21. Mary brings forth before Joseph returns.

F. Epiph. *Hom.* 329. Joseph goes to Bethlehem with his household. They hastily enter the cave. Mary bore without pangs. 332. A shepherd named Isaac, who used the cave for an ox, found Joseph outside the cave, and they witnessed the wonderful and miraculous birth. There were, hard by, shepherds in the open.

G. Asc.Is. xi. 8. *When they were alone Mary . . . saw a small baby and was astonished. 9. Her womb was found as formerly before she had conceived. 11. And a voice came to them tell this vision to no one. 12. And the story regarding the infant was noised abroad in Bethlehem. 13. Some said that the Virgin hath borne a child before she was married two months. 14. And many said, She has not borne a child, nor has a midwife gone up to her, nor have we heard the cries of pains. And they were all blinded respecting Him.*

§ 146. 1. The stillness of nature described by Joseph (A) must have been one of the marvels which occurred at the moment of the Nativity and to which allusion was made in KP *sub* Ign. *Eph.* 19 (§ 140 A). The speech, therefore, shews that BCDE are superior to PJ in making

the birth occur in Joseph's absence. Joseph doubtless gave
his account of what took place on the occasion on which
the midwife stated the results of the examination which
she made in KP, possibly that narrated in a fragment
which we shall discuss in § 151. The fact that when turned
into the third person the speech coheres with the context
is probably simply due to the fact that in KP Joseph repeated
a portion of the earlier narrative of KP.

Our attribution of the speech to KP is confirmed by its
picturesque rhetoric. With the epigram *I was walking and
not walking* we may compare two others with which we are
concerned in this section. (*a*) In VP, 24, Peter attributes
to a prophet the words, *peperit et non peperit*. This testimony
in Tert. de Carn. C. 23, is attributed to Ezekiel. There
and in Epiph. Haer. xxx. 30, and Clem. Strom. vii. 15, the
opening runs, *the heifer who*. (*b*) In PJ, xix. 2, Christ takes
the breast. Now in RobEvvC, 53, 77, we read: *I received
suck, and I am He that nourisheth all*. We may compare
KP, 2 (§ 12). Cyril who was much influenced by psMark
writes: *truly nourished by milk* (Cat. iv. 9). That this incident derives from KP is shewn by Asc.Is. xi. 17, where the
Tiamat motive is clear: *He sucked the breast in order that He
might not be recognised*. Cf. § 149 (*a*). This passage explains
an epigram which occurs in Gobar and is in the characteristic
style of KP, *He was nourished by milk and not nourished by
milk*. (*c*) We shall attribute to KP, *those whom (Antichrist)
hath summoned and those whom he hath not summoned* (§ 153).

§ 147. 2. An even clearer instance of the influence of the
myth occurs in PJ, xxii. f., where Elizabeth flies from Herod
who fears lest John should become the king of Israel.
Hard pressed, she prays to a mountain, which cleaves
asunder and receives the mother and child. The incident
is obviously based on the legend underlying Rev. xii. 4. In
each case the earth rescues the mother from the persecuting
dragon. We may find traces of the legend in EvM, 18 and
at the point in PJ, xvii. 4, where Joseph says, *whither shall I
take thee to hide (thy shame)* and finds a cave. We shall
return to this incident in § 322. Cf. § 90*k*.

§ 148. 3. PJ brings to the cave a midwife, but any man or woman would have answered the purpose of the narrative. She runs out and meets Salome, who is not said to have been a midwife, but makes an examination and refers to her cures. EvM and the Coptic (BCD) confirm the obvious conjecture that Salome was originally the midwife. The purpose of the incident is clear. The birth was miraculous and there was no need of her presence except after the event in order to make the examination, an incident which is implicit in the statement of Asc.Is. (G) that the womb was found as it was before the conception.

The invitation which Joseph addresses in PJ to the midwife is in the Coptic (C) addressed by her to the people of Bethlehem, and C is supported by EvM. The result was *no small contention* (Is. vii. 14 LXX), because of Mary, an allusion which in PJ is obscure. The incident, however, is explained by G, where Isaiah prophesies that the Bethlehemites will disagree. . . . *Some will not believe because they will not have heard the cries of labour pains.* But this, as we have already observed, was just what Ezekiel had predicted in KP *sub* VP, 24. And Peter in the same passage after citing Is. vii. says that another prophet wrote: *Neither did we hear her voice, neither did a midwife come in.* When the unbelieving Bethlehemites were denying the truth they were confirming it by fulfilling the prophet's prediction. The derivation of VP from KP is shewn by the fact that the passage contains some primitive anti-Judaic testimonies.

§ 149. 4. There were only two primary Acts which were concerned with the details of these events. If in KP the ministrations of a midwife were not needed at the birth, her testimony was required after the event to prove that it was miraculous. Leucius, on the other hand, required evidence to prove the non-Nativity. We turn, then, to the contexts of A and F expecting to find traces of QPl; and in PJ we find the following narrative: "Behold a bright cloud overshadowing the cave (as in KP *sub* Epiph. *Hom.* 329, where Jesus is born) and a great light appeared . . . and little by little withdrew itself until the young child appeared." The following matter also must be attributed to QPl:

[(a) In PJ Christ *goes* and takes the breast.

(b) The PJ priests Reuben and Samuel are not mentioned in Epiph. *Hom.*, and the names are likely to be Leucian. Samuel was suggested by KP (§ 139 (vi)) and is on a Leucian list (§ 139). Reuben is due to Leucius's addiction to using tribal names (§ 315).

(c) No one but Leucius would have made the shepherd (F) a spectator or have named him Isaac. We shall find that he named the other shepherds (§ 315 D).

(d) The worship of the animals (BD) is very characteristic of QPl (§ 265 f.). The ox is mentioned in F.

(e) In the preceding contexts of C and E Mary's face shines before the Nativity. There is a parallel in the starry light which shines in the face of Jesus when in EvH, 51, He cleanses the temple.

§ 150. The evidence shows that QPJ derived from Heg and that PJ had an independent knowledge of Heg.

(i) Epiphanius derives through Heg matter both from KP and QPl. QPJ was based on KP and had matter from QPl (D). The fact that he attributed his work to James shews that he was also acquainted with an apocryphon written by James or claiming his authority. PJ, xxv. is probably a fragment of J (§ 294). PsMatthew may also be independent of PJ and QPJ in several places.

(ii) Salome the midwife cannot have occurred in QPl, and it is in the highest degree improbable that she was named in KP, for there is no evidence that the writer invented any other names than those of Joachim and Anna, and it was necessary to name the Virgin's parents for apologetic reasons. The name comes from Heg who, for reasons which do not here concern us, named Joseph's daughters Salome and Mary (§ 286 (a)). In KP Joseph was accompanied by his sons and daughters to Bethlehem (Epiph. *Hom.* 328 f.). QPJ followed KP, but omitted the allusion to Joseph's family and compensated for this omission by naming the midwife Salome. Later when using the QPl narrative of the worship of the dragons he named Joseph's daughter Mary (§ EvM, 18). PJ in A made Joseph leave the Virgin with his sons because in QPJ Salome was not with him, having become the midwife whom he met. This, of course, was no reason for omission; he probably did not think the matter out. But his unexpected *sons* requires explanation and shews that like QPJ he used Heg.]

§ 151. The influence of KP on Heg *sub* Hist. Patr. has been already illustrated. In one of the prefaces of that work (124) we are told that there was a vacancy in the priesthood and the priests met to discuss whether they should appoint Jesus. One of them said that he was a good man, but for fear of the people because of the infants slain by Herod His parents fled to Egypt, and there was a question whether His birth was not adulterous. It was replied that Mary was descended from both tribes and decided that the question of Mary's virginity should be decided by midwives. Her neighbours bore witness to her.

There are some parallels with this passage.

(i) In Epiph. Haer. lv. the Jews say that Melchizedek was a good man, but the son of a harlot, a passage which we have concluded must derive from KP. According to Hist. Patr. this was which some said about Jesus.

(ii) Precisely the same charges are brought against Christ in EvN, ii. 3.

(iii) According to Celsus (i. 28), who probably used Heg, a Jew accused Jesus of inventing His birth from a Virgin. She was a spinner (weaver of curtains) who bore Jesus to Panthera (a charge dealt with by Heg, § 131). She was neither rich nor of royal rank (a daughter of Joachim). Not even her neighbours knew her. This charge is answered in the statement of Hist. Patr. that Mary's neighbours knew her.

The Jew of Celsus said that the name of the father of Jesus was Panther. Heg's treatment of this charge illustrates his aversion from the rejection of any written statement if he could suggest an harmonisation. He suggested that the second name of Joseph's father (Matt. i. 15) was Panther (Lawlor, 35–37).

CHAPTER IV

SOME NOTES ON APOCALYPTIC

In this chapter it is argued that KP is prior to Revelation. Readers who are not interested in apocalyptic should glance at the tables in § 161 f., for they illustrate the fact that the apocrypha are interrelated. In § 165 there is a very clear illustration of the indebtedness of Leucius to KP and, inasmuch as VP, 20 is based on QP, the parallelism of VP with AJ proves the indebtedness of QP to the source of the whole AJ context, QPl. The apocalypses are also discussed in § 101 and § 279 (vi).

---

§ 152. It is impossible to omit the subject of the uncanonical apocalyptic; but, large though the field of enquiry is, our examination of it will be very brief. While it seems clear that KP influenced Revelation, there are other contacts of the apocrypha with Revelation, and the problem appears to me to be very complex. When I deal with the subject of Papias I shall argue that that writer, Leucius and the source of Rev. xii., were influenced by the preaching of John or Ariston in the Lycus valley. It is as unfortunate as it is surprising that Charles in his great work on Revelation gave hardly any attention to the subject of the relations of Revelation to other Christian apocalyptic. For a summary of the dates of the primary apocalypses, see § 101.

We will in the first place reconstruct two passages of KP which it will be argued are used in Rev. xi.

1. We read in EP, 472: *Great numbers of the people of Jerusalem saw* (*the Ascension*) *and with them many of the unbelieving Jews. . . . And they stood . . . at the place where they could readily see . . . and fear and dismay came upon them all, and they glorified God. Then some of them who were doubtful . . . wished to go up to the Mount of Olives, and there came upon them tongues of fire and burnt up many of them* (Ex. xix. 21). That this passage derives

from KP appears as follows: (i) It is abbreviated in the preceding QP Ascension narrative (467) where we read, "And all men saw the splendour (of the cloud) and were dismayed" (467). (ii) The motive of the incident was to make the Jews witnesses of the Ascension just as they had been witnesses of the Resurrection and Joseph's ordeal (§§ 96, 135).

§ 153, 2. KP predicted the martyrdom of Enoch and Elijah in the times of Antichrist.

A. That the Antichrist legend influenced KP is shewn by Asc.Is. iv. 4, and by the fictitious testimony in Hippol. Antichr. 15, 54, where Antichrist *will gather all his forces from the east to the west: those whom he hath summoned and those whom he hath not summoned* (a curious phrase characteristic of KP (§ 146 (iii)) *shall go with him: he will whiten the sea with the sails of his ships and blacken the plain with the shields of his weapons*. The style is that of KP, and not only at the point mentioned. Like Joseph's speech in PJ, 18, it is picturesque. Moreover most, if not all, fictitious testimonies either derive from or are based upon KP. The testimony was invented to support a prediction preserved in EP, 513, where Antichrist will destroy believers by land and sea. There is no other parallel. The writer was probably thinking of Pharsalus and Actium. This interest in history is another link with KP.

B. Bousset (Antichrist Legend, 203, 288) has collected evidence for a Christian tradition that Enoch and Elijah will reproach Antichrist and be slain by him. That this tradition occurred in Heg is suggested by its occurrence in Hippol. Antich. 43 (in which work we have just found KP Antichrist matter), Tert. de Anim. 50 and Hist. Jos. 31. That it occurred in KP is proved by the agreement of EApP, 512, with QPl *sub* the Burgomil Book of John (J, 190) (where Enoch is a scribe, as in ApPl, 20: cf. II. En, 23), with EvN, xxv. and also (perhaps) with Tryph. 49.

§ 154. C. The passage with which we are mainly concerned occurs in SachauApP, 471 f., and is not cited by Bousset. It runs: *Enoch and Elias will say that the wicked Jews have crucified Him. . . . Then shall (Antichrist) slay them, and their bodies shall lie in the streets of Jerusalem, and no one*

*shall bury them. Enoch and Elias will live again and rise
again in their own bodies.* That the matter about Enoch
and Elijah derives from KP appears as follows:

(i) It influenced QPl. (*a*) The EvN narrative of the
Descensus is Leucian, and it is actually said to have been
written by Leucius and Carinus. In xxv. Enoch and Elijah
will be slain by Antichrist in Jerusalem and after three days
and a half will be taken up alive. (*b*) In psMethodius they,
with John, will convict Antichrist of fraud (99: Bousset,
205) as also in Ambros. in Rev. xi. 3 f. (one MS.). Tert. de
Anima, 50, also connects the three names with Rev. xi.
Epiphanius (*Haer.* XXIX, 5) protests against John being
ranked with Enoch and Elijah.[1] He is ranked with them
because in QPl *sub* EP, 524, he will not taste death until the
last times (§ 271). This prediction probably underlies the
late tradition that John slept in his tomb at Ephesus.

(ii) The wickedness of the Jews in slaying Christ was a
main theme of KP. (*a*) KP, 9, amended runs, *after the
udgment of Jerusalem.* (*b*) Pilate predicts this judgment in
his letter (§ 125). (*c*) In EvP, 25,[2] the Jews say, *Woe for our
sins, for the judgment is at hand and the end of Jerusalem.*
(*d*) The primitive testimony which underlies Rev. i. 7, and
Jn. xix. 37, was amended in KP, so as to make the Jews at
the second coming repeat the lamentation which they
uttered at the Crucifixion. The passage survives in a work
which is full of KP matter. In Cyr. Catech. xv. 10, we read.
*the sign of the shining cross shall go before His face. . . .
The Jews who pierced Him shall mourn tribe by tribe . . .
saying, This is He on whose face they spat, whom of old they
crucified and set at nought.* This testimony is abbreviated
in Barn. vii. 9. The epistle is based on KP.

§ 155. We will now compare our two reconstructions of
KP with Rev. xi. 3 f.: *My two witnesses* (Moses and Elias)
. . . shall prophesy 1260 *days, clothed in sackcloth. . . . The
beast shall slay them. And their dead bodies lie in the
streets of the great city . . . where also their Lord was*

---

[1] For a discussion of these passages see Zahn, AcJoh, cxvii. f.
[2] Add to Swete's parallels EP, 492; STrans, 44.

crucified. . . . Men look upon their bodies three days and a half, and suffer not their bodies to be laid in a tomb. And they stood upon their feet; and great fear fell upon them that beheld them. And they heard a voice saying . . . Come up hither. And they went up into heaven in the cloud; and their enemies beheld them. . . . There was an earthquake. . . . There were killed in Jerusalem 7000 persons; and the rest were affrighted and gave glory to the God of heaven.

That there is a close literary relation between Revelation and the two passages which we have ascribed to KP is obvious, and it is impossible to suppose that they abbreviate Revelation. On the other hand, Revelation, as elsewhere, seems to modify earlier material. Inasmuch, then, as we may safely ignore the hypothesis that the common source was a lost Christian apocalypse which was earlier than KP, and inasmuch as our citations and Revelation agree in unexpected allusions to the Crucifixion, Revelation must derive from KP. This attribution may be confirmed as follows:

(i) The allusion to the Crucifixion in SachauAP, though unexpected, is well motived. In Revelation, on the other hand, it is not only the only allusion to that event, but reads like an irrelevant splinter.

(ii) The visible ascension of the witnesses in a cloud and the killing of the Jews are badly motived in Revelation, but are explained by the passages cited from EP in § 152.

(iii) We are about to attribute the words, *come up hither* to KP.

(iv) Charles shews that Revelation identifies the two witnesses with Moses and Elijah. Now the return of Enoch and Elijah occurs in En. xi. 31, but Charles can adduce no evidence of any value for the return of Moses. On the other hand our hypothesis accounts for the allusion to him. EApP, 519 identifies the two men who appear on Olivet in Acts i. 10 with Moses and Elijah.

(v) The indirect identifications of the two witnesses and the allusions to Sodom and Egypt and the beast, are secondary as compared with the explicit allusion of our passages to Enoch and Elijah, Jerusalem and Antichrist.

§ 156. The KP apocalypse was divided into two parts: pre-Ascension discourse, in which Christ revealed the future, and the rapture of the apostles into heaven where they beheld the unseen. It will be argued in § 160 that Rev. vi. f. is influenced by the discourse. Here we are concerned with the evidence which suggests that the section of Revelation which precedes the ascension of John in iv. 2, was parallel with KP.

Revelation, like the KP apocalypse, begins with the appearance of the risen Lord on the Lord's-day (see § 86). The seven letters, so we shall conclude, have an historical basis. S. John's visits to the seven cities, a tradition of which survived in AJ (AJ, 45; EP, 502. 28), were the visitation of Christ Himself. Now in these two chapters there may survive discourse from early Resurrection and pre-Ascension discourse. They are anti-Nicolaitan, and this fact gives us a possible contact with the KP discourse, which certainly foretold lawlessness. It must also be observed that the Nicolaitans were regarded as schismatics whose errors were influencing the churches from which they had seceded (Rev. ii. 6, 15; cf. 1 Jn. ii. 19; iv. 1). All the matter cited will be discussed further.

False apostles	Rev. ii. 2 ; 2 Cor. xi. 13	H, xi. 35 ; Tryph. 35
False prophets	Rev. ii. 20 ; Mk. xiii. 22	H, Tryph. 51, 82; AknApP, 1; Did. 16; 2 Pet. ii. 1
False teachers	Acts xx. 29 f. ; 1 Tim. iv. 1	H, Tryph. 82 ; 2 Pet.
False Christs	Mk. xiii. 22	EApP, 511
Schisms and *Heresies*	Rev. ii. iii.; 1 Cor. xi. 19	Tryph. 35, 51; 2 Pet.; EP, 510
Lawlessness	Rev. ii. iii.	Did. 16; Asc.Is. iii. 24

In Acts xx. S. Paul probably refers to a lost logion. Note the prophetic *must* (Matt. xviii. 7) in 1 Corinthians.

§ 157. There is much evidence which shews that in the KP apocalypse the apostles were caught up in the spirit, which they had just received, into the seventh heaven. I propose to confine myself to the main facts.

The following passages are likely to derive directly from KP:

A. In Asc.Is. iii. 16, Christ ascends, and in iii. 24–iv. 16, there are fragments of the eschatological discourse which has just been mentioned. In iv. 18 and ix. 9, there are allusions to the garments (spiritual bodies, BDEHK: cf. 2 Cor. v. 2 f.) stored for the saints in heaven. After a digression Isaiah is caught up (vii. f.). In the sixth heaven he heard the angels praising the Father, His Beloved (E) and the Holy Spirit, and in the seventh he saw the glory and the worship of the Son and the Spirit (EGJK).

B. ApP began with the discourse on Olivet. The transportations are omitted, but the apostles saw part of what was seen in KP, Paradise, a region which was outside the world (AknApP, 15: D) where were the high priests (20: E). The tabernacles of EApP, 519, are the garments of A and the tents of E.

C. Joshophat was caught away to Paradise and brought to the city (Boisonnarde, *Anec. Gc.* iv. 280, 360).

D. Saturus (APerpet. xi.) passed the first world, and the Lord shewed him a vast space beyond the world (B). The transportation shews that ApP is not the source.

The following passages derive from QP:

E. In STrans, 64 f. (§ 99) Mary, after her death, is transported to the earthly Paradise, where she sees Enoch, Elijah, Moses, and Peter (cf. EApP), the tents (ABHK) of the sons of light, the crowns of the priests (B) being woven and the garments prepared for the day of resurrection (ACDHK), the treasure-houses of God the Father, the Beloved and the Spirit (AGJ), the river of fire, the tabernacles of the just and the sinners who were beholding, as in EApP, their prepared torments. She was sorry, and interceded. We may compare EApP, 520; ApPl, 43 f.; and K.

F. In EP, 520, Peter is said to have seen and described the heavenly Jerusalem.

G. In EvvC, 4, Peter sees the heavens opened and the Trinity (AEJK). He hears trisagios (E).

H. In MPol, 2, the martyrs gaze upon the good things

prepared for the just.   The letter is probably influenced by QP elsewhere.

J. In § 296E we shall attribute to QPl the experience of a raised man in the unseen in which the river of fire and the Trinity are mentioned.

K. We have concluded that in QPl the Father, Son and the mother spirit Mary (AEGJ), were seen in heaven (§ 120).

L. In NZos, 5, Zosimus sees the raiment of the saints in the height of heaven.   There is ground for suspecting the influence of J on this context (§ 251).

§ 158. We will now collect the evidence for three other incidents.

(i) We find tears for sinners and intercession in STrans, 66, and EApP, 520 (cf. James) and ApPl, 43 f.   The incident underlies Pist. Soph. 325 and CMystJ, 255.

(ii) The greeting given to Peter when he reached the highest heaven underlies the following passages:

(*a*) VP, 23. The raised Stratonicus heard Christ say, *Come, enter*.

(*b*) NZos, 5. *Come.* . . .

(*c*) In ApPl, 14, the Spirit greets the saved with the words, *Come, enter*.

(*d*) In ApEsdr, 21, God says to Esdras, *Thy crown hath been prepared.   Come*.

(*e*) Ign. Rom. 7. *There is in me living water (of the Spirit) saying, Come to the Father*.

(iii) The following passage occurs in the purely Jewish psPhilo.   It combines Is. lx. 4 with lxv. 15, in its description of the twelve stones found by Cenez and inscribed with the names of the tribes: *ex eo quod oculus non vidit nec auris audivit, et in cor hominis non ascendit, quo-usque tale aliquid fierit in seculum et non indigent justi opera luminis solis neque splendore lunæ, quoniam preciosissimorum lapidum lumen erit lumen eorum.*   (Thackeray, *S. Paul and CJT*, 244.)   S. Paul used the ultimate source, and that psMark did so is proved by the large influence of our citation on the apocrypha. In 1 Clem. 34, it ends in its uncanonical form *for them that await Him*.   Sometimes the allusion is to the resurrection bodies of the saints, as in STrans, 65, and Asc.Is. viii. 22 f. (*who hath prepared such lights on those who await His promises*). In CEncJB, 345, the stones are on the garments of the saints (cf. Asc.Is.). In the QP vision of Siophanes they are on the thrones of the apostles (CBRB, 208) and light up the heavenly Jerusalem; and in EP, 478, they are on the book given to Peter (John) and light up the earthly Jerusalem.

§ 159. Just as in KP the apostles received the Spirit from the ascending Christ at the dawn of Pentecost, so in Revelation John is in the Spirit on the Lord's-day. Like Peter (after matter parallel with discourse about the signs of the end) he is caught up (iv. 2) and hears the invitation, Come hither. Like Peter he sees the Father and the Son and hears the worship of heaven. Peter's tears in heaven may explain the unaccountable weeping of John which is connected with the book containing the divine decrees and judgments. As in KP we read of a mountain, a conducting angel and the vision of the heavenly Jerusalem. As in KP there are allusions to the river of fire and the trees of Paradise. The apostles and the tribes which they judge, the gates, the gems and the inscriptions, are characteristically worked into new combinations, one of which is due to Eph. ii. 20. As in psPhilo the city needs not the light of the sun. The parallels are not accounted for by Is. liv. 11 f., lx. 9 f., and Tob. xiii. 16 f.

We will now compare the following passages:

§ 160. A. 2 Pet. iii. 10. *The heavens shall pass away . . . and the elements shall be burnt and dissolved and earth shall (?) not be found* (cf. Rev. xvi. 20). 12. *The elements shall melt.*

B. 2 Clem. 16. *Ye know that the day . . . cometh even now as a burning oven, and the powers of the heavens shall melt* (cf. A), *and all the earth as lead melting on the fire.*

C. Melito (Spic. Syr.). *There was once a flood and a wind. The earth shall be burnt up . . . and the sea together with the isles . . . and a wind. . . . The idolaters shall lament when they behold their idols on fire together with themselves.*

Other woes are summarised below in Table I.

TABLE I

	D EApP	E Sib[1]	F STrans	G BaarJ	H LPP	J RSteph	K Rev	Cf.
1. Fire going before Him	513	Sib	..	..	..	159	..	Cf. L
2. The heavens folded as a scroll	513	..	..	BJ	176	..	vi. 14	..
3. Stars falling like leaves	Macar, v. 7	Sib	..	..	..	159	vi. 15	..
4. Stars melted	513	..	..	..	..	..	viii. 10	Cf. A and B
5. Sea or isles burnt	513	Sib	68	..	..	..	vi. 14 ("Moved")	..
6. Darkness	513	Sib	68	..	..	..	viii. 2	Cf. C
7. Storm	..	..	..	BJ	..	159	xii. 13	Did. xvi.
8. Trumpet	..	..	..	..	176	159	xx. 13	..
9. Sea giving up its dead	513	Sib	68	Cf. BJ	Cf. 176	..	..	..
10. Bones to bones	512	Sib	..	BJ	..	159	vi. 15	Cf. L
11. Terror of men	513	..	..	..	..	..	..	..
12. The books opened	..	..	..	..	..	159	xxii. 12	..

For D see J, 512 f., and for EJ 521 f.[1]   G = Barrlaam and Joshophat XXV.

1

L. We may add from Clem. Protrep. viii. a passage which may derive from one of the eschatological KP testimonies (KP, 9): *The sun shall fail, and the heaven shall be darkened, but the Almighty shall stand for ever: and the powers of the heaven shall be shaken, and the heavens shall be rolled up like a curtain, and stretched out and pulled in (for these are the words of the prophecy), and the earth shall flee from the face of the Lord.*

ABCD derive other matter from KP. F is certainly based on QP and H on QPl. Two important woes do not occur in Revelation, and apart from this fact the uncanonical matter seems to clearly derive from KP and not from the disordered and fragmentary predictions of the canonical apocalypse.

Charles (i. 159) holds that the case for the derivation of Rev. vi. 2–vii. 1 from the source of the Markan Apocalypse is irresistible. Now it will be shewn in the next volume that ApMk derives from ApM, and in § 90*k* (i) we concluded that Rev. xii. 4 f. is related to M. It is certain then that our parallels from Rev derive from M. But this derivation is probably through KP, for Rev and the apocryphal data agree in matter which is not likely to have occurred in ApM and the source of Rev was in the rhetorical style of KP (§§ 146, 153A).

§ 161. The reader who wishes to reconstruct the QPl and QP apocalypses may receive some help from the subjoined Tables. The only apocalypse which is certainly independent of QP is CMystJ. That apocalypse is seen by John only, who reports to the other apostles (257) just as Peter (John) in EP, 479, reports the names of the two angels. For his transportation to the east see § 188, vi.

TABLE II

	STrans	Proch	LJas	MAnd	CBRB	
Christ appears	63	..	140	..	213	..
Commissions the apostles	..	3·5	140	AA.1	213	..
Inhabited earth	..	3·5	140	AA.1	..	..
Persecution foretold	..	5·5	140	..	211	CEncJB, 345
Father Peter	64	5·7	140	AA.1	189	..
Peter leads	28	6·3	140	..	..	..
Paul present	64	SHJ	..	..	..	LT, 93, EP, 521, 1 ApPl
The Virgin	64	4·4	..	..	..	LT, 93
The Seventy	19	7·2	..	AA.2	..	EP, 467, 517
The lots	..	5·12	140	..	..	..
Complaint as to lot	..	5·13	140	AA.1	..	..
The Lord's-day	..	SHJ, 59	..	..	193	EP, 520, JosTrans (J, 217), ABarn, 24
Gift or grace of the Spirit	63	4·2	140	AA.1	202	..
Christ ascends	63	..	140	..	214	RobEvvC, 125

TABLE III

	STrans	EP, EPl	ApPl	CEncJB	
Trisagios . .	65	468	..	..	EvvC, 4
Golden girdles . .	::	::	12	345	CBRB, 207; CMystJ, 248
Eliz. John Zacharias .	58	::	C (J, 554)	345	::
David with his harp .	65	::	29	::	RobEvvC, 121; CMystJ, 248
The earthly Paradise .	64	691	::	::	LT, 93; CMystJ, 248
30 or 300 stadia .	::	692	::	347	::
Bending trees . .	::	::	24	::	ObsMar (J, 226); Narr. Zos. 3
The golden ship . .	::	(695)	23	347	::
The miraculous vine and corn	::	::	22	348	See § 369

§ 162. Budge, in *Copt. Apocr.* lxii. f., has collected parallels with his apocrypha from Egyptian apocalyptic, but most of the illustrated passages may be editorial, and, if so, the parallels do not concern us. Egyptian influences may have reached the primary apocryphists through many channels, and it is quite possible that they affected the KP apocalypse. That our conjecture is not improbable is shewn by the intimate acquaintance with Egyptian idolatry shewn in KP, 3, where the original is abbreviated. Budge cites from the *Book of Gates*, sec. iii., a passage which states that the waters of the lake of fire scald the wicked, but the righteous pass through them scatheless and drink of them. This doctrine appears very clearly indeed in CBRB, 207, where the raised Siophanes says that the river of fire was for him a river of water and that he saw the twelve jewelled thrones of the apostles. This matter must derive from the QP apocalypse, for it exalts the twelve. Again in EPl, 671, the raised young man was in Gehenna and the flaming river changed its form when a beautiful young man touched it with a staff of gold. The passage is referred to in 682, in a "Cæsarea ending," which is based on QPl. In STrans, 66, the river of fire burns nothing, and the Trinity is mentioned as in EPl, 672. The allusions to the Trinity are evidence for derivation from ĶP (§ 157 f., AGJ), and this derivation is confirmed by two writers who are certainly independent of Leucius. Cyril, who is much influenced by KP, says that the Son of Man will come with a stream of fire to test men (Cat. v. 21), and in Did. 16, where there are other contacts with KP, we read of the fire of testing. We may conclude that the testing fire derives from KP, but it is uncertain that the fuller statement of the doctrine in CBRB and EPl does so. It may derive from Cerinthus who, according to Hippolytus, came from Egypt.

§ 163. There are one or two points as to which there may be a doubt, but it is clear that the passages tabulated (Tables II and IV) derive from QP, that the work the writing of which was recorded was EvXII and that LeuciusP used KP in which Acts John Mark placed the Peter apocalypse, which he recorded in the Holy Sepulchre where were the instruments of the Passion. EvXII probably contained an apocalypse. The incident has the following history. In Ex. xxiv. 19 the seventy elders are on Sinai with Moses, who in xxv. 16 places the tables in the ark. In II Macc. iv. 4 f. Jeremiah hides the ark in Nebo, and in a later tradition (James Apoc. Anec. ii. 88) that mountain becomes Olivet.

TABLE IV

	STrans	EP	Proch	
The apostles write .	17, 62	..	..	VP, 20; CApPl, 554
Pen and ink . . .	..	(?)621	154·8	psProch, 184·22
They and the Seventy seal	19	519 f.	..	..
John takes the book to his house . . .	62	..	157·11	..
John preached its contents	..	520	157·11	VP, 20; AJ, 88 f.
Copies for the churches	18, 63	523	158·3	HE, II, xv. 2
The book placed in the cave . . .	19 f.	520–2	..	psProch, 184·7, ABarn, 24

See also Table V.

[None of our documents preserve the sequence of events clearly. Matter in which the Virgin is spoken of as dead, or in which all the apostles write, must derive from QP.

A. The whole of STrans, 62–63, 32, is based on QP, and the apocalypse follows in 64 f. All the apostles write. The words *let each of us write what the Holy Spirit is preparing by his mouth* (63), are parallel with the AJ narrative of the writing of John *sub* Murat., *what may be revealed to any of us, let each of us write*. They all certify as in the Table.

B. In QP *sub* AJ, 63 f., the death of Drusilla was originally that of the Virgin (§ 122), and the eucharist that at the Holy Sepulchre. A sermon follows, but it is based on QPl.

C. In VP, 17, there is a eucharist at the Holy Sepulchre.

In 20, Peter preaches a composite sermon on EvXII which contains a parallel with 2 Pet. i. 17 f., which must derive from KP (cf. Chase, BD, iii. 802). He says that the apostles could write no more than they were capable of writing. The AJ designations follow.

D. In ABarn, 24, Matthew puts his writings in a cave (*where the Jebusites formerly dwelt*) on the second day of the week, *i.e.* on the day after the eucharist or sermon.

I shall discuss the AJ narrative of the writing of John in the next volume. In ApocPl (J, 582) Timothy presumably represents Leucius, and Mark, who also writes the work, probably derives from ApP and is a link between ApP and KP.

§ 164. The narrative of the eucharist at which the apocalypse was preached underlies the following passages:

A. We shall conclude that the narratives of Thecla derive from a recension of QPl (QThec). In Thec, 23, there is a eucharist at a tomb which, like the Holy Sepulchre, was *new* (Arm, Gk. vl). There is a fast (CDE). A lad who was originally Christ (E) brings five loaves (Jn. vi. 9), water (VP, 2) and vegetables.

The following evidence derive from QP:

B. In a *Dormitio* (RobEvvC, 51; cf. CBRB, 192) Christ will receive the offering on the next day.

C. That there was a eucharist in the AJ narrative of the writing of John is suggested by *they rejoiced with great joy* (Proch, 157, 16; LJ, 167). The fast for three days (Mur. Proch, 152, 11) occurs in E.

D. In AJ, 72 f., the brethren go to the tomb of Drusiana (Mary) on the third day. As in B and F Christ appears as a beautiful youth, and as in the *Dormitios* ascends from the tomb. In 85, John takes bread into the sepulchre and breaks it on the slab, an incident which probably derives from KP and the Easter rite observed at the Holy Sepulchre. He then comes out and distributes it.

E. In VP, 17 (A) Peter fasts for three days and a boy gives him a wheaten loaf. The cave is the Holy Sepulchre, and Heg's description of it is used.

Leucius probably introduced into his narrative the story of the fornicating communicant whose hands were withered (VP, 2; AT, 51).]

§ 165. We will now compare the designations of Christ in the AJ and VP sermons with each other and with designations which occur in documents which derive from KP.

In AJ, 98, we read: *This cross of light is sometimes called word by me, sometimes mind . . . Jesus . . . Christ . . . door . . . way . . . bread . . . seed . . . resurrection . . . Son . . . Father . . . Spirit . . . Life . . . faith . . . truth . . . life.* In 109, John giving thanks over the bread says: *We glorify . . . Thy name of Father which was said by Thee . . . the name of Son which was said by Thee. . . . Thine entering of the door . . . the resurrection . . . Thy way . . . the seed . . . word . . . grace . . . faith . . . salt . . . pearl . . . treasure . . . plough . . . net . . . greatness . . . diadem . . . called Son of man.* To this list VP, 20, adds *water, feast, wine.*

That the designations derive from QP1 is proved by the personification of the cross, but in VP the source was probably not QP1 but QP. That QP1 derived from KP is proved by the following parallels. The influence of KP on Theophilus will be illustrated.

TABLE V

	mind	Father	Spirit	kingdom	light	power	wisdom	word
Theoph. i. 3	mind	Father	Spirit	kingdom	light	power	wisdom	word
Theoph. ii. 10	..	Father	Spirit	*arche*	..	power	wisdom	word
Hippol. c. Noet. 4	..	..	Spirit	..	..	power	wisdom	word
Ad Diogn. 9	mind	Father	Spirit	..	..	power	wisdom	word
ArmCall, 301	..	..	Spirit	..	light	power	wisdom	word
AJ	mind	Father	Spirit	*arche*	..	power	..	word
VP	..	..	..	*initium*	light	power	..	word

The following passage occurs in a context which is full of KP and is likely to be based on that work: *For one is God who formed the beginning of all things. Pointing out the first begotten Son Peter writes* (*i.e.* in his introductory letter), *In the beginning God made. . . . And He is called wisdom by the prophets. This is He who is the teacher of all things, the fellow counsellor of God* (Clem. Strom. vi. 7). In the passage from ad Diogn. cited above, Christ, as in Clement, is *teacher* and *counsellor*.

§ 166. [We may compare with the liturgical hymn in AJ, 94 f., those of the angels in CBRB, *e.g.* in 195: *Glory to Thee undying One. Amen. Glory to Thee who wast not born. . . . The alpha of the universe . . . the beginning and the end . . . sabaoth . . . Eloi . . . the king of the ages* (MPl, 2) *. . . abba abriath.* This hymn we have already ascribed to QPl. We compare also the glories in EvBart, iv. 69. It must not be assumed that the parallel in Rev. xxii. 13, is the source. Apart from the certainty that *the Beginning* occurred in KP and the probability that *the End* did so, there is evidence as to the vogue of the phrases (Charles, i. 20; ii. 220).]

In H, iii. 72, designations of Christ are transferred to the Father: *power*, *physician* (ad Diogn. 9; Ign. *Eph.* 7), *wall*, *life* (AJ), *hope* (AJ), *refuge* (AJ), *joy*, *expectation*, *rest* (AJ).

The designations Father, Son, Spirit were probably suggested by a conjecture that the Matthæan baptismal formula stated the name of the Lord into which the primitive converts were baptised.

CHAPTER V

THE ETHIOPIC NARRATIVES OF S. PETER AND S. PAUL

This chapter is of great importance for the reconstruction of
Heg, and incidentally illustrates the derivation of the western
variants in Acts from him and also the fact that he made topo-
graphical notes. It is also an introduction to an almost unknown
Acts of which we shall make much use and to the important
L group of Acts with which EP and EPl are connected.

---

§ 167. The Ethiopic MS. which contains EP and EPl
(Brit. Mus. Orient. 683), according to Budge, dates from
the first half of the seventeenth century. The Ethiopic
L group to which it belongs are translated from an Arabic
version of a Coptic collection which was made in the second
half of the thirteenth century. The original work may be
securely dated at the time when Mohammed was winning
his first victories in Arabia, for Antichrist comes from the
south (513), as he does in HEvXII, 36. Budge has not
noticed this point. Some of the L Acts are dated by Lipsius
A.D. 400–540 (i. 223 f.).

It is possible that few works could be written which would
throw more new light on problems connected with the origin
of Christianity than a critical edition of the L group. This
paradoxical suggestion is justified not only by the importance
of some of the matter which they enshrine, but also by
the light which they throw on the lost work of Heg. The
work which I desire to see published would not only collect
and discuss the variations between the different recensions
and the history of the group, but would also collect parallels
from all quarters. In its absence the discussions of the
present chapter must be very inadequate.

It will become abundantly clear that EP and EPl, like
the rest of the group, quarry much matter from Heg. My

first point is that they derive indirectly through a source which we will call QEPP. The postulation of this source is demanded by an examination of the Clementine matter in EP. This matter is found in two blocks. That in 483. 27–489. 19 is in its original position and must closely resemble the QC narratives which underlie it. The earlier block (19. 8–20. 20, 23. 5–24. 18) is misplaced and worked into a non-Clementine story which is based on QPl matter and which resembles some other narratives in EPl and EP. Now similar Clementine matter occurs in another recension of the Clementines (M), which varies with EP against R and H by naming Mattidia Mitradora, and which, like EP, cannot derive from HR. Further, EP, 488 and M, 75 vary together in an incident which cannot have occurred either in QC or HR, the miraculous transportation of Faustinianus from Rome to Syria. They derive, therefore, in common form from a lost source. To this source we must attribute the Clementising of the narratives, the conversion of QPl narratives of John and Judas into narratives of Peter and Paul, and the misplacement of a block of matter.

The case for the position that the Peter and Paul of QEPP were John and Judas in Heg's excerpts rests broadly on the position that they play parts which Leucius cannot have assigned to the former and must have assigned to the latter apostles. Unless we assume this identification QEPP, though based on Heg, is both within and without our system of interrelated documents. Apart from this there are several passages which provide definite evidence. (a) In EP, 491 the transportation of John to Antioch, an incident which cannot have occurred in KP, is combined with a KP journey of Peter to Antioch (§ 252 f.), the result being that John's name remains unaltered. (b) We then find "Peter" in Cyprus, a fact which is explained by Ac. xiii. 1, 5. Leucius brought there John the apostle and Judas Thomas Barnabas Matthias. This was at the beginning of a journey which brought John to Hierapolis and Barnabas Thomas to Rome (§ 259). (c) In a passage in which the writer of QEPP was not altering a source but writing freely the mysteries revealed to "Peter" are revealed to John (§ 120). (*d*) The Matthew of LM and the Paul of EPl seem to play the same parts (§ 177 (iv)).

§ 168. We now note the following facts with respect to the use of this lost source (QEPP) in EP and EPl.

1. In QEPP the Peter sections and the Paul sections were intermingled as they are in Acts ix.–xi. A later editor moved the Paul matter into EPl, but did not do his work completely. In EP, 483, he used a narrative of the conversion of S. Paul, which he used again in EPl, 536, and a parallel with the allusion to Saul in Acts ix. 30, survives in EP, 503.

2. Though few contacts survive, the same section of QEPP underlies EP, 6 f., and EPl, 611 f.

3. The "Peter"-"Paul" matter in EPl, 691, originally followed EP, 510.

4. The matter which in Heg followed the seventh pass-over was important and probably occurred in QEPP but it has almost entirely disappeared. [I will note one or two phrases which I have detected. (*a*) The transportation of John and Judas to Antioch, which in QPl followed the seventh passover, is telescoped into a KP journey of Peter which occurred much later, John and Judas becoming Peter and John (491). (*b*) The commission of Peter (John) to go to Antioch with "another apostle" (Judas) was moved from the seventh passover into earlier much-edited QPl sections (470, 479). (*c*) QP matter preceding 524. 9 has dropped out, and an editorial passage which contains Jerusalem matter, and which it is difficult to use (520, 4–524, 8), has been inserted.]

§ 169. In spite of these changes and the fact that QEPP abridged Heg, the analysis which follows shews that EP preserves much of the order of Heg. We learn that in a series of excerpts from the primary apocrypha Heg narrated the evangelisation of Judea and later brought the apostles to Rome. Further, in the analysis the order of the first group (A–H) suggests that Heg broke up his narrative into sections and introduced into each section the matter which referred to it in his various sources. This conjecture is established by the fact that in J and O, Peter twice journeys to the coast and in R and S he arrives twice at Laodicea and that Simon arrives twice at Rome (509, 515).

[Our hypothesis as to the procedure of Heg is confirmed by some evidence which derives from excerpts which narrated the closing events of the Cæsarea narratives. (a) We shall conclude that AThadd, 4, 5, are doublets. (b) The allusion to the destruction of idols and other evidence shews that APh, 86 originally closed a Leucian narrative. 87–91 are from the close of the KP narrative; 92–93 are from the QP narrative of the departure. (c) LJasZ, 33, is based on the KP healing of the "lad" of Theophilus, but the ordination of the servants of the temple at the end (34) is Leucian, and a doublet precedes it.] Lastly, the evidence which shews that Heg harmonised is evidence that he presented together the parallel narratives which he discussed.

§ 170. We will now analyse EP, 466–469.

1. *The Ascension and Pentecost.*

From QP. A, 466–469, 28; E, 474, 3–475, 15; G, 475, 27–477, 6.

From QPl. B, 469, 28–472, 6 (from the narrative of Good Friday much edited); D, 472, 17–474, 3; H, 477, 7–479, 21 (edited).

From KP. C, 472, 6–16 (a fragment).

A harmonisation by Heg. F, 475, 15–26.

2. *The Preaching in Jerusalem and Judea.*

From QPl. J, 479, 21–26 (the city, Joppa, Emmaus, Lydda); L, 479, 30–480, 21 (the vision at Joppa); K, 479, 26–29 (part of a Cæsarea ending: enforces circumcision and the abrogation of the law of meats); M, 480, 21–481, 2 (part of a Cæsarea ending. (?) M continues K).

From QP. O, 481, 12–17 (Peter journeys to the coast);

Y, 510, 8–513, 21 (Peter meets Satan when journeying to Cartagena (Cæsarea)).

3. *The Seventh Passover at Jerusalem.*

Z. Some matter in 518–521, a composite passage.

4. *The Journey to Antioch and Rome.*

From QP. N, 481, 2–4. Peter goes to Tyre and Sidon.

From QC. P, 481, 17–482 (much edited), Peter meets Clement.

From QC. R, 483, 27–490, 20. The journey to Laodicea. 483, 1–26, Q. The conversion of Paul.

From QPl. T, 491, 10–11. The angel sends Peter (John) with John (Judas) to Antioch. 491, 19–503, 23. They are transported thither and imprisoned. Paul worships idols.

V, 495. Peter (John) goes to Cyprus and Rome, Clement (Leucius) to Athens.

From AJ. U, 502, 28–504. Peter (John) goes to (the Asian) Laodicea.

5. *The Later Journeys of Peter.*

From KP or QP S, 483, 27–490, 20. Peter arrives at Laodicea a second time.

T, 491. Peter goes to Antioch.

§ 171. EP and EPl may be compared with two other documents which illustrate Heg's interest in topography and chronology, the two texts of "AJ," 1–17, P and V. They derive from a common source (QPV), the writer of which, like QEPP, edited an historical work which must be Heg. I shall return to the discussion of AJ, 1–17, in the next volume. Here we are concerned with some facts which suggest that QPV was in some way related to QEPP. Like QEPP it abridged Heg, sometimes edited his excerpts and was used by later apocryphists. The question therefore arises whether these two lost works were not different sections of the same abridgement of Heg.

There is positive evidence for the existence of an abridgement. The opening section of Hist. Patr. is based on Heg, and the preface contains an excerpt from KP, which we

used in § 151, which illustrates the subject of Christ's priesthood (123), and which we may assume is from Heg. The
writer then mentions abridgements of certain histories, the
first of which illustrated the points illustrated by our excerpt.
Christ was *perfect in person, pedigree and conduct*. We
then find one of the few explicit allusions to Heg (133).
Josephus is said to have dealt with the subject "in the
Books of the Captivity." Josephus is the alternative form
of the name Hegesippus, and it is applied to Heg in the
following passages:

A. The various citations of Irenæus and Josephus must
derive from a later writer who cited an author who used
Irenæus and Hegesippus. (*a*) Hippolytus did so in his
lost *Syntagma*, and his works were in the library at Jerusalem (HE, VI. xx.). There can be little doubt that this
library had much influence on the late apocrypha. There
are allusions to it in CEncJB, 343; RobEvvC, xxvi. 130;
EvInf, 1 (Lat.); EvN, xxviii. (See also F.) (*b*) The whole
of the matter cited is likely to have derived from Heg.
(*c*) E supports the view that the phrase of RobEvvC, 29, 181,
*the things which Josephus and Irenæus who were of the Hebrews
narrated in their Antiquities* may mistranslate Hypomnemata.
This work contained much archæological matter.

B. EvInf, 1, says that the work derives from *the book
of Joseph who was high priest in the time of Christ. Some
say that he was Caiaphas*. The confusion is due to the fact
that Heg described Caiaphas as Joseph C. (§ 196).

C. Jacobus de Voragine (*Leg. Aur.* lxvii.) cites Josephus
for EvH, 16, adding a detail omitted by Jerome. Cf.
E. B. Nicholson (EvH, 63 f.). Heg cited EvH (HE, IV.
xxii. 8). (See § 92.)

D. Cedrenus cites Josephus for millenarian matter
(Charles' *Secrets of Enoch*, 46). Cedrenus has a parallel
with EP, 17 f. (*JTS*, xv. 241). Presumably like EP he
derived from Heg.

E. The Paris copy of the Epitome of Heg describes it
as an epitome of the Archæology (A) of Josephus.

F. In a passage attributed to Basil of Cæsarea the library
at Jerusalem is said to have contained a copy of the work

of Josephus the compiler (Rev. de l'Or. Chrét. xxiii. (iii.), 158 f.).

G. Orosius, for my knowledge of whom I am indebted to Merill, in vii. 6, 15 cites Josephus for the expulsion of the Jews from Rome in Claudius ix. (A.D. 49–50). I may return to this passage and here only observe that Heg referred to the decree of Claudius *sub* AJ, 2. There are two other contacts of Orosius with Heg. (i) Like Heg (§ 207 f.) he brought Peter to Rome at the beginning of the reign of Claudius (vii. 6, 1). (ii) He described Nero as the first persecutor as did Heg *sub* Bodl. Epit., Melito ap. HE, IV. xxvi., Lact. de M. Pers., 2 f.

H. Jerome adv. Jovin. ii. 14 states that according to Josephus the Essenes abstained from flesh and wine. Josephus does not say so, but Heg is likely to have described them and the allusions to them in Ap. Const. vi. 6 and Epiphanius to derive from him.

We conclude that the writer of Hist. Patr. used an abridgement of Heg and that the fact favours the hypothesis that QEPP and QPV are based on an abridgement, which may be that used in Hist. Patr.

The text of Heg used by Eusebius was corrupt, and it cannot be regarded as certain that he knew the work in its original form. I shall argue that there was a Latin translation or recension of Heg.

§ 172. The following facts seem to indicate that QEPP and QPV derive from the same recension of Heg:

1. In "AJ," 5, P and V vary together in an apocryphal narrative of S. John's arrest against the AJ narrative preserved in a papyrus (J, 264). We may compare the miraculous transportation which QEPP inserted in excerpts in which the writer otherwise followed QC closely (§ 167).

2. While a comparison of V with P shews that P omitted matter which occurred in QPV the two documents read together give the impression that QPV itself abbreviated Heg.

3. V in 14, preserves the statement of QPV which P omits that John was three years in Patmos and confirms

to the chronology of Heg (§ 287). In 17 (P stops before this point), we find one of Heg's topographical notes. A chapel had been built by the men of the village near Miletus, where the apostle landed after his exile. At the season myrrh blooms for the confirmation of the faith. On the other hand, there is much editorial matter in V. We note an important contact with EP. In 5, John wears the tonsure as Peter does in EP, 494. The nearest parallel is the allusion to the building of monasteries in LLk, 152.

4. It is a contact between V and the L Acts that V occurs in a MS. of Ac. Proch., and that Ac. Proch. is found in the latter collection.

5. The Q recension of AJ, 38–54, may be attributed to the same hand or school as V. At 45 we find an important historical splinter in our rubbish. John, at Smyrna, *appointed as president (Bukolus and Polycarp and) Andronicus.* Q, or his source, interpolated a fragment of Heg into a phrase of AJ which he left in its original form. (I shall shew that the allusions to Bukolus and Polycarp in *Vit. Pol.* derive from Heg.) In AJ, 46, a priest is killed and a kinsman tells John. In Q the incident is moved to Smyrna, and "kinsman" becomes "brother." In LJ, 175, the brother comes to John at Ephesus. LJ therefore derived from a document the perversions of which Q perverted still further. Links with the L Acts are links with QEPP.

§ 173. The facts suggest that the monastery in which the L Acts were written contained either two similar recensions of Heg or that QEPP and QPV were different parts of the same abridgement. The latter is by far the more probable, and tallies with the fact that Hist. Patr. derives matter from an abridgement. Apart from the doubtful evidence of EP, 520, 6 f., the contents of EP and EPl suggest that QEPP abridged a large part of Heg. (*a*) In EP, 503, there is an edited reproduction of an excerpt from the AJ visit of John to Laodicea. (*b*) In EPl, 698 f., there are fragments of a tradition of the Lycus valley (§ 175, 24). (*c*) The allusion to Bukolus and Polycarp in V probably occurred in the same book of Heg. (*d*) The ordinations in EP, 509,

derive from the five successions which underlie the first
part of ClemBps and which probably, as their position in
EP indicates, occurred in the Rome section of Heg and at
the end of Bk. II. (e) In the same part of the work Heg
probably narrated his journey to Rome (HE, IV. xxii.)
under Anicetus. This passage probably suggested the
substitution of Anicetus for the Nicetas of QC in QEPP
sub M, 70. (f) LSim, 115 f. and LJas, 140 f., are based
on Hypomn. V.

§ 174. [A few sentences in the very late matter printed
in *Woodbrooke Studies*, III, suggest that EP and EPl have
undergone abbreviation in transmission. While this document in 368 agrees with the serious depravation of QEPP
in EP, 20, it is in several places superior to EP: (a) perhaps
in the allusion to unclean meats (316, EP, 479), (b) in *Aradus*
(370, EP, 483). (c) In 382 Stephen is Paul's nephew. (In
RSteph, 161, he is of the tribe of Benjamin.) EP and EPl
have no apocryphal matter about Stephen. Our late
document, in view of the allusion in RSteph, probably
derives from a passage of Heg, which preceded his account
of the conversion of the apostle used in EPl, 534. (d) 382
probably preserves QEPP in the statement of Paul that he
will preach with Peter and John: EP, 495, omits. In 396
Paul practises idolatry at Rome and the Emperor consults
him (§ 240 L). EP, 495, transfers the incident to Antioch.
It may be added that the story of Akrosya occurs in
Patr. Or. vii. 233.]

§ 175. We will now examine some passages which connect
QEPP with Heg and which illustrate his interest in topography and geography. We will also note some instances
of his influence on the western variants in Acts. These
variants were adapted to their new setting, and two important
illustrations of this adaptation may be mentioned. (a) We
shall attribute to Heg's citations from KP the gloss at x. 41
"we conversed with him forty days." KP had *many*, and
forty is due to Acts i. 3. (b) At xi. 27 the glossator imitated
the "we" sections. A most important argument for the

influence of Heg on the western variants in Acts is the
occurrence of two topographical notes. (*a*) At Acts xii. 12,
Peter escapes down the twelve steps. (*b*) *Sub* the gloss, at
Acts xxi. 16, Heg, when travelling to Cæsarea, had been
shewn Mnason's house.

1. In EP, 6 where the scene in QEPP was Cæsarea, there
is an allusion to the tetrapylon. Cf. *Jew. Enc.*, *s.v.* Cæsarea.

2. In 488 Laodicea is on the Green River.

3. Zion (490) is the old name for the church at Jerusalem.

3*a*. In 492 the apostles when close to Antioch meet wood-
cutters. This must be a splinter. Heg *sub Vit. Pol.* 8, said
that Polycarp, when returning from the suburbs, saw wood-
bearers.

4. In 493 Antioch is twenty days from Jerusalem on
horseback.

5. At Acts xi. 27, a gloss runs: *there was much rejoicing,
and we being assembled . . . Agabus. Rejoicing* is from QC,
as cited by Heg in his Antioch section (R, x. 70; EP, 501).
That Heg referred to Agabus is shewn by EP, 517. *We*
identifies S. Luke with Lucius of Cyrene, and connects
with the evidence which shews that, according to Heg,
S. Luke at this date resided at Antioch (§§ 19, 372). Heg
also identified S. Luke with Leucius, who is named Charinus
by Photius, Carinus *sub* EvN, xvii. and Carius *sub* EvvC, 4.
The names seem to deprave Cyrenius. Possibly the
" we " is due to the fact that they used QP and in QP
Leucius accompanied Barnabas.

6. In 509 Peter appoints Mark, the son of Ariston,
Archbishop of Alexandria, and Evodius, the son of Lendæus,
the Archbishop of Antioch. Both ordinations occurred in
Heg *sub* ClemBps. For the succession at Alexandria compare LMk, 149. For Evodius, who only here is the son
of Lendæus, see §§ 8 (iii), 288.

7. In 518 Clement builds a church in his house, which in
SolokoffAP (Lips. ii. 208) is near the forum. This is not the
site of S. Clemente, but in history there were two Clements.

8. Heg's account of the conversion of S. Paul preserved
in EP, 483, is used in 534. As in the western variant at
Ac. ix. 7 Ananias lays his *hand*.

9. In 535 the street Straight is the market-place, *i.e.* the Bazaar of the Carpenters. I shall shew that Heg went also to Samaria and Paneas.

9*a*. Lake (Beginnings . . . v. 194) infers from Gal. i. and 2 Cor. xi. that S. Paul preached in Nabatæa, that Aretas intended to arrest him at the gate of Damascus and that S. Luke transferred this plot against the apostle to the Jews. EP, 483 confirms this view by the statement that Paul preached to all the Jews and gentiles in the cities and regions round about Damascus. S. Luke's tendency to make the Jews responsible for S. Paul's troubles is illustrated. (Cf. 10.)

10. *Sub* 539 Heg, under the influence of KP, rightly distinguished Bar-Jesus from Elymas (§ 265).

11. In 540 *marvelled and being filled with astonishment* is parallel with the variants at Acts xiii. 13, *marvelled and* (DE) and *cum admiratione stupens* (Gig, Lucif.).

12. In a parallel with Acts xiii. 15 (540), we find *they entered into a church . . . the chief priests sent unto them.* *Chief priests*, like the distinction between Elymas and Bar-Jesus (10), almost certainly derives from KP. In KP the phrase was equivalent to *rulers of the synagogue* or used even more widely. (*a*) Hence it is that KP spoke of priests at Nazareth (§ 144). Compare also (*b*) AknApP, 20, *the place of your high priests.* (*c*) Did. xiii. *give the first fruit to your prophets, for they are your high priests.* There is other evidence for the influence of KP on Did. In QPl *sub* EvN, i. Jairus was a high priest, and conversely, in xiv. the priests were described as "rulers of the synagogue." Irenæus derives from QP or QPl " the daughter of the chief priest" (Jairus) under the influence of a source, probably Heg (V. xiii. 1). There is a parallel with EP in AThadd, 5. Cf. § 315 B.

13. In the Lystran healing (Acts xiv. 8 f.) EPl, 542, and western MSS. vary together. I shall argue that Heg was influenced by KP.

And he thought that they
  would give him alms . . .
In the name of the Lord Jesus   so vl. at xiv. 10.
  Christ. . . .

And straitway he rose up . . .	vl. straitway.
And whilst they were living there teaching	so vl.
Persuaded the people to entreat them cruelly, and they corrupted the hearts of the council to such an extent that they beat and stoned Paul. . . .	vl. stirred up the crowds to stone Paul.
Now when even was come his disciples went to him, and he rose up and came with them into the city.	vl. when the crowd was departed in the evening.

14. Luke the evangelist who wrote Acts (545) is said to have joined Paul at Troas (545). This is probably not editorial but due to Heg.

15. 548–591 is a chaotic cento which contains some matter which in a later chapter will prove to be important. Here I will note some indications of the continued use of Acts by Heg and of his allusions to the QPl visit of Paul to Iconium and to Thecla's lion. (i) Athens, Thessalonica (548), Festus (551), the street Straight (568), Sakentes (Secundus), Felix, Demetrius (586 f.). (ii) The seven priests and the kid (562), the lion (564, 587, 590), Iconium. Pilate (Philetus) and Hermogenes (586).

16. In 548 the apostles go to Halb (Aleppo). In Heg they went to Berœa, which Heg distinguished from the Syrian Berœa (Aleppo) as "in Macedonia" (ClemBps).

17. In 552 Timothy's house is said to have been in a garden, and his mother to have been a prophetess. Evidently her house became, to use a word used both in KP and Heg, the "hospice" of the community. Heg brought Stratæas of Lois to Smyrna (ClemBps, *Vit. Pol.* 2). "Of Lois" tallies with the unexpected allusion to her in 2 Tim. i. 5. EP refers to the death of Eunice.

18. In Acts xix. 8, Paul teaches in the synagogue. In 9, he moves to the school of Tyrannus, where he continued two years, two incidents parallel with xviii. 4, 17. At xix. 9, in a western vl he teaches from the fifth to the tenth hour. In EPl, 567, he arrives at *the tenth hour*, a

phrase which is not in the writer's manner and a splinter.
In 581 we read of the synagogue of Derson, a phrase which
probably corrupts something written by Heg.

19. In 567 Paul stays at the house of Secundus; in 579
at the school of Tyrannus; in 581 in the house of Trophimus.
We recall the fact that Trophimus was an Ephesian (Acts
xxi. 25); but our editor was the last person to put two and
two together. The allusion to Secundus, who was not an
Ephesian, imitates Heg's allusion to the house of Trophimus
who, in Heg's context, was ordained by S. Paul (591: see
21). He was probably the president of the elders addressed
by the apostle at Miletus (Acts xx. 17). The houses of the
earliest leaders of the churches probably often became
hospices. Those of Lois at Lystra, Claudia at Rome
(ClemBps), Mary the mother of Mark at Jerusalem, are
probable instances. Heg's interest in the hospice at Ephesus
explains the agreement of Abdias (v. 20) and Eusebius
(Chron. AD. 98) in the statement that John returned to
Ephesus, where he had his hospice and many friends.
(See 21 and p. 275 *ad inf.*)

20. At Acts xix. 28, a western vl adds: *they ran into
the side street* . . . (and seized Gaius and Aristarchus).
EPl, 568, is much edited but preserves Heg more fully: *a
certain man* . . . *said, I have seen the man in the house of
Sakentes; he belongeth unto the men of Iconium* (whence Paul
and his companions had journeyed in QPl) *who dwell in
the street* . . . *and they ran and seized.* An Ephesian who
knew that Paul lived in the house of Trophimus led
the mob down a side street and found only the apostle's
friends.

21. *Sub* 591, *I have fought with beasts at Ephesus* was
cited by Heg from 1 Cor. xv. 32, to illustrate an incident
which in his Ephesus section he cited from the Ephesus
section of QPl, and which will be discussed in § 269. It
underlies 587 (cf. 573). In the preceding context we find
splinters from our Heg matter, *who lives in the house of
Trophimus* (585), *went and searched and found him in the
street* (586), and the ordination of Trophimus.

22. *Sub* 595, our scribe learnt from Heg, who gave both

ancient and contemporary names to his cities (cf. Berœa,
Aleppo) that Accho was the Ptolemais of Acts.

23. In 595, Julius is the governor of the soldiers at
Sebastya. Heg so interpreted *Augustan band* (Acts xxvii. 1),
because in his time Cæsarea was sometimes called Sebaste.

24. In 698 f. there are parallels with the Khonai (Colossæ)
legend (Ramsay, *Ch. and R. Emp.* 469). It was based on
Heg.

I have omitted several allusions to Cæsarea, which will
be discussed in the next volume.

§ 176. [We will now examine a tangle which, owing to
centoising and other perversions, cannot be explained in
detail without a longer discussion than the matter deserves.
Its essential elements are as follows. (i) In QPl an apostle
met a demon in a desert near Hierapolis who made a speech
(320 A). (ii) LeuciusP moved the incident to the desert
through which Peter passed on his way to Azotus (Acts
viii. 26) when he was establishing the work of Philip, who
had journeyed to that city and thence to Cæsarea (Acts
viii. 40). (iii) Among the many corruptions of some texts
of Heg was the substitution at this point of Cartagena for
Cæsarea (ΚΑΡΤΑΓΗΝΑ ΚΑΓ-ΑΓΕΙΑ ΚΑΙΣΑΡΕΙΑ), a
corruption which accounts for the Spanish journey of James.
(iv) In this context of Heg, QEPP, presumably owing to some
textual defacement, substituted Philippi for *the city to
which Philip had gone*, and knowing that Philippi was in
the west, the editor moved a section of Heg into the Roman
section of his work.

The encounter with the demon and the movements of
Peter and Philip are of much interest.

A. In AT, 30 f., Thomas meets a black serpent
which foretells the activities of Antichrist in terms which
shew that in the underlying passage of QPl Leucius was
influenced by the mythology of the Lycus valley (§ 321).
The serpent is bidden suck the poison from a young man
whom it has killed, and then bursts. The incident is better
preserved in LBart, 73 f.

B. The setting of QPl *sub* A survives in APh, 102 f., a

QPl context where Philip, journeying through the desert to Hierapolis, meets a dragon. He engulfs it in its own fire and seals the hole. The sign of the cross is made.

C. The same setting and the use of the cross occur in the encounter with the dragon in QVitA, 578.

D. We shall conclude in § 302*b* that pseudoMark preserved a fuller account of the journeyings of Peter and Philip, which are narrated in Acts viii. ix., than did S. Luke. Here we are concerned with the fact that in QP our QPl incident was transferred from Asia to the journey which Peter made *to all cities and Azotus*. There are two other traces of this journey. (*a*) In Hist. Patr. 137, Mark (who we shall find in KP accompanies Peter to Cæsarea) is at Azotus, and the passage is shewn to derive from Heg by a topographical notice. (*b*) The editor of EP could not decipher the word Aradus: in 22 he substitutes Cyprus; in 485 he makes Peter go to Azotus. In a Greek fragment printed in Lips. ii. 233, Peter when making this journey to Azotus meets the dragon, which is in the form of an archangel and makes the speech which it made in QPl *sub* A. This combination of the KP journey with matter from QPl must be attributed to LeuciusP.

E. In EP, 510, Peter goes to Kartagon (Cæsarea), *the city whereinto Philip had gone*, and Satan appears. Peter blew in his face (an incident which is shewn to derive from QPl by EvT, xvi. 2 where Jesus breathes on the serpent which had killed James and which like the serpent of A bursts). Satan flies. As he flies he describes his eschatological activities (cf. BC). He says that death will be cast into Tartarus, that is, Sheol (cf. B). At the end of the speech Peter makes the sign of the cross (BC). Satan then flies again, designating Christ as he flies *the strength of Adonya* (cf. F). The doublet is due to the fact that the speech is editorial and substituted for that of D. The source is repeated at the point where it was left. The speech is interesting, for it is taken from the KP apocalyptic, which underlies Asc.Is. iii. 21, iv. The clergy will be covetous and corrupt. Antichrist will destroy believers by land and sea (§ 153). Like the writer of HEvXII, 32, 36, the author

P

predicts the Nestorian heresy and, identifying Mohammed with Antichrist, makes him come from the south.

F. In SHPh, 69, Christ appears by night in a vision (EP, 491) and sends the apostle to *Carthage which is in Azotus*. In 73 Ananias believes in *the Messiah thy God that He is El Shaddai, Adonai, the Lord of Sabaoth, the strong* (E, CBRB, 1963, *Thou art the strength*, 196, *Sabaoth . . . Eloi*). In 76 Philip encounters a demon, the description of whom is composite, but whose speech is influenced by QP *sub* E. He says, *Whither shall I go from this Mighty (One) . . . from this Strong (One)?* In EP, 513, Satan, as he flies, says, *O Son of the Virgin, Thou Son of the Father, Thou Word of light, Thou Strength of Adonya* (E) *. . . whenever Thou didst wish, Thou didst reveal Thy power unto me*.

§ 177. Lips. (D) and F derive independently of QEPP from Heg. The derivation of E and several other passages from a misplaced context of QEPP appears as follows:

(i) In EP, 509, Peter is at Rome in a narrative which derives from QPl (§ 236), Timothy and Simon arriving later. He ordains, stays a period in Rome, and then goes where Philip had gone, Kartagon. He then encounters Satan (E). Peter and Paul then go to Philippi. Timothy was there and Simon followed. Paul then goes to Warikon. The narrative of QEPP which followed is the only Clementised passage in EPl, and is placed in 691, where Paul (Judas) has been at Warikon and finds "me Peter" (John) at Kartagna. Peter prays that he may go to Warikon. In 700 the two angels who used to appear to him transport him (§ 105).

(ii) Our misplaced section of QEPP is used in the Acts of Paul and Philip (EPl, 611 f.), who are shewn by a slip of the pen in 656 to be Peter and Paul. There is a trace of Philippi in 613, where the apostles worship on the river-bank (Acts xvi. 13).

(iii) In LPP, 182, as in EP, 510, Peter and Paul after meeting at Rome stay for a period and then, as in EP, 513, go to Philippi. EP, 509, explains the description of the empire of the King of India.

LPP, 182. I ruled over . . .
Greece, *Nubia*, Egypt,
Syria, Iraq . . . Berbers.

EP, 509. Evodius of Antioch . . .
Mark of Alexandria, Thomas
to India, Philip to *Nubia* and
Mesopotamia, Thaddæus over
Edessa, John over Ephesus.

(iv) It is probable that LM, an Acts separated from the other L Acts by its literary excellence, originally began at 101. 31 and with Matthew's objection to his lot and his transportation to the east (El Berber = Bartos = Parthos: Lewis xix.) and that the editor of the L collection and EPl used the same section of QEPP in the introduction and in EPl, 691 f. In EPl, 700 like Matthew Paul journeys to the east and in 691 (the MS. is in disorder) tells Peter his experiences on his return, as also does Matthew in LM. Peter goes east in both works, and in both the editor shews his uncertainty as to the historicity of QEPP. In LM the apostle goes to Rome from the east, and in EPl, 700 Paul thinks that he is going to Rome. The editor may be influenced by LM in EPl, 661. The Armis of LM is Artemis.

Inasmuch as in a section of MPP Peter and Paul were originally John and Judas (§ 185 f.) that section must derive from QEPP.

§ 178. We shall conclude in § 268 f. that matter in EPl derives from a section of QEPP which narrated the QPl journey of Paul from Antioch to Ephesus.

The stories of Akrosya (6 f.), the meal provided for the apostles at Cæsarea (*twenty sucking lambs, thirty chickens*, etc.) (620) and the story of the harlot (629), are not in the manner of the writer or writers of the L Acts and may be due to a second reviser.]

CHAPTER VI

The Chronology of the First Septennium

This chapter is of special importance for the study of the Acta, for it deals with some fundamental changes in the structure of the KP tradition. Among its data are the three clues with which the writer began his decipherment of that tradition, (a) the evidence which proves the ordination of Theophilus at Cæsarea, (b) the QC list of ordinands in which he detected an historical nucleus and (c) the probability that the ordination of the Jewish evangelists of Cæsarea was an Ebionite perversion of the ordination of the converts Theophilus and Cornelius, whom we shall learn to detect beneath their various disguises. Later he found a verification of some of his critical positions in chronological notices which he attributes to Heg, and which will be discussed in this volume. In this chapter two discussions will be of special interest, that on the date of the Crucifixion and the connected subject of some traditions of the political career of Theophilus whom psMark identified with Pilate's successor Marcellus.

---

§ 179. By a great stroke of good fortune R has preserved the incident which, more than any other, is crucial for the explanation of the fundamental perversions of the history of the apostles, Saul's attack on James at the seventh passover (R. i. 43, 69 f.). The passage obviously derives from J, and a comparison of R with the QDesp martyrdom (Heg, ap. HE, II. xxiii.) shews that in J Saul killed James. Inasmuch as James was the hero of the work it follows that the main narrative ended at this passover. It will be shewn, however, that there was an epilogue. If James ousted Peter from the leadership at Jerusalem, his brother Judas supplanted the apostle as the founder of the church of Cæsarea at the close of the seventh year, and Saul having killed the one saint pursued the other to Antioch, the history of which church it was necessary for J to rewrite, and also to Rome where Judas won the martyr's crown which, in KP and in history, were Peter's.

§ 180. Leucius controverted the Christology of Cerinthus and professed to revere S. Paul; but he had probably been an unorthodox Jew, and took no interest in the apostle's polemic against the Judaisers. Though we cannot define his position, he broadly accepted the Ebionite narrative of the first seven years. The point on which it was his main purpose to insist was the lawfulness of the Nicolaitan position and of the verbal denial of the faith in times of persecution. Here he was in agreement with J and Cerinthus and also, so he held, with S. Paul, who in KP probably took no part in the proceedings of the apostolic council. Both as a Docetist and as a Nicolaitan, Leucius depreciated the twelve and the Marco-Petrine tradition. He perverted the apostolic history as follows:

1. In QPl, as in J, the seventh passover was of cardinal importance. James was murdered, though not by Saul who, at this point, appeared upon the scene and, with Christ's approval, said that the gentiles should be taught a less rigorous discipline than that enjoined by the twelve (§ 227).

2. This teaching was given on a journey which developed the J journey of Judas to Antioch and Rome.

3. The narrative of the council just mentioned telescoped the gatherings narrated in Acts xi. and xv. Judas, who in KP and J was the Judas Barsabas who went to Antioch (Acts xv. 22), became in QPl Judas Barnabas (cf. Acts xi. 22). John (Mark), who in KP accompanied Peter in Judæa and Barnabas in Cyprus, became John the apostle. The result was that John accompanied by Judas made two journeys, the first that which culminated at Cæsarea, the second to Antioch, Cyprus, Iconium, Asia and Rome. Paul, after converting Thecla, met them at Iconium, arriving later at Rome. Peter and Simon Magus followed. Apostolic history was bisected at the seventh passover and its council, and this bisection influenced Valentinus, who said that the

apostles taught before they had perfect knowledge (Iren.
I. iii. 2; III. Praef.), and also QC, in which work there were
two septennia.   At the close of the first the Clementine
Peter sent his preaching to James from Cæsarea; at the close
of the second from Rome.

4. In KP Cornelius was a subordinate figure, and was
probably a young legionary centurion who had just begun
his official career in this capacity.   The most important
convert made by Peter was his father Theophilus, who was
identified with Pilate's successor, Marcellus.   The procurator
was recalled by Gaius not long after his conversion, and
Cornelius returned to Rome with him.   The writer of QPl
observed that the J journey of Judas synchronised with the
KP journey of Cornelius, made the latter the companion
of the former.   Identifying him with the author of the
canonical Acts and with S. Paul's disciple, he named him
Leucius Cornelius Dionysius.   The distinguished young
Roman became the counterpart of the Mark of KP and of
the Ananias of J.

5. The author of the primary Acts called it the Preaching
of Peter.   The elder, imitating him, called his work the
Preaching of Paul, because S. Paul's preaching was the
climax.   There are, however, serious gaps in the evidence.
The elder reported much preaching of James, but hardly
any remains; and only one or two fragments preserve the
Nicolaitanism of the Leucian Paul.

JAMES THE LORD'S BROTHER

§ 181. Replying to QPl LeuciusP reaffirmed the Marco-
Petrine tradition and the authority of the twelve.   If
James was not killed in QP at the passover, it was partly
because he survived in KP and partly because Leucius had
identified him with the brother of John.

QP matter about James underlies the following passages:

[A. In LJas, 140, the apostles assemble on Olivet, and
when Christ appears say that the Jews seek to kill them
when they preach the Resurrection, a statement which

confirms our view of the date, for it probably refers to
Stephen (cf. *Da*). There follows a compromise with the
J-QPl tradition. The apostles place James on the throne
to which Christ had appointed him. "Throne" and an
allusion to the grave of James (HE, II. xxiii. 18) are from
Heg, whom the writer uses later, his narrative being clearly
independent of Eusebius.

B. The opening narrative of Proch will be shewn to
preserve in an abbreviated form (which omits the allusions
to Christ which certainly occurred in QP and probably in
AJ) the beginning of the latter Acts. The apostles are in
the same place as in LJas, for they meet in Gethsemane,
as they did in the KP tradition of the Ascension (cf. EP, 467).
In 4, 4, there is an allusion to the death of Mary, which
confirms our attribution to AJ, for the QP *Dormitio* underlies AJ, 72 f. (§ 122).]

The following passages shew that LeuciusJ used, and Heg
cited, the same passage of QP:

Proch 3, 5. Peter reminds the apostles that Christ commanded them to go into all " the inhabited earth ".	In LJas, 140, Christ bids them preach in the " inhabited earth ", the word used by Christ in KP, fragm. 6, to which saying there is a probable allusion.
4, 11 f. Peter reminds the apostles that Christ foretold persecution.	In LPh, 60, LT, 80, and LJas. 140, Christ foretells persecution.

The QP narrative of the lots follows. Here we are
concerned with the fact that while James is prominent in 5.7
and 6.13 (cf. EP, 475), it is he who says that Peter takes
thought for them all. The J tradition has been Petrinised.
Our passages derive from QP.

C. Heg ap. HE, II. xxiii. 4, was presumably influenced
by QP (cf. A), when he says that James succeeded Christ
(Lawlor, 15) with the other apostles.

D. The following reconstruction illustrates (i) the QP
co-ordination of Peter with James (A); (ii) the influence of
Heg on APh; (iii) the connection of the evangelisation of
Judea with the martyrdom of Stephen; (iv) Eusebius's
use of Heg without acknowledgement.

(a) APh, *Epit*. 91. After the slaying *of Stephen* and the *plots of the Jews against the . . . disciples, the rest* being all sent to the preaching, Philip received Asia from *James* the Lord's brother *and Peter*.

APh, 15. *Driven out* of Judea *they go about the world*.

HE, III. v. *The Jews* after the Ascension devised . . . *plots against His apostles. . . . Stephen was slain. . . . The rest* . . . who had been incessantly *plotted* against and *driven out . . . went unto all the nations*.

(b) APl (J, 286).   Persecuted out of Judea.

(c) According to Symeon Metaphrastes (Migne, CXIV, 123) the apostles dispersed after the death of Stephen.

(d) See also § 337 B.

§ 182. We will now examine the apocryphal evidence as to the death of James.

A. In R. i. 43–72, R derives directly from QHR, which Acts probably depraved the narrative of QC very little. The composite character of this section is illustrated by the fact that the apostles receive three invitations to discussions with the priests in the temple (43, 44, 55), and that there are three Christian protagonists, Thomas (61), Peter (62), and James (69).

To J we may securely attribute the statement of 69 f. that the preaching of James was so successful that but for Saul, Caiaphas and the people would have been baptized. In 70, Saul leads a riot, in which James is thrown headlong down the steps, and leaves him, as he supposes, dead. The disciples spend the night praying (Acts xii. 12) in the house of James, a phrase which is the J equivalent for "the church of the brethren" (44). The disciples, 5000 in number, fly to Jericho. They hear that Caiaphas had commanded Saul to go to Damascus with letters (Acts ix. 2), employing the help of unbelievers to make havoc of the faithful (Acts viii. 3). Saul hastens to Damascus, supposing that Peter (Judas) had fled thither. At this point the use of J stops and that of QP begins. James sends Peter to Cæsarea. The fact that in 69 Saul fails to kill James is probably due to the fact that it suited psClement's scheme to follow QP rather than J, in which work James was killed, as is shewn by the evidence of the passages now to be cited, and is confirmed by R's statement that Saul supposed that James was dead. B and C derive independently from QPl.

B. QDesp *sub* Heg (HE, II. xxiii.) is shewn to derive from J by a comparison with R. In each passage James wins converts from the seven sects and receives a good hearing from the people. In each his subject is Jesus. If in QDesp the phrase *the door of Jesus* refers to baptism there is a parallel in R. i. 69. In each work James is thrown from the raised place on which he speaks. In B as in A and C, he is struck, and as in C is killed by the blow. As in A the event is dated at the passover. QDesp as elsewhere derived from QPl.

C. There are two passages which preserve QPl in a form which is independent of QDesp. (*a*) In LJas, 145, the editor interpolates into the QDesp narrative an incident which he must have found in Heg: *All the scribes and the Pharisees desired that James should say . . . that Jesus was the son of Joseph and he himself his brother. And they commanded a herald to order the crowd to be silent. And they all cried, It is our duty to listen and not to oppose.* That this is from QPl is shewn by the parallels in R. i. 55, 65 and EvN (§ 131). (*b*) In STrans, 17, Antonius, the deacon of James, writes: *about the Jew who was a captain. And he struck James the bishop, and he died, because the Jews hated James greatly on account of his being the Lord's brother.* That this passage derives from QPl is shewn both by the allusion to Antonius and also by the fact that the captain of the temple is substituted for the Saul of J *sub* R, but has not become the fuller of QDesp *sub* HE, II. xxiii. 19.

THE CÆSAREA ORDINATIONS

§ 183. The seventh passover in KP, QPl and QP followed the conclusions of narratives of visits of apostles to Cæsarea. These conclusions, in epitomised or conventionalised forms, are frequent in the apocrypha and may be called "Cæsarea endings." They usually include allusions to ordinations.

Interesting instances are R. iii. 65–74 and the gloss at
Acts xi. 1. The Cæsarea ordinations are of two types.

1. The first type preserves the tradition of KP. This
survives in ClemBps, where we find the ordinations of
Cornelius and Theophilus, in LSim, 116 f., where Marcellus
(Theophilus) is ordained and, probably, in 1 Clem, 42,
where the apostles are said to have ordained their first-
fruits and KP influences the context (§ 194). (See also
§ 226 B.)

The evidence, which derives from QPl, is best explained
by the hypothesis that Leucius, having accepted as we are
about to conclude, the J tradition of the ordination of elders,
combined KP with J by giving Theophilus seven sons
and making them deacons. He intended to identify
Cornelius with Dionysius the Areopagite and therefore
made them the servants of the temple of Mars (EP, 503).
(A) In LT, 92, the six sons of the old man (Theophilus)
are ordained. One is probably omitted because the
editor names the "magistrate" Lucius. (B) In EPl, 655,
a QPl ending is conventionalised. Theodore (Leucius)
becomes a bishop and the seven priests of the temple become
priests and deacons. In PassT (Lips. i. 251) Judas ordains
Dionysius. (C) In VP, 5, Theon (Leucius) is ordained
a deacon. Theon (Theodore = § 226A) derives from QPl.
(D) The temple was mentioned in QP *sub* R. iv. 6, and
if we assume that in QP as in QPl the seven sons were
ordained deacons we account for the ordination of four
deacons in R. iii. 66. psClement subtracted the three sons
of Theophilus who journeyed to Rome. (E) In LJasZ, 34,
the servants of the temple are ordained. This reconstruction
is confirmed in § 305.

§ 184. 2. (i) J rewrote the history of the church of Cæsarea,
attributing to Judas the foundation of the church and the
ordination of twelve Jews whom James had sent with him
from Jerusalem. Hence in QC there were sixteen companions, the twelve elders of J, and the four deacons
suggested by QP. That the QC companions were also
ordained is shewn not only by the fact that they were
sixteen in number but also by the fact that in R. iii. 66, the

twelve companions "stand round" Peter (as a corona of
elders: Ap. Const. ii. 28; Ign. Magn. 13; Philad. 5; Rev.
iv. 4) and four accompany him (as deacons accompanied
bishops). In EP, 517 Thomas, who is a companion in
R. ii. 1, is an elder. It is clear, then, that in J Zacchæus was
the president of a presbytery of twelve members.

(ii) JerBps consists of three desposyni, Zacchæus and
eleven other Jews and gentiles. The first group derives
from Heg, whose episcopal lists suggested his task to the
compiler. It is obvious to conjecture that the second group
is the QPl elaboration of the tradition of J. That this is
the case appears as follows:

(*a*) When we reconstruct the Cæsarea section of KP we
shall find that seven of the names are connected with it.
It would appear, then, that the group is influenced both by
J and KP. (I had only named the Presidents.)

(*b*) The list presents the character of QPl lists. Like
those in EvN, i. ii. it quarries from KP, adds tribal names,
and, just as EvN uses the name Agrippa, so JerBps includes
the even more absurd Jew Seneca, a name which elsewhere
is only used of the statesman and his father.

(*c*) According to LagardeDAdd, 93, the sons of the
priests became companions of the apostles and after their
deaths rulers of churches. Their names are those of
JerBps, 11–15. The history of this passage is as follows.
The writer read in Heg *sub* DAdd, 27: *the children of the
crucifiers have become . . . evangelists with the apostles . . .
in all the land of Palestine and Philistia.* He also read an
extract from our section of QPl and chose the last five
names of the QPl companions as the sons of the priests.

We conclude that in QPl and QC Zacchæus was the
president of twelve elders who were ordained in Judæa.
Now there is no tradition of any ordination in Judæa other
than those at Cæsarea. It follows that QC and QPl derive
from a common source which perverted the tradition of the
ordination of Theophilus and Cornelius and which can only
be the Ebionite source J, one of the motives of which Acts
must have been the rewriting of the history of the early
years of the churches of Cæsarea and Antioch.

§ 185. 3. We shall conclude below that Leucius combined J with KP by moving back the ordination of Zacchæus to the end of the first year and leaving the ordination of Cornelius *in situ*, and that LeuciusP combined the Cæsarea narrative of KP with that of QP1 by making Peter visit Cæsarea at the end of the eighth year. This implies that he recorded in that year the ordination of Theophilus whose ordination was the climax of KP and had been omitted in QP1.

The QP narrative survives in three Acta. (*a*) The ordinands of QC were much influenced by J, but the narrative of the ordination retained much of the narrative of QP unaltered. Much of Peter's sermon and prayer survive in H. iii. 60 f. and EpClem (R. iii. 66 f.). In R. iv. 1 he is set on his way by his sorrowful converts, an incident which is certainly Leucian and which occurs also in APh, 93; AT, 68; VP, 2 f.; and EPl, 656. (*b*) The first two of these passages also preserve the QP ordination. In APh, 91 the apostle prays and a splinter of his sermon survives in the exhortation to subjection (H. iii. 66). (*c*) In AT, 67 the apostle prays and as in APh says *the peace of the Lord be with you*. In neither Acts is the incident conventionalised. There is for instance no allusion to the ordination of deacons. Only Ireos and Xenophon are ordained, and from APh, 47 Ireos has played the part of Theophilus. It is clear that psClement using J substituted the ordination of Zacchæus and his co-presbyters for the QP ordination of Theophilus and used also the QP1-QP ordination of seven deacons.

§ 185*a*. Heg treated this matter as follows:

(i) *Sub* ClemBps he gave the ordinations as *Zacchæus, Cornelius, Theophilus*. This notice presents three difficulties. (*a*) It combines a tradition that one of the evangelists who visited Cæsarea became its presiding elder with a tradition that the two most important converts were ordained. (*b*) It places the name of Cornelius before that of his more important father. (*c*) Heg held that Christ appointed James bishop of Jerusalem and that Symeon and Judas were apostles. There are ordinations of twenty-six other bishops, and in all except those at Cæsarea the ordaining apostle or *apostolicus* is given. Our reconstruction solves the three problems. (i) Leucius combined the ordination of Cornelius with that of Zacchæus. (ii) LeuciusP postponed that of Theophilus. (iii) In KP Peter ordained Cornelius and in QC Zacchæus. In QP both were ordained by Judas. Heg left the problem unsolved.

(ii) The compiler of JerBps (*a*) used Heg for his first three bishops (§ 284 f.); (*b*) used Heg *sub* LagardeDAdd for the next twelve, converting the rulers of churches into rulers of the church of Jerusalem; (*c*) derived from Heg a correct identification of Zacchæus with Zacharias (Epiph. *Haer.* lxvi. 20) and Joseph with Joses (Epiph. *Eus. Chron.*).

(iii) The phrase of HE, IV. v., *the record runs* shews that Eusebius is deriving from a document which he found at Jerusalem. It contained not only the two identifications just mentioned, but also two other notes. (*a*) We shall find that Heg was very punctilious in all matters relating to chronology, and it would be entirely in his manner to say that the twelve companion-elders who became rulers of churches did not long survive the apostles. This remark became the statement of HE, IV. v. that they were short-lived. (*b*) It is clear that Heg *sub* LagardeDAdd discussed the subject of persecution and condemned the views of Leucius (§ 253). He also said something which became in that fragment a statement that they endured bonds and in HE an allusion to their sincerity. Our examination of ClemBps will shew that Heg's lists were accompanied by discussions and notes.

(iv) A splinter of Heg's discussion of the Cæsarea ordinations survives in PassT (Lips. i. 251) where the ordination of Dionysius by Thomas is preceded by a statement that the seat of the apostle and the catholic faith remain in the city until this day. Heg appealed to the evidence of the thrones of the apostles *sub* Tert. de Praescr. 36. He mentioned that of Peter *sub* R. x. 71 and that of James *sub* HE, VII. xix. and LJas, 141.

The Chronology of the First Septennium

§ 186. Our conclusion that Leucius used the ordinations both of KP and J affects our determination of the chronology of the first septennium, for the QPl endings of the seventh year shew no trace of the ordination of the twelve elders, and this negative fact tallies with the evidence of EP, 479 f. After QPl Olivet matter Peter (John) goes to Joppa. There follows a fragment of a Cæsarea ending. [The apostle enforces the law of Moses as he does in two Cæsarea endings (AThadd, 4; EPl, 656), but he prohibits the prohibition of meats (in the Woodbrooke recension (316) the meats themselves). The Joppa vision follows, and then a Cæsarea ending, in which "Peter" teaches the faith written in the first of the eight books. Presumably the writer of QEPP moved Cæsarea matter to Joppa, when he inserted this editorial allusion to the eight books.] EP proves that there was a QPl "ending" at the end of the first year. At this point, then, we place the ordination of the twelve QPl elders.

This first year was followed by a period of four years which we are about to discuss (§ 189 f.). The length of the fourth and closing period of the septennium can be approximately determined. In KP Simon opposed Peter after he had been a week at Cæsarea, and the next incident was the ordination, which was followed by a period of three months (R. iii. 65; EPl, 656). The apostle then went up for the passover preaching in towns and villages (gloss at Acts xi. 1; LJasZ, 33; APh, 93). The period, therefore, gives the impression of lasting about four months. This leaves for the third residuary period twenty months. During this period Judas went to the east, and at the close John was transported thither and saw the second QPl apocalypse.

§ 187. If in QPl there was a J Cæsarea narrative of the first year, Theophilus and Cornelius must have come to Palestine about the date of the close of Christ's ministry. This chronology enabled the author of QPl to represent his Leucius Cornelius as one of the Greeks who would see

Jesus (J. xii. 20). This perversion underlies the following passages:

A. In EvvC, 5, Theophilus is an official in Palestine before the Passion.

B. In EusThadd, Abgar has heard of Christ's miracles and invites him to heal his disorder. Christ promises to send an apostle. Judas sends Thaddæus. Clearly in QPl Judas went himself. The whole narrative is Caesarean.

C. In QC sub M, 76, Faustinianus has heard the report (R. i. 6: of Christ's miracles in the spring).

D. In ATit Rustilius, the proconsul of Crete, sends Titus to Jerusalem before the Passion.

The derivation of this perversion from J is shewn by H. xx. 13, where Christ is said to have healed Cornelius at Cæsarea. This incident suggested to Leucius that he should make Christ journey to Cæsarea with Judas (§ 297). Heg's citations of J and QPl are combined in EusThadd, 6, 10 where Christ is invited but says that He will send Judas. J sub Heg also influences EP, 503.

§ 188. Our reconstruction is verified by two traces of its influence on the chronology of Heg.

(i) In AT, 18, Thomas promises to build Gundaphor a pretorium which would resemble that at Cæsarea as it was described by Heg. Its gate, like the tetrapylon at Cæsarea, would be on the east side of the city. The windows would catch the (sea) breezes from the west. The bakehouse would be on the south. An aqueduct (traces of which still exist) would bring the water from the north (from Carmel). The work would begin in November and finish in April. The pretorium turned out to be a spiritual one. April was the right month for its completion. November is a blunder for December.

(ii) In EP, 514, Paul (Judas) leaves Peter (John) at Kartagena (Cæsarea), goes to Warikon (the Warkan of AT, 111), and is there one year and eight months (John being transported thither on his return: EPl, 691, 700 f.). Clearly Heg calculated the periods as we have done. The calculation is certainly not editorial.

MARCELLUS

§ 189. The two last sections have shewn that Theophilus was the principal convert at Cæsarea, and the whole evidence goes to shew that in KP he lived in the pretorium and was the procurator (cf. *e.g.* §§ 220 DE, 221 F). Now in QP *sub* R. i. 44 the apostles returned from a missionary journey for the observance of the seventh passover and reported what they had done to a gathering of the church. KP therefore dated its parallel with Ac. xi. at that passover. If the crucifixion was in A.D. 29 or 30 this was about the date of the dismissal of Pilate and his supersession by Marcellus. It cannot therefore be a mere coincidence that a Cæsarea ending in LSim records the ordination of Marcellus and that in VP, an Acts which moves much Judæan matter to Rome, Marcellus is the principal convert and plays a part similar to that of Theophilus in a house which like the pretorium at Cæsarea is described, the same features being noted (§ 222 B). Our identification also tallies with the fact that S. Luke gives Theophilus the style which he gave to Festus and leaves the impression that he wrote for an imperial official.

Here we are concerned with the fact that it is possible to collect from the apocrypha a little heap of splinters which read in isolation are either of no significance or difficult to decipher but which explain each other and read together produce an account of the political career of Theophilus which shews that he was Marcellus. This evidence makes a very important contact with the chronology of Heg, and for this reason we will now deal with it.

(i) According to QPl when Theophilus returned to Cæsarea his wife refused his bed. In his rage he murdered one of his sons and then attempted the lives of the two apostles (§ 241). This story may not seem to be a very promising starting-point for an enquiry which concerns not only NT scholars but also writers of Roman and Jewish history, but such we deem it. The point is that Leucius (§ 191 D) and Kewestos (§ 191 D) is said to have been absent four years and Kewestos (E) three. The discrepancy may be due to a statement of Heg that Theophilus lived at Rome for three years. Such a statement would probably have been accurate, and it would have been in the manner of Heg. We now notice two interesting cohesions.

The period of four years which preceded this encratic incident was transferred by Leucius or by J from the KP narrative of the recall of Theophilus by Gaius on his accession and his return about four years later on the accession of Claudius. It must be observed that it is not based on Heg's calculation of the length of the reign of Gaius, for Leucius had transferred it to the reign of Tiberius. The period, therefore, is due to KP, and the accuracy of the chronology of that work is evidence for the historicity of the narrative. This transference led Leucius to omit the names of Gaius and Claudius with the result that in § 191 D and E the emperor who promoted Theophilus is the emperor who dismissed him.

(ii) LeuciusP converted the QPl journey of Judas to Rome into a journey of Peter, but the evidence shews that apart from this he made large use of KP in the period which followed the seventh passover. He used the KP narratives of the Herodian persecution and of Peter's journeys to Laodicea and Antioch (§§ 206, 252). In particular he correctly dated the troubles which led to the recall of Marcellus, for he made Peter find Philo at Rome (§ 192 J). Further, the QC journey was based on QP, and the journey of Faustinianus was based on the return journey of Marcellus (§ 191 AB). We expect then Peter to meet Faustinianus in the twelfth year. Our reconstruction therefore is established by the fact that they meet at Laodicea in R. viii. 1 and that in QC Peter spent the twelfth year in that city (§ 206). Leucius and LeuciusP made independent use of the same tradition.

§ 190. We know from Jos. *Ant.* VIII. iv., a passage which Heg used when dating the Crucifixion, that at the very end of the reign of Tiberius Vitellius the proconsul of Syria dismissed Pilate and appointed his friend Marcellus to succeed him; and we may safely conjecture that the appointment was in accordance with his policy of favouring

Q

the Jews. Gaius, not long after his accession, dismissed
Marcellus, and later attempted to enforce Cæsar worship
on the Jews. The result was rioting. An altar erected at
Jamnia by a *publicanus* named Capito was pulled down.
At Alexandria a leading opponent of the Jews was named
Apion. Philo, who was the brother of the olobarch Lysimachus and the uncle of the procurator Alexander Tiberius,
was a member of a deputation which was sent to Rome
to dissuade Gaius. Petronius, the proconsul of Syria, did
his best for the Jews; but war was about to break out when
Gaius opportunely died. Claudius reversed his policy. All
these names except the last occur in apocrypha. That of
Petronius was assigned by Leucius to the centurion of the
sepulchre. PsMark in accordance with his plan of stating
the relations of Christianity with the empire, narrated the
part which Marcellus played in these events. For the
Jamnia statue see § 222 B (*b*).

§ 191. According to psMark Marcellus, whom he identified
with Theophilus, was accused of spending imperial moneys
on the poor. He had a brother at Rome who told him
that if he refunded them the malversation would be pardoned.
Claudius, on his accession, consulted the pro-Jewish ex-
procurator, who advised him to reverse the policy of Gaius
and was then or later made a senator. Marcellus was sent
to the east with his son Cornelius, who was a legionary or
a *frumentarius* (bearer of despatches). They landed at
Seleucia, reported the welcome news at Antioch, and later
received at Cæsarea the welcome they deserved. QPl dated
the departure and return under Tiberius and spoke only
of one Emperor. We shall find that there are grounds for
identifying the stratopedarch mentioned in the gloss at
Acts xxviii. 16, with Theophilus.

The following passages derive from QP:

A. In QC Faustinianus (Theophilus) had a brother at
Rome (M, 67; R. vii. 15: EFG). In H. xiv. 7, he is said to
have landed at Seleucia, the port for Antioch (C). The
journey of Clement to Rome is the QP journey of Cornelius
to Rome, and the eastward journey of Faustinianus the
return of Theophilus.

B. In R. x. 55, Cornelius is at Antioch, having been sent to the president of Cæsarea on public business (C). In 72, Faustinianus receives the ovation which Theophilus received at Cæsarea (DE).

C. In Proch, 12, 14, Seleucus (Leucius Cornelius: for Seleucus, see Zahn, Ac.Joh. LXXXI, note) comes from Antioch on public business (B). Seleucia (A) is mentioned in 9, 7. The fact that the name Seleucus occurs also in F suggests that the text of Heg was corrupt at this point.

The next five passages derive from QPl.

D. In LT, 85, Lucius (who is only in LT Theophilus) is absent near the king four years (E). When he returned to the city all the inhabitants went out to meet him (BE). His wife was dressed in mean clothing (E).

E. Kewestos gave his possessions to the poor (FGH: cf. EPl, 668). The Emperor sent messengers bidding him come in order that he might take counsel with him about certain anxious public business, for his speech was wiser than that of any other of his senate (HL). He feared, but his wife persuaded him to borrow money from his brother (AF) in order to make a gift to the king (FH). After three years (D "four") he returned. The people of the city dressed themselves in fine apparel and went out of the city to receive him (BD), but not his wife (D) (EP, 11 f., 25).

F. In LA, 9 f., the governor has brought all his goods to the apostle (Theophilus gives much money to the poor in LJasZ, 33), and the news reached the king that he had distributed his property among the poor (GH). Seleucus (C) the vizier (who was presumably the *brother* of EG) saw that the king desired the governor's ruin and entreated the king to desist, suggesting that the governor should offer his goods to the king's treasury (EH).

G. In the parallel section of AT, for the relations of which with LA (F), see § 300 f., Thomas plays the part of Theophilus and spends the king's money on the poor (EFH: AT, 19). The brother (EFH) is mentioned (21).

H. In VP, 8, Marcellus is a senator conspicuous for his wisdom in speech (E). Nero keeps him out of office lest he should despoil the provinces by his gifts to ragamuffins.

Marcellus said, " All my goods are thine " (EF). There is
no evidence as to the source. (See § 222 B (b).)

J. We will now collect some apocryphal matter connected
with Philo. In HE, II. xvii. (HE probably derives from
Heg through Clement) Peter meets Philo at Rome as he
also does in Photius, 105. KP did not contain fiction of
this character, and the source must be QP. In this Acts
the apostle probably debated testimonies with Philo, for
John does so in Proch, 110, 9, and there is a dialogue of
Philo with Papiscus. We may safely infer that KP mentioned
the historical journey of Philo to Rome. (a) In EPl
646, 648, the proconsul Alexander of the story of Thecla
is absurdly identified with Alexander Tiberius, who was
the son of Lysimachus, and who is said to have been converted by the apostle. (b) In VP, 3, Lysimachus has been
converted by Paul. The last two passages evidently quarry
from a note on Philo made by Heg à propos of the statement
of QP that Peter converted Philo.

K. Other names occur which were connected with these
events, Jamnians, a Jewish disputant, named Apion, and, as
has been said, Petronius. (See § 315 F.)

§ 192. L. The following passages are based on a mis-
translation of the word γέρων, which may mean either senator
or old man.

(a) In both EP, 488, and R. viii. 1, Faustinianus is an
old man. In R (cf. b) he is a workman on the shore.

(b) In LLk, 153, Theophilus, who is so named, is an old
fisherman on the shore.

(c) In LT, 90, the old man whose six sons are ordained
(§ 183) is Theophilus.

(d) In VP, 3, Demetrius (Theophilus: § 226) is a senator.

M. LLk (Lb) seems to identify Theophilus with the
Faustinianus of La. The following passages seem to shew
that Heg probably recognised the identification. Possibly
in QC Faustinianus received the name Theophilus at his
baptism.

(a) In R. x. 71, a context, Theophilus who, like Cornelius,
cannot have been mentioned by his right name in QC
at this point and who almost certainly is quarried from Heg,

makes an unexplained entry into the narrative, and in 72 Faustinianus receives an unexplained ovation, which was that which Theophilus received at Cæsarea (B).

(b) In SolokoffAP, as Lipsius notes with surprise (ii. 208), Clement is a sailor. In VP, 5, Theon (Leucius) is governor of the ship.

§ 194. The interconnections of a large number of splinters and indications imply an historical tradition that Marcellus was promoted to the office of *princeps peregrinorum*, was closely connected with Seneca and was probably his brother.

A. At Ac. xxviii. 16 a western variant runs: *the centurion handed over the prisoners to the stratopedarch, but Paul was allowed to abide by himself without the camp.* According to Mommsen the stratopedarch was the *princeps peregrinorum*, who was an important officer of state and the commandant of a body of soldiers who were on detached service and who travelled backwards and forwards between Rome and the provinces and were called *frumentarii*. Their camp was on the Mons Cælia, and prisoners were sometimes placed in their charge.

B. Our reconstructions have already provided a link in the chain of evidence. Cornelius was sent to Cæsarea " on public business." He was acting therefore as a *frumentarius*. Marcellus belonged to the equestrian order, and the sons of its members often began their careers as legionary centurions (Deamberg et Saglio s.v. centurion). Moreover Marcellus was made a senator, and his services to the empire marked him out for high office. Lastly, the gloss represents the stratopedarch as very friendly to the apostle.

C. Our hypothesis explains the great consideration shewn to the apostle by Julius who would be acting under the orders of Marcellus.

D. In VP, 1 f. S. Paul's jailor is over the storehouses (cf. *frumentarii* and EJKL), becomes a Christian and allows Paul to go whither he would away from the city. The writer, who played with his sources, combined *without the camp* (A) with the tradition of the journey to Spain where

Paul says he will be one year, a sentence which is based on Heg (§ 203). We then find Marcellus at Rome.

E. In APl, 1 Paul is in a barn (AD). In 3 is said to be *over the camp* (*stratopedon*) (A), and the Christians were burnt (F) after being condemned without trial. In 6 there is a probable allusion to Seneca, for there are philosophers at Nero's court.

F. Unlike any other apocryphist psSeneca endeavours to secure vraisemblance by the methods used by modern writers. Lightfoot thinks that he sought to make Paul and Seneca write in different styles. He uses a local touch in his allusion to the gardens of Sallust. Here we are concerned with the fact that he introduces matter from an historian who can only be Heg. In letter 5 the lady (Poppæa), is angry with Paul for having left the old rite and sect. In 7 Seneca writes to Paul and Theophilus. The writer knew that S. Paul left Rome (D) and connected Theophilus with the journey. In 12 he gives details about the fire and says that Jews and Christians were executed. Nero had rejected the position of Poppæa, as Heg matter in AJ, 3 shews that he was likely to have done. Our concern is with the absence of Paul from Rome and the fact that Theophilus is with him.

G. AXanthippæ bring Paul to Spain (D). The writer probably had Theophilus in mind, and if so Paul's journey is connected with Theophilus as it is in F. His " Philotheus " is probably suggested by " Theophilus." Probus like Marcellus is a friend of the emperor (L). In 8 Probus receives Paul in the way in which in KP Theophilus received Peter at Cæsarea. We note the indication (FO) that Theophilus was connected with Spain.

H. The evidence which shews that in a narrative which mentioned Seneca S. Paul during the last years of his life was in contact with Marcellus is in a line with a vein of matter in Acts which represents the apostle as a pious Jew and the Jews as disturbers of the peace and with the no less significant omission of matter in which S. Stephen denounced Judaism and S. Peter said that he had turned from the people to the nations. Acts suggests that Theophilus was in a position to use political influence in S. Paul's behalf.

J. We now return to the *peregrini*, the *frumentarii* and their camp on the Mons Cælia.

In EP, 19, a context which we have already used for the recall of Marcellus, the emperor provides " Kewestos " with a beautiful house, *i.e.* with an official residence which Heg had seen. In 11 he opens his *storehouses* (ADEKLM). The same passage is used in 668 where (Theophilus) has many children, a fact which shews that the source was QP, in which work he had seven sons who were ordained deacons. He also had many servants (L).

K. The same context is probably used (§ 235 J) in the QP narrative of the healing of his daughter in EP, 505. There is here an allusion to the fact that the house was on a little hill (the Mons Cælia). There is an allusion to storehouses (ADJL). He loved the stranger (*peregrini*) (L).

L. In APh, 38 the story of the healing is somewhat depraved. The father was a friend of the king (G. like Marcellus). Many strangers lodged in the house (K). He goes to the barns and seeks the apostle (DEJK). There is an editorial allusion to Leucius the physician which shews that Heg in the context with which we are concerned cited Col. iv. 14. In 44 many of the children and servants believe (J).

M. In STrans, 49 Sabinus, who has played the part of Pilate, like Pilate and Marcellus is dismissed. Unlike Pilate and like Marcellus (K) he goes to a beautiful house.

N. The occurrence of the name Seneca in the list of the twelve elders who in QPl were ordained at Cæsarea at the end of the first year (JerBps) is a proof that Leucius found an allusion to a Seneca in KP and almost certainly in the Cæsarea section. The only known Senecas are Nero's minister and his father, and apart from two tribal names (tribal names do not count in QPl lists) all the names may be connected with narratives of the evangelisation. For another instance of the influence of the section of KP which he was using on the nomenclature of Leucius see § 315 A. Either Marcellus or Cornelius was named Seneca, or they were said to be connected with the statesman in some way.

O. PsSeneca (F) and AXanthippæ (G) connect Theophilus with a journey of S. Paul which in the latter work and elsewhere (*e.g.* E) was a journey to Spain. Now Seneca was a Spaniard, and the following passage, which occurs in Jerome Ep. i. 7, is an important link between Marcellus and Seneca. Jerome, who used Heg elsewhere, writes to Lucinius (who lived in Seneca's province, Bætica): *Cornelius the centurion anticipated the faith of Lucinius. Paul* (in Rom. xv. 24) . . . *shewed by such fruits what he expected from that province.* Cornelius was described as first-fruits in KP *sub* EpClem, 3, and I Clem, 42 probably alludes to the ordinations at Cæsarea.

P. An inscription found at Ostia, which is of somewhat later date than Seneca, runs: *Annæus Paulus to his very dear son M. Annæus Petrus* (Ramsay Paul the Traveller, 356) and proves the influence of Christianity on the dependants of the Annæi at a very early date.

Q. A fragment in LLk, 155 illustrates the inscription, for it shews that Christianity had spread widely in some of the *familiæ*. We are told that *the vizier . . . believed . . ., and all his servants; and their number was* 267 *men. And the emperor commanded that their names should be written down.* The persecuting emperor was Nero (153) who is said to have slain a multitude of the disciples. The large number proscribed confirms the statement that the *familia* mentioned in LLk was that of a " vizier." Was he Lucius Annæus Seneca? The " vizier " of the king in LA, 9 was originally the brother of Theophilus (§ 193 F), and his name is Seleucus, a corruption of Leucius.

R. In view of the fact that psClement used the QP narrative of the recall and return of Theophilus we note that he said that Faustinianus like Seneca was interested in philosophy and had kinsmen at Athens (M, 68, R. viii. 2 f., Tryph (§ 223)). Gallio was Seneca's brother.

S. According to Lightfoot (Philippians, 300) Seneca not improbably had a vague and partial acquaintance with Christianity, but a case is considerably strengthened if we are right in holding the early dates of Mk, Lk and of their sources. Seneca sometimes asked his slaves to dine with him, and Lightfoot suggests that some of them may have spoken to him about their religion. We have found evidence that some of them were Christians (PQ).

T. S. Paul was accustomed to make one step good before he took another. Why in the heyday of his activities in Asia, Macedonia and Achaia did he resolve upon a journey to Romanised Spain, *i.e.* to the remote province of Bætica? Why did the Greek-speaking Levantine Jew contemplate Latin-speaking Spain as a sphere of work? Why did he regard a visit to the metropolis of the empire as an incident in the evangelisation of the Pillars of Hercules? These questions are answered if the conversion of Marcellus had opened a door in the home of the Senecas.

It may be rightly objected to the view that Marcellus was Seneca's brother that Seneca is not known to have had a brother of that name, but I do not know that the argument from silence in this instance is a strong one. As has been stated, the rule as to the *tria nomina* does not hold under the empire. An A. Marcellus was perhaps *consul suffectus* with Gallio (*Enc. Bib.*, 1638).

We may now summarise the evidence which shews that in KP Marcellus was the brother of Seneca. (i) Leucius (N) connected the name Seneca with Cæsarea. (ii) (*a*) Like Seneca the brother of Marcellus held office under Gaius (§ 193 AEFG). (*b*) In two Acts the same writer speaks of the Emperor's vizier; in one he was the brother of Marcellus (§ 193 F), in the other, almost certainly, Seneca. (iii) Seneca was a Spaniard, and FGO connect Marcellus with Spain. (iv) In QC Marcellus like Seneca had kinsmen at Athens and was interested in philosophy. (v) It is very relevant that we find Marcellus in high office at Rome at the time when Seneca was in power. (vi) Our identifications agree with the probability that Seneca had some acquaintance with Christianity and with S. Paul's intention of going to Spain.

We conclude that the evidence for the career of Marcellus hangs well together and that both its internal character, the character of its source, which was written less than a generation after Seneca's fall, and the cohesions of the evidence with known facts compel us to accept it. But, while the evidence is strong that Theophilus was related to Seneca, he may not have been his brother. For the position that in KP Marcellus was the stratopedarch the evidence is decisive.

THE DATE OF THE CRUCIFIXION

§ 195. Inasmuch as Marcellus was procurator in 37, and we have concluded that in KP Peter returned to Jerusalem for the seventh passover, our evidence gives us A.D. 30 as the year of the Crucifixion. Now this is the date at which many critics have arrived on other grounds, and it may be claimed that the narrative of R. i. 43, 44*a*, derives from an historical source. It runs: ... *A week of years was completed from the passion ... the church ... in Jerusalem was multiplied ... being governed with most righteous ordinances by James who was ordained bishop by the Lord.* xliv. *But when we twelve apostles on the day of the passover had come together with an immense multitude and entered into the church of the brethren, each one of us at the request of James stated briefly what he had done in every place.* The narrative is obviously influenced by J, but it derives from QP (§ 197).

§ 196. There is however a difficulty. If there is any truth in our view of the influence of Heg on the apocrypha and patristic chronology it is quite certain that Heg dated the Crucifixion under the Gemini (A.D. 29), for that date is found in EvN, Prol.; EusThadd, 22; Clement, Tertullian, Hippolytus, Julius Africanus, Lactantius and psCyprian (Turner Hastings, BD, i. 413*b*). It is usually far more difficult to account for error than to recognise truth, but it is possible to shew both that Heg worked with our data and how he went wrong.

The date of Marcellus is known from Jos. *Ant*. XVIII. iv. Now it can be shewn that Heg used both this and other passages of Josephus. (i) We have already concluded that AJ, 1–4, derives from Heg. Now AJ, 1, is influenced by BJ, IV. i. 3, VII. v. 7. (ii) Heg's knowledge of the procuratorship of Tiberius Alexander (EPl, 646) presumably derives from *Ant*. XX. v. 2. (iii) Albinus (DAdd, 37; ParadPil; VP, 34) is shewn to derive from *Ant*. XX. ix. 1, by the fact that in Josephus the death of James is a connected subject. Heg rejected the date implied by that writer, but after his manner recorded discrepant evidence. (iv) In a note he corrected the identification of the Herods of the NT with Archelaus (Matt. ii. 22) which he found in QP *sub* EpApp, 9; AnaphPil; HistJos, 8; APh, 15; STrans, 25; and EvP, 2 ("Herod *the king*"). It is due to Heg that the Herod who killed James is rightly Agrippa in LB, 77 and VP, 35. Against QP he pointed out that according to Jos. Ant. XVII. xiii. 2 Archelaus died at Vienne. PsLinus, who derived his pseudonym from Heg, combined the deaths of Agrippa and Archelaus (LinusAP, 17).

That Heg used the *Antiquities* when dating Marcellus is shewn by the two following facts : (*a*) He referred, like Josephus, to the dismissal of the predecessor of Marcellus, Pilate (DAdd, 37; STrans, 48); and (*b*) like Josephus he spoke of Caiaphas as Joseph Caiaphas. In EvN Prol, where the Crucifixion is carefully dated under the Gemini; Joseph Caiaphas is the high priest. (See also § 171 B.)

§ 197. Heg worked back from the synchronism of the appointment of Marcellus with the visit of Peter to Cæsarea, which KP dated in the seventh year. Our hypothesis therefore involves the position that QP, an Acts which Heg accepted and attributed to S. Luke, dated the visit in the eighth year. That QP preserved this section of KP may be assumed, for it was long and important, and, if QP preserved it, it can only have been by appending it to the visit of John and Judas at the close of the seventh year and in the interpolated year which our reconstruction demands. Now as it happens the passage which refers to the seventh passover (R. i. 43) is clearly based on QP. It occurs at the beginning of an important and composite passage. Remembering that only J exalted James and only QP the twelve we compare the two following contexts:

43. The twelve meet in the church of the brethren.

71. There is a night of prayer in the house of James (Acts xii. 12).

55 f. The twelve speak in the temple.

69. James answers Caiaphas.

The matter directed against Saul in 70, and the supposed flight of Peter (in J, Judas) to Damascus, must be from J. On the other hand the narrative of the activity of Peter at Cæsarea and his evangelisation of the Syrian coast which follows cannot derive from either J or QPl and must be a continuation of the use of QP which we detected in R. i. 43. There is some dislocation of the chronology under the influence of the scheme of the Clementines, a subject to which we will return in the next chapter, but the close of R. iii. is a valuable "Cæsarea ending," and the period of three months mentioned in 68 must in QP have immediately preceded the passover which followed that mentioned in R. i. 43. R therefore shews that as our hypothesis requires, QP brought S. Peter to Cæsarea about four months before the eighth passover.

§ 198. Our reconstruction of QP from R may be confirmed and extended by a comparison of R with VP.

A. R. i. 72. Zacchæus has written from Cæsarea saying that Simon was subverting many of the people asserting that he was Stans. . . . Make no delay.

N. VP, 5. At Jerusalem . . . Christ showed . . . a vision. . . . Those that believe in me hath Satan made to fall . . . whose power Simon approveth himself to be. . . . Delay thee not (R).

O. 31. I am Stans.

B. In six days I arrived at Cæsarea.

P. 5. In six days they came to Puteoli (Cæsarea).

C. 73. When I (Peter) entered the city Zacchæus met me and embracing me brought me to this hospice in which he himself stayed.

Q. 6. Theon . . . went to the hospice (where he was wont to lodge) . . . prepare to receive Peter.

D. 74. Zacchæus . . . told me . . . Simon's doings.

R. Ariston says, . . . Simon a Jew . . . made all the brotherhood fall away. Make haste (N).

E. i. 12. The hospice . . . and standing before the door I (Clement) informed the door-keeper who I was, and Barnabas coming out rushed into my arms . . . and led me to Peter. 13. Peter ran to me and kissed me.

S. Ariston fell upon Theon's neck and embraced him and besought him to bring him to Peter.

F. APh, 65. They stood before the gate. . . . A damsel came forth and running in . . . came to Ireos (" the first man of the city," Theophilus). . . . He came forth.

T. Acts x. 25 (gloss). When Peter drew near (Gig omits " to Cæsarea ") one of the servants ran forth and announced that Peter had arrived. . . . Cornelius leapt forth and met him.

§ 199. That VP is related to R is obvious, and QP was almost certainly the main source of VP; but we must not assume that VP derives from QP, for VP will be shewn to have been influenced also by QC. The direct influence of QP on N–S can be proved as follows:

(i) F follows KP closely, and that Acts is slightly modified in T. Leucius haggadised the journey of Peter to Cæsarea (§ 297) and made the three messengers go to the hospice at Cæsarea (EPl, 619). In QP Cornelius had been converted during the seventh year and went to the hospice instead of the messengers (E). LeuciusP used the KP narrative of the reception, but there was an inevitable change of parts. We find another such change in S.

(ii) We shall conclude that in QC Simon was described in terms of Saul who, in J, was a gentile. In KP and QP *sub* Didasc. xxiii. Simon was a Jew. Again, Simon was not a demon in QC. The Satan-possessed Jew of N and R must derive from QP.

(iii) The fact that Ariston represents Zacchæus (R), illustrates the care with which names are sometimes chosen in VP. Ariston, the host at the hospice, was the father of

Mark in QP *sub* EP, 509, and therefore like Zacchæus the
host of Peter (at Jerusalem). He is the host in ABarn, 14.

§ 200. LeuciusP solved the problem of combining KP
with the double narrative of QPl by making Simon
follow John and Judas and pervert the church. Zacchæus
wrote to Peter asking his help, and Peter refounded the
church. This letter survives in R. i. 72, where it is sent
to James; in VP, 5 f., it becomes a vision and the information
supplied by Ariston. In APl (J, 289) Theophilus and other
Corinthians ask Paul to visit Corinth because Simon and
Cleobius have perverted some of the members of the church
of that city. In QP Cleobius was the companion of Simon
at Rome (§ 238). Our view that Simon and Cleobius went
to Cæsarea is confirmed by the fact that Simon is associated
with Theophilus in the title of the *Altercatio*, and the name
Cleobius with the name Marcellus in AJ, 18.

§ 201. We have proved our main point, the interpolation
of a year by LeuciusP. We can now return to the subject
of the influence of this interpolated year on the chronology
of Heg.

1. Our hypothesis accounts for the order of the names of
Cornelius and Theophilus in ClemBps (§ 185*a* (i)).

2. We shall examine at length some Armenian evidence as to the dates of the Gospels and conclude that
it certainly derives from Hippolytus who was with almost
equal certainty using Heg. Now Vardan, a mediæval
Armenian, using the same tradition, gives in his brief
tractate the *Solutions*, two dates for Mark, the eighth year
and the fifteenth. All that needs to be said here about
the latter date is that the same tradition underlies the
allusion to Claudius in HE, II. xiv. and that we shall find
that it was the year which followed Heg's date for the
foundation of the church of Rome. As regards the tradition
of the eighth year we shall presently conclude that according
to both KP and QPl, Mark was written at the date of the
apostle's visit to Cæsarea. Vardan, therefore, gives all but
explicit confirmation to our view that according to Heg,

Peter visited Cæsarea in the eighth year. The two dates for Mark are an important instance of Heg's practice of recording discrepant traditions.

3. According to Heg (§ 181 D) Stephen was stoned before the departure of the apostles to the nations. Now in a psEvodian letter cited in RobEvvC, 186, which is influenced by early apocrypha and probably by Heg, the stoning of Stephen is seven years after the Passion. The phrase is that of R. i. 43. Later writers usually dated from the Ascension. This notice involves the position that in an Acts which can only be QP a journey followed the eighth passover.

§ 202. Before we discuss some evidence for the interpolated year which occurs in AThadd we will note some traces of Heg's discussions of the journeyings of S. Peter, even though most of what will be said has little to do with the question of the interpolated year.

If the main positions which we have adopted are justified, Heg would take into account and as far as possible harmonise the following data. (A) In the introduction of KP Peter suffered at Rome under Nero but there was no narrative of his journey. (B) In QPl Peter went to Rome shortly after the seventh passover (§ 23) and probably suffered not long after. (C) In QP he journeyed to Rome after the eighth passover. (D) We shall conclude that QP narrated the Herodian persecution. (E) In KP and QP Peter after the twelfth passover evangelised the Syrian seaboard. He returned to Jerusalem and after his escape from prison went to Antioch (§ 252 f.). (F) In QC Peter left Jerusalem after the seventh passover, spent several months at Cæsarea and the twelfth and fourteenth years at Laodicea and Rome.

In his discussion of the data stated in E and F Heg was confronted with two difficulties both of which concern us.

(i) Owing to his antedating of the Crucifixion KP (and probably also QP) compelled him to suppose that Peter spent much over a year at Laodicea without going on to Antioch, and we shall find that with characteristic accuracy he noted the point (§ 253 (iii)). Unhappily he did not reconsider his preference of the chronology of QP to that of KP.

(ii) It was a more serious difficulty that, while in KP and QP Peter spent the fourteenth passover and the preceding months at Laodicea, in QC (§ 206) he spent them at Rome. But the writers who created the difficulty solved it by their narratives of miraculous transportations, and had not the angel of the Lord carried Habakkuk to Babylon by the hair of his head? This solution of the problem survives in LP, 211 and EP, 505 where Peter is transported to Rome. The transportation of Faustinianus (488) depraves the apostle's return journey to Laodicea. The incident almost immediately precedes traces of Heg's discussion of the chronology of Peter's journeys (§ 252 f.).

§ 203. Heg's discussions also underlie VP. The scheme of that work was based on the positions at which Heg had arrived as to the chronology of Peter's last visit to Rome. The Rome section of his narrative opens with S. Paul's residence in "the storehouses" after his arrival. The apostle is released and went to Spain on a journey which Heg calculated lasted a year. During his absence Peter arrived, and Nero was responsible for the apostle's martyrdom. The QP journey also influences VP, for though there is no allusion to Philo his brother Lysimachus is a convert at Rome (3). Lastly, there is a trace of Heg's discussion of the Syrian journey, for Peter's journey to Rome is explicitly dated after the twelfth passover (KP, 6). For the journey to Spain see §§ 194, 207 B.

§ 204. We can now return to our main theme and discuss the evidence of AThadd.

According to our reconstruction of QPl and QP there was at the seventh passover a council of the apostles at which they discussed the discipline which should be administered among the gentiles to whom Christ at this passover sent them. We are here concerned with two Cæsarea endings which form consecutive paragraphs in AThadd, 4 f., and which preserve a remark of Heg who had observed that in QP, though not in KP, the apostles went up to two consecutive passovers.

A. *He baptized them, anointing them with the holy myrrh
and imparted to them the mysteries . . . and delivered unto
them the law of Moses . . . according to the commandments
of the apostles, for they met yearly at the passover, and again
he imparted the Holy Spirit* (ordained).

B. *And Thaddæus . . . built churches and having ordained
. . . delivered to them the canon . . . of the liturgy and . . .
departed to Amis* (Jerusalem). . . . 8. *Beyrout.*

The fact that two endings follow each other explains the
statement that the apostles met yearly. Now this statement
occurred in Heg, for we read in EncA (Lips. i. 578): *They
met yearly at Jerusalem to celebrate Easter and Pentecost
at the house of the mother of God.* Our conjecture that
we have another trace of Heg's discussion of the chronology
of the events which followed the seventh passover is confirmed by the statement that Thaddæus was five years at
Amis (Jerusalem). The allusion is to the five years which
preceded the twelfth passover to which Heg referred *sub*
VP, 5. Our conjecture is confirmed by an allusion to
Beyrout in 8 which derives from the QP journey of Peter to
Syria. We are confirmed then in holding that Heg discussed the chronology of S. Peter's journeys, that he brought
the apostle back from Jerusalem for the eighth passover as
well as the seventh and that the KP narrative of the seventh
year became in QP a narrative of the eighth.

On a review of the whole discussion it is certain that,
using QP, Heg held that Peter met Marcellus four months
before the eighth passover, and that in KP he met him
before the seventh passover. We have gone behind Heg to
his sources and behind QP to KP, and we have found that
all the data cohere.

R

CHAPTER VII

The Ebionite Romance and the Traditional Date of the Foundation of the Church of Rome

Unhappily this is the only chapter in which our analysis of the apocrypha can be based on documents which are fairly well preserved and the proof be built up point after point without tiresome interruptions of the argument and assumptions of positions proved in other parts of the book. Our results give us an Acts which seriously depraved its main source but which was very early and sometimes preserved matter of great historical value. Our literary analysis as in the last chapter will be confirmed by the discussion of Heg's chronology, and we shall be concerned with a topic of great intrinsic interest, the traditional date of the foundation of the Church of Rome.

---

§ 205. When we analysed EP (§ 167 f.) we concluded that the writer of QEPP preserved in his recension of Heg extracts from KP, QPl and QP which narrated the period which followed the Crucifixion, extracts from QPl and QP which narrated the evangelisation of Judea, extracts from KP and QPl which brought apostles to Antioch and, later, extracts from QPl and QP which brought apostles to Rome. When, then, we find in 481 f. extracts from a Clementine document and matter from KP which brought Peter to Laodicea, there is the strongest possible presumption that the Clementine matter also was extracted by Heg. Our position may be confirmed.

(i) That it was the author of QEPP who Clementised Heg is shewn by the fact that the editor of EP and EPl moved to EPl, 691 f., matter which is shewn by Peter's use of the first person to have been already Clementised.

(ii) In EP, 466–490, apart from our Clementine matter, there is probably not a phrase which is not either taken from or suggested by Heg.

258

(iii) If Clementine matter occurred in Heg it must be earlier than what is called the Clementine *Grundschrift* and presumably derives from the earliest stratum which is peculiar to R and H, *i.e.* from the Ebionite eight books of Peter's preaching reconstructed by Waitz. Now the editor who Clementised the extracts and substituted Peter and Paul for John and Judas in his QPl extracts substituted eight books given to Peter for the one book given in QPl to John. That these books are editorial is shewn by the description of the first (520). The obvious inference that these books were suggested by the eight books of QC is confirmed by the fact that apart from any difficulties of detail, it is virtually impossible for the QEPP recension of the Romance to have derived from the *Grundschrift*. It varies from the carefully elaborated narratives of the latter in being short, simple and crude.

In this chapter our examination of the Clementines will be confined to this new matter and to some other positions which concern us in this work.

§ 206. When R and H are examined carefully it becomes clear that they derive from a source in which Peter did not return from Cæsarea to Jerusalem for the eighth passover, but journeyed to Tyre and thence after the passover to Sidon, two cities which he visited in QP *sub* EP, 481. He then, as in QP *sub* AThadd, 6, went to Beyrout, thence to Tripolis and, as in KP *sub* EP, 490, to Laodicea and also to Antioch and Rome. In these eight cities and in these only, he founded churches (R. iii. 66; H. vii. 5, 8, 12; R. vi. 15; H. xx. 23; R. x. 72; EpClem, 2). In so far as the original narratives survive, they repeat the QP account of the foundation of the church of Cæsarea. We find the same healings, the same movements of the apostle and his companions, the same topography (§ 220). In QP Mark wrote the preaching of Peter at Cæsarea (§ 333), and in QC Clement did so. We must infer, then, that the eight books of QC were written respectively at the eight cities at which Peter founded an Ebionite succession.

Our result may be confirmed. In R. iii. 75, a context

which R derives from QHR, Peter sends from Cæsarea the ten books of QHR which had been written by Clement. According to this passage James received all the books shortly after the seventh passover, but according to EpClem, 19 the books were sent from Rome. The clue to the discrepancy is in R. i. 72, where James bids Peter send an account of his sayings and doings every seven years. In QC the first book was sent from Cæsarea and the seven which contained the teaching given and written in the other seven cities were sent from Rome at the close of the second septennium.

Inasmuch, then, as in this scheme the bishop of Rome was Clement, the Clementine romance derives from the oldest stratum in the Clementines.

§ 207. Our next task is to shew the influence of QC on Heg's account of the foundation of the church of Rome and his chronology. It is neither possible nor necessary for our purpose that we should discuss all the problems which arise in connection with the notices of the first three bishops of Rome. It will be enough if we trace the more important to Heg and endeavour to ascertain his views as to the ordinations of Linus and Clement.

A. If, as we hold, ClemBps reproduces Heg, that list provides our most important evidence. It must be observed that it is a list not of first bishops but of bishops who were *apostolici*, a fact which explains the absence of Anencletus the second bishop. The first apostolic bishop is *Linus of Claudia by Paul; the second after the death of Linus Clement by Peter.* (i) *Linus of Claudia* tells us more than Heg could have learnt from 2 Tim. iv. 21 (*Linus and Claudia*). The phrase is the result of the investigations which Heg made when he drew up his "succession" on his arrival at Rome (HE, IV. xxii.). Claudia was a woman of distinction who had probably offered her home as a hospice, and her son (cf. ClemBps, *Strateas of Lois*) had become the first president of the elders of the community which worshipped in it. (ii) Heg knew that the records which he found at Rome, probably in the hospice of Claudia, were the best possible evidence.

He made, therefore, Linus the first bishop, but he harmonised the apocryphal tradition with the historical and
stated that Peter had already ordained Clement at the
fourteenth passover. (iii) It follows that the phrase *after
his death* is not otiose, but a splinter from Heg, who evidently
said that Clement did not succeed to the actual government
of the church until after the death of Linus.

B. For the use of Heg in *Haer.* xxvii. 6, see Lawlor, 73 f.
Epiphanius, who follows Heg closely, writes: *Peter and
Paul, Linus and Cletus, Clement, Evaristus, Alexander,
Xystus, . . . Anicetus.* The second "and" needs explanation, and it may be found in the preceding words. Epiphanius, like Irenæus (C), refers to 1 Clement, and he
cites it loosely. He suggests that the apostles had made
Clement a bishop-coadjutor owing to their journeyings.
Thus, for instance, Paul went to Spain. When the apostles
suffered, Clement for the sake of peace waived his claim
but succeeded *after the deaths of Linus and Cletus.* The
harmonisation is precisely in the manner of Heg, and the
phrase cited both accounts for *and Cletus* and shews that
the harmonisation derives from the same source as the
list. It also provides an unexpected confirmation of our
explanation of the phrase *after his death* in A.

Epiphanius uses the less common name for Spain, Spania,
which occurs in three allusions to the apostle's visit, which
almost certainly derive from Heg. (*a*) In VP, 1, the
chronological allusion is a strong link with him (§ 203).
(*b*) Hippolytus probably used Heg throughout the Muratorian. (*c*) The word is used in MPP, 1, a composite
Acts which in part is based on QEPP.

C. It will be argued that Irenæus in *c. Haer*, I and III,
derives much matter from Heg, and that in III. i.–iii., he is
parallel with Tert. de Praescr. In III, iii. 3, he writes:
*The blessed apostles having founded and built up the church
committed the episcopate to Linus. S. Paul mentions him
. . . (2 Tim. iv. 21). To him succeeded Anacletus; and
after him in the third place Clement was allotted the bishopric
. . . conversant with the apostles . . . their teaching in his
ears. . . . He wrote to the Corinthians, exhorting them to*

peace . . . proclaiming the one God, omnipotent, the Maker
of heaven and earth. . . . From this epistle whosoever chooses
may learn that He . . . is Creator . . . (and not) . . . another
God. To Clement there succeeded Evaristus. Alexander
followed Evaristus. Then sixth from the apostles Sixtus,
who was gloriously martyred; after him Hyginus; after him
Pius; then after him Anicetus. Soter having succeeded
Anicetus, Eleutherius holds now in the twelfth place the
inheritance from the apostles.

If Irenæus used Heg in the context he certainly used
him here. (*a*) The allusion to 2 Timothy occurs in D
(cf. A). (*b*) Like Epiphanius, he describes Clement as a
contemporary of the apostles. (*c*) Like Epiphanius he refers
to 1 Clement, but, the use to which he puts the letter against
the Gnostic dualists goes far to shew that he had not read
it. (*d*) Just as Heg, on our view, discussed the ordinations
of Linus and Clement, and especially Clement's, so Irenæus
discusses them. Then follows what is almost a bare list
of names. The close recalls Heg, ap. HE, IV. xxii. 3: *I*
made a succession as far as Anicetus. . . . And from Anicetus
Soter received the succession; after whom came Eleutherius.
(*e*) According to the numeration of our passage, Hyginus
was the eighth bishop, but the source which underlies I. xxvii. 1 and III. iv. 3, numbered the bishops
and numbered them differently. In these passages he
is the ninth bishop, because the episcopate of the two
apostles was included. That this source was Heg is shewn
by *John by me John* in ClemBps (John appoints himself:
cf. AJ, 14), by the list of Heg preserved in B (the
episcopates include that of Peter and Paul) and by the
preceding allusion to Marcellina in Iren. I. xxv. 6 (Lawlor,
75–86).

D. Eusebius uses Heg in HE, III. v. 2 (§ 181 D) and
also in iv.

5. Timothy bishop of Ep-   ClemBps.
   hesus.
Titus of Crete.   ClemBps.
6. Luke the doctor an An-   § 21.
   tiochene.

Had no mere casual acquaintance with the apostles.	In Heg he was Leucius the scribe of Peter (LLk, 152; APh, 40).
S. Paul's phrase *according to my gospel* referred to Luke.	In Heg *sub* Iren. III. i. 1 and *sub* Mur. Luke wrote the apostle's preaching.
8. Crescens to the Gauls.	ClemBps. *Crescens to the churches of Galatia.*
Linus, 2 Tim. iv. 21.	AB.
9. Clement, Phil. iv. 3.	The citation of Philippians is obviously wrong. Eusebius corrects Heg, who trusted his memory and thought that the passage occurred in Romans, to which epistle it is ascribed by Epiphanius in our context and also in Ap. Const. vi. 8, where all the matter except that from HR is likely to derive from Heg, whom the writer used in vii. 46 (ClemBps). So also Jerome de Vir Ill. 15.
10. Dionysius.	ClemBps.

This chapter, like that which follows it, illustrates Heg's habit of using Heg without citing him and his distrust of him.

E. The Roman canon mentions *Peter*, *Paul*, And, Jas, Jn, *Thom*, *Jas*, Ph, Bt, Mt, Sm, Thad, *Linus*, *Cletus*, *Clement*. . . . Later the following are commemorated: John, Stephen, *Matthias*, *Barnabas*, *Ignatius*. . . . All the italicised names are likely to derive from Heg (presumably through Hippolytus). (*a*) For Peter and Paul, cf. ABC. (*b*) We shall conclude that in QP there was only one James and an apostle named Thomas Barnabas Matthias. It is impossible not to connect these facts with the displacements of the names of the second James and Thomas in the Roman rite, and with the collocation of Barnabas Matthias. The martyrdom of Ignatius at Rome will be shewn to have been recorded by Heg *sub* HE, III. xxxvi. 3.

F. In de Praescr. 32, Tertullian, using Heg, states the ordination of Clement by Peter and of Polycarp by John.

G. Julius Africanus, who based his chronology on Heg,

dated the episcopate of Linus A.D. 68. If we deduct the traditional twenty-five years of S. Peter's episcopate, we arrive at the QC date for the ordination of Clement, for according to Heg the Crucifixion was in A.D. 29 and the ordination in QC was fourteen years later.

H. In CurSCeph, 35, Peter leaves Antioch for Rome in the third year of Claudius (A.D. 43). In QC he left Antioch after the thirteenth passover. The date is a year wrong, but the ultimate source must be QC. The statement of the Acts that the apostle built a church in Rome and in the towns and villages of Italy, occurred in Heg sub LT, 80, Hist. Patr. i. 143. I shall return to this statement.

J. In DAdd, 50, Peter is said to have been bishop of Rome twenty-five years and Nero Emperor thirteen years. For the position that Heg gave term numbers, see Lightf. AF, I. i. 67.

§ 208. The following comments may be made on the evidence.

(i) It is certain that Heg, using QC, dated S. Peter's ordination of Clement in A.D. 43.

(ii) As regards the two names given to the second bishop my only contribution to the discussion is that if he had both names Heg would have recorded both (cf. e.g. § 185 (v)) and that the text of his work was in a bad condition.

(iii) According to our best authority (A) only S. Paul ordained Linus. The statement of Irenæus that *apostles having founded and built up the church committed the episcopate to Linus* probably does not do more than connect the ordination with what Heg regarded as the joint episcopate of the two apostles. In the next paragraph still using Heg (who underlies Tert. de Praescr. 32, AJ, 14 and Q at AJ, 35) and referring only to S. John, Irenæus speaks of the appointment of Polycarp by apostles.

The argument of Heg as it may be reconstructed from HE, IV. xxii. 3, Tert. de Praescr. 19 f. and Iren. III. i.–iii., v. 1 required the ordination of a bishop of Rome by S. Paul. His point was that the successions founded by Peter and Paul at Rome and John in Asia preserved the accounts of their teaching given in the Gospels. The episcopal tradition which derived from Paul through Linus confirmed the doctrine taught in Lk.

(iv) Neither of the two surviving works of Irenæus contain a single passage which suggests that he made any investigations of his own outside the limits of the canon. In his Demonstratio he used Justin and KP or a second writer who used KP. In c. Haer. his originality is shewn in his appeal to the canonical writings and in the argument which he based upon them. For other matter he relied on Papias, Justin and Heg. It may be added that he seems to go as far as he can towards accepting the position of Heg that Clement was ordained by Peter almost fifty years before his accession but to refuse to commit himself to it.

§ 209. The argument has shewn decisively that the Clementine Romance was not introduced into the Clementine tradition by the writer of the so-called *Grundschrift* (HR) but was the setting of the eight books of the Ebionite Preachings reconstructed by Waitz. Inasmuch however as this conclusion involves a revolution in Clementine criticism our discussion must be continued.

The Ebionite origin of the Romance itself may be shewn by an examination of some interesting matter which derives from Papias.

(i) The names of Marthones of Tripolis (H. Maroones, R. Maro) and of Clement's brothers, the twins Niceta and Aquila, occur also in ClemBps, where they are disciples of Paul. Heg and psClement derived from a common source which can only be Papias. To Papias, therefore, we must assign the fact known by psClement that there was a bishop of Rome named Clement, who was also a writer, and also the fact, which he used *sub* R. vii. 8, that Flavius Clemens was related to the Emperor who had given him his wife Domitilla. 1 Clement was known to Polycarp and was likely, therefore, to have been known also to Papias. That the writer who introduced this matter was the Ebionite who used J is shewn by the fact that in the Romance two of the disciples of Paul became disciples of Simon-Saul and the other was ordained by Peter after Simon-Saul had perverted or tried to pervert him.

Hippolytus represented Cerinthus as one of the Judaisers of Acts xv. and Gal. ii., and he must have blundered in his use of a tradition, which can only have derived from Papias, that Cerinthus was an opponent of the apostolic letter. Presumably Papias when discussing the position of Cerinthus mentioned Marthones as a leading disciple of S. Paul who had played a part in the events narrated in Ac. xv. Hence in QC Peter expounded the apostolic decree to "Maroones" (R. iv. 36). Papias replied to Cerinthus and psClement to Papias. Presumably the tradition of Evodius, the son of Lendæus the first bishop of Antioch, survived in the same connection. Both names probably occurred in the KP parallel with Ac. xv.

(ii) There are few reconstructions of KP and QP more secure than the position that in those Acts Mark accompanied Peter to Cæsarea and there wrote his Gospel. Now psClement used QP and, though he gave Peter sixteen companions, he does not include the evangelist among them. He did not, however, ignore the tradition. He described Clement in terms of Papias's tradition of Mark. Clement was the apostle's scribe in the Greek and Roman tongues (EP, 482). If in Papias Mark remembered accurately but did not write in order, Clement's memory was phenomenal, and he had a special gift for orderly narration (R. i. 22–25). This matter occurs at a point where psClement was using the QP tradition of the writing of Mark (§ 333 D).

§ 210. What has been said about Marthones shews that he must have been a character of great importance in the Romance and, if the view which still remains to be argued that the Simon of QC was Simon-Saul is also valid, we should expect Peter's conflict with Simon to have taken place, not at Cæsarea, but at Tripolis. Further, in R. iii. 65, 73 these expectations are encouraged by Peter's statements that Simon has "preoccupied" him among the gentiles and that he stayed mainly at Tripolis. Now these two

passages occur in a section of R which, in our view, derives
not from HR, but from QHR and just before the summary
of the ten books of QHR. Nothing corresponds with them
in the Tripolis narrative of HR. Again, the letter of
Zacchæus which we discussed above (R. i. 72) leads us to
expect that we shall hear of the restoration of Simon's
perverts, but R and H tell us nothing. On the other hand,
their narratives of Simon, which are virtually confined to
the beginning and close of the work, suggest a possible
explanation of the procedure of HR. They are connected
with narratives of Theophilus and Cornelius which cannot
derive from QC. Now in QP, Peter confronted Simon at
Cæsarea and Antioch (§ 238). It is probable then, that
HR resolved not merely to rewrite QHR, but also to
recast the work so as to bring it into closer conformity to
the older tradition, and moved a contest which in QC
was at Tripolis back to its QP *situs* at Cæsarea.

§ 211. Our first reconstruction of QC will shew that R
derives from QHR and also that HR moved to Cæsarea,
not only the Simon contest, but also the conversion of the
twins from Tripolis. psClement probably found their
names in the same context of Papias as the allusion to
Marthones. Having read Papias for one purpose he used
him for another.

In R. ii. and H. ii. the twin brothers of Clement play an
important part, as they do in the plot of the work, yet they
are not introduced to the reader, but merely appear at the
end of the two lists of Peter's companions, where they are
described as "the friends," a phrase which receives no
explanation. Moreover, these lists present a problem, for
they vary. In R. ii. 1 there are nine Jews, Clement and
the twins, four Jews being added in iii. 68. In H. ii. 1 there
are fourteen Jews and the twins. One Jew is peculiar to R,
two to H. Now if we assume that, as was shewn in § 184,
the sixteen ordinands were originally companions, and that
R used QHR, and also assume that in QC the twins became
companions at Tripolis, the variations are explained. HR
omitted two Jews in order to insert the twins. R, who in

a long section which has no parallel in H, had been using
QHR, had the sixteen Jews of QHR before him, and remembered the procedure of HR (whose recension he was about
to use) but slightly varied, including Clement and omitting
two different Jews.

§ 212. Our view that R had been using QHR may be
confirmed as follows: In R, H and HR, Peter had been
discoursing to Clement, but R varies from H in making the
discourse include a long narrative of events (43–72). Further,
in R. i. 73, Peter narrates to Zacchæus what he had told
Clement, and adds the detail which he did not tell Clement
that James was lame in one foot. Now these facts suggest
that R was using a source in which Peter's arrival at Cæsarea
and first encounter with Clement were preceded by a narrative
section which concluded with the statement that when the
apostle arrived at Cæsarea Zacchæus told him what Simon
had been doing at Cæsarea and Peter told Zacchæus of the
attack made by Saul which had just been narrated. This
suggested to R that Peter should narrate part of the opening
section of QHR to Clement. We turn to i. 71 and observe
that we have explained the fact that Peter, who is speaking,
refers to himself in the third person as "Peter."

§ 213. We have found indications that the Simon contest
and the conversion of the twins was moved by HR from
Tripolis to Cæsarea. We will pursue the subject further.
(i) In R. ii. 5 f., the twins who had been Simon's accom-
plices expose him. In iii. 44 f., 63; H. iii. 58, Simon's
accomplice says that he fled from Cæsarea by night.
But this incident is inconsistent with the statement of
QHR *sub* R. iii. 65, that Simon went north as a propa-
gandist who understood the value of the "preoccupa-
tion" of men's ears. And why should he have thrown
his valuable books into the sea? Now Simon's flight
by night occurs in two other passages, and in each
case it is due to the action of Cæsar against sorcerers. In
R. x. 55, 57, the incident is placed at Antioch and connected
with ancient matter about Cornelius with which it has

nothing to do. The second passage is in VP. In 5, where we have assigned some of the matter to QP, there is also a QC variation from QP. Whereas in QPl and QP *sub* EP, 509, 515, Simon followed Peter to Rome, in 5 as in QC *sub* R. iii. 66, he "preoccupies" him. Now VP, 32, is similarly composite. While the narrative of Simon's fall is based on QP (§ 237 f.), where it was fatal, the VP incident of Simon's flight after his fall must derive from an altogether different Simon incident. That it is the incident with which we are concerned is shewn by the fact that as in R. iii. and R. x. he flies by night, and there is an allusion to an accusation of sorcery. Further, Simon's companion is named Gemellus ("twin") obviously because like the twins who had been *assistants of his wickedness* (R. ii. 6) he joined Peter. It is also clear that in QC Simon did not both leave Cæsarea for Syria in order that by his propaganda he might forestall Peter's preaching and also run away by night from the police after destroying the evidence which they might have used against him. HR has moved the narrative of the exposure of Simon by the twins and, presumably, from Tripolis. We turn to R. iv. 3, and find that Simon fled by night from that city. The flight is entirely unmotived, but in H. viii. 3, there is an unexplained allusion to a charge brought by Simon against Peter. Presumably in QC it was brought against the sorcerer. We conclude that HR and VP respectively moved a QC flight of Simon from Tripolis to Cæsarea and Rome. VP confirms our conjecture that the twins joined Peter after Simon's flight from Tripolis. For VP32 see § 222B (*e*).

The view that HR was influenced by a QP narrative which psClement had altered is confirmed by R. iii. 63 where the unnamed associate of Simon who joins Peter must be Cleobius who is associated with Simon in a parallel with R. i. 72 (EpCor, § J, 289; cf. § 238). This must be a restoration of QP, for psClement substituted the twins for Cleobius.

§ 214. Our canon that the apocryphists never invent was subject to qualifications. But it largely holds good even in the history of the Romance, and it would be in accordance with the methods of HR if he not only moved

Simon's departure from Tripolis but substituted the Cæsarea departure. Now in R. i. 12, immediately before an allusion to Simon, Clement comes to the hospice because he has heard from the people of the apostle's arrival. We may conjecture that Simon heard of it in the same way, and our conjecture is confirmed when we turn back to R. iv. 3. We now observe that there is at this point another instance of the exchange of narrative between Cæsarea and Tripolis. In H. viii. 3 Simon has departed from Tripolis to Syria. Clearly this is a splinter from the Cæsarea section of the source. The implications of the fact that HR did not know that Tripolis was in Syria will be discussed below.

§ 215. I shall deal at some length with the position which has been already illustrated that the settings of the eight discourses of QC were always Cæsarean. The only houses which they mentioned were the hospice and the quarters (of Theophilus) in the pretorium; and the only citizens the first man of the city, his family and the crowds. But there were in HR two exceptions. (i) At Tripolis the citizens are eager to offer the hospitality of their homes. This exceptional fact would be explained if the widow who befriended the twins lived there in QC and if HR moved her to Cæsarea from Tripolis and substituted for her hospitality that of the citizens at large. (ii) In H. iv. 1 Justa the Canaanitess is hostess at Tyre. Now her name is almost certainly editorial (§ 317, IV), and her hospitality was originally the widow's, for she shews affection for the twins and honours Clement (on their account). A later reconstruction will shew that in 10 they are substituted for Peter. HR could not transfer the incident to Cæsarea, for it was necessary to make Peter stay at the hospice. He therefore used it immediately after his Cæsarea section.

§ 216. It was Peter's practice to dine with his companions (R. iii. 74). Why, then, is the dinner of R. v. 36 recorded? Our clues are in ii. 71, where he cannot dine with the unbaptized and vii. 33, where the twins persuade their mother to be baptized in order that she may dine with them. We infer from these passages that the dinner of v. 36 is likely to have been recorded because it followed a baptism. Now the sixteen accompanied Peter to Tripolis (iv. 3), but (v. 36) nineteen dine with him, a fact which the commentators have been unable to explain, because they have assumed that the sixteen, as in the lists of R and H, included the twins. We have, however, concluded that they did not in QC do so, and we may be sure that the dinner of the nineteen was mentioned, because the twins had just been baptized and dined with Peter, Clement and the sixteen for the first time. It is true that, according to R. vi. 15, Clement was baptized after the meal. But this is merely absurd. If there were ten thousand baptisms at Cæsarea, that of Peter's most important convert cannot have been postponed. Moreover, if it had been postponed it would have occurred at the end of the work when his higher teaching was completed. As in the narrative of the departure, Cæsarea matter has been moved to Tripolis in exchange for the Tripolis matter which was moved to Cæsarea.

We conclude that the HR Romance is secondary, and that Simon was originally exposed by the twins at Tripolis. Tripolis was the scene of the Simon contest, because in Papias Marthones was a disciple of Paul and was one of the leaders of the Syrian churches who supported the apostle against his Judaising opponents.

§ 217. That the preHR recension of the Romance which our discussion postulates was that of which fragments were preserved in QEPP (§ 167) is sufficiently proved by a single fact. In M, 70, the widow lives at Tripolis and brings up the twins there. We will, however, examine the relations between the two documents further.

§ 218. 1. If we judge HR by the very low standard set by the Acta, he shewed some skill in telling his story. On the other hand, he carried to absurd lengths a tendency to over-elaborate. Now the narratives which survive from QEPP shew no trace of these elaborations, and this they would have done if they had been secondary. We will compare the two recensions at several points.

(i) In R. vii. 13 Mattidia begs, not at the gates of the city as in M, but at those of the temple. The change was due to HR's use of Heg, a matter which will be discussed below. He wished to drag in an allusion of Heg to some wonderful columns in the temple. Peter, who had just been described as a friar (6), becomes a tourist.

(ii) In M, 70 (depraved in EP, 486) Clement bursts into tears when he tells Peter of the loss of his father. In R. vii. 7 he weeps because he is touched by Peter's humility, and says that he took the place of a father.

(iii) In M seamen bring the twins to the widow, who gives them their names. In R pirates find them clinging to a plank at sea and frighten them into changing their names.

§ 219. 2. We now turn to the accounts of Faustinianus.

(i) In both R and M the Romance originates in the infatuation of the brother of Faustinianus for his sister-in-law. She left Rome with the twins, leaving Clement with his father. In R. vii. 8 f. Clement tells Peter how his father grieved when his wife disappeared, and that he went in search of her. Now we should expect this matter to be at any rate referred to in the introduction in which Clement describes his boyhood, but we hear of nothing but his interest in philosophers, hierophants and magicians, and the visit which he paid to the East after his father's departure. The account of his life, given by Faustinianus in ix. 32, is no less strange. Like his son, he was interested in magic, and was convinced by an astrologist that his wife had committed adultery with a slave. It is obvious that this story does not cohere with that of the devoted husband and father who went in search of his wife and children. We may suspect that the HR introduction and the interest of Clement and his father in magic are editorial. We turn to M, 67 f. and find that the narrative opens, as we should expect, with an account of Faustinianus and his wife, who hear Christian preaching at Rome, and with the story of the brother. Clement told Peter that his father took him with him, but lost him (M, 72). This is a plain and straightforward story which provided materials for one of the two strands which HR clumsily combined. In QC the reader's sympathy with the unfortunate family was elicited from the outset.

(ii) It was shewn in § 191 B that the companion of Faustinianus in H. xiv. 7 was originally Cornelius. Now Clement (Cornelius) accompanies his father from Rome in M, 71, but is left behind in R. vii. 10.

§ 220. Before we examine some highly probable traces of the influence of the Romance on Justin and on some writers who derive from Heg, it will be convenient that we should review the evidence for the position which has been already illustrated by the eight ordinations and the eight books, that the settings of the eight books were Cæsarean.

A. Peter was accompanied by his converts (R. iv. 1, vii. 1: cf. QPl *sub* EPl, 656, 682; AT, 16 and QP *sub* APh, 93; also VP, 3 and AT, 68). He was met at the gate of the city (R. i. 73, iv. 1 f.; H. vi. 26), whence he was conducted to the hospice (H. vi. 26, viii. 2; R. i. 73, vii. 2). In R. vii. 2 the hospice is near the gate, but in EPl, 617 (probably = QPl), in the market-place. There is also an allusion to the gate in M (§ 218) and in VP, 17.

B. Peter was then invited to a house with his companions (R. viii. 36, ix. 38; H. viii. 1).

C. Here there were preaching and healings (R. ii. 70, iv. 6; H. vi. 26, viii. 6; R. iv. 37, viii. 36; H. xv. 11; R. x. 70). The crowds were bidden assemble next day (R. ii. 70, iv. 37, v. 37), an incident which occurs in EusThadd, 20.

D. The host (B) was a great man. In the citations he is contrasted with the people. In R. viii. 35 he is the chief man of the city, in H. iv. 10 a rich man, in EP, 501, the Emperor. Maroones was evidently a man of importance. In LPh he was "the governor" (§ 167 A).

E. The host's house was that of a man of high rank. In EP, 501 and R. x. 71, it is a palace. In R. ix. 38 we find one of a series of parallels with the description of the

S

pretorium which Herod (who also built that at Cæsarea) built at Jerusalem in the fact that there was accommodation for many guests (Jos. Ant. XVI. ix. 6; BJ, V. iv. 4). In R. iv. 6 f. we read of a garden within the house, *i.e.* a piazza, which was approached by a passage through which the people streamed. Peter preached from a pillar in the court, where he had confuted Simon (iii. 64), and later dined (ii. 70, so v. 36). The waters mentioned in R. iv. 6 refreshed the trees mentioned in H. x. 26. For the scene cf. H. iv. 10. In H. vii. 1 Peter preaches from a stone, and in H. viii. 8, where the incident is not mutilated, from the base of a (fountain) statue.

§ 221. Our discussion may now be extended.

F. In R. ii. 70 those whom Peter had begun to teach dine in the court, but inasmuch as they were unbaptized, Peter did not eat with them. In v. 19 he dines and discourses in the garden with the nineteen (cf. iii. 74). In EPl, 619 f. (=QPl), the apostles (John and Judas) dwell in the market-place, are summoned to the palace, where they teach Thewodas and his friends, who dine in the garden; but the apostles ate nothing that day (*i.e.* they ate with Theodore after his baptism). In a much edited parallel Thomas is summoned from the hospice to the palace and does not eat at the banquet (AT, 5). On the other hand in a section of LJasZ, which derives from KP, Theophilus invites the apostle(s) to eat after the healing (33).

G. EP, 502-4, is obviously a cento. In 502 there is an allusion to a "fountain," which is mentioned also in 490 and 655, and which we shall conclude was the traditional scene of the first baptisms at Cæsarea. It lay to the east of the city, and in the time of Heg it was known as "Peter's birket" (490).

In 503 there occurs the following passage: *he* ("the Emperor," *i.e.* Theophilus) *began to build the church which is known as Kuesyan (?) in the name of his son, whom Christ raised from the dead, and he called it after me, Peter. And he built another church by the city wall towards the east, and he called it after the name of Saint Paul, and he turned the great*

heathen temple which the ancients had built in the name of the
planet Mars into a church, which was dedicated in the name
of Saint John our companion.

(i) The writer of QEPP, as elsewhere, introduced Peter
and Paul, but also, as in 491 and 520, allowed S. John's
name to remain. The temple of R. iv. 6 was that of Mars
(cf. § 226 H), because Leucius identified Cornelius with
Dionysius, the Areopagite, and made Theophilus and his
sons priests (§ 183 (i)). In QEPP it became a church
dedicated to S. John, because in QPl S. John went to
Cæsarea.

(ii) *After me Peter* is obviously an editorial addition to
the statement of Heg that Theophilus built a church, the
name of which he gave as Kuesyan(?). *Whom Christ raised*
depraves Heg *sub* H. xx. 13, where Christ is said to have
healed Cornelius. The original nucleus is preserved in
APh, 84–88, where the son (in KP, the "lad") of Theophilus
(whose name in APh is transferred to his "son") is healed
as he is in LJasZ, 32 f. Nereus (Theophilus), after the
healing, builds *a synagogue or bishop's house in the name of*
Christ, the allusion to Christ being editorial. There are
two parallels. (*a*) *He appointed them a bishop who was the*
ruler of the synagogue (LSim, 116). (*b*) In VP, 9, Peter
goes to the house of Marcellus from the synagogue. In
QP he went from the hospice. Such variations are
frequent in VP.

The evidence then shews that there were two primitive
churches at Cæsarea, the synagogue built by Theophilus
and the hospice to which S. Peter went in QP on his arrival
at Cæsarea and where he lodged in QPl, and which was
in J called *the house of the community* (*sub* QPl *sub* EP, 480).
It was doubtless originally the house of a Christian, who,
I shall suggest, was Tobias, the father of Tabitha (STrans,
25), and who was the apostle's host, and had become when
psMark visited Cæsarea the hospice of the church, like the
houses of Mary, the mother of Mark, Lois, Claudia and
Priscilla (Rom. xvi. 3), which became the *hospitium Bethy-*
norum (cf. VP, 4). Cf. § 175, 19.

The two primitive churches mentioned in Heg were

doubtless used by Greek- and Aramaic-speaking con-
gregations respectively. Many of the Jews would worship
in the house of their compatriot who had received the
apostle. Theophilus built the synagogue primarily for the
use of his household, Christian officials and other Greek-
speaking worshippers. He and his son Cornelius naturally
were among its first zekanim.

Most, if not all, of the topographical matter which we
have collected is earlier than Heg, but when we collect and
discuss the allusions to the topography of Cæsarea, his
interest in the subject will be clear. Some other topographical
allusions occur in the writers who on our view were influenced
by QC.

§ 222. The following passages shew the influence of Heg's
excerpts from QC.

A. In LPh, 62, the apostle and his disciples lodge with
Marwan, the governor of the city. The L Acts seldom use
names that were not in the source. The splinter almost
certainly refers to Maroones. The statement that he was
a governor occurs neither in R or H. But the governor
of Tripolis must have been mentioned if Simon was
exposed there. (See also § 220 D. For "lodged," see
§ 220 B.)

B. We will now turn to VP and (diverging from our
present task) note some topographical allusions to Cæsarea
which derive from passages of QP which were parallel
with QC.

(a) In VP, 6, Peter takes up his abode with the elder
Narcissus, who represents Zacchæus. In 9 he goes from
the synagogue (§ 221 G) to the house of Marcellus (§ 220 AB).
The passage continues the QP parallels with R given in
§ 198. For Marcellus and his house see also § 225 B.

(b) In one of the confused centoistic stories of VP (11)
there is a statue in the house of Marcellus and an allusion
to water running down. For Marcellus, cf. § 225 KLM; for
the statue, cf. § 190. This matter seems to be combined
with the story of the statue erected at Jamnia (§ 190).
Marcellus is afraid lest the Emperor should hear of the

destruction of the statue by a young man, for it was a statue of the Emperor. The suggestion is confirmed by a splinter in H. ii. 1, where among some absurd designations we unaccountably read of the Jamninians. In 14 and 19 there are allusions to porticoes (the piazza) and the outer gate (the door of 11) of the house of Marcellus.

We must attribute the following matter to the influence of Heg's citations of QC.

(c) In 5 Simon "preoccupies" Peter. (See § 213.)

(d) In 6 an unmotived incident (Ariston day after day questioned sailors) is from QC *sub* R. vii. 10; M, 71.

(e) In 17 a confused story combines matter from two incidents in Heg. The following elements in the narrative derive from the Tripolis section of QC. (a) Peter has driven Simon out of Judæa, where he has been working magic. (b) Simon has robbed a widow named Eubola (the widow of Tripolis). Peter goes to her (the widow of T entertained him). (c) Apparently in Heg two young men (the twins) stole her property. (d) A gate, a pretorium and a ruler (Marthones) are mentioned. (e) The name Italicus may be suggested by Aquila. Antulus may be suggested by Antonius, Simon's father (R. ii. 7). (f) The sequel of the story is used in 32, where Gemellus (twin) deserts Simon for Peter in a context which certainly derives from the Tripolis section of QC (§ 213).

C. In AAM, a composite Acts based on Heg, the apostle sits behind an alabaster statue, from the mouth of which water pours (22, 29). But KP or QP are possible sources as well as QC.

D. We now turn to a context of AT, in which we have already observed the influence of Heg (§ 188), and compare with 18 H. iv. 9 f., where the rich man of Tyre says:

Let us choose some place for private conference... (away) from the city. They sat down in a place where there were streams...and all sorts of trees.	AT, 18. The king took him outside the city gate and began to speak to him.... The place was wooded and there was much water. A description of the Cæsarean pretorium follows.

There can be no doubt that there is a literary relation. The point is that it is very improbable that in QP Theophilus (or even Cornelius) invited Peter to leave the city (*i.e.* the hospice) to go to the garden-court for the purpose of *conversation*.

§ 223. There is one probable instance of the influence of QC on patristic which is earlier than Heg. In R. viii. 1 f. Peter finds on the shore a distinguished old Roman who had come to doubt the existence of God and was there in quest of his wife and children. We now turn to the setting of Trypho, a work which is much influenced by KP and here and there by QPl. We remember that fictitious settings of such works were customary and that the Christian writers of Justin's time had no capacity for invention. (*a*) In 1 Justin describes his philosophical difficulties and studies. I do not suggest that this is nothing but fiction, but it is also a contact with QC. In 8 he describes himself as meeting near the sea an elderly man of grave disposition who said that he was anxious about some members of his household who had left him and whom he was seeking. These incidents are entirely irrelevant to Justin's purpose, and we find them in the Romance. (See § 219.) (*b*) In QC *sub* H. iv. 9 f. Peter, like Thomas, was invited for a discussion in the garden. In H Simon has companions. In Tryph. 9 Trypho has companions, and Justin suggests that they should withdraw to a spot where they might rest. They go to a colonnade (the piazza and the *porticatio* of VP). In 142 Justin is expecting to embark at once. In QC Peter went from city to city.

§ 224. We noticed in § 214 that, in a context where H preserves HR better than R, Simon goes from the Syrian Tripolis to Syria, a fact which shews that HR was not acquainted with the Syrian coast. Now he found in QC allusions to five towns in Syria and the island of Aradus, that island being mentioned in connection with the shipwreck. PsClement, however, only selected from QP the geographical matter which was required for the scheme of his work, the narrative of which, apart from the plot of the romance which he doubtless adopted from some novel, was plain, straightforward, and simply told. Now HR contains topographical and geographical matter in which the writer is merely elaborating and displaying his knowledge. It must derive from the source of the allusions to Theophilus and Cornelius, *i.e.* from Heg.

We will examine this non-Clementine matter in detail.

1. That Simon was born at Gittæ (H. ii. 22) was probably stated in KP (Just. Ap. i. 26), but it is very improbable that KP stated that Gittæ was six schœni from Samaria.

2. R. iv. 1. Peter first stays in a small town called Dora.

3. H. viii. 1. People follow from Byblus.

4. R. vi. 15. Clement was baptized in the fountains adjoining the sea. This is in the very manner of Heg. He would describe the traditional site of S. Paul's baptism of Marthones.

5. H. xi. 36. Peter, who is at Tripolis, sends the forerunners to Antioch in Syria, after bidding farewell to the people in Tripolis of Phœnicia. That a writer who was describing the journey of Peter from Jerusalem to Antioch should say at this point which Antioch he means, requires explanation. Moreover, "Tripolis of Phœnicia" at this point is absurd, as indeed it would have been at the beginning of the Tripolis section. No other Tripolis was possible. We must connect these two facts with viii. 3, where, though Peter is in the Syrian Tripolis, HR sends him to Syria. Now, such definitions were in the manner of the travelled Heg. In ClemBps we find Cæsarea of Palestine, Laodicea in Phrygia, Berœa in Macedonia, and the very phrase which H uses in connection with Marthones, Tripolis in Phœnicia. For the occurrence of "Antioch in Syria" in Heg, see § 373.

6. R. vii. 1. The first halt was at Orthosias, not far from Tripolis.

7. R. vii. 13. Antharadus is not more than six furlongs from the coast. Columns of vinewood and works of Phidias adorn a temple which we know from M, QC did not mention. Heg had seen the statues of Phidias in a temple at Athens.

8. R. vii. 25. Balaneæ, Pathos, and Gabala are mentioned.

9. See § 257.

We may safely assign all this matter to the notes which Heg made in the course of his journeys to Rome and Damascus. (Cf. § 175, *ad init.* and 1–4.)

§ 225. Theophilus and our identification of him with Marcellus played an important part in our discussions, and this will be a convenient point at which to collect the occurrences of the two names.

A. ClemBps states the ordinations of Cornelius and Theophilus at Cæsarea.

B. Cornelius and Theophilus entered HR together (R. x. 55, 71) in connection with matter which implies the identification of Theophilus with Marcellus (§ 191 D).

C. In QPl *sub* EvvC, 5, Theophilus was an official of rank stationed in Palestine.

D. In LJasZ, 33, Theophilus is a chief magistrate in a Cæsarean narrative.

E. A parallel narrative of the healing transfers the name Theophilus to the healed lad (APh, 84).

F. In LLk, 153, Theophilus is an "old man" (senator, § 192) as Marcellus is in VP, 8 and Kewestos in EP, 11.

G. The Altercatio collocates Theophilus with Simon.

H. The signature of Theophilus to Ep. Cor. connects him with Cæsarea, Simon, and Cleobius (§ 200).

J. PsSen Ep, 7, connects Theophilus with Paul, Seneca and the apostle's journey to Spain (§ 194 F).

K. In a Cæsarea ending (LSim, 116), Marcellus is ordained. (Cf. A.)

L. In VP, 8, Marcellus is a senator who was too kind to the poor when he held a provincial appointment. For his house, cf. § 222 (*b*).

M. In AJ, 18, the names Marcellus and Cleobius are collocated.

§ 226. We will now examine some evidence which shews that in QPl Theophilus was also named Demetrius and Cornelius Dionysius. The latter was baptised by Judas Matthias and received the name Matthias, which was identified with that of Matthew and also Græcised as Theodore (Theodas, Theon).

A. In EPl, 620 f., Thewodas (F) is the governor of the city and his son's name is *Theodore*. The parallels shew that *Thewodas* is the *Demetrius* (HK) of 641. In 586 *Demetrius* of Ephesus is a priest, because his namesake was in QPl (§ 183). In 518 *Dionysius* (Cornelius: GHJK) is the son of the heathen high priest, and in 520 Paul has revealed the mysteries to him. In 17 *Demas* in a context related to EPl, 620–641, is a priest. For Leucius Cornelius Dionysius see also the Table in § 259.

B. In AT, 4 f. the king's daughter is married instead of his son (Leucius Cornelius). The story of the Encratite marriage in which Christ appears (11) underlies 154, where it is told of Ouazanes, the king's son (139). In 169 Siphor (Theophilus) and he are respectively ordained priest and deacon by Judas just before his death. In MM, 28, the king and his son after the apostle's death are ordained priest and deacon by *Matthew* (Matthias), and after receiving at their baptism the name *Matthew* (so in A they are named Thewodas and Theodore: see also CF). They had married Wisdom and Understanding who, in EpApp, 44, are two of the virgins of Matt. xxv. I shall have something to say about a difficult tangle of sources which lies behind this incident. We may compare Jerome, who says (Cornelius) *virgo sortiretur uxorem* (Migne, I. 499), with AT, 150, where Ouazanes (the king's son and Cornelius) says that before he married he knew no woman. In AT, 138 Siphor (the father of Ouazanes) like *Marcellus* (VP, 20: cf. § 222 B (*a*)) provides a triclinium, which is also mentioned in R. viii. 38 and in which as in R and VP the apostle teaches. We are confirmed therefore in our identification of Marcellus with Theophilus. For the ordinations and *Thion* (A) see § 183 and § 225 K.

C. In the matter added to the AT matter in LT the name *Lucius* is transferred to the king, who later is named *Matthaus* (98, BF).

D. In LJas, 145 f., LSim, 115, a story is derived from Heg (cf. Proch, 74, 5 f.) which probably began its history in J. The wife is *Theopiste* (E), because in 116 Marcellus is the ruler of the synagogue. Leucius coined this name for his wife on the analogy of Theophilus.

E. In an Arabic Synaxary (Patr. Or. iii. 208 f.), *Theopiste* (D) is the wife of *Theodore* (AF).

F. Basilides spoke of secret discourses which were communicated to him by *Matthias*, who heard them from the Saviour. Hippolytus [1] blunders. Basilides claimed to have heard them from Cornelius Theodas (*i.e.* Matthias, BC), who heard them from the apostle whose name he had received at his baptism. Similarly Valentinus claimed to have heard *Theodas* (A), the disciple of Paul (Clem. Strom. vii. 106). This is an important clue for the reconstruction of QPl. The disciple of Matthias became the disciple of Paul.

G. The bridegroom of B is in the Latin AT named *Dionysius* (AGJK, Lips. i. 251). (See § 185 (vii).)

H. By a slight blunder *Dionysius* (AGJK) becomes in the ActaSS (Propyl. Nov. 1) the son of Cornelius, but in the Constantinople Synaxary he is rightly the son of *Demetrius* (AK). In the Arabic Synaxary (Patr. Or. iii. 208, Nov. 19) he adores the stars, was ordained bishop and baptized the governor *Demetrius*.

J. According to the Armenian Synaxary [2] *Dionysius* (AGHK) went to the house of the Virgin whose mysteries (revealed to John in EP, 520) were known to him. According to ps*Dionysius* (Dict. Christ. Biog., i. 484*a*) he was present at the death of the Virgin, as in STrans, 32, JosTrans (J, 217) is *Leucius*.

K. Leucius accompanied Paul to Rome (§ 259 f.). Now in VP, 3, we find among the disciples of that apostle at Rome a *Dionysius* and a *Demetrius* who, like Marcellus, was a senator.

[1] Ref. viii. 20.   [2] Patr. Or. v. 376.

CHAPTER VIII

The Apostolic Council. The Journeys of Judas and Simon. The Neronian Persecution

§ 227. The concentration of our attention on the influence of the primary Acts on the chronology of Heg has resulted in omissions in our study of the evidence for the first septennium. We will at the outset continue our reconstruction of some of J's structural perversions of KP.

The Apostolic Council of the Seventh Year

The evidence for the incident which Leucius substituted for the apostolic council is small in quantity, but it is very clear.

A. The statement of AThadd, 4, that the apostles met annually at the passover is connected with an allusion to the decrees which they enacted (§ 204).

B. In SObsBVM, 42 (J, 224), Paul asks the twelve what they will preach when they go forth, and is answered by Peter, John, and Andrew. He recommends a gentler policy, and they are angry. While they dispute, Christ appears and supports Paul. The incident underlies STrans, 63, where the dispute is at the mouth of the cave (sepulchre), and in psMelito, 5. No apocryphist who was later than Heg would have invented the contention between S. Paul and the twelve, and it is evident that the three *Dormitios* derive in common from an excerpt in Heg.

C. PsCyprian (§ 23) says that Peter and Paul met at Rome after a comparison of the preaching.

The distinction which Leucius drew between the position of Paul and that of the twelve had some slight justification. S. Paul in KP took no part in the proceedings of the apostolic council and in 1 Corinthians both transgressed the letter of

the decree and wrote, *all things are lawful*, a position which
he asserted in the first lost letter and which had been
misunderstood. The tradition that the founder of the Asian
churches was at variance with the twelve had deepened,
and Leucius was insisting on some fundamental opposition
to the apostolic letter. This cannot have concerned circumcision, for there is no evidence or probability that he took
any interest in the matter, and, if his position had been
that of Cerinthus, it is obvious that he would not have
made S. Paul the hero of the work. It follows that he
rejected the apostolic decree as to *eidolothuta* and *suffocata*,
as also that, like the Nicolaitans, Leucius attributed to
Paul a view as to *eidolothuta* which varied from that which
the church of his time and place attributed to the twelve.
Now this inference tallies with our earlier conclusion that
he held the Elkesaite position that in times of persecution
a Christian might dissemble his faith and also with a narrative
which we shall assign to QPl in the next chapter and which
represents Paul as worshipping in a heathen temple at
Antioch with the result that John was saved from persecuting
magistrates.

§ 228. Cerinthus could not and did not evade the problem
of the apostolic letter. J narrated how James taught the
law in its true form as it had been republished by Christ
on Olivet, and shewed that James rejected both the interpolations of later Judaism and the heresy inculcated in the
letter attributed to the apostles. The decree, however,
found a place in the disciplinary system of J. According to
R. iv. 35 f., a passage which clearly derives from J, Peter
bade Maro believe no teacher who was not authorised by
James or his successor (Judas). The things which pollute
the wedding garment given in baptism are the rejection
of the true Prophet, the non-observance of the law as to
such matters as murder and adultery *and not to partake of
the table of demons, to taste things sacrificed or blood or a
carcase which is strangled or if there be aught else which is
offered to demons. This is the first step which brings forth
thirty commands, and the second sixty, and the third one*

hundred. Peter then says that he will explain the matter more fully, a promise which he does not keep. A comparison with H. xi. 35 shews that R has used QHR.

The derivation of our passage from J is shewn not only by its strong assertion of the authority of James but also by the influence of the matter of which it formed a part on QPl.

(*a*) The thirty commandments when broken became the thirty snakes which fill the mouth of Judas in CBRB, 185, and the thirty devils which build the house of torment in LA, 7.

(*b*) The Naasenes who used the QPl discourses of James (§ 128) preserved the threefold gradation of J in their three churches which were respectively angelic, psychical and earthly, and the names of which were elect, called, captive (Hipp. Ref. v. 6). For "elect" compare *the elect Thomas* (JamesAT, 45), *Peter my chosen* (LJas, 140).

(*c*) Papias ap. Iren. V. xxxvi. 1 f. describes the triple division of the saved thus: *Then those who are deemed worthy of an abode in heaven shall go there, others shall enjoy the delights of Paradise and others shall possess the splendour of the city; for everywhere the Saviour shall be seen according as they that see Him are worthy.* Three striking contacts with R follow: *This is the distinction between those who produce an hundredfold . . . sixtyfold . . . thirtyfold . . . the guests who are invited to the wedding. . . . They advance by steps.* If this passage derives ultimately from J it must be through Leucius, who elsewhere influences Papias and to whom we shall attribute the words *they shall see who are worthy* (§ 367). We may also compare with Papias R. i. 51, where (Enoch and Elijah) are translated to Paradise and those in whose flesh some evil remains are kept in good abodes (the city of Papias). For the connection between rewards and discipline we may compare the relation between the injunctions preserved in Didache and the torments described in ApP.

§ 229. It is obvious to suggest that inasmuch as the gradations or steps of R. iv. 36, in the discipline were fundamental in J and that work on our view contained discourses of James, Epiphanius referred to it when he wrote (§ 24):

Certain supposititious Steps or Discourses so called do (*the Ebionites*) *produce in the Steps of James*. This identification may be confirmed.

(i) Both the Steps and J were important works. If the Steps was not J it did not influence the apocrypha. If J was not the Steps it was not mentioned by any of the writers who speak of the Ebionite literature.

(ii) Cerinthus only accepted the law in part. The Steps and J (R. i. 37) rejected the law of sacrifices.

(iii) In the Steps James is represented as speaking against the temple. It will be shewn that the James of J was based on the Stephen of KP and that Stephen in KP might be understood to have attacked the temple. Cf. R. i. 37 and Acts vi. 14.

(iv) Both works were violent in their antagonism to S. Paul, and some of the attacks of the Steps on the apostle almost certainly underlie the apocrypha. The accusation of the Steps that Paul was circumcised because he wanted to marry the high priest's daughter (§ 24) somewhat resembles a passage which may be assigned to QPl in which the Jews say to the apostle: *thou art from Tarsus, and because thou art a poor man thou hast taken the name of the Messiah, and thou art a freeman by it* (STrans, 28). It will be observed that in this passage "Tarsian" is used as a term of reproach as it was in the Steps. Other instances occur in EvvC, 8; RSteph, 160; EP, 498. (See also § 240 K).

(v) M probably taught a graded discipline (§ 90*r*, p. 125).

§ 230. We will now retrace our steps.

It was to Cerinthus and Leucius that Papias refers when he speaks in his preface of men of many words who put forward alien commandments. Cerinthus wrote with the purpose of discrediting not only the apostolic view of Christ but also the apostolic discipline. With this purpose he rewrote the histories of the churches of Jerusalem, Cæsarea, and Antioch. At Jerusalem James supplanted Peter, and his deacon, Ananias Antonius, was a counterpart of Mark. The J Cæsarea narrative perverted KP. Ananias in KP was one of Peter's six companions, and in the same list Cerinthus found Joseph and Judas Barsabas

(§ 310 E), who were identified with the Lord's brethren. We are not concerned here with the historicity of this identification, but it may be observed in passing that it is supported by 1 Cor. ix. 5, where Peter is said to have been accompanied as he was in KP by his wife on his missionary journeyings, as were also the brethren of the Lord by their wives. Further, if Judas Barsabas was both the brother of James and one of the founders of the church of Cæsarea, we understand why he was chosen to take the apostolic letter to Antioch. Leucius explained away the tradition that Judas was the Lord's brother by saying that he was also named Thomas, because spiritually he was the Lord's twin brother (§ 272).

As has been said, if Judas supplanted Peter at Cæsarea and James was killed at the seventh passover, the conclusion of J was inevitable. The history of the Primitive Church had been a tragedy. At the very moment when James had all but persuaded Caiaphas and the people to be baptised (R. i. 69 f.) and Judas, perhaps, had reported the success of his missionary work, Saul had murdered the Lord's brother. The rest was epilogue and must have been concerned with Judas. Nor can there be any doubt as to how the epilogue began. J had just narrated a gathering of the church for the passover, and this event in KP was followed by the journey of Barnabas to Antioch (Acts xi. 22). J telescoped these incidents into his substitutes for the apostolic council and the journey of Judas Barsabas. Judas went to Antioch after the passover and Saul pursued him with a view to continuing the persecution and to perverting the Antiochene converts.

§ 231. Our conjectural reconstruction tallies with the following facts:

(i) We have already concluded that a council at which the disciple was discussed occurred in QPl.

(ii) We shall find evidence that KP had a section parallel with Acts xii.–xv.

(iii) There is evidence for the succession of Judas to James. R. iv. 35, a context which we have just assigned to J, speaks of the successor of James. (See also § 274.) This evidence is evidence for J. Apart from it it seems to be a secure position that the structural depravations in the QPl narrative of the first eight years are due to that Acts.

(iv) Our hypothesis will enable us to explain the origin of the following two apocryphal apostles, each of whom occurs in QPl contexts, Judas Thomas and *Barnabas Matthias, who was chosen in the place of Judas* (R. i. 64). (See § 274 f.)

§ 232. We now return to the J matter in R. i. at the point where Saul attacked James. In 71 the brethren go to the house of James (a J phrase). Saul hastens to Damascus, intending to employ the help of unbelievers against the faithful (a J calumny) and supposing that Peter had fled thither. Peter cannot have been Saul's quarry in J, and psClement must have substituted Peter for Judas. Our passage shews that in J Judas left Jerusalem and suggests that Saul pursued him to Antioch. But the climax of J cannot have been at Antioch. If Judas supplanted Peter as the founder of the church of Cæsarea he must have reached Rome, have suffered and have robbed the apostle of his martyr's crown ("AJ," 4), and it is antecedently probable that in J Saul consummated his crimes by playing the part of which historians suspect Poppæa.

Conjectures which are based on a few facts and the logic of J's procedure explain the journey of Peter to Rome under Gaius which we have discussed, and the visits of Barnabas, of Thomas, of Judas and his sons. Moreover, they also explain Simon's. If Cerinthus accounted for S. Paul's journey to Rome by making him pursue Judas, Leucius, who said that James was murdered by the captain and not by Saul, must have substituted another pursuer, and Simon, who in KP followed Peter to Cæsarea and opposed him there, would be the inevitable substitute. In QPl and QP Simon followed the apostles to Rome; in QC he "preoccupied" Peter, as he did at Cæsarea.

§ 233. The position that in J Judas and in QPl Judas and John went to Rome and were tried before the Emperor is confirmed by the following passages:

A. QDesp ap. HE, III. xxvi. 4. *The sons of Judas when asked about Christ and His kingdom . . . replied that it was not of this world* (Jn. xviii. 36), *nor earthly, but angelic, (and) that it would appear at the end of the world . . . when He would come to judge the quick and the dead.*

B. AJ ap. "AJ," 8. *Art thou John who said that my kingdom would speedily be uprooted and that another king, Jesus, would reign instead of me? . . . Out of heaven shall come a king, eternal, true, the judge of quick and dead.*

C. MPl, 2. Nero said, *Shall the king of the ages overthrow all kingdoms? . . . Barnabas* (Gk. Bars.) *Justus. . . . 3. Nero said to Paul, thou art the great king's man. . . . 4. . . . not the king that cometh from earth but from heaven . . . cometh as judge.* Barnabas was another name of Judas.

These passages must derive from a passage of QPl in which Judas and John impressed the Emperor as John impressed Tiberius (EvvC, 4), and were acquitted. In C the phrase "the great king" is a contact with J as is also the unexpected allusion to Barsabas Justus (Lat Barn). Apart from these contacts with J, evidence for the acquittal of John and Judas in a QPl Rome narrative is evidence for the condemnation of Judas in J.

§ 234. In the most important document for the reconstruction of the Rome section of J, Simon Magus plays an important part, and we will now turn to the subject of this strange figure. Happily it will not be necessary to discuss all its ramifications.

1. No one would have invented the tears attributed to Simon in the western gloss at Acts viii. 24, and we may safely attribute this incident and Simon's association with Cleobius to KP. In KP the Samaritans were one of the seven sects of the Jews, and Simon may have gone to Cæsarea as an "apostle" of the Sanhedrin. There is no evidence which suggests that in KP he left Judæa.

2. There is an antecedent probability that J would transfer Simon's misdeeds to Saul, and we may plausibly account in this way for the fact that in RSteph, 160 (a composite

T

Acts), Saul is at Cæsarea. The conjecture is confirmed by the fact that he is described as a Tarsian (§ 24).

§ 235. 3. Leucius treated the Simon matter which we attribute to KP and J as follows:

(i) If in KP Simon opposed Peter at Cæsarea and in J Saul took his place and stirred up persecution, we have accounted for some eschatological midrash which occurred in QPl *sub* EPl, 622 and LPP, 182, in which Acts a demon king who has come from the east and represents Antichrist stirs up persecution against the apostles. Leucius may have found the Nero Antichrist myth in KP, for it influences AscIs iv. 2–4. At any rate he used it *sub* AT, 32, where the persecuting dragon says that he is kinsman to him who is to come from the east. The influence of J on QPl is also shewn in the identification of the kings who will accompany Antichrist with the tares of the parable in EP, 513, 520. In J *sub* R. i. 70 and EpClem, 2, Saul was the *inimicus homo* of Matt. xiii. 25. Cf. also §§ 228, 240 H.

That the demon of QPl *sub* QEPP *sub* EP and LPP was the Simon of KP is shewn also by two details. (i) As in R. i. 20 Peter's contest with Simon will be a week after his arrival and in VP, 15, on the next sabbath (VP usually disarranges and modifies his source), so in EPl, 622, the demon arrives a week after the apostles. (ii) In LPP the demon weeps, an inadequately motived detail. In Proch 37, 12, a weeping demon has come from "Palestinian Cæsarea," Heg's phrase *sub* ClemBps.

(ii) We shall conclude that just as in J Saul played the part of Simon at Cæsarea, so in the QPl Antioch and Rome narrative Simon played J's Saul.

§ 236. (iii) The story of Simon's statue must be a midrash attacking Cæsar worship and the invention of Leucius. It was probably suggested by KP *sub* AscIs iv. 11, where Antichrist will set up his statue in every place. The QPl statue was inscribed with words which travesty similar phrases which were carved on countless statues of the Roman emperors and their sons, *to Simon the new god* (VP, 10). Justin (Apol. i. 26) would not have identified the statue to Semo Sanco with Simon's unless he had already read and accepted the story. There are other traces of the influence of QPl on his works (§ 331). The Antichrist myth was used at Rome as at Cæsarea.

In the next chapter we shall conclude that the arrival of Paul from Athens in EP, 509, is from QPl, and the later arrival of Simon must be from the same source. The allusion to Jannes and Jambres in connection with the enchantments by which Simon led men astray confirms this attribution (§ 315 H).

§ 237. (iv) The QPl narrative of Simon's death underlies Hipp. Ref. vi. 15 and runs: *Journeying as far as Rome he fell in with the apostles* (John, Judas, Paul, and Peter). *Peter opposed him. His death was as follows. He said that he would rise the third day. Accordingly having ordered a trench to be dug by his disciples he directed that he himself should be interred there.* This story evidently suggested that of the death of S. John, who in AJ, 111, bids the young men dig a trench, lies down in it, dies and is buried. Leucius represented Simon as practising once too often the art of suspended animation which was and is believed to be still practised in India. Peter, according to psCyprian (§ 23), was at Rome, but it is surprising that he is the protagonist. Hippolytus may be guilty of a slip due to the story of QP. In this incident Simon is a false Christ as he is in R. ii. 9, where he claims to have worked the miracles assigned to Jesus in EvT, 12 and EvM, 34.

§ 238. 4. In KP Saul opposed Stephen at Jerusalem. QP substituted Simon and Peter (Table § 118). The KP conflict at Caesarea was postponed to the eighth year (§ 200). QP probably made Simon follow Peter to Antioch. In EP 515 just as in QPl he followed John. In EP, 515, Simon arrives in Rome a second time in a narrative which must derive from a section of QP which underlies the following parallels:

	H and R	VP	Didasc 24	EP	
A. Simon at Jerusalem	..	23	D	..	
B. Simon follows Peter	..	..	D	(?)5[15]	
C. Representing the Jews	..	..	D	..	
D. Contest the next sabbath	R. i. 20	18, cf. 7	..	(?) QP	
E. He is a ravening wolf	H. xi. 35	8	::	..	
F. And false apostle	R. iv. 34, H. xi. 35	..	D	..	(probably) QP *sub* Heg ap. HE, IV. xxii. 5 f.
G. An ox is raised	..	::	::	5[16]	Photius, Slav AP (Lips. ii. 212)
H. The statue	R. iii. 65	10	D	..	HE, II. xiv.
J. He falls and dies	..	32	D	5[17]	MPP, 55 f. Philastr.
K. Cleobius	..	3	D	..	Heg ap. HE, IV. xxii.

The narrative underlying Didascalia must be that of QP. On the one hand, the story of Simon's death imitates that in QPl; the statue is Leucian, and probably also the raised ox. On the other hand, our discussion has shewn that Cleobius cannot have occurred in QPl at this point. He was probably like Dositheus an historical heretic mentioned in KP. (Cf. § 213.)

§ 239. 5. Our discussion of the activities of Simon at Tripolis and of his relations with Marthones and the twins must be added to the arguments for the view that the Clementine Simon sometimes caricatures S. Paul. Some of Headlam's objections to this position (BD, iv. 524*b*) have been implicitly met, but not that from the distinction between Saul and Simon in R. i. 69. The text here is impossible. No apocryphist could have made Saul describe the disciples as perverts of Simon. He must have said that James was misled by a magician (Jesus: cf. EvN, i. 1). The true text is preserved in Abd vi. 3, where *Simon* is omitted.

MPP

§ 240. Our view that Simon, who in QPl followed John and Judas to Rome, was the Saul of J is confirmed by MPP, in which work Peter and Paul were originally John and Judas, a fact which shews that it is based on QEPP.

We will note in our MPP context some passages which must derive from QPl.

A. It must have been Leucius who rewrote the words spoken by Christ at S. Paul's conversion: *I am the truth* (Jn. xiv. 6) *whom thou persecutest* (39). . . . *Go forth, for I will be with thee; and all things as many as thou shalt say and do I will justify* (38, Lat). Christ in QPl fulfilled this promise when in the QPl apostolic council Paul advocated a less severe discipline (§ 227).

B. In 57 Nero orders Simon's body to be kept for three days. In QPl Simon met his death by being buried after saying that he would rise again (§ 237).

C. In 24, as in QPl *sub* EP, 509, Simon is compared to Jannes and Jambres. (See §§ 236 (iii), 315 H.)

D. Just as in QPl Christ appeared sometimes as a child, sometimes as a youth, and sometimes as an old man (§ 22 and *passim*), so Simon appears in these forms to Nero, who supposes him to be the Son of God.

E. It is a contact of MPP with QPl that in MPP, 4, Peter and Paul meet and embrace, for psCyprian says that Peter and Paul met each other at Rome. It is true that he adds that they did not know each other, but this criticism may be suggested by QPl *sub* EPl, 665, or, inasmuch as Leucius was given to repeating himself, by a parallel passage. Paul asks Peter and Andrew who they are. Matter in 677 suggests that in the original narrative he knew who they were.

The following matter shews the influence of J on QPl *sub* MPP.

F. Simon in MPP stirs up mischief with Nero against the apostles, just as in J Saul stirred up the magistrates of Antioch (§ 256) and intended to stir up those at Damascus (R. i. 71). (See L.)

G. In 45 Simon is accused of having caused the circumcised to be put to death. The allusion must be to Christians, and only in J and QC and passages of QPl based on J would they be described by our phrase. The only possible explanation of these words is that Simon was originally Saul.

H. In 39 and 43 Paul is as he was in J, an "adversary" (§ 235).

J. In 39 Simon is *a false Christ, a false apostle, and a false prophet*. This passage explains the origin of the designation of Simon as a false apostle which we find in QP (§ 238, Table). The designation is not explained by KP, in which work Simon was an apostle of the Jews (§ 234). Cerinthus, on the other hand, adopted the position of the earliest Judaisers that Saul was no true apostle. Hence Peter, in a passage much influenced by J, warns Maro against *false apostles and false prophets* (R. iv. 35), *i.e.* against such teachers as Simon-Saul. Leucius added *false Christs*. (Cf. D.)

K. J stated that Saul was a gentile from Tarsus who had been circumcised because he wanted to marry the daughter of the high priest. In 43 Peter says: *Simon was circumcised because not otherwise could he have deceived simple souls, unless he feigned himself to be a Jew and made a show of teaching the law of God.* The reply of Leucius to J occurs in 35, where Peter says: *It was necessary to have in readiness this man who from his youth up set himself to no other thing than to search out the mysteries of the divine law, by which he might become a vindicator of divine truth.*

L. Our reconstruction is confirmed by Woodbrooke Stud. iii. 396, where Paul preaches idolatry at Rome and Peter has an audience with the Emperor, who consults with Paul. EP in 498 transfers this incident to Antioch. There may be a trace of the QPl dissimulation of Paul in MPP, 1, where the Jews ask his help against Peter. (See § 174.)

M. The fact that in the Simon section of MPP the part of Paul is very subordinate is due to the fact that he represented in QEPP the Judas of QPl in which Acts Judas was subordinate to John.

The Burnings at Cæsarea and Rome

§ 241. We will now reconstruct the QPl narrative of the burning of John and Judas at Cæsarea. Our main source will be a long passage of EPl, where the scene was originally laid at Cæsarea, a placing which is confirmed by AT, LT, and MM.

A. Thewodas ordered a pillar of wood to be set up (EPl, 641).

B. Pegs or nails were driven into the hands or feet of the apostles (EPl, 639, 641; MM, 19; RSteph, 162).

C. They prayed in Hebrew (EPl, 635; LPP, 187).

D. They were encased in iron (EPl, 635; AT, 140; LAB, 18; LPP, 187).

E. Pitch and other substances were poured in (EPl, 642; RSteph, 162).

F. The fire was lit (EPl, 572, 642; AT, 21; LAB, 18; ArmPhoc, 180).

G. Their skin peeled off (EPl, 644; LAB, 18; AT, 21; LT, 87).

Christ and two angels appeared in the fire (EPl, 572), Christ (EPl, 635, 644) and the angel of the Lord (LPP, 187; LAB, 18; RSteph, 162). Phocas prayed that the Lord would send an angel (ArmPhoc, 18). For their survival, cf. AT, 140; MM, 19. For Christ and the angels, cf. 297.

H. A summary account of the martyr's tortures survives in QDesp ap. HE, III. xxxii., where Simeon is said to have been tortured in various ways so that the judge was astonished, and at the last to have been rewarded with an end similar to the Lord's.

§ 242. Burning was not a recognised punishment in the first century, and the fire which burnt Judas at Cæsarea was lit by Nero at Rome. (a) In EPl, 642, the apostles suffer in the garden which was in the midst of the city. That the garden was Nero's is shewn by FrankoAP, 323, where Nero commands that Peter should be crucified in the midst of the city. (b) In EPl, 639, nails are driven through the hands of the martyr, and in RSteph, 162, through his feet. These details are explained by a passage from QP. In EP, 524, Peter says: *It is for me to be crucified, even as my Lord was crucified, and they shall pierce my hands and my feet with nails*. The last phrase is based, like the incident of QPl, on a combination of two testimonies, Ps. xii. 16 and Ps. cxix. 120. This latter passage is used in Barn. v. 13, Iren. Dem. 79, and Cypr. Test. ii. 20, and derives from KP (§ 52). (c) In EP, 641, there are *heaped up round* (the apostles) *vine branches and plants of flax* whereon the flowers still remained. Nero made his victims represent mythical characters, *e.g.* Orpheus and Daedalus (Lightfoot on 1 Clem. 6). *Sub* EP they represented Bacchus and the Fates spinning destiny.

§ 243. PsMark was probably influenced in his treatment of the martyrdom by the story *Domine, quo vadis?* Leucius carried the assimilation to the Crucifixion still further. In the fragment of this story which Origen (in Joh. t. xx. 12) attributes to the Acts of Paul, Christ says: *I am about to be crucified again* (ἄνωθεν). The treatment of the phrase in QPl *sub* VP, 38 f.; MA (359); APh, 129, was characteristic. Ἄνωθεν was interpreted as meaning *from above* and *head downwards*, and the incident was spiritualised. [The narrative must be read in the light of the phrase of the Coptic EvN, *the prayer of the Saviour on the cross concerning Adam* (J, 104), and the Naasene doctrines stated in Hipp. Ref. vii. 7. Behind the midrash is the identification of Christ with the cross in QPl (369) and the fact that He was Alpha (CBRB, 195). As Peter in VP, 38, draws a lesson from the fact that the cross consisted of two pieces, so in EvT Lat. vi. 8 Jesus in his exposition divides the first letter and in EvT Lat. vi. 5, when reciting the alphabet, stops at T, a letter which closely resembled ancient crosses.]

§ 244. The story *Domine, quo vadis?* cannot be the invention of psMark or any other apocryphist, and in the next volume I shall argue that in VP, 36, it is rightly placed in a narrative of the Herodian persecution (the name Agrippa actually occurs). In KP the narrative influenced the account of Peter's death as follows: (i) As we have concluded, Peter was said to have been burnt when nailed to a cross. (ii) Christ shortly before the martyrdom appeared to the apostle and told him that his death was to come quickly. Peter referred to the incident in a letter which was in the introduction of KP and in which he bade Mark write his preaching. The passage survives as follows:

2 Pet. i. 1. *Symeon Peter.*	EpClem, 1. *Simon.*
14. *Knowing that the putting off of my tabernacle cometh swiftly.*	2. *I have been taught by (Christ) that the day of my death is approaching.*
15. *I will give diligence that at every time ye may be able after my decease to call these facts to remembrance.*	19. *Whensoever I depart this life . . . send to James an account . . . of my discourses.*

I only know of one or two passages in Greek apocrypha in which Simon or Symeon occurs, and they probably derive from KP. PsMark presumably derived "Symeon" from S. Mark's narrative, *Domine, quo vadis?* (Cf. Ac. xv. 14.)

§ 245. We must assign to the KP narrative two sayings discussed by von Dobschutz (das Ker, 109).

A. Gregory N and Elias Cret. attribute to Peter the words

A weary soul is near God. Hermas, who is full of chips from his predecessors, has *weary in soul* (M. viii. 10).

B. Didymus and Origen ascribe to Christ the words: *Near me, near fire; but he that is far from me is far from the kingdom.* The epigrammatic style favours our ascription of the words to KP, and the parallel in Ign. Sm. 4 is decisive. We there read, *Near the sword, near God.* The two parallel phrases refer to S. Peter and S. Paul.

§ 246. [We can now deal with the problem of the history of the narrative, *Domine, quo vadis?*, the scene of which was on our view, according to KP, in the neighbourhood of Jerusalem. Inasmuch as Leucius cannot have narrated the Herodian persecution, the incident cannot have occurred *in situ* in that Acts. Presumably he substituted it for the Rome incident, adding at the close Christ's ascension, which occurred in QP *sub* VP, 35. LeuciusP moved back the incident as it was told in QPl to its original place and continued with the narrative of Peter's arrest and imprisonment (EpApp, 15). VP transferred much Palestinian matter to Rome, and naturally restored the QPl narrative preserved in QP back to its original QPl position. In VP the introduction to the martyrdom is transferred from the matter which preceded the QP martyrdom of James, but, like almost all the VP narratives, it has been rewritten.]

The Eastern Journey and Letter of Judas

§ 247. We will now complete what remains to be said about the first septennium.

That Judas Barnabas Matthias went to the east in a primary Acts which can only be QPl is clear from AT, EusThadd, 11; ABarn, 7; R. ix. 30; LM, 100, as also from the EP journey of "Paul" to Warikon. Now analogy shews that this journey is likely to have originated in J, and we are about to attribute to J a description of the ideal life of the ten and a half tribes who had not been influenced by the Judaism which the writer attacked. The account of them was in a letter which Judas sent to James.

This letter cannot have been suggested by a similar letter
in KP. On the other hand, it is likely to have been suggested
by the organisation of contemporary Judaism. The essential
fact is that the synagogues of the dispersion were organised
and kept in touch with the authorities at Jerusalem by
"apostles" who carried to and fro formal correspondence
(Harnack, *Expansion*, i. 67). The Ebionite view was that
the church of Antioch and the other churches of the Christian
dispersion should have been organised on similar lines.
Judas therefore reported to James, and James presumably
wrote himself, and is the more likely to have done so in
view of the part which he must have played in the KP
parallel with Acts xv. We may thus account for the fact
that in R. i. 72 James bids Peter send him an account of
his sayings and doings.

§ 248. The following passages must pervert a primary
incident in which James wrote a letter. It may have been
suggested by that of Peter in KP (§ 244).

A. DAdd, 16. *James, the director of the church in Jerusalem
...gave a written account and sent it to the apostles ... in
their cities and in their countries. And also the apostles themselves gave written accounts and made known to James whatsoever Christ had done by their hands.*

B. In STrans, 17, James writes to the convent at Sinai.

C. There is an allusion to a writing of James in Lagarde
DAdd, 93.

D. The only surviving apocryphon attributed to James
is PJ.

§ 249. The evidence for a letter which Judas wrote to
James from the east is as follows:

A. In R. ix. 29 Thomas (Judas) has written a letter
which described his work in the east. HR used Bardaisan
in his matter about the east, but we may observe that in
19, where he describes the Seres, he speaks of them as living
at the beginning of the earth and that in EPl, 671, Paul
(Judas) goes to Warikon, which is at its limit. There is
another contact with J in the fact that Elkesai was received

from Seræ, a town in Parthia (Hipp. *Ref.* ix. 12). In QPl Judas Matthias went to Parthia, a country which later became Berber.

B. In NZos, 7, the blessed (ed. for Judas) write an account of themselves, which they send to the west. We shall find matter from J in this work.

§ 250. We now turn to the problem of the contents of the J letter of Judas.

In LM, 100 f., the members of the ten and a half tribes have described their life to Matthew (Judas Matthias), who in 80 has gone to Persia and in 110 goes to Parthica. They praised God at midday with the 144,000 infants whom Herod slew. (These infants occur also in AMM, 3; RSteph, 159 f.; ApPl, 26, a fact which proves derivation from Heg.) In an interesting Utopia Judas reproduced the account of their lives which the tribes gave him : *As for silver and gold we do not wish for it in our country. We eat no flesh and drink no wine in our country; but honey is our food and our drink. We do not look upon the faces of our women with desire; the first boy who is born we present him as an offering to God, that he may serve the temple all his life when he is three years old. Our drink is not the water which overfloweth from Paradise. We do not wrap ourselves in clothing made by the hands of men; but our clothing is from the leaves of trees. Our country heareth no lying speech, and no one knoweth of it. No man weds two wives in our country; and no boy dieth before his father. And the younger speaketh not in the presence of his elder. Lions dwell with us in our country; they hurt us not, and we hurt them not. When winds blow we smell from them the scent of the garden of Paradise. There is no cold in our country, and no snow, but a breath of life; and it is temperate.*

There is a parallel passage in NZos, x. which we will discuss at the same time. The Rechabites describe their life in a letter as follows: *We are pious but not immortal. For the earth brings forth sweet-smelling fruit; and there comes from the trunks of trees water sweeter than honey, and these are our meat and drink. . . . There is no vine with us nor*

*ploughed land, nor works of wood and iron, nor silver nor gold,
neither heaviness nor keenness of the air; nor do we marry
wives except for the purpose of begetting two children.*

§ 251. Subject to the proviso that there may be some
editing in NZos we must attribute these two passages to J
for the following reasons:

1. This is an instance in which we may use the argument
from elimination with security. Our LM passage is obviously
an excerpt, and it is used in Commod. Instr. ii. 1 f., Carm.
Apol., 94, 1 f. KP was concerned neither with the topics
of our passages, nor with Judas, nor with the East. The
statement of Photius that Leucius condemned the pro-
creation of children proves that our passages do not derive
from QPl. J, therefore, is the only apocryphon possible.

2. In NZos, 1, Christ is described as the Great King,
a title which we have attributed to J and QPl.

3. Our matter has contacts with other matter which
derives from matter which Leucius derived from J. (*a*) The
Rechabites provide priests in the QDesp martyrdom preserved by Heg MJas, 17. (*b*) The dedication of the eldest
sons to the service of the temple at the age of three is clearly
suggested by the dedication of Mary, and it also provides
a contact with the James of J, who in QDesp was represented
as the ideal Ebionite saint and who served as a priest in
the temple. (6) Again, like the members of the tribes, James
did not marry a second time (§ 284 L).

4. Our matter also influenced QPl as follows:

(*a*) In making up his name-lists Leucius used the names
of nine or ten tribes (§ 315).

(*b*) Zosimus, like the Judas of J and QPl, went to the
east. Christ appeared to Zosimus as the angel of the Lord
just as He appeared as an angel to Peter (John) and transported him to Warikon (EPl, 691).

(*c*) The words of LM, 105, *O fire which destroyeth all
fabricated goods*, which are shewn probably to derive from
QPl by the context and especially by the phrase *Lord and
God* are clearly suggested by the attack on the arts of
civilisation in our passages.

(*d*) Leucius played with this attack. The apostles were

in a spiritual sense bankers (AT, 146), craftsmen who made spiritual ploughs and yokes and built spiritual pretoria (17 f.), fishermen (CBRB, 211; EvvC, 5), merchantmen (H. v. 208, APA, 3), farmers (APA, 3), vine-dressers (LBart, 70), gardeners and dealers in vegetables (CBRB, 201), makers of the apparel of priests (EPl, 661).

It is in accordance with J's outlook (as it was exhibited in our passages) that Leucius emphasised the poverty of the apostles. The influence of Matt. x. 9 f. is seen in H. xii. 6; QDesp ap. HE, II. xxiii.; Epiph. *Haer.* lxxiii. 13 f., AT, 20; and of Mk. vi. 8 in VP, 5; AAM, 6. In H. xii. 6 the apostle bread and olives. Cf. SHJ, 8; AJ, 5; and Proch, 48, 2; also HE, where James eats no flesh. This view is condemned in Ap. Const. vi. 10, 26, where it is connected with the Encratite heresy and the view held by Leucius and, probably, by J, that animals had rational souls (§ 265). For the use of bread, water and salt at the eucharist, see H. xiv. 1; AT, 29; VP, 2; Thec, 25. Cf. AJ, 6. According to Jerome (in Gal. i. 18), the Clementine Peter was bald; in MPl, 2, Judas flat-footed; AT, 37, and CBRB, 213, Thomas little; in Thec, 3, Paul bandy-legged; in Hipp. Ref. vii. 39, Mark stump-fingered (§ 332). We note that John, whom Leucius had seen, is not described. That his "low appearance" in AJ, 5, was borrowed by the editor from some other apostle, is shewn by the Coptic fragment (J, 264 f.).

CHAPTER IX

The Journeys of S. Peter to Syria and of S. John and S. Paul to Iconium, Ephesus, and Rome

The chapter begins with a detached discussion of S. Peter's journeys to Syria, which touches other reconstructions at three important points. (*a*) It confirms our view that in QP the apostle evangelised the Syrian coast and that QP derived from KP. (*b*) It gives us another contact with the chronology of Heg. (*c*) It seems greatly to strengthen the case for the early date of Acts. We will then weave into a narrative many fragments of evidence which, when brought together, shew that in QPl John and Barnabas journeyed after the seventh passover to Antioch where Paul played a part which shews that Leucius was a Nicolaitan. They then visited Cyprus and met Paul at Iconium where Leucius became his disciple and was rebaptized by him. John journeyed through Hierapolis to Rome. In the Iconium section of his narrative Leucius told the story of Thecla, existing recensions of which derive from an orthodox version which both abbreviated and expanded QPl. The lion which licked Thecla's feet followed Paul to Ephesus, where it was baptized by him, an incident which Jerome rightly attributed to the elder who wrote the Acts and who was unfrocked in the presence of John. This last incident coheres with our view that Leucius was a Nicolaitan and also with a very important passage of EP which states that John would survive to the Second Coming and then be martyred.

§ 252. When we discussed the QC journey of Peter we concluded that psClement derived his knowledge of the Syrian coast from QP, in which work he found visits of Peter to Tyre and Sidon, Beyrout, Tripolis, the island of Aradus and Laodicea. The visits to Tyre and Sidon survive independently in EP, 481, and that to Beyrout in AThadd, 6. Now LeuciusP was hardly more than a compiler, and he probably lived in Asia. This matter, therefore, derives from KP.

In EP Peter, who has already arrived at Laodicea in a QC narrative, arrives again, converts multitudes, stays two years and returns to Jerusalem. Now all the allusions of the Acta to periods which we have tested have been found to derive either from Heg or KP. We attributed to KP the seven years between the Passion and the return from Cæsarea and the four years of the absence of Theophilus, and to Heg periods of twenty months and four months which followed his return and a period of five years which separated the twelfth passover of KP, 6, from the return from Cæsarea. It may be expected then that the two years of EP, 490, derives either from KP or from Heg.

In EP, 491, Peter is sent to Antioch and complains: *I am an infirm old man, and the road to Antioch is exceedingly long; why didst thou not give me this command when I was at Laodicea where the road would have been shorter for me?* That the apostle's geographical knowledge is borrowed is shewn by the fact that the editor's insertion of a passage from AJ in 501 shews that he confused the Asian with the Syrian Laodicea. We infer that Hegesippus stated that Peter reached Laodicea and did not go on to Antioch and that he calculated that the apostle remained at Laodicea two years. He then said that though Antioch is near Laodicea, Peter did not reach that city until after a return to Jerusalem.

§ 253. Matter such as this cannot be apocryphal, and the statements of EP make striking adhesions.

(i) In KP, 6, we read: *If any of Israel will repent . . . his sins will be forgiven: and after twelve years go ye into all the inhabited earth. . . .* The preceding words evidently bade the apostles witness to the Jews, and the whole passage was parallel with Lk. xxiv. 47. The writer edited his source in terms of a journey of the twelfth year which he was to narrate and like S. Luke in Ac. i. 8 made the logion programmatic. The passage implies the narrative of a journey of Peter outside Palestine which followed the twelfth passover. Now there is no tradition of a journey of Peter to Egypt or the east. It follows that according to KP Peter went to Syria in A.D. 42.

(ii) The rapid growth of the Syrian churches must have given rise to many problems, and no one could speak to the Syrian disciples with an authority equal to the apostle's.

(iii) Herod's attack brought S. Peter back for the passover of A.D. 44. He cannot therefore have been two years at Laodicea. Probably KP stated that he spent a considerable time there. The statement of EP is based on a calculation made by Heg whose twelfth year was a year too early and began in A.D. 41. But, though the chronology of our passage coheres with the chronology of Heg and with the historical situation, it is improbable that the apostle would be three years in Syria without visiting Antioch. On the other hand this improbability disappears if the period is reduced by a year, for according to QP Peter evangelised the cities on the Syrian coast, and he may not have reached Laodicea until after the thirteenth passover. We are confirmed therefore in our view that Heg dated the Crucifixion a year too early.

(iv) We know from Gal. ii. 11 that he visited Antioch, and if we adopt Turner's suggestion (Hastings' Bib. Dict., i. 424a), a suggestion which I shall defend against Chase (ib., iii. 765a), the emissaries from James (12) were the Judaisers of Acts xv. 1 and the apostle's journey, as in Heg sub EP, 491, was before the apostolic council.

§ 254. These cohesions cannot be accidental. But there is a difficulty. Why does not S. Luke in Acts xii. 17 tell us that Peter went to Antioch? He was beyond doubt very interested in the place, and one of the few editorial notes in 1 Acts which add substantial matter to the sources tells us that the disciples were first called Christians at Antioch (xi. 26). But if the omission of the name of that city in xii. 17 is strange, it is not stranger than the narrative which that verse closes. The story of the apostle's escape has no bearing whatever on the development of the theme announced in i. 8, and the important Herodian persecution would have been entirely omitted if a word or two about it had not

U

been necessary in order to shew how the apostle came to be in danger. The fact is that a second theme has already begun to exercise a disturbing and unfortunate influence on the work, the comparison of S. Paul to S. Peter, and also a decision to make the close of the work a long story of his escape from danger after danger. S. Peter's escape anticipates the last eight chapters. *To another place* anticipates the emphatic adverb with which Acts closes and which should be translated *without let and hindrance*. S. Luke omitted S. Peter's important visit to Antioch in order to emphasise as the culminating parallelism between the careers of the two apostles the fact that both escaped martyrdom. Inasmuch then as both were martyred at Rome not long after S. Paul's release Acts *must* have been written immediately after the last event which S. Luke records.

§ 255. We have once again vindicated the value of the apocrypha for the reconstruction of the chronology of Heg and also the historical value of the only citation of Clement from KP which contains or implies narrative. We have shewn that KP underlies QP and that the narrative of QP underlay QC. We must now resume our task of examining the methods by which Cerinthus and Leucius made havoc of the priceless historical materials which they were using.

We have concluded that the section of QEPP which narrated the seventh passover is almost entirely missing from EP and EPl. The QPl departure after the passover only survives in three passages. In EP, 470 and 479, two contexts in which splinters and fragments of QPl are depraved and disarranged, Peter (John) is promised a companion apostle (Judas) and is sent to Antioch. In 491 the apocryphal journey of John and Judas is misplaced and combined with the KP journey of Peter to Antioch: *The angel who had often appeared unto me* (here both Peter and John) . . . *said*, . . . *Go unto the city of Antioch and take with thee John* (Judas).

§ 256. In the much edited narrative which follows, the two apostles are cast into prison. Christ appears and repeats the promise which He made upon Olivet (479) that He would be with the apostle to the end of the world, and says that He will send Saul, "whom I have named Paul in baptism" (a very Leucian sentence: § 260). When Paul arrives he acts as he did in J *sub* R. i. 71 (where he seeks the help of unbelievers at Damascus) and in the QPl Roman section (where he practised idolatry and the Emperor consulted him (§ 240 L)), and converses with the heathen magistrates and worships idols in a temple. It was, however, with good intent : the people thought that he was praying to the idols, but he was praying secretly in his heart unto the Lord that He would help him. The result was that the apostles were released and there were conversions.

The incident is obviously based on J's version of the events of Acts xv. 1 f., but Leucius derived from J not only the story of the persecuting idolator which he rewrote, but also the suggestion as to how he should rewrite it. There can be no doubt that the Elkesaites derived from J their position that a discreet man will sometimes deny the faith with his mouth (Orig. ap. HE, VI. xxxviii.). Not only does this position underlie our narrative, but in R. i. 63 Gamaliel, who we concluded was one of J's *dramatis personæ*, on the advice of the apostles conceals the fact that he is a disciple. If Cerinthus,[1] according to Philaster, blasphemed the martyrs it was probably because of the obstinate stupidity with which they brought trouble not only on themselves but on their fellow-Christians. In our narrative, then, Leucius admits the truth of the statement of J that Paul made friends with persecuting magistrates at Antioch and worshipped in their temples, but also affirms that he acted in accordance with the views of Cerinthus and the practice of Gamaliel.

Cerinthus and Leucius were not the first heretics to pervert the story of the events at Antioch which occasioned the apostolic council. The Nicolaitans had claimed to have derived a true account of S. Paul's views from Nicolas, the Antiochene proselyte. Inasmuch, then, as Leucius taught Nicolaitan views in his Antioch narrative he was

---

[1] Dionysius, probably influenced by Hippolytus, connects his charge of "carousals" with "festivals and sacrifices" (HE, VII. xxv. 3).

presumably a Nicolaitan. Our reconstruction involves the
position that at this point Cerinthus and the Nicolaitans
were at one, and it explains the statement of Papias *sub*
Iren. III. xi. 1 that S. John wrote against Cerinthus and
the Nicolaitans. His preface shews that Papias envisaged
the controversies which prevailed at the close of S. John's
life from the standpoint of the discipline. His standpoint
was that of Rev. ii., iii. and the three epistles.

§ 257. There is not only disorder in our context of EP,
but also there are omissions. John suspects that the
idolatrous Paul was Simon ... *in the form of Paul ... by
magic, that he might be an adversary unto us* (497). Simon
is not mentioned elsewhere in this narrative, but this sentence
implies that he was in Antioch. He had doubtless followed
the apostles just as he followed them at Rome, and it was
due to the fact that he had taken the part which J assigned
to Saul that the apostles were imprisoned. The allusion to the
inimicus homo of the parable shews that Leucius was using J.

[In J Saul, exposed in the very scene of his supposed
triumph, was compelled to confess his misdeeds. In matter
omitted in EP Simon played Saul's part. In QC this incident
was doubtless told of Simon-Saul. All this might have been
conjectured and is only worth mentioning because it
accounts for the absurd story of the transformation of
Faustinianus with which R and H close. HR was using
Heg and observed the suspicion of John and Judas that
Simon had taken Paul's form. He combined the transformation thus suggested with QC and made the seeming
Simon confess that he was the enemy, a seducer and a
deceiver (R. x. 61).]

§ 258. Our next task is to reconstruct the journey of
John and Judas from Antioch to Cyprus, Iconium, Ephesus
and Rome. Inasmuch as Leucius Cornelius was his com-
panion, at any rate during the first part of the journey,
our first authority shall be a depraved passage of Symeon
Metaphrastes, who says that Cornelius came to Phœnicia,
Cyprus and Antioch and again set out with Peter and
Timothy to Ephesus (Migne, CXIV. 123).

In EP, 503, Peter (John) spends twenty-three days in Cyprus. Leucius did not invent details of this sort, and the period must derive from KP. Peter's transportation is editorial (§ 202). In QPl Leucius, who became Clement in QEPP (*e.g.* in 466), must have remained the companion of John until he qualified himself for writing the Acts of Paul by becoming that apostle's disciple.

§ 259. Before we attempt the reconstruction of the journey we will collect the names of the companions who ultimately arrived at Rome:

EP, 509	Barnabas	Timothy	Titus	Clement
EP, 517 f.	Barnabas Thomas [1]	Timothy	Titus	Dionysius
EP, 519	..	Timothy	Titus	Luke (Leucius)
LP, 211	Thomas	..	..	..
MPl, 1, 2	Barnabas Justus	..	Titus	Luke (Leucius)
VP, 3, 4	Barnabas	Timothy	..	Dionysius
Symeon M	..	Timothy	..	Cornelius

In the passage just cited Symeon brings the party to Ephesus. The following passages shew that in QPl John went to that city through Hierapolis. A–D cannot derive from AJ, in which work John did not visit Hierapolis.

A. In APh, an Acts of which we are about to make important use, John arrives at Hierapolis (128), where Philip is. For Philip, see BCD and § 319.

B. John visits Hierapolis in TransPh (James, Apoc. Anec. i. 162).

C. In MirKh John comes to Philip at Hierapolis. The source is certainly Heg. MirKh influences EPl, 699.

D. In SHJ, 8, John, on his way to Ephesus, arrives at the city of the priests (Hierapolis). In 43 he will not let the governor (Philip: cf. APh, 131) slay the priests. In the Arabic recension the ruler who brings John into the desert is named Philip (LJ, 166). The desert must be that of APh, 102 f.

E. At AJ, 57, where John returns to Ephesus, two MSS. give the heading *from Laodicea a second time*.

The evidence then indicates that Leucius, Dionysius,

---

[1] *Elder* is editorial.

John and Judas joined Paul in Asia Minor and travelled with him through Athens to Rome, that John and Barnabas journeyed as the latter does in Acts xiii. from Cyprus to Antioch and Iconium, and that in this way Paul became acquainted with the distinguished gentile convert whose instruction in the faith he completed by revealing to him his mysteries. The apostle rebaptized and renamed him.

§ 260. The following instances of rebaptism and renaming survive in matter deriving from QPl.

A. We observed that Leucius received the name Matthias or Theodore from the apostle who baptized him (§ 226 A), and that the editor used the name Theodore before Leucius had received it. Now the Cæsarea ending with which the narrative closed survives not only in EP, 655 f. but also in 681 f., but in both places it is edited. In 681 the apostles make the governor bishop and change his name to Paul Leucius, being referred to in the next sentence. We must infer that at this point the editor found the statement that the apostles named Leucius Theodore, and again anticipating the future he substituted "Paul." Our hypothesis explains the colophon at the Coptic APl, *the Acts of Paul according to the apostle*, and this in spite of the fact that APl recorded his martyrdom. The writer of the colophon knew that (Leucius) Paul had written an Acts of Paul.

B. The mother of Leucius received the name Theopiste (§ 226 E).

C. EP, 494. Saul was named Paul at his baptism.

D. AThadd, 1. Lebbæus (Judas) received the name Thaddæus when he was baptized by John and the name Nathanael when he was rebaptized by Christ (§ 275 (a)).

E. This last incident may underlie the tradition of the baptisms of the apostles. PsEvodius (RobEvvC, 186) says that Jesus baptized Peter.

F. PsCyprian attacked Prædicatio Pauli on the ground that it encouraged rebaptism.

§ 261. The evidence has shewn that when Leucius became S. Paul's disciple he was rebaptized and renamed. Leucius using KP had brought John and Judas Barnabas to Cyprus, and using Acts xvi. f. was bringing Paul to Athens and Rome. The two parties therefore must have met in South Galatia, and, inasmuch as we shall conclude that Leucius made Paul convert Thecla, they presumably met at Iconium. The story of the meeting survives in a passage of ABarn, which as it stands is almost unintelligible:

2. *I, John* (*Leucius:* the writer used Acts xiii.), *the servant of the high priest* (§§ 183 (i), 221 G), *received the gift of the Spirit* (ed) *through Paul . . . who baptized me in Iconium. After I was baptized, I saw a certain man in white raiment, and he said, Be of good courage* (LT, 88), *John* (*Leucius*), *for thy name shall be* (*hath been*) *changed to Mark* (*Paul*). . . . *There hath been given thee to know the mysteries. . . . I went to the feet of Barnabas* (*Paul*) *and related to him the mysteries* (*vision*). *And he said tell no man the miracle which thou hast seen. . . . A time will come for thee to reveal the* (*mysteries*). 5. *I having been instructed . . . remained many days in Iconium, for a pious man entertained us whose house Paul . . . sanctified* (*Onesiphorus*).

In 12 Barnabas (Paul) and Mark (Leucius) meet two men (? John and Judas). After a greeting Paul said: 12. *If you wish to know who and whence we are, throw away the clothing which you have and I shall put on you clothing which never becomes soiled. . . . 13. And having taken from me* (*Leucius*) *one robe he put it on the one and his own robe he put on the other.* (Cf. EPl, 661; LM, 102.)

The writer probably used Heg, [for in 7 *in Antioch on the first day of the week they took counsel . . . Lucius of Cyrene* is parallel with the gloss at Acts xi. 27. In 19 the temple of Apollo falls as in QPl *sub* LM, 109; APl (J, 285). In 7 a journey to the east is suggested. In 14 Ariston the host is Mark's father (VP, 5; EP, 509). In 22 Barnabas labours with Matthew because he was Barnabas Matthias. (See § 231 (iv).) I shall argue the influence of Heg on 23. The knowledge of the topography of Cyprus which the Acts shews is the writer's.]

§ 262. The fact that our context of ABarn makes the apostle reside at Iconium and meet Paul there and the probable allusion to the Onesiphorus of AThec raises the question whether AcPl et Thec (Thec) derive from QPl. But this derivation, which we are about to argue, involves the further hypothesis that the existing recensions derive from an orthodox recension (QThec). QThec is best preserved in the Armenian which, as Conybeare shews, supports Ramsay's corrections of the Greek but very depraved narrative found in APl.

That QThec was influenced by QPl is sufficiently proved by the following facts: (i) The narrative of the eucharist is Leucian (§ 164). (ii) For the Encratite beatitudes in 5 (*. . . keep the flesh chaste . . . possess their wives . . . as having them not . . .*) compare EP, 7. (iii) The description of the bandy-legged Paul in 3 must be Leucian (§ 251 (*d*)): for his angelic face cf. EusThadd, 13). (iv) For the appearance of Christ in the form of the apostle (21) cf. AJ, 27 f., 87; AT, 11. (v) Titus acts as Paul's precursor (2) as he does in ATit, an Acts which is influenced by QPl (§ 187).

§ 263. My next point is that Thecla matter survives which is independent of QThec.

(i) A passage which is attributed to Chrysostom (Conybeare, ArmThec, p. 60) tells us that not only Thamyris and Thecla's mother used their influence to persuade her to marry, but also her relations and the servants. While in Thec, 21 Castelius condemns her to be burnt, psChrysostom tells us that the magistrates threatened and then released her, an incident which Ramsay (398) regards as likely to be historical. She sought for Paul, and Thamyris pursued her. When she was about to become the victim of his violence she prayed. At this point the fragment breaks off.

(ii) Curiously enough the incident which I am about to claim for the story of Thecla connects with psChrysostom's allusions to the servants and the violence of Thamyris. In AT, 94, Thomas preaches a sermon which very closely resembles that of Thec, 5. In the next chapter we read: *Charisius found (her) not in the house; and he inquired of all that were in the house: Whither is she gone? And one of them answered: She is gone unto the stranger. And when he heard this of (the) servant, he was wroth . . . and he sat down and waited for her. And . . . when she came into the house, he said unto her: where wast thou? And she answered and said, With (the apostle). Charisius was very angry . . . but he answered nothing, for he was afraid; for she was above him both in wealth and in birth: but he departed to dinner, but she went into her chamber. 96. And Charisius when he heard that she would not come out of her chamber went in. . . . 98. And she cried out: Save me from the shamelessness of Charisius . . . and fled from him naked, and as she went forth she pulled down the curtain of the bed-chamber and wrapped it about her; and went to her nurse and slept there with her. 120. And she awaked her nurse saying unto her Narcia, my mother and nurse.*

These fragments seem to belong to what was originally the same narrative, and no one who was familiar with a copy of AT which was without them would attribute them to its writer. The incident presumably underlies Thec, 8–10, *Where is Thecla, my betrothed, that I may see her . . .?* In ArmThec, 9, Thecla's mother says: *Do thou Thamyris, go in and talk with her, for she is betrothed to thee to be thy wife.* It is probable that the purpose which we attribute to Thamyris was suggested by Thecla's mother as the only way of curing her of an enchantment and infatuation. The words are otherwise rather pointless. Moreover, there are two sentences in AT which are much more likely to have been written of a man of the people who was in the home of his future bride than of a kinsman of the king (95) and a husband in his own house: (*a*) *He sat down and waited for her;* (*b*) *he was afraid, for she was above him both in wealth and birth.* Again, while it would be unnatural in an Acts to introduce her nurse into the home of a married woman, the servants are prominent in psChrysostom and in QThec, where they are much concerned about the unhappy situation (10). Lastly, the visit of Mygdonia to the apostle in his prison and the bribing of the gaolers (AT, 118, 151) are suggested by Thec, 18. Another instance in which LeuciusT incorporated into his work an incident recorded in an earlier Acts almost *verbatim* will be given in the next volume. His most probable source is Heg, and we shall find Thecla matter in APh and EPl, where he is certainly the source.

(iii) The attempt to burn Thecla was probably editorial in QThec. (*a*) The statement of psChrysostom that the magistrates only threatened Thecla, who sought the apostle and was pursued by Thamyris, is not only superior to our AThec but explains the extraordinary phrasing of a sentence in Thec, 21, which as it stands can only mean that Thecla sought Paul with her eyes: *As a sheep wandering among the hills in search of a shepherd, even so Thecla sought for Paul. She saw the Lord sitting opposite her in the likeness of Paul* (Arm). Probably in QPl Christ saved Thecla from Thamyris when she was seeking Paul. (*b*) In 22 young men and maidens bring wood for the fire. This is much more likely to be suggested by 41 than to be original. (*c*) In 22 Thecla is naked as she is in 34, and the judge laments like the women of the latter passage.

§ 264. We have concluded that QThec was influenced by QPl and that it derived from a source which was used by psChrysostom and LeuciusT. The following evidence shews that this source was QPl:

(i) The narrative reads, especially at the beginning, as if QThec were excerpted from an Acts of Paul, and if this is the case the Acts must be QPl.

(ii) The incident occurred during the apostle's first missionary journey, but the first reviser moved it into a journey in which he was travelling west (Ramsay, 390). We have concluded that a similar edited journey occurred in QPl, and in ABarn there is a prolonged residence in the house of a holy man at Iconium (cf. AThec, 2, 42).

(iii) The nomenclature of QThec is decisively Leucian. Probably all the names in the early Acts which derive from the Pastorals do so through QPl (§ 315 H). Now QThec had the names Onesiphorus, Titus, Demas, Hermogenes and (probably) Philetus and Zeno(nia) (ArmThec, 1).

(iv) Ignatius, who was acquainted with QPl, probably alludes to Thecla in Rom. 5: *I will entice* (*the beasts*)

. . . not as they have done to some refusing to touch them through fear.

(v) Ramsay (416) attributes the first revision to an Asian and, suspecting a tendency towards Montanism, suggests the date *c*. A.D. 130, but says that the story that the writer was degraded by S. John is quite possible though ill attested (414).

(vi) When we examine QThec for traces of the motivisation of its source we notice in the editorial matter the two following tendencies: (i) In 5 we find the influence of the Encratite preaching of John at Cæsarea (*sub* EP, 7 f.), and observe that the story obviously lends itself to the purposes of an Encratite writer. (ii) The source exalted the ministry of women. (*a*) In psChrysostom and the Greek horologion Thecla is described as an "apostle." This suggests that she received a commission from Christ. Now in ArmThec, 40, Thecla says to Paul, *he that commanded thee to preach commanded me also to baptize.* (*b*) In ArmThec, 40, as she was on our view in the source, Thecla is the leader of a band of young people. (*c*) In 41 Paul commissions her to preach in Iconium.

To say that no early writer is so likely as Leucius to have used the story for the enforcement of Encratism is an understatement. That Leucius advocated the ministry of women appears from the following evidence: (*a*) In APh, 94, Mariamne prepares bread and salt in the breaking of bread while Martha is busy feeding the multitudes, a perversion which is undoubtedly from QPl and which is very characteristic. (*b*) Celsus, who probably used Heg, knew of Christian sects which derived their names from Mariamne and Martha (Orig. c. Cels. v. 62). (*c*) In an interpolation in the Syriac Didascalia (iii) John says that when Jesus asked for the bread and the cup he did not allow deaconesses to remain. The laughter with which Mary greeted this remark is very characteristic of QPl. (*d*) In MM, 28, Matthew ordains the wives of the king and his son to be a presbyteress and a deaconess.[1] There is editing. Leucius cannot have made an apostle ordain a presbyteress, for

---

[1] In PassT (Lips. i. 251), the bride of Dionysius becomes a nun.

his two great heroines Mariamne and Thecla were only deaconesses. (e) Leucius brought seven women to the tomb (§ 315 A) instead of the three of the Gospels because he held that Christ instituted the order of deaconesses.

We observe that our hypothesis accounts for the introduction of the story of the eucharist in the tomb. Doubtless Thecla assisted at it.

§ 265. We will now examine some QPl matter the purpose of which was to shew that the beasts lead a simpler and more religious life than civilised men. In what he wrote Leucius was amplifying the views of Cerinthus. We recall our conclusion that in his J letter Judas said that lions did not hurt the ten tribes.

There survives an amusing midrash on the message sent from Joppa to Peter in the KP parallel with Acts ix. 38. All the birds of the city were anxious to take it. But the raven was told that he lost his character in the days of the flood, a sparrow that in morals he was no Encratite, and that he would be detained on the way by hens. Only the dove was worthy (LA, 5). James was *inspired by the Holy Ghost with a knowledge of all languages . . . the tongues of the birds . . . and the creeping things and the wild beasts when they chattered in their own language* (LJasZ, 35). In CMystJ, 254, the birds, beasts and reptiles pray, and it was Leucius who brought the animals to worship in the cave of the Nativity (EvM, 14, 18 f.). In AJ, 112, John prays to God (Christ) saying: *Thou that madest thyself known through all nature, that proclaimest thyself even unto the beasts.* The Ophites who held that Christ's mundane body was of the same nature as that of the animals (Iren. I. xxx. 14) certainly did not derive the Christological side of their interesting speculation from QPl, but inasmuch as the next sentence tells us that Christ remained on earth eighteen months after the Resurrection and one of their æons was named Wisdom (cf. MM, 28 and EpApp i. 43; I. xxix. 2, 4), they were probably influenced by such passages as those cited. See also CMystJ, 256.

§ 266. The Oxyrrhynchus Sayings (J, 25) were addressed to Thomas, who in 11 is almost certainly Judas. White is probably right in his emphasis on their relation to the Alexandrian EvH, and this Gospel on our view derived matter from QPl. Inasmuch, then, as Thomas was prominent in QPl and the combination Judas Thomas was due to QPl the case is already very strong for the position that the collection is based on QPl. The position is strengthened by several parallels with John: *ye are . . . of the Father* (ii), *of the truth* (v), *he . . . shall not see the Father* (vii). We are concerned with the second saying which runs: *who are they that draw us . . .? the kingdom that is in heaven, the fowls of the heaven, whatsoever is under the earth, the fish of the sea.* This last saying became in QPl the motive of an haggadic narrative (§ 320). In AT, 30, Thomas near the second milestone of the Eastern road meets a dragon (§ 247) which in APh, 110 (where the apostle is approaching Hierapolis) is described as having no shape and as shunned by beasts and birds. In the wilderness of dragons Philip meets a leopard who seized a kid but spared it when it appealed to its conscience. The two animals fulfil the Oxyrrhynchus saying and go before the apostle to the city. In AT, 39, after the dragon incident, Thomas is a fellow initiate with a colt. In 69 he is again at the same place, and the wild asses fulfil the saying and draw him to the city.

§ 267. Our argument has shewn that in QPl John and Judas Barnabas travelled together to Cyprus with Leucius Dionysius, that John passed through Hierapolis to Rome, where he was joined by Paul, who was accompanied by Timothy, Titus, Barnabas and also by Leucius, who had become his disciple and been rebaptized at Iconium. Paul had travelled from Antioch to Lystra and Iconium, where Thecla heard him preach. QPl added to a narrative of Thecla which had come into the elder's possession the Encratite preaching at the beginning, Titus, Demas and Hermogenes, the intervention of Christ who saved Thecla from Thamyris and the commission of Christ to Thecla to carry out all the duties of a deacon's office and Paul's recognition of this commission. The writer of QThec was not concerned to record the arrival of John and his companions. We have also learnt from APh that a leopard in an haggadic narrative led the apostle to the city (Hierapolis and the heavenly Jerusalem) whither he was journeying. Philip in APh travels with Bartholomew, who may be Paul with whom he is associated in EPl, 611 f. It must be also observed in passing that the connection of Philip with Hierapolis is historical and evidence that "Leucius" was an Asian.

§ 268. The reviser of QEPP moved into EPl matter which Heg excerpted from the QPl narrative of S. Paul's journey from Antioch to Ephesus. In 611 Christ bids Philip go to Lystra and Iconium, and he is associated with Paul. In 629 two bracelets clumsily introduced into the story of the teaching given by the apostles to Euphemia (it was Encratite in QEPP) were suggested by the bracelet which Thecla gives the door-keeper in ArmThec, 18. In 549 Leucius and Timothy, who arrived with Paul at Ephesus (Symeon M.) and Rome (sub EP, 509), are at Iconium. In 567 f. Pilate and Hermogenes are connected with Iconium. The two names are evidence that the writer of QEPP found in Heg a narrative of Thecla which was not that of QThec. We compare:

A. 2 Tim.	Alexander the coppersmith	Demas	Hermogenes	Philetus
B. Thec, 1	.. the coppersmiths	Demas and Hermogenes	..
C. EP, 17; EPl, 567	..	Demas	Hermogenes and Pilatus

In 646 the governor is Alexander, the name of the governor who condemned Thecla to the lions. He is stupidly identified with Tiberius Alexander.

§ 269. We will now observe that EPl has parallels with the kid and the leopard which in APh accompany the apostle to the city, with the Hierapolis priests of APh and SHJ and with the allusions of these two Acts to a desert.

In 564 a lion carries a priest as if he were a kid and follows Paul from a city to a desert. In 565 we are told that we shall hear of the lion again. In 573 the lion, like the leopard of APh, announces its faith in Christ. In 587 the apostle is thrown to the lions, and a lioness licks his feet. It was the lioness which licked Thecla's (Thec, 33), for it is said to have lived in the days of Alexander. In 590 a fountain springs up in its lair, and the people are baptized, though they are not said to have been converted and play no part in the story. In view of its confession of faith we may be sure that it was the lion that was baptized. Happily we can complete the argument by shewing that in QPl the people of Ephesus, where the incident took place, were baptized not in the lair of the lion but in the sea. The incident of the lion which licked Paul's feet was known to Hippolytus (in Dan. iii. 29), who presumably derived it from Heg as also, probably, did the author of APl, who also used it (J, 291 f.). Now in APl (where the scene was at Ephesus as it was in Heg *sub* EPl) the people are baptized in the sea. That APl is at this point based on QPl is shewn by the parallels in ArmPhoc, 16, where the baptisms are in the sea, and AT, 118. The fact that the lion spoke to the people was known to Commodian (Commod. Cv. Apol. 624 f.).

§ 270. We will now compare our reconstruction of QPl with two patristic passages.

A. Tert. de Bapt. 17. *Since those who read the writings falsely attributed to Paul support the right of women to teach and baptize by an appeal to the precedent of Thecla, they must be told that the elder who wrote that work in Asia was deposed for attributing to the apostle matter of his own, and that after his conviction he had admitted that he had done so out of love for the apostle.*

B. Hier. de Vir. Ill. 7. *We regard as apocryphal the Acts of Paul and Thecla and all the story of the baptized lion.* Jerome then cites Tertullian but adds *convictum apud Johnannem.*

Our passages cannot refer to APl. An Asian elder of

the second century would have been less likely to have been unfrocked for writing that Acts than a clergyman of the twentieth. There can be no doubt that the passages refer to the heretical Acts of Paul which were attributed to Leucius. But how can we account for Jerome's additions to Tertullian which are the stranger as he remembers Tertullian's words, writing *confessum se hoc* (Tert. *id se*) *Pauli amore fecisse, loco excedisse* (Tert. *decedisse*)? The simplest answer is that Tertullian, who we shall find used Heg, knew of the deposition from him and that Jerome combined his recollections of Tertullian with his recollections of that writer's source. The fact that Hippolytus, whom Epiphanius uses in *Haer.* li. 12, knew that Leucius was a contemporary of S. John and an opponent of Cerinthus, confirms our view that Heg was the source of Jerome and Tertullian, as also does the fact that the occurrence of the story of the baptized lion in Heg *sub* EPl. At any rate Jerome's phrase *convictum apud Johannem* authenticates itself. A blunderer or a romancer would have inevitably written *a Johanne*. The incident took place in S. John's extreme old age when he was very feeble and, possibly, very deaf, a conjecture which bears on the criticism of the Fourth Gospel.

Our conclusion tallies with Ramsay's view that the reviser of the story of Thecla was an Asian who lived *c.* A.D. 130 (or, possibly, was a contemporary of S. John), with our view that Ignatius attacked Leucius and probably derived from him an allusion to Thecla's lioness and with evidence which we have already considered which proves that QPl was written not long before S. John's death. If I am right in holding that Leucius was one of the elders of Papias and that Papias at a later date directed much of his polemic against him, Heg probably derived from Papias the allusion to the elder's deposition which we have attributed to him.

§ 271. Our view that Leucius was a contemporary of S. John is confirmed by EPl, 524, where Peter says: *I have to drink the cup which the Lord drank. . . . It is for me to be crucified, and they shall pierce my hands and my feet with nails.*

X

... Paul the apostle will they also slay with the sword. But John the beloved shall not taste death except at the time of the second coming. ... My God said unto me ... No man shall bury the body of John.

It is an illustration of the neglect of the NT apocrypha that this passage, so far as I am aware, has never received any attention. It is difficult to imagine that it can have been penned after S. John's death, and the *prima facie* view of it is confirmed when it is examined more closely. As has been already shewn (§ 155), it is an adaptation of an eschatological tradition which Rev. xi. 8 f. derives from KP. Its application to John also occurs in psMethodius who, as we saw, says that Enoch, Elias and John will convict Antichrist of fraud, and the parallels involve their subsequent martyrdom. That Leucius held that John would survive to the last days is also shewn by a QPl passage which we have already used in which Christ says: *the clouds which covered me shall not leave thee until the day of my second coming* (EP, 479; cf. 493 f.). Leucius and other leaders of the Asian churches had found it hard to reconcile the saying about John's tarrying till Christ came with Matt. xx. 23. In Jn. xxi. 23 it is suggested that Christ had not actually said that John would tarry until the Coming. Leucius took the opposite view and combined it with the prediction that John would drink the cup in the same sense as James. The evidence suggests that his knowledge of the saying about S. John's tarrying was independent of the Gospel. I shall discuss at some length in the light of the apocrypha Papias's treatment of the problem suggested by Matt. xx.

It is not clear whether EP derives from QP or QPl. The parallels in EpApp, 15 and AA, 20 (J, 344 ; cf. Apoc. Anec. II. xxx.) perhaps favour derivation from QP. The hypothesis implies that LeuciusP had not heard of S. John's death, but this fact presents little difficulty. The publication of QPl must have aroused some excitement in the Asian churches, and LeuciusP may have felt that it demanded an immediate reply. He was a mere compiler, and it would not have taken him long to write QP.

§ 271a. I will now tabulate the journeys which we have reconstructed according to the years of the Passion:

1.
A. In QPl Judas went to Cæsarea (depraves G).
B. QP followed A.

2–5.
C. In QPl Theophilus went to Rome and returned (depraves J).

6 and 8 months.
D. In QPl John and Judas were in the east. There is no direct evidence for the date of the J journey of Judas.
E. QP at least to some extent followed D.

7. The last four months.
F. In KP Peter evangelised western Judæa and went to Cæsarea. Simon followed.
G. In J Judas probably went to Cæsarea in this year (depraves F).
H. In QPl John and Judas went to Cæsarea (based on F and G).

8–12.
J. In KP Theophilus and Cornelius went to Rome and returned to Cæsarea.

8.
K. In J Judas went to Antioch (R) and Rome. Saul followed.
L. In QPl John and Judas (depraves K), Leucius (depraves J), Paul (depraves K) and also Simon (depraves F and K), went to Rome.
M. In QP Simon, who was at Cæsarea (F), perverted the church. Peter went there and returned to Jerusalem (depraves F).
N. In QC Peter went to Cæsarea (follows M) and Tyre (depraves M and Q), proceeding in the subsequent years to Laodicea (Q), Antioch (S) and Rome (O).

9.
O. In QP Peter went to Rome. Simon followed (depraves L).

13 and 14.
P. In KP Peter evangelised the Syrian coast as far as Laodicea, returning for the fourteenth passover (A.D. 44).
Q. QP followed P.

15.
R. In KP Peter went to Antioch.
S. QP followed R.

CHAPTER X

Various Studies

I. The Names of the Leucian Apostles

§§ 272–275e are wholly concerned with the eccentricities of
Leucius and LeuciusP in naming the apostles. It is shewn that
the Barnabas who accompanied John was Barnabas Matthias
Judas Thomas. Several points of interest arise. (*a*) It is clear
that in J Judas the Lord's brother was the apostle and the son
of Cleopas. (*b*) The title of EvT was expanded by LeuciusP
into an eccentric list of the apostles which stood at the head
of EvXII. (*c*) Both in QPl and QP John took precedence of
Peter, a fact which implies that both writers identified the
evangelist with the apostle and suggests that both were Asians.
Among the more interesting instances of this precedence are those
in §§ 275 (Table), 275*b*, 275*e*.

---

§ 272. We will now return to the subject of Judas Thomas
Barnabas Matthias.

1. That Leucius identified Matthias with Matthew
appears as follows: (i) The Martyrdom of Matthew derives
from the same source as the Acts of Andrew and Matthias.
(ii) In CBRB, 204, Matthias forsakes his riches. (iii)
According to Clem. Strom. iv. 6 some persons said that
Lk. xix. 2 f. was told of Matthias the chief of the publicans.
(iv) In EvvC, 8, Matthias is one of the twelve before the
Passion. (v) In ABarn, 11, Matthew is connected with
Barnabas because Barnabas was originally Barnabas Matthias.
(vi) We shall conclude that in QPl Matthias was the author
of a Hebrew gospel.

2. The apostle Judas was in J the Lord's brother. Leucius
therefore shewed that the relationship was spiritual. He
might have quoted the saying of Christ preserved in
Mk. iii. 35, but he belittled the Markan tradition and
characteristically preferred to express Christ's thought in

terms borrowed from Jn. iii. 3 f. Jesus was the Son of
God and born of the Spirit Mary. His brethren were those
who were born of the Spirit. In a Leucian Epiklesis the
Spirit is *the holy dove that beareth the twin young* (AT, 50).
So in APh, 115, Mariamne says, *one mother bore us both as
twins*. One MS. rightly paraphrases, *daughter of the Spirit*.
So again in the Alexandrian EvH Christ speaks of *my
mother the Spirit*. It was in this sense that Judas was
the Lord's twin brother and Thomas, and John like his
brother James was the Lord's brother (CEncJB, 345, where
the Baptist was obviously in the source the apostle). His
brethren precisely resembled Christ as in the instances of
John (AJ, 27, 87) and of Thomas (AT, 11). We may suspect
that Leucius had read S. John's words, *we shall be like him*.

§ 273. 3. That James the bishop of Jerusalem was in
QPl the son of Zebedee, appears from the following evidence.
It must be read in the light of the strong motive which
Leucius had for proving that James was not the Lord's
brother after the flesh. (i) In LJasZ, 35 a very Leucian
context which we have already used, the son of Zebedee
goes to the twelve tribes and in Abd iv. 1 obtains Judæa
and Samaria as his lot. (ii) In HEvXII, 26, James and
John are the only two apostles who are of the same tribe.
James must be an editorial insertion, and there can have
been only one James in the underlying list. (The source
stated the tribe each apostle judged.) (iii) In a QP list
which we are about to reconstruct there is only one
James. (iv) Commenting on a QPl non-Ascension tradition,
Clement (§ 275*b*) says that there were two Jameses and
distinguishes between the Lord's brother, to the Heg
narrative of whose martyrdom he refers, and the James
who was beheaded. Clement is using Heg, whose source
must have identified the two Jameses

§ 274. 4. Both Judas Thomas and Barnabas Matthias are
actually found in existing Acta. That they were originally
the same apostle is proved by the fact that if we make the
assumption our analysis explains the data with which we
are concerned and that if we do not there is a whole block
of apocryphal matter which must remain a chaos. As in

the case of the angel Spirit who became Mary the mother of
Jesus we cannot expect the positive evidence for so flagrant
a departure from the NT to be either plentiful or easy.

The more the Acta are studied the clearer it becomes
that the fundamental depravations of the narrative originated
in the exigencies of the Ebionite polemic. We are here
concerned with the following facts. (i) In KP Judas
Barsabas, the brother of James, brought to Antioch the
letter which embodied the views of James and in which
the twelve rejected the position of the Judaisers who claimed
that James had authorised their visit to Antioch. (ii) Judas
therefore in J became the great missionary who brought to
the gentiles the true faith which had been revealed to his
brother and his brother's successor. (iii) Cerinthus would
have a strong motive for identifying with Judas the Matthew
or Matthew-Matthias to whom was attributed the Gospel
which he commended to his followers.

There is positive evidence that Barsabas Matthias occurred
in J. In Chron. Pasch. (A.D. 107) the third bishop of Jerusalem is *Justus Barsabas who was chosen in the place of Judas.*
Now this bishop was Judas Justus (§ 284 DE). It is clear
then J identified the Judas who succeeded James both with
Barsabas and Matthias. I may add that Justus Barsabas
survives also in MPl, 2. It was Heg who made Judas the
third bishop (§ 275 A).

Leucius, who had no special interest in Judas but who
largely based his narrative on J, observed that by an alteration
of a letter Judas Barsabas could become the Barnabas, could
become the companion of his heroes Paul and John, the latter
of whom had been originally John Mark. The change was
probably suggested by the fact that at the point which he
had reached in KP Barnabas went to Antioch (Ac. xi. 22).
That he made this change and invented the apostle Judas
Barnabas Matthias appears from the following evidence.

(i) At Ac. i. 23 we find the variant Barnabas.

(ii) In R. i. 60 we find an apostle who was evidently
suggested by the Judas Barsabas of Chron. Pasch., *Barnabas
Matthias who was chosen in the place of Judas.* Further,
the list in which he occurs runs *Matthew (And, Jas, Jn, Ph,*

Bt, Jas, Lebb, Sim) *Barnabas Matthias who was chosen in
the place of Judas, Thomas* (*Pet*).   This list clearly expands
Judas Thomas Barnabas Matthias.   [Its history was probably
as follows.   PsClement found speeches of Peter and James
in the composite narrative of QP.   Under the influence of
J he (*a*) retained the J reply of James to Caiaphas *sub* 69
and (*b*) substituted Judas for the Peter or James of QP,
describing him in the terms of QP, which Acts he mainly
followed and which followed QPl.   The antiMarcionite
editor of QHR was interested in the twelve whose authority
had been attacked by Marcion and whose presence in the
temple occurred in QC (R. i. 44, 55).   He therefore expanded
Barnabas Matthias Judas Thomas into a list which was
normal but for the order of the names and the description
of Matthias.]

(iii) Leucius replied to the Cerinthian Gospel in a Gospel
which asserted that Jesus was the Word and work for
miracles before his baptism.   There is a presumption that
he would claim that he and not Cerinthus preserved the
true teaching of Matthew-Matthias.   Yet in the surviving
recensions his Gospel is attributed to Thomas.   Our
hypothesis explains his procedure.   Moreover in the introduction to EvM we are told that Matthew wrote in Hebrew
somewhat secretly, and it is suggested that Leucius introduced heretical matter into his translation.   EvM then implies
that Leucius attributed evangelical matter to Matthew.

(iv) The Judas Thomas of AT was the Matthew of MM
(§ 226 C).   The writer of LT when introducing QPl matter
named the king Matthaus (88) rightly.

The ordination in MM 27 is influenced by that in AT. 169.

(v) In LM, 100, Matthew like the Judas of J and QPl
goes to the east.   ABarn 7 connects Barnabas with the east
(7) and with Matthew (23 f.).

The discussions which follow supply more evidence.

§ 275. [We will now reconstruct the common source (D)
of the lists of apostles, which occur in EpApp, 2 (A),
Const. Clem. (*ad init.*) (B), the Syriac interpolation of
Didasc. vi. (Gibson, Hor. Sem. II. 12) (C).

A.	Jn Thomas	Pet An Ph Bt	Matt Nath Jud-Zel		Cephas	Bt	
B.	Jn Matthew	Pet An Ph Sim Jas	Nath	Thom	Cephas	Bt	Jud of J	Matthias
C.	Jn Matthew	Pet Ph An Sim Jas	Jud-of-J Nath	Thom		[Bt]	
D.	Jn Matthias	[Pet An Ph Sim Jas]	Nath Jud-Zel	Thom	Cleopas		

E. EvT inscr. Thomas the Israelite, the philosopher.

F. LSim, 115. Simon the son of Cleopas called Jude who is Nathaniel the Zealot ... bishop of Jerusalem.

(i) A copied D but after Ph continued in the familiar order. Finding that he had written Matt twice he corrected his first Matt into Thomas, whose name follows Matt in Mk. iii. 18. He did not, however, observe that he had omitted Sim and Jas, with the result that he gives only ten apostles.

(ii) B omitted and C corrected the impossible Judas Zelotes who is explained by F and occurs also in the old Latin variant at Matt. x. 3 and in a dictum of Bar Kappara which will be discussed and which is based on KP (§ 311). The blunder represents a misreading which substituted ' O KAI for KAI ' O.

(iii) D expands an erratic nucleus.

§ 275*a*. The clue to the Nathaniel of D and F is in E. In view of the facts which connect renamings with the QPl baptisms (§ 260) and the fact that the Prædicatio Pauli brought the Lord's brethren to the Baptist (§ 23) we may conjecture that combining J with Jn. i. 41 Leucius named Judas Nathaniel. This incident almost certainly underlies AThadd, 1, where an Edessene named Lebbæus (Judas) is baptized by John and receives the name Thaddæus (Nathaniel). The incident gives us another contact with Cerinthus, in whose system the baptism of Christ was of great importance. In J the brethren were present.

Thomas was a philosopher because in QPl the apostles were peripatetic teachers of religion. In EPl, 620, they teach Theodore as philosophers. We have already concluded that MM is in part parallel with our section of EPl, and our incident suggested to the editor that he should name his bishop Plato. In MPl, 2, philosophers are at Nero's court, and Barsabas (Lat Barn) is a courtier.

Assuming that either LeuciusP or the writers who used his list omitted the obviously impossible but undoubtedly Leucian Barnabas, we attribute to QPl a letter the inscription of which ran thus: *Barnabas Matthias Judas Thomas who was also named Nathaniel and Simon the Zealot, the son of Cleopas.* Whatever objections may be alleged against our conclusion, it must not be said that this is too absurd for QPl.]

§ 275*b*. In EP, 466 f., Christ upon Olivet bids Peter summon James, John and Andrew, and they summon the rest of the twelve and the seventy-two. This passage, to state too briefly a matter which we will discuss at length, derives from the common source of Mk. xiii. 3, 32 and Acts i. 6*a*, 7, where Pet, Jas, Jn and An are separated from the rest of the twelve. Our passage must derive from KP, but the separation of Peter and the contextual influence of QPl shew that the source is QP. Our hypothesis is confirmed by the influence of the source of QP on what appears to be a QPl Ascension tradition with the Ascension omitted.[1] In Clem. Hytyp. VII. ap. HE, II. i. 4, a passage which, as has been said, derives from a source which identified the two Jameses, we read: *The Lord after the Resurrection committed the gnosis to James the Just, John and Peter, they to the other apostles and these to the seventy of whom Barnabas was one. But there are two persons named James, he who was cast down from a pinnacle . . . and beaten by a fuller's club, the other who was beheaded.*

The list is eccentric in the exaltation of James, the superiority of John to Peter and the inclusion of Barnabas. The two last facts confirm our attribution of our matter to QPl, and the first indicates that Leucius was using J. We also observe that while Leucius evidently used the passage of KP which underlies QP *sub* EP he has only three names, and we ask how he came to make Barnabas one of the seventy, a group in which he nowhere shews any interest. Clearly Heg made a second harmonising correction. Barnabas was not one of the twelve, but he might have been one of the lesser apostles who according to the tradition of QP were present on Olivet. In QPl, then, there was a quaternion which consisted of Jas, Jn, Barn-Matt, Pet. Where then was Judas Thomas whom Leucius undoubtedly exalted? We reply that he was the same apostle as Barnabas. [P.S.—I now think that the matter is somewhat more complex, and that the four apostles mentioned were those of the QP recension of QPl. The argument is still valid.]

---

[1] Leucius had substituted an ascension on Good Friday for the KP ascension at Pentecost (§ 101 f.).

§ 275*c*. [HE, I. xii. 2 cites Clem. Hytyp. V. for the position that the Cephas of Gal. ii. 11 was not Peter but one of the seventy and that *it is recorded of Matthias who was numbered among the apostles in the place of Judas and of him who was honoured by being voted on along with Matthias that they were deemed worthy of the same calling*. (i) Clement used the context of Heg which he used in the passage cited above, and Heg accepted the variant at Acts i. 23 *Barnabas*, and solved the problem of the apostle Barnabas Matthias by making both Barnabas and Matthias members of the seventy who in QPl and QP were on Olivet. (ii) The text used by Heg was influenced by QPl *sub* R. i. 60, *Barnabas Matthias who was chosen in the place of Judas*. (iii) Clement's suggestion that Cephas was one of the seventy must be another correction of our QP list; but, inasmuch as there is no ground for supposing that Clement would have interested himself in the matter, he is probably using Heg, a view which is confirmed by the allusion to Gal. ii. 11. (iv) The writer of EusThadd, who derived his date of the Crucifixion from Heg, solved the problem of Thaddæus on the lines suggested by Heg's treatment of Barnabas and Cephas and made him a member of the seventy.

§ 275*d*. The following passages shew that the QPl apostles were prominent in the QP *Dormitio*:

A.	Greek.	*Jn*, Pet, *Th*, *Jas*, *Matt*.
B.	Joseph.	*Jn*, *Jas*, Pet, Pl, An, Ph, *Lk*, *Barn*, Bt, Mt, *Matthias Justus*, Sim, Jd, Nicodemus Maximianus.
C.	STrans, 27 f.	*Jn*, Pet, Pl, *Th*, *Mt*, *Jas*, Bt, An, Ph, Sim, Mk.
D.	STrans, 37.	Pl, Pet, *Jn*, *Th*.
E.		Pet, *Jn*, Pl, *Th*.
F.	psMelito.	*Jn*, Pl, Pet.
G.	RobEvvC, 29.	*Jn* summons Pet and *Jas*.

The quaternion mentioned in Clement's non-Ascension narrative occurs in A and B. In DEF Paul pushes out James. In B we note Matthias Justus and compare J *Barnabas Justus* (§ 237 G) and MPl, 2 (*supr.*). Lk (B) is Leucius.

The two facts with which we are most concerned, the primacy of John and the importance of Thomas and Matthew, are the clearest.]

§ 275e. EvEb (J, 8) represented a standpoint which was similar to that of QC (Waitz, 128, 141) but had contacts with QPl in (a) its rejection of animal food and (b) sexual intercourse and (c) in its allusion to the fire on Jordan (§ 23). (d) Christ, as in effect He was in QPl, was an archangel. We learn from fragm. 2 that the Gospel was attributed to Matthew. Christ says: I chose *John* and Jas . . . Sim, An, Thadd, SimZ, JudI and thee *Matthew*. It will be observed that John again takes precedence over Peter.

II. A NOTE ON THE GOSPELS OF THOMAS AND THE TWELVE

I have merely collected a few data for the convenience of scholars. Probably almost all CBRB and much of HEvXII derives from EvT and EvXII.

---

§ 276. Our analysis of the evidence has shewn that Leucius attributed his letter Gospel to Matthias Thomas. We have also concluded that LeuciusP, assigning like Leucius the primacy to John, expanded this title, and we must infer that it stood at the head of the section of the work which underlies EvP. Our examination of the title of EvT has brought us to the subject of the uncanonical Gospels.

1. We have accepted and illustrated Schmidke's explanation of the origin of EvH. That work was an interpolated translation of Matt, and not strictly an uncanonical Gospel.

2. The parallels of EpClem with 2 Peter printed in § 244 shew that KP in its introductory matter included a letter written by the apostle. Moreover, in this letter he referred to the apocalypse which he saw on Olivet. Further, we have attributed protevangelical matter to the introduction. It is highly improbable that there was a KP Gospel, but

there was matter which may have suggested the idea of a letter Gospel.

§ 277. 3. We have accounted for the Gospel which Leucius attributed to Matthias Thomas. A few words may be said as to its contents.

(i) It contained the Leucian narrative of the non-Nativity.

(ii) *Sub* EvInf, 1, Christ proclaimed Himself the Logos when in the cradle.

(iii) Matter which is abbreviated and expurgated in our EvT followed, and also an incident in Christ's Ministry as a priest in the temple (§ 151).

(iv) PsCyprian shews that QPl contained the J narrative of the Baptism and the light on Jordan.

(v) We shall conclude that there was a narrative of the Adulteress.

(vi) We must attribute to EvT the Matthias matter cited by Clement. There are contacts with QPl. (*a*) The substitution of Matthias for Zacchæus (Strom. iv. 6) is Leucianic. (*b*) For *wonder at the things before thee* (ii. 9). (See § 114.) (*c*) *Chosen one* (iv. 6) is a Leucianism. (See index s.v. "elect.") (*d*) *Abuse the flesh* (iii. 4) is connected with a story of Nicolas. He had a beautiful wife and, being accused by the apostles of jealousy, offered her in marriage, saying that men ought to abuse the flesh. Leucius was interested in Nicolas and an Encratite. Moreover, the story is rather in his manner. It is possible that Clement cites Matthias at second hand.

(vii) We may place towards the close of EvT the story of the fishing devil (RobEvvC, 178 f.) to which there is an allusion in EvB, iv. 44.

(viii) Some or all of the Oxyrrhynchus logia are Leucian.

(ix) Almost all the M and docetic evangelical matter survives in the apocrypha.

§ 278. The following facts shew that the Gospel of the Twelve was the QP analogue to EvT.

A. LeuciusP exalted the Twelve.

B. The expanded title of EvT implies a QP gospel.

C. For the existence of an EvXII there is the evidence of Orig. in Lc. i.

D. EvP, which is based on QP, is written in the first person plural.

E. In VP, 20, Peter finds a Gospel being read and says *we wrote*.

F. The main incident of the *Dormitios* has been shewn to derive from QP. STrans is attributed to the Twelve, who wrote it in Hebrew, Greek, and Latin.

G. HEvXII begins with a summary of Christ's life, and in 27 there is a "we." We have already concluded that it is probably influenced by QP. The title runs: *the Gospel of the twelve holy Apostles together with the revelations of each one of them done from Hebrew into Greek and from Greek into Syriac*. (Cf. E.)

H. CEncJB, 343. *Let us describe . . . the honours bestowed on John (the Baptist) according to the statements that we have found in the ancient manuscripts which the apostles wrote and deposited in the library of the holy city Jerusalem*. QP apocalyptic follows (§ 161). Was it the writer or Heg who found the MS. of QP in Zion?

J. The heading of EpApp runs: *the Book which Jesus Christ revealed unto His disciples and how that Jesus Christ revealed the book which is for the company* (James adds in brackets *college*) *of the apostles, the disciples of Jesus Christ, even the book which is for all men. Simon and Cerinthus, the false apostles. . . . Like as we have heard we . . . have written for the whole world. . . . Let grace be multiplied upon you.* 2. *We, John, Thomas. . . .*

This passage must be based on Heg. (i) (*a*) Heg divided heresies into two groups, those which descended from Simon's activities in Palestine and Rome and the Asian heresies of Cerinthus and the Nicolaitans. Nor can we otherwise account for the allusion to Cerinthus. I have indeed argued that Cerinthus wrote a preface to J in his own name, but there is no evidence for the position that LeuciusP used J, and "Leucius" cannot have mentioned Cerinthus. He must have dated his work, as did psMark, not long after his hero's death. Lastly, the matter is really settled by the fact that EpApp, 7, makes Cerinthus and Simon contemporaries, Cerinthus being placed first. The writer blunders in the use of a work which dealt with the subject of the origins of the heresies. (ii) The run of the passage suggests that it is composite. (*a*) The ten are both "disciples" and "apostles." (*b*) The apostolic "college" is not a conception which belongs to the apocryphal tradition and probably derives from Papias through Heg. (*c*) There is an allusion to the book which Christ in QPl gave John on Olivet. The apostles have both read what Christ wrote and heard (cf. 13 f.) what He said. We have already concluded that the list of the apostles in EpApp, 2 derives from QP.

K. CHistJos inscr. (RobEvvC, 130). *Our Saviour told the apostles His life on Olivet; and the apostles also wrote these words and left them in the library at Jerusalem.* (Cf. G.) The writer certainly used Heg (§ 284 Q).

§ 279. We will now briefly enquire what were the contents of the letter Gospel (EvXII) which we have with complete security assigned to QP.

(i) The apostles recorded their recollections of the Ministry from the time of their call. EvEb (J, 9) starts at this point. A section of their narrative underlies EvP.

(ii) They also stated that Christ appeared to them. At this point EpApp, 11 f., becomes parallel with the Syriac Testament of the Lord.

(iii) Immediately before His ascension at Pentecost Christ sat on Olivet and narrated His life (HJ). Part of this narrative survives in EpApp, 13 f., where Christ says how He descended through the heavens and appeared to Mary in the form of Gabriel. The passage is evidently the QP substitute for the book which in QPl Christ gave John on Olivet. The fact that Christ Himself at this point used the protevangelical narrative of KP tallies with two facts. (*a*) We found no protevangelical matter assignable to QP. (*b*) EvXII was the record of the experiences of the apostles and could not include the matter which preceded their call. This position, again, tallies with the fact that EvEbion begins with that event.

(iv) The conversation which followed contained some

sentences which are common to AT, 60 f. and HEvXII. (See Harris, 23.)

(v) For the conclusion see § 63.

(vi) The strangest feature of EvXII was the fact that it contained an apocalypse, that seen after the appearance to the eleven.

(*a*) In EpApp, 12, Christ says: *rise up. I will reveal unto you that which is . . . in heaven. . . . For My Father hath given Me power to take you up thither.* An hiatus follows, and we then learn not what the apostles saw when they were taken up but part of what Christ told them about His life (K).

(*b*) In VP, 20 (E) Peter describes some of the contents of EvXII, and the words *we wrote what we contained to write* refer to an apocalypse, for in a parallel context John after referring to the fact that Christ chose the twelve says that he is unable to set forth and *write* the things which he heard and saw (AJ, 88). Some things the apostles could and others they could not write.

(*c*) STrans (F) closes with the eastern apocalypse.

(*d*) HEvXII (G) is an apocalypse. *They went whither Jesus directed them* and *suddenly there were set before them tables full of good things* (30: cf. CBRB, 179) are splinters from an earlier apocalypse.

(*e*) EvP is based on EvXII, and in the Akhmim papyrus is followed by a distinct fragment of an apocalypse written like EvP in the first person plural. James (J, 90) writes, "It is either as I now think a second fragment of the original gospel or a piece of ApP." Both views may be right.

The existence of letter Gospels containing apocalypses is a fact which demands explanation. Now the apocryphists were very conservative in matters of this kind, and there is a presumption that, like most of the important eccentricities of the primary apocrypha, that which we are considering had its roots in J. Cerinthus, we concluded, in that work attributed the apocalypse to Judas whom he sent to the east. That apocalypse was undoubtedly influenced by the apocalypse Baruch who writes a letter to the nine and a half tribes. I suggest that in J a letter of Judas narrated what the tribes said about their manner of life and also an apocalypse which like Enoch he saw on the mountains which overhung the earthly paradise. Leucius combined the letter of Judas with the Gospel (CerM) of Matthew (Matthias) and made Judas Matthias write a letter Gospel in which he narrated how John was caught up during the three hours' light (darkness) and saw Mary in the tabernacle of light with the Father and the Son (§ 121). LeuciusP substituted the twelve for Judas, Easter for Good Friday and modified the apocalypse.

III. " QDESP "

The combination of matter from QPl with historical traditions of the Desposyni which we find in Heg's accounts of them cannot be due to that writer but may be plausibly attributed to Ariston of Pella. An interesting little fragment of history occurs in the narrative cited in § 281 (iii).

---

§ 280. It has become clear that Heg never compiled a narrative which he knew to be in any way fictitious. Inasmuch then as his accounts of the Desposyni combine fragments of historical tradition with matter derived from QPl we must attribute them to the source which I have called QDesp. The high value which Heg attached to it is shewn by a single fact. In J and QPl James was killed at the seventh passover. In QP he survived the attack made on him and suffered under Herod. According to Jos. Ant. XX. ix. 3, a passage which refers to the appointment of Albinus and was known to Heg, he suffered in A.D. 61. Heg on the other hand in HegMJas, 18, accepts the statement of QDesp that James suffered immediately before the siege.

§ 281. There is evidence which shews that QDesp was not a mere apocryphal Acts of the Desposyni and suggests that it may have been an historical work of a very inferior type.

(i) The allusion of HegMJas to the siege connects with

Y

the Pella matter which Epiphanius and Eusebius derive
from Heg (Lawlor, 28 f.). It is not improbable then that
Heg's source was more than a history of the Desposyni.
Pella suggests Ariston of Pella. Was he the author of
QDesp? That he wrote an historical work is indicated by
the fact that Eusebius cites him for the revolt of Bar Chochba
(HE, IV. vi.). Some, at any rate, of the writers who refer
to his dialogue, Celsus, Clement, Origen, Tertullian, Euse-
bius, Jerome, are more likely to have derived their knowledge
of it through Heg than directly. Further, the notices give
us two slight contacts of the Dialogue with QDesp. (*a*)
Like QDesp it contained some matter of poor quality (Orig.).
(*b*) Clement's suggestion that it derived from S. Luke
(Clement) may be due to the fact that Heg, who identified
Leucius with S. Luke, recognised that, like QDesp, the
Dialogue contained Leucian matter.

(ii) The statements that James suffered, if not immediately,
not long before the siege and that he was stoned are historical,
and inasmuch as in QPl he was killed by the captain of the
temple it is just possible that Heg's allusion to the fuller
(HegMJas, 18) may derive from tradition.

(iii) Heg is cited in HE, III. xx. as follows: *But there
survived of the family of the Lord the grandsons of Jude, His
brother after the flesh as he was called. These they informed
against as being of the family of David; and the "evocatus"
brought them before Domitian.* . . . *For he feared the coming
of Christ as did Herod also.* . . . *They said that between the
two of them they had only* 9000 *denarii* . . . *in* 39 *plethra of
land, so valued, from which by their own labours they both paid
taxes and supported themselves.* . . . *They adduced the hardness
of their bodies and the callosities of their hands* . . . *as a proof.*
. . . *And when asked to speak about Christ's kingdom, they
replied that it was not of this world* (Jn. xviii. 36) . . . *but
angelic.* . . . *He would come in glory.* . . . *Domitian* . . . *despised
them as of no account, let them go free and by a decree caused
the persecution* . . . *to cease.* We shall find that Heg named
these Desposyni James and Zoker and said that they were
the sons of Judas. It is very clear that the names and the
unheroic story of the farm and the acquittal are not

apocryphal. James and Zoker were probably acquitted by Cuspius Fadus who was appointed procurator on the death of Agrippa I. QDesp combined the QPl narrative of the acquittal of Judas with a detailed story of the close of the persecution. There is no other date at which an acquittal on a political charge is likely to have marked a reversal of the official policy.

(iv) We need not doubt that a Symeon of Cleopas was martyred under Trajan (HE, III. xx.) or the historicity of Thebuthnis.

§ 282. We will now collect the apocryphal matter.

(i) I shall argue that, the matter mentioned above excepted, the whole of the matter in HegMJas is from QPl.

(ii) The gathering of the Desposyni and disciples to elect a successor to James (HE, III. xi.) must derive from QPl or QP narratives of the seventh passover.

(iii) The trial of the sons of Jude before Domitian and their conversation with him (HE, III. xix. 3, 4) are from QPl (§ 233).

(iv) In III. iii. 6 Symeon at the age of one hundred and twenty is tortured for many days and crucified because Judas Symeon in QPl so suffered at Cæsarea.

IV. The Desposyni

Heg was acquainted with two traditions as to the relationship of His brethren to Christ. In the wholly unhistorical protevangelical narrative of KP they were the sons of Joseph by his first wife. On the other hand the tradition which Leucius derived from J and the tradition which preserved the account of the trial of James and Zoker and the martyrdom of a Symeon of Cleopas made them apostles and the sons of Cleopas. Heg attempted to harmonise the two traditions by the hypothesis that Joseph made a levirate marriage. This section reveals Heg as a painstaking and accurate historian, and it also illustrates his influence on later writers.

---

§ 283. Before we attempt a reconstruction of Heg's solution of the problem of the Lord's brethren, something must be said about his sources.

(i) PsMark collected topographical and other data in Palestine. On the other hand his position that the brethren were the sons of Joseph by his first wife is part of a narrative which at no point has any vraisemblance and the whole purpose of which is to fabricate evidence in support of the position that Christ was born of a virgin and without labour pains.

(ii) In view of the fact that Cerinthus held the Ebionite position that Jesus was the son of Joseph, that he exalted His brethren and that he was entirely unscrupulous on questions of fact, we should have expected him to make the Lord's brethren His younger brothers, but there is no trace of a tradition that he did so. On the other hand the inscription of EvT, which described Judas as the son of Cleopas, is a sufficient proof that he was so in J. We must hold, therefore, that the Cleopas tradition was generally held by the readers for whom Cerinthus wrote. In his time James and Zoker were still remembered and that a Symeon of Cleopas was still living. Further, inasmuch as Cerinthus rejected the authority of the Twelve his attribution of apostleship to Judas the Lord's brother implies that it was traditional. Our result tallies with the conclusion at which Chapman arrives in a brilliant article after a most thorough examination of the canonical evidence (*JTS*, Apr. 1906, 412 f.).

§ 284. Heg accepted the authority of the KP tradition as to the brethren as it was reproduced in QP (*sub* EvP: Orig. in Matt. t. x. 17). On the other hand he accepted the Cleopas tradition. Later writers quarried from the materials which he collected and his discussion of them, but they could not accept his complicated and impossible solutions. The result was that the surviving data are in utter confusion. All the notices which follow probably derive directly or indirectly from Heg.

A. The heading *Simon of Cleopas . . . Judas . . . the zealot, bishop of Jerusalem* is found in LSim, 115, and derives from the inscription of EvT (§ 275); but under the influence of Heg, who made Simon and Judas consecutive bishops

(D–J), the narrative distinguishes between Simon and Judas.

B. In Eus. Chron. the second bishop is Symeon or Simon (AHNOST).

C. In Heg ap. HE, IV. xxii. Symeon is the son of Cleopas, Joseph's brother and the Lord's cousin (N), and Judas is *called Christ's brother after the flesh* (N).

D. In HE, III. xxxv. the third bishop is *a certain Judaios named Justus* (EGJQ). *Judaios* obviously depraves *Judas* (AEFHJM).

E. In Epiph. *Haer*. lvi. 20 the third bishop is Judas Justus (D).

F. In ClemBps the second bishop is Symeon of Cleopas, and the third Judas of James (H).

G. In MPl, 2, the Barsabas Justus (D) of the Greek and the Barnabas Justus (J) of the Latin was in QPl Judas. (See also § 224 B.)

H. In Chron. Pasch. A.D. 104 the third bishop is Simon Canaanites called Judas (A) of James (F). (Cf. § 206 F.)

J. In Chron. Pasch. 107 the third bishop is *Justus* (D) *called Barsabas* (GQ) *who was chosen in the place of Judas.* Cf. R. i. 60: *Barnabas called Matthias who was substituted in the place of Judas.*

K. In the Bodleian Epitome of Heg (Lawlor, 42) the *sons* of Judas are James and Zoker (LMN).

L. Epiph. Mon. V. Virg. 14: *James had a wife two years, and when she died he had not another.* The ultimate source is J (§ 251.3). Judas had two sons *James and Zoker* (K).

M. Lawlor (44) cites Matthæi's Menology (May 26) for the statement that *Alphæus had two sons James and Zoker* (K). *Judas was the third bishop* (D). The indebtedness of the context to Heg is very clear.

N. PsEpiphanius (Lips. iii. 159): *Judas the Lord's brother* (Jude 1, C) *and Symeon his cousin* (C) *preached . . . in all Judæa and Samaria* (LSim, 115), *wrote the catholic epistle and early in life had two sons James and Zoker* (K).

O. Abd vi. 1: *Simon, Judas and James were brothers (german) sprung from Cana* (SV), *their parents being Alphæus and Mary of whom the last was by the same mother but of a different father,*

James the Just . . . the three (became) apostles of whom the youngest (P)-*James. . . .* "German" obviously makes nonsense of the sentence. The source stated that the three were uterine brothers and that Simon of Cana and Judas were the sons of Alphæus. The context is discussed in § 92.

P. The editor based LJas on Heg, inserting some matter from Heg's context. In 144 he writes: *This James was the youngest* (O) *of the sons of Joseph the carpenter. And Joseph had four male children and two daughters* (QST) *and all the children of Joseph were married* (KLMN) *except this James, and he was orphaned of his mother* (QR). *And when the Lady Mary was espoused to Joseph she found him in the house; and she brought him up. . . . Therefore she was called the mother of James* (Q).

Q. HistJos 4: *Mary found James the little* (O) *in his father's house* (OR) *broken-hearted because of the loss of his mother* (P), *and she brought him up. Hence Mary was called the mother of James* (P). In 2 the names of Joseph's children are Judas, *Justus* (D), James, Simon, Assia, Lydia (P).

R. In Epiph. Hom. 322 Anna is the daughter of Cleopas, and Joseph has four sons and three daughters (P). Mary nurses Joseph's wife Marem and her baby James (P). The view of Jewish chroniclers (*sub* PQ) that Marem was dead is rejected. Marem survived the Annunciation (326, 328). In 326 f. Joseph goes to Jerusalem with the Virgin for the ordeal, his sons, his wife Marem (the order and the fact that Heg held that "Marem" was dead prove that in Heg "Marem" was Joseph's daughter *Mary*) and his daughter *Salome* (STUW).

S. Epiph. *Haer.* lxxviii. 7: Joseph was the *brother of Cleopas* (C) and the *son of James Panther*. (This is a curious instance of Heg's (Lawlor, 35 f.) practice of accepting as far as possible all the matter that came to his knowledge; Panther in a Jewish slander was Christ's father.) James is said to have been called the Lord's brother because he was brought up with him (PQR). In 8 Joseph's sons are James (whose position is inconsistent with the view stated in 7), Joses, *Symeon* (BT) and Judas, his daughters *Mary and Salome* (RTU). He was forty when he begat James.

The fact that Heg adduced it shews both his readiness to accept the narratives of QPl and the thoroughness of his discussion. Rufus was probably the seventh child of Joseph mentioned in R. *Daughter* may be a correction of the Armenian translator.

(*d*) On the other hand Heg must have rejected the evidence of QPl *sub* V, for it implies the survival of Mary and Cleopas. The statement of S (lxxviii. 13) that Joseph and James were absent shews that Leucius, doubtless in EvT, told the story of Simon-Judas. His purpose would be Encratite, and Heg would regard the incident as heretical. The misinterpretation of "Chananæan" (H, O) was probably due to Leucius, who seems to have been given to interpreting words of Hebrew origin.

(*e*) We shall ascribe the Muratorian to a context which Hippolytus based on Heg, and it will be argued that Heg held that only those writings were canonical which embodied the preaching of the apostles. The fact, then, that the Muratorian accepts the Epistle of Jude which Heg probably mentioned *sub* N and omits that of James confirms our view that Heg regarded the former brother of the Lord as an apostle but did not so regard the latter.

(*f*) James, the son of Alphæus, presented a difficulty, for there is no indication that Heg identified Alphæus with Cleopas. Heg's solution survives in M. He availed himself of the fact that Judas had a son named James (KLMN) and gave Judas the name Alphæus. Judas of James meant "father of James," and the ninth apostle was one of the *Desposyni*. Heg was a careful scholar who knew the importance of chronology. He noted, therefore, that his view was only possible if Judas married early (N). Our attribution of this position to Heg is confirmed in § 289.

(*g*) N explains the distinction which C seems to draw between the relations in which Symeon and Judas stood to Christ. "Cousin" was the more accurate definition, but Judas was *called Christ's brother after the flesh*, as was proved by his epistle.

(*h*) Our assumption that Heg availed himself of the levirate is supported by the fact that Julius Africanus used the same expedient when discussing Christ's descent (HE, I. vii.). Heg is almost certain to have discussed the subject, and the fact that Julius refers to the Desposyni in his context suggests the antecedently probable position that he was using Heg.

(j) Our attribution of ClemBps to Heg is important. We may observe, therefore, that this list runs: *James the Lord's brother and after his death second Symeon the son of Cleopas and after him the third was Judas of James.* The constitutor must have used Heg here, for our data shew that many variations were possible. We note the parallels: Heg ap. HE, II. xxiii., *James the Lord's brother succeeded* ap. HE, IV. xxii., *And after James had suffered . . . Symeon the son of Cleopas . . . the second bishop* DE; *Judas (H) of James the third bishop.*

V. THE DATES OF S. JOHN, IGNATIUS, SIMEON AND THE ANNUNCIATION

In this section we return to the subject of the chronology of Heg.

§ 287. (i) Lawlor (40 f.) compares HE, III. xvii.–xx. with the Bodleian Epitome and shews that the two derive independently from Heg. We shall confirm his view by a comparison of these passages with others, among them with Abd v. 1 and AJ, 14. In HE the persecution is dated in the fifteenth year of Domitian, Nerva is said to have recalled the exiles, and John to have returned from Patmos at this time. The parallel passage in QPV *sub* AJ, 14 stated that John returned under Trajan, and that the Exile lasted three years, *i.e.* a year and portions of the preceding and subsequent years. These statements agree with those of Eusebius but they are independent.

Further, the chronology is in accordance with a topographical allusion in AJ, 17, which on our view must be attributed to Heg. We are there told that a chapel was built on the place where John landed and that flowers bloomed at the time. The apostle probably returned not long after Nerva's death, which was in January. His return, therefore, was probably in the spring.

According to the documents which on the view just stated derive from Heg, John wrote his oral teaching on his return from Patmos, *i.e. c.* A.D. 99. This date can be shewn to have been the date which underlay a passage in the lost Heads against Gaius in which Hippolytus was using Heg. The Armenian colophons date John in the fifty-third year of the Passion, and the importance of this evidence can be shewn by his other allusions to the Gospels. Here we are concerned with the fact that the impossible date must derive from the Heads. Chapman (*JTS*, 1919, 588) has shewn that in this work Hippolytus omitted seventeen and a half years from the period which preceded Trajan. Now if we add that period and fifty-two and a half years to A.D. 29, which we have concluded was Heg's date for the Crucifixion, we arrive at the traditioned date of the Gospel.

§ 287a. Both Chapman's hypothesis and our view that the chronology of Hippolytus was based on Heg (§ 372 f.) are confirmed by the extraordinary chronology which we find in Proch. 162 where John is said to have been A. 15 years in Patmos, B. 9 years in Ephesus before the exile, C. 26 years at Ephesus after his return and D. to have been 50 years and 7 months when he came from Jerusalem to Ephesus.

We will take for our starting point a passage of Theodore of Mopsuestia (Zahn Ac. Joh. XL), who says that he cannot accept the position that John was the first to preach at Ephesus. John beginning from Nero, in whose reign was the Jewish war and the departure from Judæa, continued until Trajan. Paul appointed Timothy over the church of Ephesus. Theodore used Heg. (*a*) We shall conclude that John's continuance until Trajan and Paul's appointment of Timothy were both in Heg. (*b*) Theodore's source accepted an apocryphal journey of John. This may have been a journey which followed the QPl lots and the passover of the non-Crucifixion (SchmidtEvvC, 1: cf. Proch. 6. 8) or that of the eighth year (§ 181 D). (c) Theodore used Heg *sub* HE, III. xi where the apostles gather after the death of James, an apocryphal incident (§ 282) which implies their departure and occurred just before the war (A.D. 69).

§ 287b. Returning to Prochorus we observe the following facts. (i) If we add 9 years (B), the exile of 3 years and the $17\frac{1}{2}$ years of the error of Hippolytus to A.D. 69 (Heg *sub* Theodore) we arrive at A.D. 98 for the return from Patmos, and this is the date which we have attributed to Heg. (ii) Victorinus (in Rev. x. 11), who I shall shew was using Hippolytus, says that when John was exiled he expected to die, a statement which was based on the tradition that he had the mind of a martyr and was prepared for death. We infer that Hippolytus is likely to have said that he survived 26 years (C) (A.D. 78–104). Prochorus (C) supposed that the period was calculated not from the exiling but from the exile. (iii) The seven months of D shews that Prochorus connected John's age with that of Christ who in Papias and Heg was seven months in the womb (§ 290). There are two blunders. The Baptist and the apostle are confused, and the Annunciation is supposed to have immediately preceded John's birth. If then psProchorus had read that John arrived at Ephesus a year after the Crucifixion (§ 299) we have accounted for D, for according to Hippolytus Christ suffered when He was 49 (Chapman, *JTS*, viii. 597). (iv) If Hippolytus said that John lived to be about a hundred, Prochorus would assign 50 years to his residence at Ephesus. That he did this is shewn by the fact that if we deduct the 9 years of B and the 26 years of C and the 50 years of D from 100 we arrive at the 15 years of the exile (A). This calculation postulates the identification of the two arrivals, but both Hippolytus and Prochorus were blunderers, and the former writer may have confused the latter.

There are some other indications of the influence of Hippolytus on Prochorus. (i) In 129 Noetianus is the father of a Polycarp. In Hipp. Ref. ix. 2 Noetus is a Smyrniot. (ii) "Epicurus" (51) may be from Ref. i. 57. (iii) As Zahn points out the statement that Aquila was of Sinope in Pontus and was a Greek (81) occurs in Epiph. de Mens. 14, but the common source may be Heg. Some of the works of Hippolytus were in the library at Jerusalem (HE, VI. xx.).

§ 288. (ii) According to Abd v. 22 John died at the age of ninety-seven and he is supported by Mellitus (Zahn Ac. Joh. 258 *n*.). Now Epiphanius (*i.e.* Hippolytus) says in Haer. li. 12 that John was more than ninety (just past ninety) when he wrote. If we conjecture that he was ninety-one or ninety-two in A.D. 99 he died in A.D. 104 or 105. We will now examine the data for the deaths of S. John, Symeon, and Ignatius.

A. Eus. Chron. attaches the martyrdoms of Ignatius and Symeon to the Olympiad, A.D. 104–107, *i.e.* Traj. viii.–xi.

B. The Roman Acts of Ignatius give Traj. ix.

C. The Antiochene Acts agree with the Roman in this date and in nothing else.

D. APh, 107, gives Traj. viii. for Symeon and Philip's circuit of Asia. The only traditional circuit was that of John in AJ, where it immediately precedes his death, which therefore in the source was in Traj. viii.

E. Chron. Pasch. gives Traj. viii. for Simon "Judas of James " (§ 284 H) and John.

F. Chron. Pasch. gives Traj. ix. for Symeon and Ignatius. The consuls are correct.

The evidence may be thus summarised:

		A	B	C	D	E	F
John	Traj.	..	..	..	viii.	viii.	..
Symeon		viii.–xi.	..	..	viii.	viii.	ix.
Ignatius		viii.–xi.	ix.	ix.	..	..	ix.

The agreements are very striking and prove derivation from a common source which can only be Heg. The dating of Ignatius a year later than Symeon has the appearance of historicity. The two arrests were in A.D. 104, but Ignatius was taken to Rome and suffered some months later. We conclude that John was born in A.D. 7 and died in A.D. 104.

§ 289. (iii) According to the harmonising scheme of Heg Judas was the father of the apostle Judas of James (M). This position raised the question of the date of the birth of Judas. Heg started with the assumption that John was the youngest of the apostles, a tradition which probably reached Jerome (adv. Jovin. i. 26) through him. James, therefore, was not born later than A.D. 6. On the other hand Heg would not be likely to date his birth earlier. His tendency would be to assume that the children of Mary of Cleopas followed each other at intervals of about a year, and he would wish to diminish rather than increase the longevity of Symeon. At any rate his wish to put his dates as late as possible is proved by his statement that Judas married early in life (N). We may safely assume then that he dated the marriage of Judas about A.D. 5 and his birth about 15 B.C. He would therefore date the birth of Symeon, whose name preceded Judas in the misreading Symeon-Judas and who preceded Judas as bishop, in 16 B.C. Heg felt that the calculation could not be exact and therefore said that Symeon was *about the age of* 120 when he died. On this view, then, his death was in A.D. 104 and all our data tally.

§ 289a. The evidence has shewn that Heg was intimately acquainted with the traditions of John of Ephesus and that he identified him with John of Patmos, who according to Justin was the apostle. In the next volume it will be shewn that Heg derived his traditions from Papias, but that his evidence has an independent value. These facts are the more important as we have confirmed the view which Lawlor (40 f.) bases on the Bodleian Epitome that Heg described John as the apostle and evangelist. The Archæology of Josephus which is epitomised in the Paris MS. was the Hypomnemata of Heg (§ 17 1E). This MS. shews no knowledge of the Eusebian parallels.

I will now digress and summarise the other new evidence as to S. John's identity which I have adduced or intend to adduce.

(i) In opposition to Cerinthus Leucius asserted the doctrines taught in the Fourth Gospel as to the deity of Christ. He was the Only-begotten, the Word and "my God and my Lord." Christ in the form of an angel gave John the apostle this revelation on Olivet, and John revealed

the names of the two angels to the other apostles. Christ
promised that the cloud which bore Him would not leave
the apostle until the Second Coming. Leucius reconciled
this position (cf. Jn. xxi. 23) with Christ's words to James
and John by predicting that in the last days John would be
killed by the Jews at the same time as Enoch and Elias. In
QPl John the apostle went to Ephesus.

(ii) In the reply to Leucius which he probably wrote
immediately after the publication of EvT and the Preaching
of Paul and which was at any rate earlier than QC and
AJ, LeuciusP placed John at the head of his list of the
twelve.

(iii) It will be shewn that LeuciusJ used the passage of
Papias misquoted by Philippus Sidetes. Commenting on
Matt. xx. 23 Papias said that John had the mind of a martyr
and drank the cup of suffering.

(iv) Polycarp used this and another passage of Papias in
the Fuerdentian fragments. These fragments were excerpted
by Heg.

§ 290. Our discussions of Epiph. Hom. have shewn that
the dating of the Annunciation on Kyriake, the day of
light, and in A.M. 5500, may be safely attributed to Heg.
This position as regards the day is confirmed by the fact
that the source derived the day from Papias (Chapman,
JTS, viii. 594). The year like the day was arrived at by
a discussion of the Hexæmeron and must also be attributed
to Papias, an inference confirmed by Iren. V. xxiii. 2,
xxviii. 3, for almost all the matter in Iren. V which is due
to a source is likely to derive from Papias. Papias may
also be the source of the millenarian passage in Tryph. 81,
where *in Jerusalem* is not accounted for by Rev. xx. 4 f.;
still less is the probable allusion to the division of the land
in the millennium (113, 3). Heg gave the date A.M. 5500
sub LP, 210, and the allusion to 5500 healings which occurs
in STrans, 44, was suggested by it.

Hippolytus derived not only the day from Heg but also
the year. (*a*) Syncellus gives it when using him (Chapman,
JTS, viii. 595). (*b*) Photius ascribes it to him (cf. Dict.

Christ. Biog., iii. 104*b*). (*c*) In EvN, 28, the same date as supported by the same argument from the ark.

§ 291. [The ultimate sources of Christian views as to the millennia of the history of the world were Jewish. According to Jubilees, iv. 30, Adam died on the day in which he ate the fruit in accordance with Gen. ii. 17, and in 2 Enoch xxxiii. the days will be *after the fashion of seven thousand*, for *a thousand years are as one day*. It is possible that 2 Enoch influenced Christian thought through KP, for iii. f. may have suggested the ascension of Peter, and a variation (*the day of the Lord*) from the Hebrew and the Greek of Ps. xc. 4 (*as yesterday*) occurred in a source common to 2 Pet. iii. 8 (*one day with the Lord*), Barn. 15, and Papias. We find this variant in Iren. V. xxiii., xxviii. If Tryph. 81 does not derive from Papias, the case in view of the great influence of KP on Justin is strengthened. This variant also occurs in Hippol. in Dan. 23, 24. Victorinus when using our context of Papias in de F. Mund. has *in Thy eyes, Lord, a day.* . . . PsMark attacked Judaism, and "sabbatising" was its most marked characteristic (cf. Ign. Philad. 8). He would accuse the Jews of misunderstanding Gen. ii. 4.

§ 292. The conception of the world week was based on Gen. ii. 17 as interpreted in Jubilees and ii. 4. Eusebius in HE, III. xxxix. 13 supposes that Papias directly affected later writers. He is doubtless right in respect to Irenæus, and he might have added Victorinus. But it is probable that almost all later writers were influenced by Papias indirectly through Heg. This statement is at any rate true of the two following contexts:

(i) Cedrenus, as we have already concluded, uses him when he writes: *On this account was the day called the sabbath as being the day of rest and a type of the millennial seventh day and of the consummation of sinners, as Josephus testifies* (p. 9).

(ii) According to Lact. vii. 14 f. there will be six millennia (Ps. xc. 4) and Adam lived a thousand years, a position attributed to "some" in Iren. V. xxiii. 3. In 26 Lactantius speaks of the millennial reign of Christ. This will be as it is in "Josephus" the sabbath rest of God, and all wickedness will have been abolished (cf. "consummation of sinners") (14).

§ 293. Lactantius used Heg elsewhere. (*a*) In vii. 17 *persecute the righteous* has parallels in Heg ap. "AJ," 2 and the western variant at Acts xiv. 2, and (*b*) the statement that Antichrist *will enwrap righteous men in the books of the prophets and will burn them* explains two passages in Acts which are based on Heg, APh, 143 and MM, 18. (*c*) In iv. 10 the Crucifixion is under the Gemini. (*d*) in 21 Peter and Paul are the founders of the church of Rome. (See § 378.) I shall return to this passage. (*e*) *When Nero had put them to death Vespasian....* (*f*) We must attribute to Heg the prolonged influence of KP in the preceding context. (*g*) In de M. Pers. 2 the Crucifixion is under the Gemini (*c*). (*h*) Peter was bishop twenty-five years. (*j*) In 3 Domitian is another tyrant no less than Nero, a statement which occurs in the Epitome of Heg (Lawlor, 44). (*k*) *Persecute the righteous* occurs. (See (*b*)). I shall shew that the recision of Domitian's decrees occurred in Heg.]

VI. The Flight to Jericho

The whole of this section should be read. It is argued that the R narrative of the flight of Peter (Judas) and the five thousand has an historical basis.

———

§ 294. The J narrative of the attack of Saul on James which was based on the KP martyrdom of Stephen closed *sub* R. i. 71 with a narrative based on the KP narrative of the Herodian persecution. The brethren went to the house of James (Mary) and spent the night in prayer (Acts xii. 12). *Then before daylight we went down to Jericho, in number 5000. Then after three days one of the brethren came to us from Gamaliel ... bringing secret tidings that the enemy had received a commission from Caiaphas ... to go to Damascus with his letters, and ... employing the help of unbelievers* (§ 256) *to make havoc among the faithful* (Acts ix. 1 f.) *and that he was hastening to Damascus chiefly on this account, because he believed that Peter had fled thither. And about thirty days after he stopped on his way while passing through Jericho. . . . At that time we were absent, having gone to the sepulchres of two brethren which were whitened of themselves every year, by which miracle the fury of many against us was restrained, because they saw that our brethren were had in remembrance before God.*

The message of Gamaliel is the J version of an incident which occurred in the Herodian persecution (§ 309 (*h*)).

The flight of the five thousand to the neighbourhood of Jericho cannot be apocryphal. (*a*) The fords of Jordan were the nearest point of safety, and the wilderness of Judæa abounded in caves. (*b*) We shall assign on other grounds the Markan apocalypse to the eve of the Herodian persecution, and the flight must be that enjoined in Mk. xiii. 14. (*c*) We shall conclude that S. Peter had fled to the fords of Jordan a few days earlier.

The narratives of the flight to Jericho and the tombs underlies the following passages:

A. We found grounds for holding that PJ derives from Heg. Now the work closes with an account of its origin: *I, James, who wrote this history in Jerusalem, when there arose a tumult when Herod died, withdrew into the wilderness until the tumult ceased in Jerusalem.* I suggest that Cerinthus in order to account for the origin of J made Ananias (§ 127) write, "I, Annanias Antonius, who wrote what James taught in Jerusalem" (R. i. 69) "fled into the wilderness until the tumult" (that caused by Saul) "ceased." The allusion to Herod is due to editing in PJ (Matt. iii. 19).

B. In STrans, 16, where the source is certainly Heg, a letter is brought from Sinai (in the wilderness) in which Antonius writes about the death of James.

C. The following splinter survives in EvN, 17: *two . . . brethren. . . . We were at their falling asleep and at their burial. . . . Go (to) . . . their sepulchres.*

All three passages derive from Heg's excerpt of a J passage in which Ananias said that he wrote his narrative of James in the wilderness. The fact that the whitening of the tombs continued long after the supposed date of J tallies with the fact that the contacts of the incident with the flight of Peter

(Judas) are artificial and prove that psClement introduced matter from the preface in which Cerinthus claimed to have received J from the faithful community which told him the story (cf. § 109 f.). He may have actually heard it from an Ebionite community which used M, for M exalted the Baptist, whose followers are likely to have been numerous in the neighbourhood of Jericho. On the other hand he may have derived it from psMark, who collected Palestinian traditions and introduced them with topographical matter into his work and who, as I am about to shew, used another tradition connected with the locality.

§ 294*a*. The story of the tombs provides two confirmations of the historicity of the flight of the five thousand.

(*a*) The tombs must have been earlier than the fall of Jerusalem and the cessation of the passover pilgrimages, for it was only at the passover that tombs were whitened, the purpose being that the pilgrims might not be defiled (Abrahams Studies, ii. 29).

(*b*) Inasmuch as tombs were only whitened at the passover and the commemoration must have been at the date of the deaths of the disciples, they must have died at the time of year when on our hypothesis the flight took place.

(*c*) The explanation of the cessation of the persecution credits the observers of the rite with the impression made in history by the piety of the refugees. Herod's attack on the church may have pleased the hierarchy, but the mass of the population can have had no love for him. After the passover there was a reaction and the refugees returned to their homes.

§ 294*b*. In an account of S. Mark which is based on a passage of Heg, who was using KP (Hist. Patr. i. 131 f.), we are told that Mark the son of Aristobulus (EP, 309) carried the jar of water to the house of Simon of Cyrene where the Last Supper was held (so the Book of the Bee, 107), that after the Resurrection he entertained the disciples at his house (VP, 6; ABarn, 14) and slew a lion at the fords of Jordan. Now as is shewn by 1 Sam. xvii. 14 this last incident was not impossible. Lions frequented the thickets of the Jordan (Jer. xix. 19, 1, 44; Zech. xi. 3) and were still found in Palestine in the twelfth century (Reland, i. 274). The story is at any rate Palestinian and heard by psMark almost within the evangelist's lifetime, nor is it the sort of story that anyone would have been likely to invent. Its occurrence in KP is shewn by the fact that it was twice used by Leucius. (*a*) In AT, 8, a cup-bearer, who represents S. Mark, is killed by a lion when he goes to draw water (§ 332). (*b*) In EvT, 11, EvM, 33, Christ draws water and encounters a lioness by the banks of the Jordan. This last phrase gives us a link with R and we will complete the incident. Peter fled during the night from the house of Mary and was naturally accompanied by her son. They hid near the fords of Jordan waiting for an opportunity to cross, and there Mark encountered the lion. The five thousand fled a few days later. They would mingle with the Galilean pilgrims who were returning after the conclusion of the feast.

VII. THE HEALINGS

This study illustrates the relations of the four primary Acts and the indebtedness of QC to them.

§ 295. If the reader compares some healings which are scattered about the Acta, *e.g.* those in LJasZ, 32 f.; APh, 84 f.; VP, 25 f.; Proch, 12 f. and EusThadd he will find that they derive from a simple story which closely resembled the healings at the Beautiful gate, Lydda and Lystra. A lad was lame in his feet and gazed on the apostle who laid his hands on him in the name of the Lord Jesus Christ. He leapt; and Theophilus prostrated himself, worshipped Peter as divine, was rebuked by the apostle and gave much money to the poor. Later the apostle dined with Theophilus and his friends. There were other healings and the people cried, There is one God (cf. KP, 7).

In the next volume we shall discuss the relation of this incident to the N.T. parallels and the healing of the centurion's servant. Here we are concerned with the light which the narratives throw on the history of the depravation of KP.

I. A. In LJasZ, 32 f. Theophilus is the lad's father, and this section of the Acts derives through Heg from KP. In APh, 84 the name Theophilus is transferred to the lad.

II. B. As has been shewn, the Clementine narrative hardly ever leaves Cæsarea and the chief convert always plays the part which J and QP assigned to Theophilus.

In R. ix. 38 the wife of the householder who had invited Peter to leave the hospice (which therefore occurred in KP: § 220 BD) prostrates herself and beseeches him to heal of an unclean spirit her daughter who is bound with chains (Mk. v. 4) and shut up in a chamber. One of the servants says that she had been wont to bite and even tear in pieces all who attempted to approach her (Mk. v. 4). The healed girl prostrated herself before the apostle (A) and asked him to keep her deliverance feast (A). That this narrative derives from J is shewn by the fact that psClement used J elsewhere and by the adaptation of the incident to the Encratite motive by Leucius in H. There are no parallels in Matt. and Lk. Cerinthus preferred Mk.

C. In EPl, 672 the governor says that his brother has a son who has been kept dumb by Satan thrown by him into the fire and the sea (Mk. ix. 22: B) and but for eight servants who guarded him (B) would have been destroyed. No other healing so closely resembles B. The "governor's" brother (§ 191 AEFG) is editorial for Theophilus.

D. In the Cerinthian Matthew Christ healed Cornelius (H. xx. 13).

§ 296. III. Leucius used both KP and J.

(i) E. The son of Theophilus was killed in order that he might be raised and report what he had seen in the unseen world. In 633 Theodore (655) is killed, in 650 raised and in 651 tells his vision, another part of which is used in LA, 7 (§ 300). See also SHJ, 25; EvN, xvii.; and EP, 499, where the source of QC is uncertain.

(ii) Leucius used the J healings as follows:

(*a*) F. Christ (D) accompanied the apostle to Cæsarea (§ 297).

(*b*) G. We have concluded that the J Cæsarea narrative was preserved in the first year of QPl *sub* EusThadd. The healing, therefore, of Abdus son of Abdus (*ebed ben ebed*, *i.e.* the lad of Theophilus: 13) derives from J. This healing underlies the raising of the home-born slave in "AJ," 13 (where it is from AJ). In common with QPV, MPl, 2 derived from AJ (in the raising of Patroclus).

(*c*) H. In an Encratite story which underlies AT, 62 f. Leucius applied his haggadic methods to B. The wife (AB) of a captain of the king went to a marriage feast (B) with her daughter (B). Many servants (B) accompanied her. They were attacked by demons (B) and had since then been shut up in a room (B).

(*e*) J. In LPP, 178 f. the girl who was shut up in a stable was originally the emperor's daughter. Her eye was plucked out by a bird who itself became blind (probably in QPl when the eye was healed) (cf. LB, 76; AT, 33). The incident underlies APh, 140 f.

IV. K. The QPl healing *sub* H was used in QP *sub* EP, 505, where a leprous girl hides her hands when she pours water over the apostles. The story also occurs in Stud. Sin. vi. 53 and LP, 212, where we learn that the leprosy attacked the girl on the night of her wedding (H). (See § 194 KD.)

L. That CBRB, 207 preserves E as retold in QP appears from the allusions to the twelve and the context.

The apocryphists were not the miracle-mongers that they seem to be. Most of the healings and raisings in the Acta descend from the very simple story of the healing of the lad of Theophilus. In J he became a demonised son and daughter. In QPl the elaborations were midrashin.

VIII. Two Voyages

§ 297. The first journey with which we are concerned brought Judas and John to Cæsarea in QPl and underlies the following passages:

	AT	EPl	LMatt	AAM	VP, 5 f.
"Thy will be done".	3	..	126	..	..
No passage money, etc.	3	..	126	6	50, 12
Christ on board .	..	615	127	5	51, 1
They slept . . .	..	616	128	16	51, 11
A favourable voyage .	3	616	128	..	51, 11
The hospice . .	4	617	..	..	51, 15

[We note the freedom with which the author of VP used his data. To these parallels we may add that (a) in VP as in EP, 480 at Joppa, Peter relates the vision to his brethren.

In QPl Christ was accompanied by two angels one of whom, Michael, in FrankoAP, 318, is baptized by the apostle, an incident which underlies VP, 5, where it is transferred to Theon.

With the selling of Thomas in AT, 2 we may compare the story of John and the Ephesian bath-woman. In FrankoAP Peter sells Christ.]

§ 298. The voyage is a midrash on Peter's journey to Cæsarea. The three messengers who went to Joppa became Christ and two angels, with the result that the messengers went to the hospice at Cæsarea (§ 135). Not only the narrative but also the theme of the midrash derived from KP. Melito, whose fragments contain clear traces of KP, collected testimonies to shew that Christ was *the fashioner of men . . . pilot to Noah, the divider of the inheritance with Jesus the son of Nun* (Cur. Spic. Syr., 53). This incident was also used in a QPl prayer: *I am piloted by the Lord. Suffer not Thy ark to be wrecked of which Thou art captain and pilot. . . . Keep my spirit as Father, as God, as Lord, as shepherd lest there breathe on me the dragon* (ArmPhoc, 15). [There are parallels with this prayer in AT, 144, 167 (*let not the children of the dragon hiss at me*) and also in APh, 144, where the dying Philip refers to the dragon. Leucius also taught the presence of Christ with the apostles in EPl, 479 and EPl, 700 (§ 105). MPol derives from this midrash (probably through QP) in 19, where Christ is the helmsman of bodies and shepherd.] In J Christ went to Cæsarea before the Passion (§ 187).

§ 299. A second voyage introduces a contrasted theme. The ship resembled not the fishing-boat of Galilee but that which carried the disobedient Jonah. The apostles had been unwilling to go to their allotted regions, and each in the extant recension (QP) was encouraged by Peter. Peter and John wept (APh, 94; Proch, 8, 10). Thomas objected that he was a Hebrew (AT, 1): James desired to go to the gentiles (LJas, 140). The parallel in SchmidtEvvC, 1 dates the incident after the first passover.

Like Jonah, John (Peter) went to Joppa and took a ship which was sailing west (Proch, 7, 5) and which came from Alexandria (Acts xxvii. 6). Like Jonah (i. 3) the apostle paid his fare, a fact which may be inferred from the fact that in the other story the apostle pays no fare (AAM, 6: cf. VP, 5). In FrankoAP, 318, when the storm falls on the ship he is bidden, Arise and call upon thy God (Jon. i. 6). The story of the whale was used. In FrankoAP we read, *on thy account was the sea stormy*. In Proch, 48, 4 a young man is cast into the sea and in 50, 1 a wave casts him up alive. In 51, 7 there is an allusion to *three days and three nights* (so LAB, 14). In LAB, 12 a fish throws the apostle up outside the harbour. At this point Leucius shewed his knowledge of Hebrew, for *a wave spat forth* the apostle (Proch, 13, 10: LXX *cast forth*). Acts provided not only the ship but also the plank on which the passengers escaped (Proch, 8, 9; APh, 33; R. vii. 32; EP, 20). LeuciusJ used this incident in his narrative of the arrival of S. John at Ephesus (§ 287b; Proch, 13, 10; ATim Lips, iii. 375).

The passages which refer to the leadership of Peter must derive through QP.

IX. THE PREACHING OF ANDREW

§ 300. Like LLk (§ 21 f.) LA illustrates the fact that the Acta are compilations. [Much of the matter is so splittered, depraved and disordered that if it were worth describing it would hardly be possible to describe it. Yet it contains passages of interest and value. (i) 1, 24–3, 17 is influenced by the martyrdom of James the son of Zebedee. (ii)

5, 25 f. is based on the passage of QPl in which Theophilus after his return to Cæsarea in his rage slew his son who when raised describes his experience when dead (§ 296 D). *In the name of Jesus Christ arise* is from KP (§ 296). (iii) The attack of the devil on (the wife of Theophilus) (8, 16–9, 32) influences AT, 64 and the devil's speech must be compared with that in Lips ii. 233.]

The matter about the raised son is of interest, for it influences AT, 18, 21 f. and follows QPl very closely. In 7 the raised son says, "O my father! if thou wouldest give "half of what thou possessest to the orphans and the widows "and the poor.... For what thou hast given to the needy, "thou hast given it for thyself.... People came to me winged "like the eagles; and they took my soul to ... Gehenna. "And I looked to a large house being built of sulphur and "pitch. And the number of the builders was thirty and they "had great burning lamps. Some commanded ... to set "it on fire with lamps. He said unto them, ... By the time "that the owner dies shall ye burn it.... I asked him for "whom this house was built and why it was built of sulphur "and pitch. And he said, These are the sins which thy "father hath committed; and it will be built until the time "that he shall die. They will toss him into it.

"And when I heard these things I wept sore.... And "he who was walking with me said, Weep not. And ... "he approached with an aged man and a young man whose "age was twelve years, very beautiful in appearance, and "he conversed with the master of the builders in a speech "which I did not understand. And thereafter he commanded "that the house should be pulled down; and he commanded "the angel who was walking with me to bring me out into "a very wide place. And another man came with a golden "reed of three colours in his hand, and he laid the foundations "of a large house in thy name, the height of each of its walls "was a hundred reeds at the further end; and its breadth "and its length the same.... The master of the building "(said), ... When the wheat has come to the storehouse "we will finish." 9. The governor distributed all that he had to the poor. When the king heard, the vizier saw that he desired the governor's ruin and interceded for him, suggesting that he should deliver up all his goods.

EP, 671 (§ 295 F) preserves some matter omitted in LA.

X. Hebrew and Liturgical Matter in QPl

§ 301. i. That Hebrew matter occurred in QPl appears from the following passages in EvN.

[A. In i. 4 the Jews cite the Hebrew of Ps. cxviii. 25. Derivation from QPl is shewn by the fact that Pilate asks what the words mean. We compare EvN i. 4, *What are proselytes?*: MPP, 18, *What is a Nazarene?* and ApPl, 30.

B. In xi. 1 Jesus calls *with a loud voice* (Mk. xv. 34) the words of Ps. xxxi. 5 (Lk. xxiii. 46). That the passage derives from QPl is strongly suggested by the fact that the Coptic and Latin name the two thiefs and Gk B the centurion (Longinus). The Coptic depraves the Hebrew words but is superior in the interesting phrase *Father, Abi* (Gk, *Father*). The Coptic continues:

C. *Adonai, aroa sabel louel.*

D. *Eloi, Elemas, abaktanei. Eli, Eli, . . . sabachthani.*
(*My power, my power, thou didst forsake me.*)

Leucius's translation (Cf. § 115 (iv)) survives in EvP, 10.

C in QPl may have preserved the Hebrew for *Father forgive them, they know not what they do.* (*a*) Leucius would be almost certain to use the saying, for a docetic interpretation could be given to its final words. (*b*) It is the only other saying addressed to God. (*c*) *Sub* Heg MJas, 16 he put into the mouth of James the words *God Father, forgive.* . . . The opening phrase may have dropped the initial *Lord* which may survive in the Coptic *Adonai.* Compare Ecclus. xxiii. 4, *Lord, Father, God.* (*d*) The words which follow seem to be gibberish like the concluding *orioth.* . . . The Coptic translator or a scribe not understanding that the passage preserved the Hebrew and unable to decipher his MS. felt free to write according to his fancy.]

The incomplete notes which follow may perhaps be of some service.

ii. The following proper names occur in QPl matter:

	MM	EvN	CBRB	SHPh	EPl	APh	Celsus (1.24)	
Adonai .	21	11	:	69	5¹³	:	(C)	EvM, 12; EvT (J, 69).
Eloi .	21	11	196	:	:	132	:	
Sabbaoth .	21	:	196	69	:	132	(C)	
Shaddai .	:	:	:	69	:	:	:	
Abi .	:	11	:	:	:	:	:	
Baruch .	:	:	:	:	:	129	:	Valentinus (Iren. II. xxiv. 2). Cf. Hipp. Ref. v. 24 f.
Marmari .	21	:	:	:	:	115	(C)	
The Highest .	:	:	:	:	:	:	:	MA, 55, 4; AT (9 times).
Gehenna .	3	:	:	:	671 f.	:	:	AJ, 11, 114; AT, 74.
Sheol .	:	:	:	:	673	:	:	

E. In ApPl, 30 the interpretation of Alleluia is said to be *thebel marematha* (*praise: the Lord is at hand*), the words being Hebrew which is the speech of God (EPl, 621, *the tongues of angels*). Compare MM, 21, *Adonai, Eloi, Sabaoth, MarMari marmunth*. In Did, 10 *Maranatha* occurs in a eucharistic prayer which seems to be editorial, but the preceding *Hosanna to the God of David* probably belongs to the same early stratum as Maranatha. The influence of QPl is highly improbable, that of a eucharistic prayer in the Cæsarea section of KP probable. In MM there is a eucharist in 25. See also § 320C.

F. For the use of the Hebrew of Jonah, see § 299.

§ 302. A. Leucius used the contemporary rite in his descriptions of the worship of the angels. In EP they sing *trisagios* (so EvvC, 4). In EP, 471; CBRB, 207 and ApPl, 12 they wear inscribed girdles or robes. (In MM, 27 the bishop puts on splendid garments.) For hymns consisting of glorias followed by designations, see § 166. For instances of the Amen and Alleluia, see CBRB, 191; ApPl, 30; LM, 100; MM, 25. In MPP, 25 the broken loaf drives away dogs (devils). Rites are described in AT, 27, 49 f., 120 f., 144, 156 f. Leucius narrated a baptism *sub* FrankoAP, 318 and VP, 5.

B. For the primitive rites at a tomb near Jericho and at the Holy Sepulchre, see §§ 294, 164. A tomb rite is described in MM, 25 f. Heg referred to a service at the tomb of Bucolus (*sub* Vit. Pol, 20: cf. Polycrates).

C. A primitive rite on Olivet on the traditional site of the Ascension suggested the statement of KP that the apostles after Christ ascended remained praying (EP, 475; EApP, 519). S. Sylvia of Acquitaine refers to this rite and says that it was observed on the afternoon of Pentecost and that the scriptures read at the preceding eucharist narrated the Ascension.

D. Ps. xxiv. was an Ascension psalm in the time of psMark (EApP, 519; EP, 468; Iren. *Dem.* 84). Leucius transferred it to the ascension from hell (EvN xxi. 2 f.).

XI. S. PETER'S COMPANIONS

This section is of great importance for the criticism of the NT and supplies important data for the determination of the date of Mk and the identification of the sources of Acts. We shall be much concerned with lists of names most of which contain fictitious elements, but if our postulate that in the NT apocrypha no matter is apocryphal which is not obviously apocryphal is valid the historical value of our results is secure apart from their contacts with the NT.

---

§ 302a. 1. In Ac. iii. 1 a John accompanies Peter to the temple, in viii. 14 that apostle to Samaria and in xiii. 6 Barnabas to Cyprus. In xiii. 13 S. Luke tells us that John returned to Jerusalem and that he was Mark. But for viii. 18 no one would have doubted that it was Mark who went up to the temple and to Samaria. Now there is ground for thinking that in this verse S. Luke may have blundered.

Lk. viii. 51, ix. 28 and Ac. i. 13 vary from all other canonical passages in the order *John, James*. This variation must be motived, but it is not due to a wish to exalt John above James, for in LLk. v. 10 and MLk. vi. 14 we find *James and John*. The problem is solved when we compare the two lists of the twelve.

Lk. vi. Pet, And, Jas, Jn.
Ac. i.   Pet, Jn, Jas, And.

S. Luke varied the order when *James and John* was preceded by *Peter*. He knew that *sub* LLk. x. 1 (cf. Mk. vi. 7, Matt. x. 2 f.) Jesus sent the twelve two by two before his face, and he inferred that John was sent with Peter from the fact that in Lk. xxii. 8 Christ sends those two apostles in advance. The evidence shews that if his source associated an unidentified John with Peter S. Luke would be likely to assume that this John was the apostle.

If S. Luke had any tendency to connect the gift of the Spirit with the apostles his tendency would find both confirmation and expression in the narrative of the visit of Peter and John to Samaria (Ac. viii. 18). Now we concluded that S. Luke, misinterpreting his source, supposed that

Christ bade the eleven to wait for the gift of tongues and connected it with their mission to the world by his editorial list of the tongues. Further, while Acts leaves the question open whether the gift was confined to the apostles, in EP, 470 a narrative of Pentecost, which is one of a series of excerpts from QP, says that many of the men who were with them spake in divers tongues. It would appear that S. Luke's omission of this incident must be connected with his other editings. If this is the case it is clear that the phrase "of the apostles" in Ac. viii. 18 is very likely to be editorial. Lake on other grounds holds that the possibility must not be excluded that the John of Ac. viii. was Mark. That something of the nature of glossolaliai occurred at Samaria is shewn by the fact that Simon saw that the spirit was given.

§ 302*b*. 2. S. Luke's narrative of the activities of Peter and Philip in Judæa seems to abbreviate a source. (*a*) We first hear that the apostle had companions in x. 45. The allusion to them in xi. 12 is evidently misplaced. It is probable that Peter followed up the work of Philip just as he followed up that of the Cyrenians and Barnabas in Syria after a delay which may in part be due to the controversies of the period and the anxieties caused by Gaius (§ 252 f.). Just as Philip went to all cities (viii. 40), so Peter went through all parts (ix. 32). He followed Philip at Samaria, Joppa and Cæsarea; on the other hand Philip is not said to have gone to Lydda or Peter to Azotus.

The apocrypha agree with Acts as follows:

A. In a narrative which was independent of Acts KP brought Peter to Samaria (§ 234 f.) and Cæsarea.

B. In Proch, 7, 5 John (in QP Peter) goes to Joppa.

C. In APh, 33 Philip goes to Azotus and in SHPh to Carthage (Cæsarea) in Azotus. There is no trace of the influence of Acts on these Acts.

D. In a fragment of QP (§ 176 D) Peter *went through every city and region*, a phrase which occurs in one or two Cæsarea endings.

E. QPl *sub* LA, 5 was parallel with Ac. ix. 38.

3. The following notices preserve matter omitted in Acts:

F. According to APh, 108 Philip went to Lydia (Lydda).

G. In an abbreviated QPl narrative we read: *And the first city which we entered on the coast was Joppa, and we also arrived at Emmaus* (Nicopolis) *and at Lydda* (EP, 479). Heg seems to have distinguished this visit from the QPl visit narrated *sub* E. Leucius had no conceivable motive for varying from Acts, and as a matter of fact he was using J. He is perhaps supported by QP *sub* A where Peter stayed for three days with Tabitha. If this was on the occasion recorded in Acts S. Luke abbreviated the source of KP.

H. H has a parallel in LB, 76 where the apostle goes to the cities on the shore. The phrase would hardly have been used if Cæsarea was the only city on the shore which Peter visited besides Joppa.

J. In QP *sub* D Peter went to Azotus and he goes there also EP, 483. The name is here substituted for Aradus as is Cyprus in 22 (cf. 505).

§ 302*c*. 3. The following evidence refers to S. Mark:

K. In Hist. Patr. i. 36, a context which will be shewn to derive from Heg and through him from KP, Mark is with Peter at Azotus.

L. In a QPl list of companions, which is of considerable historical value, we find a John (§ 312). Leucius who exalted John cannot have intended this John to be the apostle.

M. We shall conclude that Mary the mother of Mark went to Cæsarea, and other evidence will bring Mark there (§ 332 f.).

§ 303. The Clementine lists of Peter's companions run as follows. The six deemed historical are italicised:

H. ii. 1		R. ii. 1; iii. 68	
1. *Zacchæus* once a publican	JBps	1. *Zacchæus*	
2. Sophonias his brother		2. Sophonias	
3. *Joseph*	JBps BarK	3. *Joseph*	
4. Michaias his foster brother		4. Michaias	
5. Thomas (*Judas*)	JBps BarK	5. ..	
6. Eliezer his twin brother	Josephus	6. Eliezer	
7. Æneas	Ac. ix. 35	7. ..	
8. ..		8. Phinees	EvN

H. ii. 1		R. ii. 1 ; iii. 68	
9. Lazarus the priests	EvN	9. Lazarus EvN	
10. Elisæus		10. Helissus	
		The four substitues	
11. *Benjamin* the son of Sapprus	JBps BarK	11. *Benjamin* the son of Sab a	
12. *Rubelus* and	BarK	13. *Rubelus* the brother of Zacchæus	
13. Zacharias the builders		14. Zacharias the builder	
14. *Ananias* and		12. *Ananias* the son of Safra	
15. Haggæus the Jamninians		15. ..	
A. ..		A. Clement	
B. Niceta and		B. Niceta	
..		16. Nicodemus	
C. Aquila the friends		C. Aquila	

Some of the descriptions have become attached to the wrong names.

(*a*) The Thomas of the apocrypha is always Judas Thomas who was spiritually a builder and the twin of Christ. Hence the designations in 6, 13 and 14. (*b*) *Son of Saba* misapplied in 11 shews that Joseph (3) and Thomas (Judas: 5) were originally the Barsabasses. That this designation derives from KP is shewn by the parallels in § 310 (ii). (*c*) *The priests* in H (= HR) refer to Æneas and Lazarus, but R preserves from QHR the original sequence, Phinees, Lazarus who are in the same list in EvN, ii. 4.

The fact that Zacchæus (1), Joseph (3) and Judas (4) were historical persons and that fictitious brothers have been assigned to them suggests the conjecture, in which this work had its origin, that psClement expanded an historical nucleus which named the six companions of Ac. xi. 12.

§ 304. We will begin our study of the names by eliminating the companions who cannot be historical.

1. The first two fictitious brothers are prophets. In the same vein psClement added to the nucleus Elisha (10) and Haggai (15).

2. Æneas (7) cannot have been one of the six, but in Ac. ix. 35 all Sharon is said to have seen him and turned to the Lord. He became a companion, and the healing confirmed the word.

3. Zacharias (13) was the same person as Zacchæus (1), a fact which the compiler of JerBps learnt from Heg (§ 185). Similarly Eliezer Lazarus became Eliezer (6) and Lazarus (9). We compare Simeon Simon, Saul Paul and Joseph Joses. These duplications were a feature of I Ac. Mc.

§ 305. 4. PsClement found in QP a statement that priests or the sons of the priest (Demetrius § 226A) accompanied the apostles (§ 183) and quarried from the list of priests in a parallel with Ac. iv. 6. The historical value of the source is proved by Josephus.

Ac. iv. 6	..	Annas	Caiaphas	..	..	John	..	*Alexander (and as many as were of the kindred of the high priest)*
Ac. iv. 6 (D)	..	..	..	..	..	Jonathan	..	
QC	..	..	..	..	..	..	..	Eliezer	Lazarus	Phinees
EvN, 1, 2	..	Annas	Caiaphas	Gamaliel (Nicodemus)	..	..	Alexander	..	Lazarus	Phinees (who in 14 is a priest)
LagardeDAdd, 93	..	Annas	Caiaphas	Gamaliel	Nicodemus	..	Alexander	..
EPl, 549 f.	Ananias	Hanna (Annas as in EvN is a ruler of the synagogue)	..	..	..
Josephus	Ananus	Annas	Caiaphas	..	..	Jonathan	..	Eleazar	..

§ 306. The Nicodemus of EvN and LagardeDAdd derives through QPl from Jn, but the Nicodemus of our list (16) was quarried from the context of QP with which we are concerned, as is shewn by the table in § 310, and was a companion because his daughter was a companion in QP. The tradition survives in STrans, 25 where we read that there accompanied the Virgin *Calletha the daughter of Nicodemus* . . ., *Neshra the daughter of Gamaliel, the chief of the synagogue of the Jews* . . . *and Tabetha the daughter of Tobia, a man of comitian rank* . . . *of the gens of the house of Herod.*

The description of Gamaliel is intended to be an equivalent to " the high priest " and is an indication of derivation from KP. Our fragment, which the writer derived from Heg and which cannot be apocryphal, explains the tradition that the children of the crucifiers accompanied the apostles (§ 185c).

That the fragment accounts for the occurrence of Nicodemus in the QC list is shewn by the allusion to women companions in the context of the list (R. ii. 1). This tradition underlies also R. ix. 38 where Peter's wife is with him. In APh, 30 the apostle is accompanied *by his disciples and certain* (their names were known) *women.* A fragment is inserted in 142 which implies a tradition that Peter was accompanied by his wife. We shall conclude in § 261 f. that Peter in KP was also accompanied by Mary Mariamne, the mother of Mark.

§ 307. The tradition of the women companions may be confirmed.

(i) In 1 Cor. ix. 5 Peter and the brethren of the Lord are said to have been accompanied by their wives and other women when on their missionary journeyings. It will be argued that S. Paul's opponents at Corinth derived arguments to his disadvantage from I and II Ac. Mc. We learn from ClemStrom, vii. 63 that Peter's wife was with him when he was martyred. The incident has no parallel in the Acta and probably derives from Papias.

(ii) The tradition of Calletha is confirmed by the fact

that the writer of the primitive gospel which underlies Jn. vii. 50 was acquainted with the words spoken by Nicodemus in Christ's behalf (§ 352).

(iii) A reconstruction of a tradition of Mary Mariamne tallies with the tradition that Mark was a companion (§ 336 (iii)).

(iv) Peter like his Master was accompanied by women who ministered to him of their substance (Lk. viii. 3).

§ 308. (v) There is much to be said about the tradition of Tabitha and Tobias.

(*a*) The statement of STrans that he was of comitian rank and of the house of Herod explains the QC designation *foster-brother* on which word it is a gloss. *Manaen the foster-brother of Herod* (Ac. xiii. 1) gives it vraisemblance.

(*b*) That Tobias was mentioned in KP is shewn by the occurrence of his name in JerBps (§ 310). Apart from the tribal names all the names in this list can be connected with Cæsarea, and Tobias is also connected with that city by the fact that the apostle stays at his house in EusThadd, 11. It was therefore the house in the market-place which in the days of psMark had become the hospice of the church. The fact that he could entertain Peter and his companions and that his house became the hospice agrees with the tradition that he was a man of rank (p. 275 *ad inf.*).

(*c*) The tradition that the apostle stayed at his house agrees with the statement of Proch, 7, 6 that John (Peter) stayed at Joppa in the house of Tabitha. The tradition is quite consistent with the statement of Acts that Peter stayed in the house of Simon the tanner. He may have been her husband or a relation. There is evidence which indicates that Tobias, who as a man of rank would know the procurator, had told Theophilus of the healings of his daughter and Æneas and that Theophilus had invited the apostle to Cæsarea in order that he might lay hands on his " lad." Tabitha accompanied the apostle from Joppa just as Æneas had accompanied him from Lydda.

(*d*) The description of Tobias is certainly pre-apocryphal.

EusThadd, 11	Tobias	the son of Tobias	
Mk. x. 46		the son of Timæus	Bartimæus
QC		the son of Saba	
Acts			Barsabbas

§ 309. (e) It will be argued that the narrative of II Ac. Mc. sub Ac. xiii.–xv. was assimilated to that of I Ac. Mc. sub Ac. x. under the influence of Peter's appeal to what God had wrought at Cæsarea (xv. 7 f.). The impression made on Sergius Paulus was overstated because he was the counterpart of Theophilus. Elymas was another Simon who tried to turn the Roman magistrate from the faith. Barjesus who in KP was distinguished from Elymas was another Tobias. It is clear that in the following passage the bracketed matter was added by the late reviser who inserted long passages of Acts in EP1: *they came to Yafus (that is to say, Paphos) where they found a certain Jew (who was a magician and false prophet); he was a servant of the governor, and his name was Baryasa, (that is to say Baryasos) . . . he said . . ., There is a certain wise man whose name is (Paul); send and fetch him* (EP1, 539 : cf. § 175, 10). There are indications that in Ac. xiii.–xiv. Luke edited II Ac. Mc. with a view to leaving the impression that the Jews were S. Paul's enemies from the very beginning of his missionary work.

(f) In VP, 35, a context which is based on the QP narrative of the Herodian persecution, the wife of " Cæsar's (the king's) friend " (Tobias) warns the church of the impending attack. The same narrative underlies the story of Charisius (AT, 138), a story which has other contacts with the Herodian persecution. In 95 Charisius like Tobias is the king's kinsman and friend.

The J version of the warning sent by Tobias is used in R. i. 71 where the warning another of the three fathers, Gamaliel, sends one of the brethren with secret tidings of the coming persecution.

A comparison of AT, 138 with 95, where the same section of the source is used again, shews that the house of Charisius was in the source in the market-place. The apostle left it to go to the house of Siphor, who may be safely identified with Theophilus if only because the apostle ordained him and his son (§ 169). The tradition therefore is that underlying AT, 3 f. where Thomas goes to the hospice and then to the palace. AT, 3 is parallel with a context of EP1 (§ 297) which we are about to use. In 618 f. the apostle lodges in the market-place and then goes to the house of Thewodas (Theophilus). The same tradition in a purer form underlies the QP passages collected in § 220. It is certain then that in the source the apostle stayed in the house of the friend and kinsman of the king before he went to the pretorium. Now in AThadd, 11 Thaddæus stays with Tobias before he goes to Abgar. Tobias therefore was the friend and kinsman of the king who in KP *sub* AT persecuted James and was Herod. We conclude that we have reconstructed part of the source of STrans.

There is however in our tradition an element which is not likely to be primitive. When psMark wrote the house of Tobias had become the "hospice" or "house of the community" (EP, 480: part of a JCæsarea ending). It was near the gate (§ 220a) and the church built on the east side of the city and mentioned by Heg (EP, 503).

Two of the blocks of names which we have been examining are historical as also the companionship of Æneas. We will now collect the passages in which occur the names which remain in the QC list when we have removed the prophets, the priests, Æneas and Nicodemus, who is accounted for by his daughter.

§ 310. Leucius in his lists of the companion elders (JerBps) and the shepherds of Bethlehem derived in common with QC from the KP Cæsarea narrative. JerBps runs:

4. *Zacchæus* (HE)	QC		10. Seneca		
Zacharias (Epiph)	QC		11. *Justus*		BK S
5. Tobias	§ 309		12. Levi		
6. *Benjamin*	QC BK		13. Ephres		
7. John		QPl	14. *Joseph* (HE)		QC BK S
8. Matthias (Judas)	(QC BK)	QPl	*Joses* (Epiph, Hier. Chron.)		S
9. Philip		QPl	15. *Judas*		QC BK

BK = Bar-Kappara (§ 311).   S = Shepherds.

The shepherds in the Book of the Bee, 81 are Asher, Zebulon, *Justus*, Nicodemus, *Joseph*, *Barshaba*, *Jose*, Isaac.

It was the custom of Leucius to use tribal names in his lists. If these tribal names are omitted we obtain two very interesting results.

(i) All the remaining names in JerBps may be connected with Cæsarea. The most interesting name, Seneca, has been at any rate connected with Theophilus. For Philip we may compare Ac. viii. 40. Matthias who in the list of the Jewish watch (§ 315) is collocated with Barnabas must be suggested by Judas Barnabas Matthias.

(ii) We must connect the following facts: (*a*) The last four names of JerBps give us Justus Joseph-Joses and Judas. (*b*) In QP *sub* QC Joseph and Judas were brothers and in the same order. (*c*) The shepherds include Justus and the collocation Joseph-Barshaba-Joses. (*d*) In Acts Joseph Justus Barsabbas has a brother named Judas. (*e*) Matt. xiii. 55 and Mk. vi. 3 give us two brothers Joseph-Joses and Judas in the QC and QPl order. (*f*) In QC Joseph and Judas were the sons of Saba. (*g*) QDesp and other documents identified Judas the Lord's brother with Justus Barsabas (§ 284 DEGJQ). (*h*) In BK Joseph is Justus.

The following table states part of the evidence:

JerBps	Tobias	Justus	..	Joseph-Joses	Judas
Shepherds	Nicodemus	Justus	Barshaba	Joseph Joses	..
QC	Nicodemus	..	son of Saba	Joseph	Thomas (Judas)
BK	..	Justus	..	Joseph	Judas
Matt Mk	..	..	..	Joseph-Joses	Judas
Acts	..	Justus	Barsabbas	Joseph	Judas

We conclude that psMark identified Joseph and Judas the Lord's brethren with the two Barsabasses and made them companions of Peter at Cæsarea and in the same context named the women companions. Before we consider the contacts of this tradition with other historical documents, we must endeavour to identify the Benjamin and Reuben of QC. We have already identified Ananias with Ananias of Damascus and concluded that his second name was Antonius (§ 128 f.).

§ 311. The most important clue to the identification of Benjamin and Reuben occurs in an unlikely place, the Talmud. I am indebted to Mr Travers Herford for the verification of my reference and for some interesting notes. Mr Herford tells me that Bar-Kappara lived at Cæsarea, his death being in A.D. 219. There are grounds for thinking that he engaged in controversy with Christians.

In the Midrash Vajikra Rabbah, p. 47*b*, occurs the following: Rab Huna said in the name of Bar-Kappara, *On account of four things the Israelites were redeemed from Egypt: they did not change their names ... they did not call Judah Rufa, nor Reuben Luliani, nor Joseph Listis nor Benjamin Alexandri.* The same passage is found in Shirha-Shirim Rabbah, § 4, p. 28, where however the names are slightly different, viz.: *Reuben, Rufus; Simeon, Luliani; Joseph Listis; and Benjamin Alexandra.* Mr Herford says that neither series is quite correct in its statement of equivalent names. " Rufus corresponds to Reuben, Luliani (= Julianus) to Judah, Listis to Justus. A comparison of the two lists seems to shew that the four Romanised names were known as having been referred to in Bar-Kappara's dictum, while the compilers of the Midrash were not certain of the Hebrew names to which they were severally equivalent. Bar-Kappara was plainly condemning the practice of Jews taking gentile names. He did not merely take four well-known gentile names and give, out of his own knowledge, the common gentile equivalents of them."

So far Mr Herford. I will add that if Bar-Kappara was attacking Christians his opponents almost certainly used KP or a work based upon it and that it follows that he was not unlikely to have read it himself. It must also be noted that his four Jewish names occur in the Clementine list and that Justus also occurred in KP. Again, the confusion in the reports of the dictum can on our view of its origin be at one point explained. We have found that Judas in a very early misreading was Simeon Judas (§ 275 (ii)). Further, such duplications were a characteristic of the matter which KP derived from I Ac. Mc.

§ 312. Our reconstruction will be complete if we can find evidence that in KP Alexander and Rufus were companions of Peter. This proof is provided by the documents which preserve the names of the QP companions. The lists run as follows:

	Andrew	John	Philip	Matthias	Some of the Seventy	
EP, 481	Andrew	John	Philip	Matthias	Some of the Seventy	
LA, 1 f.	An	Jn	Ph	Matt	Alexander	Rufus
LM, 100 f.	An	..	..	Matt	..	..
LP, 211	An	Jn	..	Thomas	..	..
APA, 3	An	..	..	Matt	Alexander	Rufus
QVitA, 576 f.	An	Jn	Ph	Matt	Some of the Seventy	
RobEvvC, 50 f.	..	..	..	..	Alexander and Rufus are members of the Seventy-two.	

That these parallels derive from a common source is obvious. That the source was QP is sufficiently shewn by the fact that it combined historical names with Leucian (JerBps, 7–9), by the fact that the passage in EP abbreviates one of a series of extracts from QP and by the allusion to the presence of members of the Seventy-two on Olivet in a QP narrative of the Ascension (EP, 467).

To the evidence for the nucleus of historical names we must add the allusion to (Antonius: § 129) Ananias the "apostle" of the church of Jerusalem (LP, 175) and an allusion to Benjamin Judas who are mentioned in FrankoAP, 316 shortly before Peter (John) sails with Christ (originally to Cæsarea: § 297). The evidence may be tabulated thus:

QC	Zacharias Zacchaeus	Joseph ..	Judas	Benjamin ..	Reuben ..	Ananias	
B-Kapp	Zacharias-Zacchaeus	Joseph-Justus	Judas	Benjamin-Alexander	Reuben-Rufus	..	
JerBps	..	2 Joseph 1 Justus	Judas	Benjamin ..	..	..	
QP	..	..	Matthias	.. Alexander	.. Rufus	..	
LPP FrankoAP	..	..	Judas	Benjamin ..	..	Ananias	
NT	.. Zacchaeus	Joseph-Justus	Judas	.. Alexander	.. Rufus	Ananias	Antonius

§ 313. The Acta contain some other passages which refer to the companions of Peter. In one of a series of parallels with Cæsarea endings John returns from Patmos with Prochorus and six other disciples (Proch. 162, 12). The companions occur in two other Cæsarea endings, AThadd, 8 and APh, 93. We observed above the allusion to these companions at the outset of a journey (APh, 45) to Nicatera where Ireos plays the part of Theophilus. In 64 f. the incident of Peter's arrival at the pretorium is used (§ 135 F). There are seven men at the gate (Peter and the six). The evidence then shews that the number of the companions was six, a number which corresponds with that of the nucleus which we have just reconstructed.

According to LPP Ananias was an apostle. This fact suggests that the companions were named in a narrative which stated their dismissal, and this conjecture is supported by the most important of the QP passages, EP, 481, where Peter goes to the coast with named companions. Cf. Ac. xiii. 1 f.

§ 314. We now return to the NT and observe that Peter's companions went to the pretorium with him (Ac. x. 45, 48) and that they were six in number (xi. 12).

Peter's speech is clearly editorial, and we may conjecture that I Ac. Mc. mentioned the companions as follows. They were named in the narrative of their dismissal. As in APh it was stated that the six went to the pretorium with the apostle and, as in the Cæsarea endings, that they returned with him to Jerusalem. The work closed with the statement that Peter declared what God had wrought (Ac. xiv. 27, R. i. 44). The Acta preserve the original positions of the allusions to the six.

Another contact with Acts is the fact that in xiv. 4, 11 Barnabas and Saul are designated " apostles." The Cephas party at Corinth probably had twitted S. Paul with the fact that he was not the apostle of the mother community at Jerusalem. In 1 Cor. ix. 6 he refers to his journey with Barnabas. He replied that he was an apostle in a still higher sense.

§ 314*a*. It only remains to note the allusions to the six companions in the NT. (*a*) The fact that Zacchæus had " restored fourfold " was probably known at Cæsarea. He may have known members of the administration personally. He must have been able to speak Greek easily. (*b*) Joseph's alternative name Joses shews that he was the Lord's brother. In 1 Cor. ix. 5 we learn that the brethren were accompanied by their wives when making their missionary journeys. Moreover the fact that the Joses of Mk becomes Joseph in Matt must be added to the evidence for the influence of I Ac. Mc. on Matt. Chapman has anticipated my view that the Barsabbasses were the brethren (*JTS*, 1906, 429). He observes that no man would be a more suitable bearer of the apostolic letter than the brother of James. The force of this contention is strengthened if Judas had helped to found the first gentile church and knew Theophilus who was almost certainly at the date of the council a leading member of the church of Antioch. (*c*) Mk. xv. 21 shews that Alexander and Rufus had visited the Greek-speaking church for which the Gospel was written. We shall find below that KP stated that Mk was written for the newly founded church of Cæsarea. (*d*) Ananias was a leading Christian who had baptised the foremost opponent of the faith. He is likely to have returned to Jerusalem soon after the baptism and to have been chosen as one of the six.

The discussions in this section are from the writer's standpoint crucial. The name lists and ClemBps were the Rosetta stones which enabled him to decipher the relations of the primary apocrypha. If, unless it be at points which are obviously of minor importance, he has wrongly interpreted them it appears to him that almost the whole of his work on the apocrypha falls to pieces. On the other hand he holds that the contacts of the various items of the evidence are so many and so striking that they cannot be fortuitous and that unless his positions are demonstrably erroneous they must be provisionally accepted until they are supplanted by a more plausible group of hypotheses.

The evidence which bears on Markan problems is of

special importance. (i) It will be shewn that psMark and Heg stated that Mark wrote his gospel at Cæsarea (§§ 333, 372 f.). Now this statement makes the following undesigned cohesions. (*a*) We have concluded that S. Mark was with S. Peter in South Judæa, and (*b*) with Alexander and Rufus (Mk. xv. 21) at Cæsarea. (*c*) We shall support the evidence of KP from Papias and by an argument from the priorities (§§ 379*a*–382), and (*d*) we have ground for thinking that Mk was written on the same ground plan as an Acts which ended with S. Peter's return from Cæsarea. (ii) A detailed analysis of Acts will shew that the whole of I Acts is accounted for if we postulate the use of Acts of Peter and Barnabas. That these Acts were Markan appears as follows: (*a*) The way in which as is shewn in this section KP supplements Acts shews that psMark used S. Luke's source. Now both writers used S. Mark's gospel, and (*b*) there is evidence that the writer of KP claimed to be Mark. (*c*) In KP John Mark and in Acts a John accompanied Peter. In Acts John Mark accompanied Barnabas. The source narrated a visit of Peter to his mother's house, named her maidservant, and at the close referred to the close of the Acts of Peter (cf. Didasc. xxiv.). The twelve allusions of Acts to a John who is a lay figure are best explained by the hypothesis that he was the author of S. Luke's sources.

Lastly, the investigations recorded in this volume finished at the point at which they began. The hypothesis that the attacks on the eleven in Mk were in some way connected with the controversy mentioned in Ac. xi. 2 and the presence of Joseph and Judas at Cæsarea led to the discovery of the influence of M on our Mk and a confirmation of the very early date of protoMk.

XII. THE NOMENCLATURES OF QPl AND SOME OTHER ACTS

§ 315. We have already attributed to Leucius an apostle named Barnabas Matthias Judas Thomas and concluded that he named Cornelius Leucius Dionysius, giving him also the baptismal names Theodore and Paul, and that he named Theophilus Demetrius. In his addiction to multiplying names and to naming persons unnamed in the Gospels and in his other sources he was unique among the apocryphists. His nomenclature is characterised by some other peculiarities.

A. In CBRB, 187 there are at the sepulchre *Mary Magdalene*, *Mary* the mother of James whom Jesus had delivered out of the hands of Satan, *Salome* the temptress, *Mary* who ministered unto him (APh, 94), *Martha*, *Susanna*, the wife of Khousa who had refused to share his bed, *Berenice* (1*), the woman with the issue, *Leah*, the widow of Nain (2*), and *Philogenes* (3*) the gardener. (See § 136.)

B. We will now return to the lists in EvN i., ii. (§ 131 f.). The first runs *Annas*, *Caiaphas*.... 5. *Gamaliel*.... 9. *Alexander*: the second, 1. *Lazarus*.... 9. *Phinees*. In the QC list Phinees and Eliezer were collocated and described as priests, and Lazarus was also mentioned. These priests were historical and derive from KP. (See § 305.)

Our lists also contain some unhistorical priests. *James* (4*) is suggested by the fact that James was a priest in J (*sub* HegMJas). That Leucius is quarrying from J is proved by his collocation with *Antonius* (5*: cf. § 129). *Samuel* (6*) is a priest in PJ x., a fact which is part of the evidence for the influence of QPl on that work. In PJ i. we also find the priest *Reuben* (7*), a name likely to be Leucian because it is tribal. *Ze*(cha)*r*(ia)*s* was a high priest in KP *sub* EpiphHom, 321. The fact that "ruler of the synagogue" and "high priest" were in KP convertible terms, accounts for *Jairus* (8*) and *Crispus* (9*).

The interest of J in the tribes led Leucius as in the instance of Reuben (7*) often to use their names. In EvN we find *Nephtalim* (10*).

It has been observed in § 143 (*c*) that the following names derive from the debate with the seven sects: *Semes* (11*), *Asterius* (12*), *Dathaes* (13*), (J)*Amnes* (14*), *Judas* (15*), *Levi* (16*) (§ 143).

The absurd *Agrippa* (17*) like *Berenice* (1*) is from Acts.

C. Just as in the B lists Leucius used the KP priests as a nucleus for his list, Judas, Levi, Nephtalim, and the absurd Agrippa, so in his list of the Cæsarea companion-elders all the names were connected with Cæsarea in KP (in QPl Matthias (cf. 39*) as in QC Thomas was Judas) except Levi and Ephres, whose names are tribal. (See § 310.)

D. Nobody but Leucius would have named the shepherds of Bethlehem and the Jews who watched at the sepulchre. In the Book of the Bee, 81, 94 they are: (i) *Asher* (29*), *Zebulon* (30*), *Justus* (31*), *Nicodemus* (32*), *Joseph* (33*), *Barshaba* (34*), *Jose* (35*), *Isaac* (36*) (the shepherd of the cave in EpiphHom, 331 (§ 149): he is another link with QPl). (ii) The Jewish watch are *Issachar* (37*), *Gad* (38*), *Matthias* (39*), *Barnabas* (40*: note the collocation Matt-Barn), *Simon* (§ 41*).

E. According to EvT vii. a *Zacchæus* (42*: cf. 18) and in EvT *sub* EvM, 38 a *Levi* (43*: cf. 12*, 26*) taught Christ. In EvN xvi. 2 a Levi shews a knowledge of the home at Nazareth. *Zeno* (44*) occurs in EvT, 9. See 54* (H).

F. *Petronius* (45*) who is the centurion of the sepulchre in EvP, 31 was probably suggested by the proconsul who opposed Gaius (§ 190). It is probable though not certain that the names of the twelve gentiles who are bishops 16–29 in JerBps are from a Leucian list, and if so they may be the names of the soldiers of the Roman watch. We note in the list Gaius (50*), Capito (51*) and Apion (52*), three names which KP is likely to have mentioned in the same context as Petronius.

G. The following passages come from the same workshop:

(*a*) In a QPl context we read: *If at any time He were bidden by some one of the Pharisees* (AJ, 93).

(*b*) *Akrosima* (53*) *the wife of Simon* (54*) *the Pharisee* (the Book of the Cock: J, 150).

(*c*) *A Pharisee a high priest Levi* (55*) *by name* (Ox. Pap. J. 29).

(*d*) In Didasc xxi. Jesus appears in the house of *Levi* (cf. 55*, § 95).

(*e*) In EvvC, 5 Jesus when at Jerusalem stays in the house of *Irmeel* (56*).

(*f*) In DAdd, 3 Jesus goes to the house of Gamaliel the chief priest.

(*g*) EvN xiv. *A certain priest named Phinees* (cf. 6*) *a teacher, Addas a teacher and Aggæus* (57*) *a Levite.* In

DAdd, 39 Aggai succeeds Addai. The influence of STrans on DAdd may be an element in the solution of an unimportant but curiously complex problem.

(*h*) PsBasil mentions the work of *Nicodemus the Levite* (§ 171 F).

H. Probably all the proper names in the apocrypha which derive from the Pastoral Epistles so derive through QPl. *Titus* was S. Paul's precursor in Galatia, and with *Timothy* and *Luke* (Leucius) arrived at Rome with him (§ 259). (*Alexander*) *the coppersmith, Demas, Hermogenes and Philetus* were at Iconium (§ 268) as also *Onesiphorus*. *Zeno* (54*) or Zenonia was used as a fictitious name (Thec, 1; EvT, 9). *Jannes and Jambres* occurred in QPl *sub* EP, 509; MPP, 34 and EvN v. *Eubulus* (54*a**) occurs in EpCor and VP, 17. Both Acts quarry names from QPl. In VP, 4 Timothy is from *Macedonia* and in MPl, 1 Titus comes from *Dalmatia* and Luke from *Galatia*. Philetus, Hermogenes and One-siphorus occur in Abd iv. 1 and APA, 13. (See also § 268.)

J. *Longinus* (55*) is the centurion of the cross in EvN xvi. 7, the Book of the Bee, 94 and Patr. Or. V. 317, and the name was borrowed in APl (J, 287). In MPl, 2 f. Longus is connected with a centurion in a narrative influenced by the Crucifixion. In the Book of the Cock (J, 150: cf. G(*b*)) we find *Paul of Tarsus, son of Josue Almason, the son of Cardafana* (56*) and compare *Rufus the son of Cleopas* (57*: § 137). Leucius must have been using J in the context of the description of Saul, for Saul plots with Iscariot. The J designation "the Tarsian" occurs in the context. In R. ii. 7 *Antonius* (58*) and *Rachel* (59*: cf. Leah, 2*) are Simon's father and mother. In EvN ix. 5 *Gestas* and *Dysmas* (60*) are the two thiefs. *Theopiste* (61*: § 161) was the wife of Theophilus. *Decalius* (62*: LLk, 153) was probably suggested by Deucalion who may have occurred in KP (R. viii. 50; Theoph. iii. 18). An *Isaac* (63*) is associated with them. In RSteph, 164 *Abibus* (64*) is the son of Gamaliel.

§ 316. The following names are given to two or more persons: Antonius (5, 58), Isaac (36, 63), Joseph (28, 33),

Judas (15, 28*a*), Justus (25, 31), Levi (16, 26, 43, 51), Matthias (22, 39*), Simon (41, 50), Zeno (44, 54). If allowance is made for the fact that Leucius probably used KP very frequently and Acts very seldom, probably thirty names are from KP, but nine are given to unhistorical persons. Nine names are tribal; fourteen from the Pastoral Epistles. If we add *Dionysius* (65*) and *Demetrius* (66*) there are five names from II Acts. There are seven names from the O.T. The following names occur in matter which shews a knowledge of the traditions of the Lycus valley: John, Philip, Hierapolis, Apollo, Artemis.

§ 317. Some notes may be made on the names used by some other writers.

I. It is important that there is only one instance in which there is ground for suspecting the creation of fictitious persons in KP, J and QP. That psMark invented *Joachim* and *Anna* is shewn by the agreement of PJ, 1 with EpiphHom, 321. As a rhetorician he was compelled by the rules of his art to describe fully the origin of His divine Hero, and his account of the Virgin involved the naming of her parents.

II. In the next volume I shall argue the influence of Papias on AJ and ascribe to it the writer's knowledge of the names of the seven cities and of the Ephesian deacon Byrrhus. Though the point cannot be proved, the style of 18 and 59 where there are two name lists suggests that LeuciusJ is using Papias. In 18 the names *Cleobius*, *Marcellus* are probably due to the influence of QP.

III. The influence of the nomenclature of QPl on APl was shewn in § 315 HJ. The writer in his Thecla narrative perhaps substituted Lectra for Zenonia (ArmThec) as the name of the wife of Onesiphorus. *Stratonice the wife of Apollophanes* (EpCor) imitates the manner of Leucius.

IV. QC was strangely defective in personal names. Peter's wife and the other women companions, the leading converts at Tyre and Laodicea and the widow who befriended the twins are all unnamed. PsClement probably derived his knowledge of Flavius *Clemens* and of the fact that the bishop of Rome was a writer as he derived his knowledge of *Niceta*, *Aquila* and *Marthones* of Tripolis from Papias. In view of these facts and the QPl identification of Berenice with the woman with the issue the allusion of H. iv. 1 to *Justa* the Canaanitess and her daughter *Berenice* were probably quarried by HR from Heg. The list of companions is an important exception and due to psClement's interest in ordinations. In this connection he took trouble with his names.

V. The nomenclature of AT also is rather meagre. There are unnamed *dramatis personæ, e.g.* in 4, 5, 6, 8, 13, 30, 62. In view of this fact we may perhaps add *Gad* to our list of the tribal names of QPl. Some of the names prove that the writer lived in the east. *Mygdonia* like Bardaisan is the name of a river in eastern Syria (Burkitt, *Early Eastern Christianity*, 25 f.). In 65 the apostle leaves the church in the charge of the deacon Xanthippus (Syr). Now Burkitt points out that Ptolomy Euergetes according to Hier. in Dan. xi. 9 left a Xanthippus in charge of the provinces which lay beyond the Euphrates and that *Tertia* is the only other name which is likely to be western. We find Ptolomy and Xanthippe also in VP. All three writers used Heg. *Gundaphor* reigned in the first century as Hyndopheres (J, 365).

VI. VP aims at a good style and the names are numerous but not too numerous. The copious nomenclature in 1–5 may have been suggested by Rom. xvi., which chapter provides *Quartus* and *Narcissus*. Heg certainly suggested *Albinus* and probably *Ptolomy, Xanthippus, Pompeius legatus, Castor* and *Balbus*. From Acts cited by Heg he derived *Lysimachus, Marcellus, Cleobius, Ariston, Demetrius, Dionysius, Theon, Timothy, Barnabas* and the suggestions of *Italicus* (?Aquila) *Antulus* (?from Antonius), *Gemellus* (from the QC twins). (See § 190 (*e*).)

VII. The nomenclature of STrans has points of interest. *Flavia* and *Sabinus*, as the context shews, were suggested by an allusion of Heg to Flavius Sabinus (DAdd, 21 is influenced by STrans). For James and *Anton*, see § 129. For *Caleb*, see § 134. *Calletha* the daughter of Nicodemus,

Neshra the daughter of Gamaliel and *Tabitha* the daughter of Tobias are from KP. The instances of *Nonnus* are Syrian or Egyptian.

VIII. QEPP probably did not alter or invent names. There are probably not more than a dozen editorial names in EP, EPl and the L Acts.

XIII. THE CONNECTION OF LEUCIUS WITH THE LYCUS VALLEY

The proof that Leucius J and Heg derived in common from Papias (§ 320 G) should be noted, as also the evidence which shows that Leucius and the writer of Rev were acquainted with the Lycus valley (§ 320*a*).

§ 318. We have found decisive evidence that Leucius was an Asian and strong evidence that he was one of the informants of Papias. The evidence now to be adduced connects him with the Lycus valley.

I. The following table is a far from complete statement of the parallels which shew that the documents derive from the passage of Heg with which we are concerned. The AJ parallels shew that the incident is Leucian.

	AJ	APh	LM	Proch	LP	EPl	APl(J)	LAB
A. A festival	38				213			
B. Festival dress	38		102	118, 10	213	661 f., 677		
C. Philip's wrath		14, 128			214			
D. Priests cursed		23, 129		129, 11	211		284	18
E. Christ appears		20, 127	102					
F. Lk. ix. 54 f.		135				678		
G. "Be patient"		121	102	128, 10	214			19, AAM, 27
H. Imprisoned in temple							284	
J. Temple	38	144	102			661	284	
K. Apollo			103					
L. Artemis	46		103			661, 681	284	
M. Earthquake		21, 124	105			677		23
N. Temple falls	42	133	109	128, 17		678	284	24
Q. Church takes its place		146	109			681		LB, 72, LPh, 63
P. Seven priests	42			128, 6		562		7, AAM, 7
O. Priests punished	46	23 f.				562, 673		LB, 74
R. Dead man raised	46	26 f.	108			?		

Among the parallels which I have omitted are allusions to the neglect of the temples in AAM, 23 and APh, 126. Again there are traces of haggadic treatment of some incidents, e.g. *I am from Egypt* (LM, 103: cf. AT, 109). In QPl *sub* EPl, 661 f. Paul offered sacrifice at Hierapolis just as he did at Antioch. In 656 under the influence of the context in (Heg § 320) he himself is to be offered.

§ 319. The following matter is Leucian and shews a knowledge of the Lycus valley.

(i) There can be no doubt that like Papias Leucius brought Philip to Hierapolis. John visited Philip at Hierapolis in Heg *sub* APh, 128 and MirKh, and the three names are brought together in TransPh and *sub* SHJ, 8 (§ 260 A–D). Further, Philip is a leading apostle in several other Acts which derive from our context of Heg (the Acts of Paul and Philip (EPl, 611 f.), SHPh, LPh, 61 f.). The incident of the wrath of Philip (Table C) occurs in a Gospel fragment (J, 32) which is not in the least likely to have been influenced by APh and is likely to be Leucian, for it is influenced by Jn and grossly perverts the Gospels. Moreover, the transference of the incident of Lk. ix. 54 (Table F) from John to another apostle would be wholly in the manner of Leucius. It is clear then that Leucius was acquainted with the historical fact that Philip had lived in the Lycus valley.

(ii) Hierapolis was famous for its devotion to the Leto myth and for the number of its priests. The priests are prominent in our documents (BDP) in a way which is not likely to be due to the fortuitous agreement of the editors. Artemis was also prominent and Apollo may have been mentioned (KL).

(iii) Hierapolis, like the other cities of the Lycus valley, must have suffered badly in the earthquake of A.D. 60. The allusion of QPl to an earthquake (M) is a contact with fact.

(iv) The incident of the conversion of a temple into a church (O) must have occurred in QPl, for like that of the seven priests we found it in QP moved to Cæsarea (R. iv. 6).

It may have some basis in fact. Rev. iii. 14 f. suggests that for some reason Christianity had spread very rapidly in the Lycus valley. The use of the temple as a prison (H) probably has some contact with fact.

§ 320. II. A. We concluded in § 176 f. that in QPl *sub* AT, 31 and a fragment of QP an apostle encountered Satan near Hierapolis. I will print the AT speech, adding variant matter of interest from the Lipsius fragment.

I am the son of him which hurt the four brothers which stood . . . which girdeth about the place which is outside ocean, whose tail is in his mouth.

I entered through the fence . . . and spake with (Lips *seduced*) *Eve. I inflamed Cain to kill his own brother.*

I cast down the angels from above and bound them in lusts for women . . . that children might be born of them and I might work my will on them.

I hardened Pharaoh . . . (suggested) *the calf . . . inflamed Herod . . . Caiaphas . . . Judas.* (Lips) *Through me they slew the prophets.*

I am the lord of the 600 *angels which fell. I am kin to him that is to come from the east . . . to do what he willeth. . . .*

In Lips Peter chains him for seven days (the depravation of an allusion to the millennium) during which time there are no sins upon earth.

In Enoch vi. 6 the angels are not as in QPl 600, but 200 in number. A splinter from the speech which survives in VP, 8 and CBRB, 213 confirms our view that AT derives from Heg. For the seduction of Eve see Thackeray S. Paul CJT, 50 and for the fall of the Satans and Gen. vi. 1 f. see Charles on Enoch vi. and Rev. xii. 9 and Thackeray 160.

The evidence now to be adduced shews that the Leucian dragon derived from the mythology of the Lycus valley, but it presents a very complex group of problems, some of which I have not solved.

B. In PistSoph, where the influence of QPl is shewn by the allusions to Mary and Martha, *the outer darkness is a great dragon whose tail is in his mouth; it is outside the world and surroundeth it completely* (287a). In 23 we are told that *when Adamas and all the tyrants warred against the light, Christ took away the third part of their powers.* The two passages recall not only A but also the dragon of Rev. xii. 3 f., whose tail draws a third part of the stars of heaven.

C. Irenæus in *Dem.* 16 f. writes of Satan's fall as follows: *so* (by tempting Eve) *the angel was struck down . . . and caused man to be cast out of Paradise. . . . He was called Satan according to the Hebrew word, that is Apostate . . . also Slanderer. God cursed the serpent . . . and the angel hidden in him . . . 17 . . . filling Cain with his spirit he made him a fratricide. And so Abel died, signifying that certain should be oppressed and slain* (the prophets: cf. A). *. . . And God raised up another son, 18 . . . a very small seed of righteousness. The angels brought presents to their wives.* Irenæus is probably using Justin whom he uses elsewhere both in Dem. (Robinson, 6) and in c. Haer. Moreover, Justin dates Satan's fall from the temptation of Eve in Tryph, 124, 3 and interprets Satan as Apostate in 103, 5. He derived from a writer who like Leucius (§ 301) displayed his knowledge of Hebrew, for according to that passage *sata* means Apostate and *nas* Serpent. But he also probably used Papias, *e.g.* in Tryph, 81, 4. The description of the descendants of Seth as a small seed probably derives from an early exegesis of Genesis which was used by S. John and underlies 1 Jn. iii. 1–12.

D. Andreas in Apoc. c. 34: "Thus saith Papias (I quote him word for word): *To some of them* (clearly the angels who at first were holy) *He gave dominion also over the arrangement of the universe, and He commissioned them to exercise their dominion well.* And he next says: *But it came to pass that their array came to nought; for the great dragon, the old serpent, who is also called Satan and the devil, was cast down, yea, and was cast down to the earth, he and his angels with him.*" This fall was not that of Rev. xii. 9 but that of A.

E. The myth in its original heathen or in a synthetic form underlies Celsus (v. 54 f.) who as elsewhere was using Heg and says Celsus refers to a statement that sixty

(A, 600) or seventy angels were cast under the earth and chained; *and hence it is that the tears of these angels are warm springs*. There are hot springs at Hierapolis, and those at Laodicea were connected with Poseidon who was one of the Titans (Leucius, die Anfange des Heil. Kults, 268). Probably their bitterness was supposed to be due to some connection with the sea. If so we have accounted for a statement of SHP, which Acts was much influenced by our context of Heg, that a water-pipe bore the body of Ananias from the synagogue to the sea. The Lycus was supposed to flow underground, and this fact suggested a connection between the springs and the sea.

F. Leucius referred to an incarceration of the dragon or Satan in (APh, 134), and in EPl, 677 the earth covers him up. This incident must be distinguished from the parallel with Rev. xx. 1 f. which occurs in EP, 512 and at the close of the devil's speech (A). It had been effected by S. Michael, for whose aid the apostle prayed (673) and who in another QPl context (APh, 137) will protect the gate of Paradise. Inasmuch as S. Michael is very prominent in the traditions of the Lycus valley (J) the presence of Michael matter in QPl is a link between Leucius and that region.

G. Papias narrated the story of an historical flood which probably was due to the earthquake of A.D. 60 and the damming of the Lycus by a landslide. This incident was preserved by Heg in a passage which underlies MirKh, EPl, 697 f. and AAM, 29 ("canal": cf. MirKh, 469, 471), which narrated the miraculous protection of the church at Colossæ from the flood. This incident shews traces of a mystical passage in which Papias spoke of the flood of persecution. His story of the flood also underlies AAM, 30 f. and Proch, 120 f. It killed cattle and children, and, following as it did an appalling earthquake, created a paroxism of terror which led the people to contemplate the sacrifice of some girls to the god Lycus, possibly the virgins devoted to the temple service (AAM, 22 f.; Proch, LP, 211: for the virgins, cf. also APh, 134). The Christians of the district intervened and owing to their prayers Christ sent Michael who opened a chasm in the ground through which the flood escaped. For the survival of human sacrifices, see Lewis (Myth. Acts xxiii.). For the intervention of Michael and the chasm, see Hartley, Researches in Greece, 53 and Laborde, 103.

That this matter occurred in Papias is shewn by the fact that LeuciusJ *sub* EP, 503 f. used it in the Laodicea section of the circuit of Jn: *The unbelieving men that were in Laodicea sent messages . . . saying, The waters of the Kesaros* (Chryses in MirKh) *have risen and drowned many men and cattle* (AAM) *. . . and they asked Peter* (John) *to entreat GCt to turn away the waters of the flood from overflowing its boundaries. . . . He said unto one of the lambs* (Christ: originally Michael), *Go thou to river Kesaros and say unto it, Peter* (John), *the disciple of the Lord* (from Papias) *hath sent us unto thee, and he telleth thee that thou art bound by the word of God* (Rev. xix. 13) *and that thou shalt never again pass over thy boundary* (Freer extension) *until the day of the Resurrection. . . . The flood went back to its limit.* The mystical flood of persecution is combined with the historical Lycus flood.

§ 320*a*. H. There is a vein of matter in Rev which shews a knowledge of the Lycus valley and of the traditions used by Leucius, Papias and Heg. I shall suggest that some of it may have been derived by Papias and the author of Rev from the preaching of Ariston.

(*a*) None of the seven letters shews such an intimate local knowledge as that to Laodicea. It probably embodies some of S. John's actual preaching there.

(*b*) viii. 11. Pliny describes the bitterness of a lake in the valley to the wormwood growing round it.

(*c*) ix. 1. The smoke from the abyss may be suggested by the vapour which rose from the Chaironion which Strabo says could kill sparrows. Springs giving forth hot vapours are characteristic of the valley.

(*d*) Moffat plausibly conjectures that Apollyon in ix. 11 caricatures Apollo. In xii. 1 the woman is described in terms of a goddess. Charles cites Dieterich for the statement that among the Greeks Leto wears a veil of stars, and holds that the myth underlying Rev. xii. closely resembled that of Leto whose worship was very prominent in the valley.

(e) The tendency to angel worship which is twice rebuked in Rev. (xix. 10, xxii. 8) seems to have specially marked the Lycus valley. Michael (xii. 7) was honoured there.

(f) In xii. 16 the earth comes to the help of the woman against whom the dragon has cast the river from its mouth. The myth, here, has assumed its canonical form in a district in which the rivers disappeared in the soil and not e.g. in Palestine or Egypt. That the Lycus was believed to disappear into the soil at some point is shewn by the express statements of Herodotus, Pliny and Strabo. Ramsay says that the Chrysorhoas disappears at Hierapolis.

XIV. The Date, Destination and Identification of QPl

§ 321. QPl has occupied so central a place in our reconstructions that it may be well that I should collect the evidence for its date and destination.

I. The internal evidence shews that QPl was written by an Asian shortly before S. John's death.

1. In the last section we concluded that the writer was acquainted with the Lycus valley. In the next chapter we shall conclude that he was acquainted with S. John's midrashim.

2. QPl was directed against Cerinthus.

3. The writer rejected the apostolic decree and was almost certainly a Nicolaitan.

4. Ramsay dated the reviser of the story of Thecla A.D. 130 or earlier.

5. The fact that QPl taught a docetism of the most extreme type favours its very early origin (Lightfoot, *Ap. Fath.*, II, i. 368).

6. While the writer used the Fourth Gospel he wrote before S. John's death. (a) He attributed to Christ the promise that He would not leave him until He came again

(EP, 470, 493). (*b*) In those last days John would taste death and no man would bury his body (§ 271). The writer took the view implicit in Jn. xxi. 23 or one similar to it.

§ 322. II. The external evidence confirms the internal, for it attributes a Preaching of Paul to a heretic named Leucius who was an Asian and a contemporary of S. John.

1. Photius attributes an Acts of Paul to Leucius, and his account of the Leucian Acts closely corresponds with our reconstruction of QPl. It contains matter which is not accounted for by AJ, AT and VP, and the two latter Acts were influenced by Heg.

2. In EvN, 17 f. matter deriving from QPl is ascribed to Lucius and Carinus.

3. The preface of EvM implies that the Matthew (Matthias) Gospel used by the writer (EvT) was very heretical and condemns the doctrines of Leucius.

4. PsMelito attributes to Leucius a narrative of the departure of the Virgin which was gravely heretical. Such a narrative found its place in our reconstruction of QPl.

5. PsCyprian describes an heretical Preaching of Paul which precisely corresponds with QPl.

6. Epiphanius, blundering in his use of Hippolytus, speaks of a Leucius who belonged to the circle of S. John who was an opponent of Cerinthus. Tertullian attributes to the author of an Acts of Paul the story of a baptized lion which we have attributed to QPl and says that the writer was deposed in the presence of S. John. (See § 270.)

§ 323. III. We are brought to the same conclusion by an examination of the priorities of QPl.

1. The work was used by LeuciusP whose early date is shewn by his influence on QC and AJ. That LeuciusP was an Asian is shewn by the fact that he gave S. John the first place in his list of the apostles as did the writer of EvEb who like LeuciusP was influenced by QPl.

2. QPl was almost canonised by the earliest heretics. Evidence has been adduced which indicates its influence on Valentinus, the Naasenes, Basilides and Marcion.

3. On our view QPl was written about a year before Ignatius passed through Hierapolis on his way to Rome. Papias had begun to collect the materials for his book before S. John's death. Presumably then it was from Papias that Ignatius derived his knowledge of the Asian situation and of the vogue of docetism. Moreover there is positive evidence that Papias referred to Ignatius. LeuciusJ, who it will be argued used Papias referred to Byrrhus the Ephesian deacon who befriended the martyr (ad Sm, 12; AJ, 36, 111; OxPap (J, 266); LJ, 169; ZahnAcJo, 245, 1). The following evidence shews that Ignatius had some knowledge of QPl.

(i) We have attributed to Ignatius a knowledge of the story of Thecla.

(ii) We have already concluded that Ignatius was influenced by QPl in Sm, 3, *spiritually united to the Father* (§ 93).

(iii) *Keep your flesh as a temple of God* (Philad, 7) is a Leucian commandment which underlies *blessed are all they that keep the flesh chaste, for they shall become the temple of God* (Thec, 5; EP, 7).

§ 324. (iv) A KP allusion to the freeing of the sleepers underlies the following passage which is cited from an elder in Iren. IV. xxvii. 2, *the Lord descended (into hell) preaching His advent there also.... Now all those believed Him who had set hope towards Him ... the righteous men, the prophets and the patriarchs....* There is an allusion to the underlying passage of KP in Barn, 6, *Abraham, Isaac and Jacob who set their hope on Christ shall live for ever.* That Christ in KP preached in hell is shewn by a fictitious testimony which occurs in Tryph, 72, Iren. III. xx. 4 and IV. xxii. 1, *The Lord God remembered the dead, and He descended to preach His own salvation.* Christ was *the Lord God* in KP *sub* EpiphHom, 324. The *Descensus* occurred in KP *sub* AscIs, xi. 19.

Sub the following passages Leucius combined Jn. x. 9 with KP *sub* Barn, 6 and the QPl revision of KP is used.

A. IgnPhilad, 5. *The prophets set their hope on Him and awaited Him.... 9.... being the door of the Father through whom Abraham, Isaac and Jacob enter in and the prophets.*

B. LPP, 181 (a Leucian context) . . . *the door of God. By Him the just enter. He is the hope of the pious.*

C. HermS, ix. 12. *The gate is the Son of God through whom the saved enter.*

In QPl *sub* AJ, 109 Christ was designated " hope."

§ 325. (v) We concluded in § 98 that according to KP angels were present at the cross, and we cannot but connect this fact with the position of KP that the cross was pre-figured by Jacob's ladder (Tryph, 86, IrenDem, 45, STrans, 42, where Gen. xxviii. 12 f. is used in controversy with the Jews). Moreover in Tert. adv. Marc. iii. 24 and Aug. c. Faust. xii. 26 (I use Bernard on Jn. i. 51) Jacob's ladder is described as a way, and in one or two of the passages about to be cited the cross is a way leading up. These passages shew that in QPl the cross was described as a ladder or way by which the sleepers ascended from Hades.

A. EvN, xxv. 2. *The Lord stretched forth His hands and made the sign of the cross over Adam and over all the saints, and He took the right hand of Adam* (EvB, i. 8, 21 f.) *and went up out of hell, and all the saints followed.*

B. APh, 130. *The Saviour stretched out His right hand and drew a cross descending from the height to the abyss, and the abyss was filled with light, and the cross was the likeness of a ladder with steps.* . . . 141. *And the shining cross brought us to the light.*

C. LPP, 181. *He is the ladder which leadeth up to the height,* because He was in QPl the cross (§ 165).

D. In LM, 106 Christ is *the ladder which reacheth up to the sky.*

E. AT, 10. *Thou didst open the doors of hell . . . and shewedst them the way that leadeth up into the height.*

F. IgnEph, 9. *Stones . . . borne up to the heights by the engine of Jesus Christ which is the cross. . . . Love is the way that leadeth up. Engine* is substituted for *ladder* owing to the influence of Eph. ii. 20 f. on the context.

(vi) Our passage of QPl was also used by Papias for the following passage of Hippolytus is shewn by Armenian evidence to derive from him (ZahnForsch, vi. 128). In Antichr, 59 the church is compared to a ship *whose pilot is*

Christ. She bears in her midst a trophy . . . the cross. Her prow is the east, her stern the west, her hold the south, her net the laver of regeneration, her anchor the commands of Christ. . . . The ladder leading up to the sailyard is an emblem of the passion of Christ which brings the faithful to the ascent of heaven.

§ 326. (vii) Photius complained that Leucius made Christ appear sometimes as an old man, sometimes as a youth and sometimes as a child. Instances occur, *e.g.* in AJ, 27 f. and VP, 20. Probably the motive of Leucius was no more than a wish to explain away the tradition that Jesus grew, but he hit on the striking phrase *the polymorphous Christ* (AJ, 82; MM, 15). The reply of Papias was that Christ passed through all the phases of human life *to save all . . . an infant for infants . . . a child for children . . . a young man for young men and an elder, a perfect Master for all* (Iren. II, xxii. 4). The last phrase was probably based on the phrase *the perfect man* which we may attribute to KP on the strength of its occurrence in IgnSm, 4 and the Syriac Melito fragm. B, *being at once God and perfect man.*

§ 327. For reasons which have been already given the evidence of Ignatius and Papias must be read together and in connection with the antecedent probability that they directed their polemic against Leucius. Ignatius attacked a heretic who like Leucius denied that Christ was born and that He suffered and rose. Papias must be thinking of Leucius when he speaks in his preface of popular and verbose writers who advocate an alien discipline. The eccentric list of apostles which follows (And, Pet, Ph, Thom, Jas, Jn, Matt) seems to be influenced both by Jn. i. and QPl. Thomas in QPl was also Nathaniel (§ 275a). It may be added that Papias is the only writer who is likely to have preserved the tradition of the deposition of Leucius from the presbyterate.

§ 327a. I Clem, 49 is a tissue of allusions and probably is influenced by S. John: *let him that hath love in Christ fulfil His commandments. Who can declare the bond* (Col. iii. 14) *of the love of God?* [For the connection of the love of God with commandments we must compare 1 Jn. v. 3,

this is the love of God that we keep his commandments.] ...
The height whereunto love leadeth up. ... [This striking
phrase is not in Clement's manner but has two close
parallels. In QPl Christ was the *way* or *ladder that leads up
to the height* (§ 325 C–F), and in Ign. Eph. 9 we read, *to
the height* ... *love is the way that leadeth up.*] Allusions to
?1 Pet. iv. 8 and 1 Cor. xiii. follow. *In love were all the
elect of God made perfect* (also in 50, *they that were perfected
in love*). [We must compare 1 Jn. iv. 18, *he that feareth hath
not been made perfect in love.* ...] *For the love which He had
towards us* ... *our Lord* ... *hath given* ... *His flesh for our
flesh and His life for our lives.* [The only parallel with *hath
given His flesh* is in Jn. vi. 52. Jn. xv. 30. *greater love* ... *lay
down his life for his friends* is a closer parallel to the whole
sentence than Mk. x. 45, the only place where Christ is said
to have *given His life.*]

The following positions may be affirmed: (i) The contacts
of Clement with QPl and Ignatius are not likely to be
fortuitous. (ii) Doubtless there was a copy of 1 Clement
in Asia and Papias knew of its existence but the hypothesis
of its direct or indirect influence on both Leucius and
Ignatius may be safely dismissed. We may conclude that
our cumulative argument for the influence of S. John on
Leucius otherwise than through the canonical books is
strengthened. It is probable that Clement was influenced
by a lost letter of the apostle which contained some such
sentences as these: "This is the love of God that we keep
His commandments, and He that loveth Him is made
perfect in love. He laid down His life for us, and His love
leadeth us to the height (cf. Jn. xii. 32). Seeing then
that we are flesh and blood He gave His flesh and blood
for us (cf. Heb. ii. 14)." Leucius, knowing that *His love
leadeth to the height* was one of S. John's phrases and connected by him with the Passion, deliberately used it in
another context. I shall return to the subject of the lost
epistle.

CHAPTER XI

SOME GOSPEL PROBLEMS

I. THE FOURTH GOSPEL

§ 328. Our reconstructions of QPl have shewn that Leucius was an Asian and a contemporary of John of Ephesus and that he identified him with the son of Zebedee. On the other hand the Fourth Gospel cannot be the work of an apostle. From our standpoint these facts present no difficulty. The Gospel was the work of a blundering editor who used papers which preserved the oral teaching of S. John. The Gospel is what the external evidence suggests it was likely to have been. At the date of his return S. John was over ninety and presumably in broken health (§ 287). There were no spectacles in those days, and it is improbable that he could see to read, and not improbable that he was also very deaf. Nor is there any evidence that the editor did his work at Ephesus. We shall conclude that the bishop most responsible for its publication was Gaius of Pergamum. S. John's only part in the matter was to give his reluctant consent to the publication of his oral teaching the tradition of which survived from Papias in Heg *sub* HE, III. xxiv. 7 and AJ, 14.

As has been shewn, it was S. John's practice to comment on a lost Gospel (X) and many of his midrashim were preserved. There was, however, no system in the preservation either of the passages expounded or the expositions. Some of the papers contained much X and little midrash. In some the midrash followed the excerpts from X. In others fragments of it were interpolated into X. Others were merely midrashic expansions of Christ's sayings.

The papers were in great disorder. Neither the person who collected them in the hospice at Ephesus nor the editor had any clues as to their order, and the latter for the most part merely strung them together with connecting matter of his own with a view to producing a continuous and readable narrative somewhat resembling those of Mk and Lk. He probably omitted valuable fragments and sometimes he tampered with the narratives which he preserved. The X narratives of the Last Visit are scattered over chs. ii.–xii. The last discourses are almost entirely pre-Ascension midrashim: xvii. for instance is a sermon on X *sub* Lk. xxiv. 51, *he blessed them*. When the editor had completed his work a small bundle of papers came into his hands which contained two fishing narratives, one of which was a Resurrection Appearance and also a third paper which narrated a conversation which followed the Last Supper. In spite of the fact that the story of the large catch preceded the X narrative of the call of S. Peter (*sub* Mk. i. 16 f., Lk. v. 1 f.), a fact which the editor probably knew, he combined the two fishing stories and made the conversation a sequel.

It would appear from these facts that there was more than one collection of papers available and that in vii-xxi no importance attaches to the order of Jn. The former inference is confirmed by the fact that Leucius was in possession of several papers and the latter by the disorder of Jn. xx. (§ 44) and by the fact that when the sheets of his MS. fell into disorder the editor was either unable or did not think it worth while to restore them to their original order. Matters were made worse by the editor's repetitions and introduction of connecting matter which was in some sense his own. His editorial methods demand a more thorough and detailed examination than I have been able to give them, but several points are clear. (i) He inserted allusions to visits to Jerusalem and enumerated the appearances after the Resurrection. (ii) He used his recollections of Mk. (iii) He amplified his matter by moving, sometimes with careless rapidity, sentences or small blocks of sentences from other contexts. (iv) He interpolated comment, *e.g.* at vi. 6 and 11*c*. He doubtless had immense respect for S. John and regarded the main credal facts as of supreme importance. But he had no adequate conception of the importance of truth in the writing of a Gospel. The Gospel is what it is in spite of the evangelist.

II. The Cup-bearer and the Stump-fingered Mark

This section introduces the subject of the destination of Mk, the discussion of which is continued in § 371.

§ 332. This volume comments on most of the matter in the first three Acts of Thomas and shews that LeuciusT used the excerpts of Heg as much as any other apocryphist. He was only exceptional in the elevation of his thought and the skill with which he used his borrowed matter.

In the KP Cæsarea narrative a sermon immediately followed or preceded the healing and the meal. In AT, 5 f. this meal became the banquet at the Encratite marriage of Theodore (Cornelius: § 226 BG). In § 294*b* the cup-bearer of AT was shewn to have been originally Mark. The apostle cursed him because he wrote the Gospel preferred by Cerinthus, and a black dog brought his hand because it had held his pen. This midrash underlies LLk, 155 where S. Luke's hand is cut off because he wrote his Gospel with it. This incident must have been suggested by something in Heg, and our interpretation of AT accounts for it. It is improbable, however, that the writer of LLk would have understood the excerpt if the point had not been made clearer in QPl than it is in AT. (ii) Hippolytus writes: *When Marcion or some one of his hounds barks against the Demiurge . . . we ought to reply that neither Paul the apostle nor the stump-fingered Mark announced such tenets* (Ref. vii. 30). Hippolytus seems to have borrowed the phrase *the stump-fingered Mark* from Marcion, who based it on the story of Leucius. "Marcion's hounds" was probably suggested by an allusion of Marcion to the dogs of QPl. For Mark's presence at Cæsarea see § 302 (*c*).

§ 333. Our passage derives its point from the fact that in KP Mark wrote his Gospel at Cæsarea. The evidence of the Cæsarea endings and of the Acts which derive from QP is very clear.

A. Many Cæsarea endings refer to a Gospel or a manual being left with the newly constituted church. The following refer to a Gospel: LT, 82; LThadd, 125; LMatt, 135; EPl, 563, 615, 682; DAdd, 34. In LJasZ, 34 Peter (Mark) interprets James (Peter).

B. We have already used an Armenian tradition which was based on Hippolytus and which dates Mk in the eighth year. Hippolytus has been shewn to have used Heg who, we concluded, based his chronology on the QP narrative of S. Peter's visit to Cæsarea (§§ 196 f.).

C. According to R. iii. 74, where we have found R follows QP closely, Clement wrote at Cæsarea the first volume of the apostle's preaching. Further, we concluded that psClement described Clement's capacity for this task in terms of Papias's tradition of the writing of Mk.

D. That LeuciusJ in some sections of his narrative used QP was shewn in § 122 f. That he used the QP tradition of the writing of Mk *sub* Proch, 149 f. is shewn by the parallels given below. As in QP the incident of the writing of the Gospel (Jn) immediately precedes the departure of the apostle (for his circuit through the seven cities). I shall argue that the narrative is influenced also by Papias, but this matter does not concern us here. The reader will notice the important parallels with Clement.

149, 8. John teaches from the scriptures.	Clem. Hytyp. (Lat). *Adducing publicly many testimonies to Christ in the presence of imperial knights.*
151, 11 f. John decides to depart.	So Peter in R. iii. 69.
We implore and beseech thee, Hand down in writing. . . .	Clem. Hytyp. ap. HE, II. xv. *With all kinds of entreaties they besought him to leave them in writing . . . the teaching.*
Many tears.	R. iii. 70. The tears of the people.
154. Prochorus writes.	R. iii. 74. Clement writes.
He bids them bring pen and ink.	EPl, 621. Philip (Thomas) bids them bring pen and ink.
157, 8. An ordination.	R. iii. 68. An ordination.

158. John bids the brethren publish his Gospel for the churches.	HE, ii. xv. Peter authorised the work for the use of the churches.
151, 14. Influence of Acts xxi. 13.	R. iv. 1. Influence of Acts xxi. 5.

Clement is parallel with the apocryphal evidence at two other points. (i) His imperial knights were Marcellus and the other magistrates stationed at Cæsarea (LJasZ, 33; EPl, 620 (*seven nobles*); EP, 7). Origen says that Mk was read in the assembly of princes (Hist. Patr. i. 172). In EPl, 620 we note the parallelism of *his friends and acquaintance* with Ac. x. 24. (ii) With Clement's statement that the apostle adduced many texts we may compare EPl, 618 where Paul (John) teaches and Philip (Judas Matthias) writes texts (testimonies) for the hearers, LJasZ, 34 (a Cæsarea ending) where James reads the prophets and Ac. x. 43.

§ 334. The following evidence shews that Leucius was acquainted with the traditions which Papias cited and which stated that S. Mark interpreted the Hebrew of Peter and that Matthew wrote in Hebrew and others translated. (i) In EPl, 621 the apostles bless Theodore in Hebrew, but he knew not what they were saying. In our context Thomas sings his psalm (the sermon) in Hebrew and only the flute-girl understands it. (ii) (*a*) In a context which is likely to derive from Heg and after an allusion to the writings of Leucius the preface of EvM claims that the Gospel is translated from the Hebrew. EvN is based on QPl and is translated by Ananias. (*b*) LeuciusP said that EvXII was translated (HEux 11 25, STrans. 62). It would appear then that Leucius was acquainted with the tradition which was later used by Papias that Matthew wrote in Hebrew and that others translated what he wrote and that he supposed that the tradition referred to a Gospel. Our reconstruction tallies with the conclusion at which we are about to arrive that Leucius was acquainted with oral traditions of the sayings and teaching of S. John and was a source of Papias.

III. THE FLUTE-GIRL, THE ANOINTERS AND THE ADULTERESS

§ 335. If Matthias Thomas and John used at Cæsarea a language which Leucius Cornelius Theodore did not understand, who translated their preaching? The only answer which the Acta give is that suggested by the statement of AT that the flute-girl alone understood the Hebrew of Thomas. Who then was she?

The clue to our problem is to be found in two unmotived splinters of QPl which survive in AT, 16. We here learn that the flute-girl, like Peter and his companions in KP, was at the hospice [1] and that she was grieving that the apostle had not taken her with him to India. It would appear then that in QPl she accompanied John to Cæsarea. Now it is surprising that these statements should have been made of a flute-girl whose conversion had not been recorded. The significance of the word is sufficiently illustrated by OxPap (J, 29), *flute-girls and harlots*, a phrase which passed from QPl into EvH, 11. In view then of the great influence of QPl on AJ we must identify the flute-girl who was a companion of John at Cæsarea with *the chaste harlot* who accompanies him in AJ, 59. The flute-girl was an important woman companion.

§ 336. The Acta only mention one QPl woman companion, Mariamne, whom we find accompanying the apostles in APh, 94 f., a QPl context. She is there identified with Mary the sister of Martha, who is said to have been called by Christ *chosen among women* and to have been present at the sepulchre (CBRB, 187). The following facts suggest her identification with the flute-girl.

(i) As has just been said she was, so far as we know, the only woman companion in QPl.

(ii) James gave her the books of his preaching (Hipp. Ref. v. 7). This was presumably with the intention that she should take them with her on a missionary journey, and

[1] AT, 4, EPl 619, § 220 A.

the only journey which he can have had in view was that to Cæsarea. The second journey of QPl followed his unexpected murder.

(iii) In KP Peter was accompanied by his wife and other women and also by John Mark. Now we shall find evidence that Mary the mother of Mark was related to the apostle's wife. Mary therefore is likely to have accompanied her son. Moreover, the companions were like John Mark doubly named, and Maria Mariamne (Miriam) would be precisely parallel with Antonius Ananias (Hananiah). Just as Leucius converted the John who went to Cæsarea and Cyprus into the apostle so, if he wished to make Mary his heroine and the interpreter of the apostle, he would be likely to make her supplant Mark and his mother and to call her Mary Mariamne. It may be added that our hypothesis tallies with the evidence which will suggest that the Drusiana who accompanies John in AJ, 59 was also suggested by Mary the mother of Mark. Our solution of the problem of the flute-girl solves also the problem of Mary Mariamne.

§ 337. We have already concluded that Heg's excerpts from QPl exercised much influence on later writers. We must connect then with the journey of John and Mariamne to Ephesus *sub* APh, 94 f. some notices which I owe to Mayor (Hastings' Bib. Dict. 284 f.).

A. Evidence which begins with Epiph. *Haer*. lxxviii. 30 (Zahn Ac. Joh. xxx., clix.) brings the Virgin Mary to Ephesus. We account for this blunder if in an early and influential document another Mary went there. Jn. xix. 27 is not by itself sufficient.

B. According to late western traditions Lazarus with his sisters and Maximin a member of the Seventy fled from the persecution which followed the death of Stephen. Mary, who is confused with Mary Magdalene and is said to have been a wealthy and wicked woman, died at Arles. James (J, 217) identifies Maximin with the Maximianus of Jos Trans, where his name occurs in a list influenced by QPl (§ 210).

C. According to the Greek tradition and Gregory of

Tours, who was at any rate in one place influenced by Heg,[1] Mary Magdalene died at Ephesus.

This evidence is decisive. (*a*) The journeyings which ended at Cæsarea followed the death of Stephen and were connected with it (§ 181). (*b*) The sister of Lazarus went to Ephesus and was confused with other Maries. (*c*) Like the flute-player companion of the apostles she had led an evil life. (*d*) The statement that she was rich is in the manner of Leucius.

D. The fact that Leucius attributed an evil past to Mary can only be explained by the hypothesis that he identified Mary the sister of Lazarus who was the anointer in Jn. xii. with the anointer of Lk. vii. Now we find this identification in three writers who have been or will be shewn to have been influenced by Heg, Victor of Capua, Tert. Pudic. 11, Clem. Paed. ii. 61.

We conclude that Leucius following Jn identified the anointer with Mary of Bethany and that he also identified her with the sinner of Lk. vii. and that he made her accompany John and Thomas to Cæsarea.

§ 338. There is no need for me to repeat the arguments which convince Bernard and Streeter that the two Anointers are identified in Jn. Our task is to account for the identification and also for the fact that Leucius identified them.

No one who has studied Leucius and his methods will be ready to suppose that his careful reading of Lk and Jn enabled him to anticipate the conclusions of the modern critics just cited. The facts suggest that he was influenced by one of the papers which contained S. John's midrashim and we shall find that positive evidence supports this view.

The position is similar with respect to the evidence of Jn. Almost all the data which all but convince Streeter that the editor used Lk are evidence for the influence of X, and even if we assume the influence of Lk it is improbable that the editor would have identified the disciple who sat at Christ's feet with the sinner of Lk. vii. The facts suggest that he knew no more about the Anointer than he records

[1] In H. Franc. i. 21. See E. B. Nicholson on EvH (p. 61).

and that the identification with Mary is due either to the fact that he remembered that she lived at Bethany or that the paper contained an allusion to her which he misunderstood. This latter hypothesis is very possible, for it was in the direct line of S. John's thought to observe that when Mary sat at Christ's feet the unction flowed from the Head to one of His members. If the editor used papers at all the case is strong that it was not he himself but one of his papers that was responsible for the identification of the two Anointers.

§ 339. That the parallels of Jn. xii. with Lk. vii. are not editorial but derive from a paper is shewn by the fact that his midrash turned on the word *feet*, which is emphasised by repetition, a fact noticed by the editor (xi. 2), and reminds the reader that S. Mark wrote *head*. What then was the mystical teaching which S. John illustrated from these facts?

If the apostle expounded the Anointing he can only have dealt with one topic. He is the only writer of the N.T. who uses the symbolism of unction. In 1 Jn. ii. 20 he writes, *ye have received an anointing from the Holy One*, and this passage like others in his epistles and our context of Jn presupposes oral teaching. S. John then must have compared Mk with X and said that both Gospels were right and that the connecting link was Ps. cxxxiii. 2, the unction had flowed from Aaron's head to the skirts of his clothing and even to his feet. It is possible that it was in this connection that S. John said that Mark made no mistake.

That we have rightly interpreted the emphasis on *feet* is shewn by a midrashic phrase which survives in Jn, *the whole house was filled with the odour of the ointment*. This sentence obviously allegorises the fact that in the words of Acts ii. (S. John doubtless used the source) *the gift* which the *Anointed poured forth* (33) *filled all the house where they were sitting*. The interpretation of *feet* is suggested by Joel and Eph. iv. 4–13, a passage which was known to S. John's hearers and influenced S. John *sub* Jn. xvii. 11. The unction passed from the Head to His members.

§ 340. We will now collect some patristic comments.

A. Ign. Eph. 17. *The Lord received the ointment in order that He might breathe incorruption.*

B. H. xiii. 5, 6. A chaste woman is said to *myrrhise* the church and to be desired by *the great King*, a title which Leucius borrowed from J.

C. In Iren. III. xi. 8, a context which is influenced by Papias, the Gospels are said to *breathe incorruptibility*.

D. In Clem. Paed. ii. 8 the Anointing teaches not only the passion but also the teaching of Christ.

E. Orig. in Cant. i. 12. *The fragrance of the Spirit fills the house of the church and of the world.*

F. Orig. in Cels. vi. 79. Celsus has objected that Christ ought to have breathed His Spirit into many bodies. Origen replies that the ointment descended from the Head to the church.

The question is whether this matter derives from S. John's midrash and, if so, whether it is independent of Jn.

A refers to our incident and interprets it on our lines; but two facts suggest independence of Jn. (*a*) The mystical meaning of Jn. xii. 1 f. would not be obvious to anyone who was not acquainted with the apostle's oral teaching, and it must be remembered that Ignatius wrote rapidly. (*b*) A introduces the Inflation, an incident which was only in the background of S. John's thought and not in his thought at all unless the Pentecostal "filling of the house" was as it is in the uncanonical tradition very closely connected with it.

B confirms our view of S. John's midrash and suggests that it occurred in QPl, a work which Ignatius used.

C like A alludes to the Inflation and connects it with the gift of incorruption. If Papias was independent of QPl our main argument would be strengthened.

D confirms our exegesis.

E suggests that Origen interpreted the allusion to Christ's feet as referring to His members and this position very clearly underlies F.

§ 341. We now turn to the evidence of the extant apocrypha which we anticipated in B.

G. The following passage suggests that Leucius in EvT telescoped the two suppers of the Last Visit: *If at any time He was bidden by some one of the Pharisees* (Lk. vii.) *and went, and there was set before each one of us a loaf . . . His own would He bless and part among us: and of that little everyone was filled* (AJ, 93). Leucius is probably using a tradition that the disciples went with Christ to the Anointing. If so, *one of the Pharisees* is a link between Lk. vii. and the Last Visit.

H. Our conjecture is confirmed by a passage in which the QPl supper is better preserved. In EvvC, 8 Jesus and the apostles are at table. He and they partake. A burlesque follows. Matthias told Him that the Jews said that the blood of his Master would be shed like the cock's. (Not Jesus but the unbelievers foretold His death.) Jesus smiled (His docetic smile) and bade the cock come to life again and announce the day on which He would be delivered up. So far we only have a travesty of the Last Supper; but in the Book of the Cock which is read in the church of Abyssinia on Maundy Thursday, Akrosina the wife of Simon the Pharisee buys the cock. Jesus blesses the bread and gives it to Judas into whom Satan enters (Jn. xiii. 25 f.). Simon is clearly the Pharisee mentioned in AJ and Lk. vii. Leucius identified the two Anointings and the two Suppers.

J. The anointing itself Leucius moved to Cæsarea where it was introduced into the story of the Encratite marriage of Leucius Cornelius.

In LT, 90, a context which undoubtedly derives from QPl, Christ appears to the son of the old man (Theophilus) just before the wedding (§ 332): *a sweet scent issued from His mouth and filled the whole house with the odour* (Jn) *of its fragrance. . . . And He said, . . . Keep thy body pure. . . .* Every word of this passage is Leucian. Now it is parallel both with the patristic evidence (see especially E) and with Jn. It cannot however be supposed that Leucius detected the doctrine underlying Jn and gave fresh expression to it on his own lines. This would have been entirely alien from his methods, and if he had attempted the task, he would have bungled and exhibited one or another of his many eccentricities. Moreover for him the Spirit of God was no more than a female angel.

K. LT is parallel with AT, 4, 5, 11 and the two contexts must be read together. AT perverts QPl, but much of the latter Acts survives. We read that when they had dined *every man took the unguent, and one anointed his face and another his beard* (Ps. cxxxiii. 2) *and another other parts of his body; but the apostle anointed the top of his head ... his nostrils, ears, teeth and the parts about the heart.* The flute-girl (*i.e.* the Anointer) played at the apostle's head, and in his song he says that the chamber of the daughter of light *giveth out a sweet smell of myrrh* (cf. B). This passage is the depravation of a depravation, but it is clearly midrash, and it is difficult to imagine any teaching which it can convey other than that which is suggested by the emphasis or " feet " in Jn. The chrism passed from the Head to the whole body. As in AT, 11 Thomas was Christ's counterpart.

The related passages J and K derive from the midrash which underlies Jn. xii., but the fact that Jn does not preserve any teaching about the unction of the Spirit and other indications shew that the report of S. John's teaching used by Leucius was fuller than that used by the editor of Jn.

§ 342. Our discussion has led us to the conclusion that S. John commented on a narrative which placed the Anointing of Lk. vii. in the Last Visit, and the hypothesis of a lost source is confirmed by the fact that Jn dates the Anointing six days before the passover. We now turn to the synoptic evidence.

(i) It is difficult to believe that Lk. vii. 36–47 has been edited; at any rate the influence of Mk is highly improbable. Yet the contacts are striking. (*a*) In each case a woman enters a room where Christ is at meat and anoints Him (*b*) using an *alabastron* of myrrh. (*c*) In each case the host is named, and in no other passage in the Gospels is a host named *qua* host, and in each case the name is Simon.

Moreover, it is strange that in Mk where nothing is said about him he should be named and distinguished from other Simons as *the Leper* and that in Lk where he plays an important part he is not introduced to the reader, and we only learn his name when Christ rebukes him. Lk explains the introduction of Simon to the reader of Mk, and Mk shews that, as we should expect, Simon had been introduced before Christ called him by his name. (*d*) The phrase *a woman in the city* suggests that the scene was Jerusalem. In MLk. viii. 27, 34, 39 *the city* is due to Mk. v. 14, 20. In LLk. xix. 41, xxiii. 17, xxiv. 49 the allusion is to Jerusalem, and in xxiii. there is no guidance from the context. Taylor (*Formation of the Gospel Tradition*, 154 f.) rejects the hypothesis of the influence of Mk and suggests a transference of details in the course of oral tradition.

The narrative of Lk must be a torso. Christ's parable shews that the woman had been already forgiven in a section of the story which has been omitted and which, if it survived might throw light on Simon's strange discourtesy. At the close where on our hypothesis the disciples complained of the waste, S. Luke inserts an editorial and misplaced narrative of the forgiveness. Our view that Lk transfers the incident from the Last Visit is confirmed by the fact that the Gospel has no parallel with Mk. xiv. 1 f. This omission is not explained by the consideration that he might refrain from narrating a similar incident in order to economise space. Only one of S. Mark's seven verses is in any way parallel with Lk. vii.

(ii) Matt attributes to the disciples the censure of the woman (Mk *certain*). This is so entirely contrary to his very marked tendency to "spare" the disciples that we may be sure that he is influenced by M. "Disciples" is a contact with "Judas" (Jn. xii. 4).

(iii) S. Mark's editorial encomium of the Anointer requires explanation. It distracts attention from the Central Figure, and shews that the evangelist was for some reason very interested in her. We may suspect that the encomium is due to the same cause as his omission of the part of the narrative which revealed the fact that she had been a conspicuous sinner and S. Luke's transposition and abbreviation of the incident.

Our discussion has shewn (*a*) that the editor of Jn used a paper which contained some matter from the X Anointing and S. John's midrash on it, that Leucius used a longer and fuller paper, and that Mk, LLk, Jn and M are likely to have derived from a common source.

§ 343. We can bring our hypothesis to two other tests. (i) Our view that the Markan apocalypse is an interpolation (§ 79) may carry with it the position that the chronology of Mk was tampered with and that it had contacts with that of Jn. (ii) Inasmuch as Lk presupposes a narrative of the Anointer's forgiveness and the Pericope Adulteræ must be placed early in the Last Visit we must also enquire whether the Anointer was not the Adulteress. The two problems are connected by an argument which will shew that the two incidents occurred on the same day. Our task therefore involves a very thorough discussion of the narratives of the first two days of the Last Visit.

We will now trace the activities of the interpolator of Mk.

(1) After the apocalypse the narrative of Mk is resumed with the statement that the Anointing was two days before the passover, and the teaching narrated earlier is confined to a single day. Now this chronology is inconsistent both with the statement of Jn that the Anointing was six days before the passover and with Mk. xiv. 49, *I was daily with you in the temple teaching.* Moreover, xiv. 1*b*–2 seem to describe a period of fruitless plotting which followed the teaching. Lastly, we shall conclude that Mk dated the Anointing on the evening which followed xiii. 2 and that the interpolator moved the crucial sentence. He inserted his date in compensation and because he had interrupted the narrative of his MS. with a very long insertion.

(2) In 12 we find a chronological note which blunders badly: *on the first day of the week when they sacrificed the passover.* Josephus shews that the whole period covered by

the two feasts might be designated by the name of either, but it is improbable that S. Mark would have written 12 in any context and impossible that he should have written that verse when aiming at precision (xiv. 1) and dating a series of events within the whole period. The passage is strong evidence for the activity of a gentile reviser (GMark).

§ 343a. We must now enquire whether the interpolator has interfered with the matter which precedes the apocalypse.

No commentator has made sense of the narrative of the fig-tree. It is not simply an acted parable, for Christ is said to have been hungry, nor can the writer have supposed that Christ meant to eat the green knops of the fig-tree, for in this case he would not have misled the reader by writing *he found nothing but leaves, for the time of figs was not yet.* Moreover, the practice of eating knops is authoritatively denied. All these difficulties are solved if we suppose that the writer misunderstood a parable which stated that the lord (of a vineyard) found a fig-tree with nothing but leaves, spoke words of warning and on returning condemned it (cf. Lk. xiii. 6 f.). The motivisation of the incident is in agreement with the hostility to the hierarchy which was a marked feature of M. For the conversion of a saying into a miracle we may compare a miracle which is peculiar to Matthew and likely to derive from M, the Stater in the fish's mouth (xvii. 24). The influence of M on Mk. xi. 23–25 has been shewn in § 91, *c.* 5.

Our hypothesis may be confirmed. (i) Inasmuch as Christ's return to Jerusalem was on the same Jewish day as the departure S. Mark would not have written in xi. 12 *on the morrow* but as he does in 20 *in the morning.* Like the date in xiv. 12 the phrase is the blunder of a gentile. (ii) *No man eat* (14) is the only optative in our Mk. (iii) It is virtually impossible that S. Mark could have written *your Father which is in heaven* (25). The other instances of Father in Mk are *in the glory of the Father* (viii. 36), *Abba Father* (xiv. 36). We may contrast Matt and Lk.

	Matt	Lk
Your or *thy Father* . .	16	4
My Father . . .	16	2
Father in heaven or *heavenly*	18	1
The Father . . .	4	4
In vocative . . .	11	3

(iv) The following glosses cannot like Mk have been written for readers who lived in Palestine: (*a*) *For the time of figs was not yet* (13) must have been written for readers who did not live in Palestine or Syria. We must also assign to him three similar notes which occur later. (*b*) *Two mites which make a farthing* (xii. 42) is presumably meant for Roman readers and is omitted in Lk. xxi. 2. (*c*) There is no parallel context in Lk with Mk. xv. 16, *the court which is the prætorium*. (*d*) Lk omits Mk. xv. 42, *the Preparation, that is, the day before the sabbath.*

§ 344. We will now endeavour to reconstruct the original Mk at one or two other points and to determine its relations.

A. xi. 11*a*. *He entered into Jerusalem into the temple and looked round.*

B. 11*b*. *At eventide he went out to Bethany with the twelve.*

C. 12 f. *On the morrow* the cursing of the fig-tree.

D. 15 f. The Cleansing.

E. 19. *When it was evening he went forth from the city.*

F. 20. *In the morning they saw the fig-tree withered.*

G. 28. *By what authority doest thou these things?*

H. 29–xiii. 2. Continuous teaching in the temple.

J. xiv. 1*b*–2. (*They*) *were seeking how they might take him with subtilty and kill him.*

K. 3–9. *And while he was in Bethany. . . .*

L. 10. *And Judas went away unto the chief priests.*

(1) That there has been disarrangement is shewn by the fact that a night (E) has been placed between D and G. The priests must have acted very soon after the challenge of the Cleansing, and the phrase *these things* shews that they did not wait until the next day. Clearly the interpolator

has moved the departure in order to bring as close together as possible the two parts of the story of the fig-tree.

Matt. xx. 18 f. is nearer M, Man is Mk. M gave the impression that the fig-tree was struck at once and stated that the disciples saw it withered when they returned on the morrow, *i.e.* that evening.

(2) The original position of the second departure (E) was probably after the parable of the Husbandmen,[1] which probably connects with the discussion as to Christ's authority (§ 350). On the other hand the questions which follow were probably asked on the day which followed the Cleansing. (*a*) They are parallel with the incident of the Adulteress which we shall assign to that day and which cannot have occurred on the previous day. (*b*) Owing to the immense impression which Christ had made by His courage and eloquence on the day of the Cleansing the high priests had been able to do nothing and during the night they thought out plans for trapping him and undermining His prestige.

(3) B also presents difficulties. (*a*) The evidence shews that the party of pilgrims who accompanied Christ bivouacked in Gethsemane (LLk. xxi. 37, xxii. 39: § 362) and the apostles according to the apocrypha returned there at Pentecost. They would probably go there on the evening of their arrival at Jerusalem. (*b*) According to the chronology which we shall adopt that evening was the beginning of the sabbath and Bethany was more than a sabbath day's journey from Jerusalem. Now the interpolator had no motive for inventing B. He probably replaced a simple statement that Jesus went out to Olivet with the more interesting splinter which he can only have taken from the Mk narrative of the third departure. Knowing that Bethany was on Olivet (xi. 1) he regarded the first verse of the apocalypse as an equivalent.

(4) Thus corrected the narrative suggests that the Anointing occurred about a week before the passover, and

---

[1] In the next volume I shall suggest that S. Mark edited the parable under the influence of S. Stephen as under the same influence he edits in XIV. 62 X *sub* LLK. xxii. 69.

that Mk is merely less exact than Jn. The narrative would run: A. *And as he left the temple one of his disciples....* B. *And he went forth to Bethany with the twelve.... C. And the chief priests were seeking.... D. And when he was in Bethany in the house of Simon ... and sitting at meat....* This reconstruction gives the impression of disarranging a source. We conjecture that S. Mark's motive was to use a narrative of the Anointing, which originally may have been longer, as an introduction to his narrative of the Passion and to make the love of the Anointer a foil to the treachery of Judas and that the original order was ABDC. Now our rearrangement gives us a scheme. The temple ministry closed with the Anointing and Christ's anticipation of failure and death. The priests continued to plot but without success. A third period, that of the Passion began when Judas left Jesus and "went away" to the priests. We may also conjecture that the source stated not only that the priests continued to plot as they did immediately after the Cleansing (protoMk *sub* Mk. xi. 18) but that He continued to teach and perhaps that the people continued to be astonished at His teaching (*ib*.).

§ 345. We will now compare Lk with the section of Mk which we have been examining. On our hypothesis the evangelist used the interpolated Mk and also derived from its ultimate source X. His agreements then with our reconstructions whether of pMk or of X will be evidence for our hypothesis.

1. At the point at which on our hypothesis the X Passion began we find in Lk the emphatic phrase, *And Satan entered into the heart of Judas*. This sentence is also shewn to derive from X by its parallelism with Jn. xiii. 27, where Satan enters into the heart of Judas on the occasion of his second visit to the priests.

2. The following table shews that L summarised the period which followed the last day of recorded teaching and the Anointing and that this summary is related to Mk.

2 D

LLk. xix. 47. *And he was teaching daily in the temple. . . . All the people*

Mk. xi. 19 (E). *When it was late he went forth from the city.*
20. *And in the morning*
19. *And all the multitude were astonished at his teaching.*
xiv. 1. *And the chief priests and scribes were seeking how they might take him by guile and kill him, for they said, not on the feast day, lest there be an uproar of the people.*

48. *All the people were hanging upon him listening.*

LLk. xxi. 37 f. *And during the days he was teaching in the temple.*
During the nights he bivouacked in the Mount of Olives.
And all the people came early in the temple to hear him.

And the chief priests and scribes were seeking

how they might destroy him,

for they feared the people.
And Satan entered into Judas.

In xix. S. Luke substitutes a fragment of the summary for the misplaced departure of Mk (see below). In xxi. he omits the statement of the summary that the people continued to be deeply impressed. The resemblance of the phrasing of the LLk summary to that of Mk. xi. 18 f. is due to the fact that X was stating that Christ, the people and the priests continued to act as they acted on the day of the Cleansing and the next day.

§ 346 (3) We will now collect S. Luke's omissions and substitutions.

(i) Lk omits the narrative of the fig-tree.

(ii) Lk omits the night spent at Bethany (§ 344 B).

(iii) For the misplaced departure (§ 344 E) Lk. xix. 47 f. substitutes a fragment of the summary which does not commit him to a decision.

(iv) In xx. 1 S. Luke corrects the misdating of *by what authority* (G) by writing on *one of the days when he was preaching*. Again he does not commit himself to the chronology of either of his sources.

(v) Lk omits the introduction to the apocalypse because

it was inconsistent with the statement of L that *he went out to Bethany with the twelve*.

(vi) The erroneous date in Mk. xiv. 1 becomes the statement that *the feast was drawing near*.

(vii) Lk omits the Anointing which in Mk is misplaced.

(viii) He omits the impossible date in Mk. xiv. 12.

(ix) The following omission of matter which occurs in our Mk and which is better placed in Lk. x. 25 provides a confirmation of our main position which is independent of our previous arguments from chronology and the evidence for interpolation.

Mk. xii. 18. *Then came the Sadducees. . . .*	Lk. xx. 27. *Then came Sadducees. . . .*
27. *Ye do greatly err.*	
34a. *Thou art not far from the kingdom of God.*	
34b. *No man durst after that ask him another question.*	40. *They durst not. . . .*

Clearly *durst not* followed not as in Mk the commendation of the scribe but the crushing refutation of the Sadducees. Our conclusion is confirmed by the fact that in Lk at its close Christ's answer is independent of Mk.

We have arrived at the startling result that in no fewer than nine places S. Luke, using a document which must have been largely parallel with Mk, corrects either Mk or our recension of Mk. Further Mk. xii. 28 f. adapts to its present position a narrative in which as in Lk. x. 25 f. the Scribe answered.

§ 347. We will now examine the evidence of Matt as to the two days of the Temple Ministry. We recall our conclusion that this Gospel shews a knowledge of M in the preceding narrative of the Children and in the subsequent narrative of the Anointing.

(i) In § 355 f. we shall conclude that the allusion of Matt to healings on the day of the Cleansing is supported by X matter in Jn.

(ii) The verse which immediately follows (xxi. 17) is parallel with Mk. xi. 11 and 19 and runs: A. *he left them*,

B. *and went forth of the city* (C) *to Bethany,* D. *and lodged there.* E. *Early* (Πρωΐ), F. *returning to the city.* .... C derives from Mk. xi. 11 and BF may derive from 19 and 27. ADE are probably from M. A does not adhere at all well to the previous narrative of the children of Jerusalem and is explained by a passage which occurred in this point in X *sub* Jn (§ 357 D). The parallel "lodged" in S. Luke's summary is not likely to be a fortuitous coincidence. E varies from the interpolator's inaccurate "morrow" and like D is parallel with the LLk summary where, however, S. Luke substitutes ὄρθρου, a Lukanism. Assuming our later results we may reconstruct the X narrative of the departure thus: *And they took up stones to cast at him* (Jn. § 357), *and Jesus left them* (Matt) *and went forth from the temple* (Jn). *And they departed each to his own house* (Peric. Adulteræ), *and Jesus went out* (Mk, Peric) *to the Mount of Olives* (Peric). *And early returned* (Matt, Peric) *to the temple* (Peric).

§ 348. The relation of the uninterpolated Mk to X at the close of our section may be stated as follows: Mk. The Tribute money . . . the Widow's mite. . . . *And, as he went forth, one of his disciples.* . . . Mk. xi. 11. *And, it being now eventide, he went out unto Bethany with the twelve* Mk. xiv. 3. *to the house of Simon the leper.* LLk. vii. 37 f. *who had desired him to eat with him.* . . . When therefore the woman which had committed adultery knew, she came from *the city* and *brought an alabaster cruse . . . loveth little.* Matt. xxvi. 8, Jn. xii. 4. But *Judas* Mk. xiv. 4 f. *had indignation.* . . . Jn. xii. 1. *Now it was the sixth day before the passover.* LLk. xxi. 37 f. *And he was daily teaching.* . . . Mk. xiv. 1 f. *And the chief priests were seeking . . . saying, Not during the feast.* . . . LLk. xxii. 3. *And Satan entered into Judas.* . . . LLk Mk. xiv. 10. *and he departed unto the chief priests.* . . .

§ 349. S. Mark preserved hardly any X narrative of the first two days of the Last Visit; Matt adds very little and

S. Luke contented himself with correcting Mk and adding the summary. Much X narrative, however, survives in Jn scattered over chs. ii.–xii. in the greatest possible disorder.

It has escaped attention that the narrative of the Cleansing in Mk. xi. 15 f. abbreviates and at two points depraves that preserved in Jn. ii. 13 f. The two narratives may be compared as follows:

Jn.   *And he found   in   the temple   them that sold* ..
Mk. A. *And he entered into the temple C. them that sold and*

.. .. .. *oxen and sheep   and doves and the changers of*
them that bought .. .. *doves* .. ..

money[1]   *sitting.   And he made a scourge of cords   and*
.. F.   *the seats of* .. .. B. *and*

.. .. *cast all out, both the sheep and the oxen, and he poured out*
began to cast .. *out* .. ..

.. *the changers' money   and overthrew their tables,   and to*
E. *of the moneychangers* D. *and overthrew the   tables* G. *and* ..

them that sold doves he said.   Make not. . . .
them that sold doves .. ..

Christ only rebuked the sellers of doves and bade them leave the temple. The overturning of their seats in Mk is due to abbreviation. S. Mark's statement that Jesus cast out the buyers is an overstatement: they were the victims of the system against which Jesus protested. It is probably an echo of *cast them all out* (Jn).

(2) In Jn Christ attacks the use of the temple for the purpose of buying and selling the animals required for the sacrifices: *make not my Father's house an house of merchandise.* With this agrees: Mk. *my house shall be called an house of prayer for all nations*, an allusion to the fact that it was the Court of the Gentiles in which, owing to the existing system, prayer was difficult. But in Mk the emphasis falls on the phrase *but ye have made it a den of thieves*, with the result that Christ attacks not the system but its abuse. Mk, however, supports Jn by stating Christ's enforcement of the rule against making the Court of the Gentiles a short

---

[1] Κολλυβιστῶν may be due to the influence of Mk.

cut (xi. 16). In other words Mk itself shews that, even if the words *ye have made it a den of thieves* are authentic, Christ must have made His purpose clear in words similar to those which are attributed to Him in Jn.

Our conclusion that Mk and Jn preserve the same narrative of the Cleansing involves the position that no importance can be attached to the order of the matter in Jn. iii.–xii.; and, inasmuch as it is impossible either to base on these chapters a coherent history of the ministry or to harmonise them with the synoptists, we will regard the series of allusions to feasts as merely editorial and treat the Jerusalem matter in this section as parallel with Mk. xi.–xiv. 9.

§ 350. We will now endeavour to reconstruct the narrative of the events which followed the Cleansing.

We compare:

A. Jn. x. 23. *And Jesus was walking in the temple. The Jews therefore came round him.*

B. ii. 18. *What sign showest thou unto us seeing that thou*

doest these things.

D. Mk. x. 27. *And as he was walking in the temple there came to him the chief priests.*

E. 28. *By what authority doest thou these things?*

F. xii. 1. *He began to speak to them in Parables.*

G. The Husbandmen.

C. x. 24. *How long dost thou hold us in suspense? If thou art the Christ, tell us plainly.*

X. viii. 20. *in the treasury.*

Z. xii. 41. *over against the treasury.*

(i) C refers to the method which Christ is said to have adopted in F and G.

(ii) In view of the paucity of S. Mark's narrative the fact that Jn has contacts with it (A–D, X–Z) is noteworthy.

(iii) In each Gospel the priests ask Christ on what he grounded his right to *do these things* (BE). For the connection of " authority " (E) with " signs " (B) we may compare Mk. ii. 10. Christ claimed authority in parables

(G) and worked signs (Matt, Jn, § 355), asserting that they were God's witness in His behalf. But the priests complained that His words were not explicit (C) and that the healings were infringements of the law of the sabbath (§ 335 A). A few weeks later S. Peter preaching to the same crowds reasserted Christ's claim: *Jesus of Nazareth, a man approved of God unto you by the mighty works and wonders and signs, which God did by him in the midst of you* (Ac. ii. 22). A doctrine which determined the scheme of Mk and I Ac. Mc. (§ 29) was derived by the apostle from Christ Himself.

§ 351. Some facts may now be noted which illustrate the relation of Jn to the underlying papers.

The confusion of the Jerusalem matter in our section may be illustrated as follows. Two consecutive sentences of X underlie the following passages. A. Jn. vii. 30, B. 31, C. 34, D. 44; U. Jn. viii. 20, V–Y, 21–29, Z. 30: AD. *They sought to take him*, ADU. *but no man laid hold of him*, AU. *for his hour was not yet come.* BZ. *But many believed on him.* This incident is parallel with Mk. xi. 18. The special sense of " hour " occurred in X *sub* Mk. xiv. 35, 41. About the time that the attempted arrest failed Christ uttered the *double entendre*, C. *Ye shall seek me and shall not find me.* S. John used this saying twice, (i) in the midrash V–Y, (ii) in his own *double entendre, he was hidden* (§ 357). The reconstruction which follows may perhaps be placed a little earlier in X.

§ 352. X may be reconstructed thus. When Christ had spoken the parable of the Husbandmen His opponents, who perceived that it was directed *against themselves, left Him* (Mk. xii. 12) and Jn. xi. 47 *gathered a council, and said, What do we? for this man doeth many signs. If we let him alone the Romans will come and take our place and nation.* vii. 50. *Nicodemus saith, Doth our law judge a man, except it first hear from a man and knoweth what he doeth? They answered and said unto him, Art thou (also) of Galilee? Search and see that out of Galilee ariseth no prophet....but* some said, He hath done nothing worthy of death. xi. 49. *The high priest ... Caiaphas, saith, Ye know nothing*

*at all, it is expedient for you that one man should die ...
and that the whole nation perish not.* vii. 32, also 30 and 44.
*They sent therefore officers to take him. And some of them would
have taken him, but no man laid hands on him.* 45. *The officers
therefore came to them; and they said unto them, Why did
ye not bring him? The officers answered, Never man so spake.
They said therefore, Are ye also led astray? Hath any of
the rulers believed on him, or of the Pharisees? But this
multitude which knoweth not the law is accursed.* ... xi. 53.
So from that day they took counsel to put him to death.

The following points may be noted. (i) According to
our scheme iii. 1 must be dated during the night which
followed the Cleansing. (ii) Our reconstruction coheres
with the fact that in KP the daughter of Nicodemus became
a disciple. She was presumably the oral source of X.
(iii) His introduction of his question is closely parallel with
Mk. xii. 14. (iv) The allusions to signs in iii. 2 and xi. 47
confirm our view that Christ healed on the day of the
Cleansing.

§ 353. The incident of the prophecy of Caiaphas (Jn.
xi. 47–52) is a paper which is almost in its original form.
But it is abbreviated and incoherent in 47–48. The discourse in 47*b*–48 was probably spoken by Caiaphas or
Annas. The words of an objector have dropped out before
49. The bracketed phrase in *it is expedient for you that one
man should die (for the people) and that the whole nation
perish not* has been moved into X from S. John's midrash
where it is found in 51.

§§ 354–5. The healings in v. and ix. are connected with
each other and with the Last Visit (*a*) by the length
at which they are narrated, (*b*) the fact that Christ met
both the healed later in the day (v. 14, ix. 35), (*c*) that in
each case that day was the sabbath and (*d*) that the midrashic expansion v. 30–47 is similar to ix. 39–41, the allusion
to judgment in 39 being expanded in v. 22–30. Our
reconstruction of X is supported by two other documents.
(i) According to the M context in Matt *the lame and the
blind came unto him and he healed them* immediately after the
Cleansing (xxi. 4). The diseases correspond with those in

Jn. (ii) The gloss interpolated at v. 4 *the angel of the Lord went down at certain seasons into the pool* . . . is likely to be primitive and like the *pericope adulteræ* from X. If this is the case the healing occurred at the Last Visit, for X narrated no other ministry in Jerusalem.

§ 356. The close of the Day of the Cleansing was occupied with a controversy between Christ and His opponents which was concerned with the healings and the claim implicit in the parable of the Husbandmen. Christ spoke of His works and their witness which was His Father's. S. John taught that His words implied a unique relation to God.

A. v. 17 f. *My Father worketh hitherto and I work.* (S. John's midrash). . . . *They sought the more to kill him, because he not only brake the sabbath, but also called God his own Father making himself equal with God.* For matter as to His works add 31–32, 36–37. In 45 f. Moses is said to accuse the Jews. The explanation is found in vii. 22. For *Moses* compare Mk. xii. 19.

B. viii. 20. *In the treasury* (cf. Mk. xii. 41). *No man took him* (cf. § 351 ADU). 13. *Thou bearest witness of thyself.* . . . 58. (a midrash) *Before Abraham was I am.*

C. x. 23. *Walking in the temple* . . . *in suspense.* See § 350 AE. 36. Christ had been accused of the blasphemous claim to be the Son of God (*i.e.* in the parable). 39. *They sought again* (as they did when they sent the officers) *to take him.* 32, 37–38: Works and their witness. In 30 there is the midrash, *I and the Father are one.*

D. xii. 37. *Though he had done so many signs before them.* . . . 42. *Nevertheless even of the rulers many believed on him but because of* * (Jn *the Pharisees*) *they did not confess it.* Midrash. *For they loved the glory of men more than the glory of God.*

§ 357. The above passages are connected with each other and with the first day by depravations of the same narrative of a departure from the temple which cannot be that narrated in Mk. xiii. 1 f. They shew that the matter which precedes them refers to events which followed the Cleansing :

viii. 59. *They took up stones to cast at him, but Jesus was hidden from them (i.e. by God). And went out of the temple.*

x. 31. *The Jews took up stones to stone him.*

19. *He went forth out of their hand.*

xii. 36. *and was hidden from them.*

He departed

Was hidden is S. John's midrash on the fact that Christ escaped from His enemies. There is a *double entendre* : He escaped because He was the Son of God and His hour was not yet come. In another sense He was hidden from them because they did not recognise Him. The X narrative is reconstructed in § 347. The statement that the hour had not come (viii. 20) is a link in our reconstruction, for it occurs in vii. 30. The word was used by Christ in the X Gethsemane narrative (Mk. xiv. 41).

§ 358. When on the following morning Christ announced his intention to return to the temple the disciples tried to dissuade Him, saying that on the previous evening His enemies had tried to stone Him. The editor inserted the protest in the Raising of Lazarus and, inasmuch as he had just before made Jesus journey beyond the Jordan, altered "yesterday" into "recently." X can be reconstructed with some security and in part the midrash on the passage. Our matter probably derives from more than one paper.

(i) X ran: A. xi. 8. *Yesterday the Jews were seeking to stone thee.* 9. *Jesus answered, Are there not twelve hours in the day?* B. ix. 4. *I must work the works of him that sent me. The night cometh when no man can work.* B is inserted in the Healing of the blind man.

(ii) The midrash ran somewhat as follows: viii. 12, ix. 5. *When I am in the world I am the light of the world.* viii. 12. *He that followeth me shall not walk in darkness, but shall have the light of life.* xi. 9b. *If a man walk in the day* (an allusion to the twelve hours of 9a) *he seeth the light of the world. But if a man walk in the night, he stumbleth because the light is not in him.* viii. 12. *He that followeth me shall not walk in darkness but shall have the light of life.* In another paper

John commented on Christ's saying, "Are there not twelve hours?" and on similar lines: xii. 35 f. *Yet a little while is the light among you. Walk while ye have the light, that darkness overtake you not* (an allusion to "the night cometh"): *and he that walketh in darkness knoweth not whither he goeth. While ye have the light, believe on the light, that ye may become sons of light.*

Another discourse or another section of our discourse connected the ideas of light and judgment (iii. 19 f., xii. 46).

The return to the temple is also found in vii. 14: *in the midst of the feast Jesus went up to the temple and taught.* Only two days of the teaching in the temple were recorded, and our passage must refer to the second. It paraphrases X *sub* Peric. Adult.: *and early in the morning he came up into the temple . . . and taught.*

§ 359. Jn preserves some comments made by the pilgrims during their journey and the two days. In the papers used in vii. 1–13, xi. 54 f. Christ went to Jericho through Samaria and Ephraim, His brethren in the caravan. For "Jews" and "Pharisees" substitute "Herod." Erase "temple."

(i) The journey. Jn. vii. 11 f. *Where is he? . . . He is a good man. Not so, but he leadeth the multitude astray. Howbeit no man spake openly for fear. . . .* xi. 56. *What think ye? Will he not come up for the feast? . . .*

(ii) First day. vii. 31. *Many believed on him; and they said, When the Christ shall come, will he do more signs than this man hath done? . . .* 40. *This is of truth the prophet. This is the Christ.* 20. *Thou hast a devil who seeketh to kill thee?* viii. 48. *Say we not well that thou art a Samaritan and hast a devil?* ix. 16. *This man is not from God because he keepeth not the sabbath. How can a man which is a sinner do such signs?* x. 20. *He hath a devil and is mad: why hear ye him? These are not the sayings of a man possessed with a devil. Can a devil open the eyes of the blind?*

(iii) Second day. A. vii. 14 f. . . . *The Jews therefore marvelled* (cf. Mk. xi. 20) *saying, How knoweth this man letters having never learned?* B. 25. *Is not this he whom they seek to kill?*

And lo he speaketh openly, and they say nothing. Can it be that the rulers indeed know that this is the Christ? Howbeit we know whence he is: but when the Christ cometh, no one knoweth whence he is. 41 f. *What doth the Christ come out of Galilee? (and not) . . . of David and from Bethlehem?*

A is connected with the second day by *in the midst of the feast.* We learn from Mk. xii. 35 f. that the objection stated in B had been suggested by the scribes.

§ 360. Our discussion of the temple matter in Jn has been of value in several ways. (i) It has confirmed our view that S. John commented on X and (ii) that Matt. xxi. 15–16 derives from XM. (iii) It has been shewn that the editor of Jn misplaces the narrative of the Cleansing which was used by S. Mark. (iv) Jn confirms our arguments at a vital point, the chronology. (*a*) In X *sub* Jn the healings were on the sabbath (v. 9, vii. 23, ix. 14) and on the day of the Cleansing. (*b*) X narrated a departure from the temple on that day.

§ 361. The most thorough discussion of the Pericope Adulteræ is McLachlan's (S. Luke . . . 257–282). His exhaustive study of the wording shews that it must be attributed to S. Luke, and that the Ferrar group is almost right in inserting it at the end of Lk. xxi. On the other hand McLachlan completely fails to account for its omission. If then the Pericope is Lukan it must derive from an earlier recension of Lk. Moreover the insertion of the Pericope in our Lk would involve changes greater than those which would have been required if it had been excised.

The Pericope is connected with the Last Visit as follows:
(i) We compare:

Mk. xii. 14. A statement of the case prefaced by *Master*.	*that they might catch him.*
xii. 18. A statement of the case prefaced by *Master*.	
Pericope. A statement of the case prefaced by *Master*.	*tempting him that they might have whereof to accuse him.*

(ii) We are especially concerned with the following contacts:

Peric. *And they went every man to his own house, but Jesus went into the Mount of Olives.*	In Matt, Mk and Jn Jesus left the city on the evening of the Cleansing.	LLk. xxi. 37. *Every night he went out . . . Olives.*
And early in the morning he came again to the temple.	Mk. xi. 20. *In the morning* Christ returned to the temple.	38. *And early*
And all the people came unto him.		*all the people came to him.*

§ 362. X was written from the standpoint of one of the pilgrims who accompanied Christ from Galilee, and it narrated the goings to and from the bivouac on Olivet and, later, to and from the upper room. The following fragments of this scheme survive. We will reckon backwards from the passover using Jewish days and enumeration. 9th. the Entry. 8th *sub* Mk. xi. 11. *In the evening he went out to Olivet.* 12. *morning* (GMk. *morrow*). 7th, Peric. *to the M of Olives.* Mk. xi. 19. *When it was evening he went forth out of the city* (so Matt and Jn), Peric. Mk. xi. 20. *in the morning.* 6th. Reconstructed Mk. *went out to Bethany* (so Jn. xii. 1). 5th–3rd. Lk. xxi. 37 f. *Every night . . . in the morning.* 2nd, Mk. xiv. 26. *they went out to the M of Olives.* Mk. xv. 1. *in the morning.* Lk. xxiii. 54. *the sabbath drew on.* Mk, Lk, Jn. *early.* Jn. xx. 19. *when it was evening.*

All the authorities for the Pericope except the Ferrar group place it after Jn. vii. The interpolator recognised the fragment of X which narrated the meeting of the Sanhedrin which preceded the departure with which the Pericope begins. The fact that the excerpt begins with the beginning of a Jewish day suggests that the excerptor was a Jew.

Our prolonged enquiry has shewn that all our documents derive from a document in which Christ's comings and goings in the evenings and mornings of the Last Visit were carefully recorded and in which the Cleansing was on the sabbath and the eighth Jewish day before the passover, the departure mentioned in the Pericope on the seventh and the Anointing on the sixth. The Adulteress therefore was forgiven on the morning of the Anointing (Jn. xii. 1).

§ 363. Our chronological results bear directly on the problem of the Anointings. X, whose interest in women was one of its outstanding characteristics, would be likely to tell its readers what the modern reader desires to know, the effect of Christ's refusal to condemn her on the woman. On the other hand we have concluded that the Anointing presupposes an earlier narrative of forgiveness. Inasmuch then as both events occurred on the same day and in the same city we may without hesitation identify the two women, and the cohesion of the two narratives may be regarded as confirming the main positions adopted in the course of our discussion.

Both the strength of the cohesion and its value for the critic will be augmented if we return once more to the evidence of the apocrypha. The following passages prove that Leucius narrated the incident of the Adulteress.

AB. HE, III. xxxix. 17. A. (Papias narrated) *another story about a woman who was accused of many sins before the Lord.* B. *which the Gospel of the Hebrews contains.* *Many sins* is evidence that there was a variant version of the Adulteress, an inference which is confirmed by C.

C. The Eçmiadzin codex (Conybeare, Expositor, 1895, 406) has the narrative in the following form: *A certain woman was taken in sins* (pl) *against whom all bore witness that she was worthy of death . . . to see what he would command. . . . He bowing his head was writing . . . to declare their sins; and they were seeing their sins in the stones. . . . Go in peace and present the offering for sins as it is written.* The allusion to Ariston after Mk. xvi. 8 in this MS. is a link with Papias. The variations are in the manner of Leucius, especially the senseless phrase, *seeing the sins in the stones.*

D. According to Lake (Stud. Bibl. ii. 173) an Athos MS. states that the incident occurred in EvT. This settles the question of the source.

E. In RobEvvC, 30 Christ writes on a penny. This incident in the manner of Leucius combines the Tribute Money and the Adulteress. It suggests that Leucius found them both in the same context.

In this matter there is a phrase of the first importance. Leucius must have read the words *this woman hath been taken in adultery in the very act*. Why then did he write *many sins*? It can only be because in the sequel Christ said, *her sins which are many*.

§ 364. There are two difficulties about which something must be said.

(i) We have not yet accounted for Simon's rudeness to his guest, a rudeness which in the east would be regarded as justifiable only by most exceptional circumstances. The solution is suggested by the words of the Pericope, *tempting him that they might have whereof to accuse him*. The high priests were afraid of the people and much depended on the Pharisees who were divided as they were a few months later. There were among them men of the type of Nicodemus and Gamaliel, and Simon impressed by the unexpected success of the Nazarene prophet on the day of the Cleansing was inclined to throw in his lot with them and invited Jesus to meet some of his friends the next evening. But the arrest of the Adulteress gave Christ's enemies their opportunity. They had brought her to the Winebibber on the off chance that He might be mad enough to give colour to the scandalous stories told about His attitude to such people. It was no temptation to Christ to think of Himself, but the question arose whether for the sake of His disciples and His people He must not avoid misunderstanding. He pondered and played with His fingers with the dust as He sat on the temple floor. He concluded that He would leave questions of policy in the hands of God, and, if possible, save the woman who stood before Him. Simon, who at once heard a hostile version of what had happened, concluded that he had made a fool of himself and received his guest with studied discourtesy. Jesus, who had known what His refusal to condemn the sinner might involve, saw that the tide had turned against Him and, when she anointed Him, said that she had done it for His burial.

§ 365. (ii) The treatment of X in Mk and Lk is very remarkable. Neither Gospel refers to the fact that the Anointer had that morning been convicted of adultery and forgiven by Christ. Mk only states that a woman anointed Christ's feet and this with a view to her exaltation. Lk omits the narrative of the forgiveness which he had recorded in protoLk and this though the omission made his narrative unintelligible and compelled him to compose a substitute and insert it in the wrong place. Both evangelists are concealing the identity of the Anointer, and S. Mark is for some reason commending her to his readers at Cæsarea, with whom he connects the incident by the words, *wheresoever the Gospel shall be preached throughout the whole world.* The converts at Cæsarea were the firstfruits of the gentiles.

The last fact gives us our clue. Like Alexander and Rufus the Anointer had visited Cæsarea. KP mentioned the wife of Theophilus, and there is an indication that she was a Jewess. The Anointer therefore was known to her. Proto-Lk had not been written for Theophilus, and when S. Luke rewrote his Gospel he concealed the identity of his Anointer by moving the incident. But it is interesting to observe the point at which he inserted the narrative. He could have placed it anywhere in LLk. vi. 20–viii. 3, ix. 57–xviii. 14. It can hardly be an accident that he places the incident immediately before the list of women who accompanied Christ when he *went about through cities and villages.* S. Mark used that phrase of S. Peter's evangelisation of the eastern Judæa (*e.g. sub* I Clem. 42), because the apostle had adopted his Master's methods.

We now recall the fact that in QPl the chaste harlot accompanied John and Thomas to Cæsarea and stayed in the hospice. Leucius either found the identification in one of the papers which preserved S. John's midrashim or learnt from X the name of the Anointer and from KP the name of the companion.

§ 366. The subjoined table states some of the more important contacts of the sources which we have used.

	Matt	Mk	Lk	Jn	Notes
The Cleansing		Mk		Jn	
The paralytic and blind man healed	Matt			Jn	the gloss at Jn. v. 4
On the sabbath				Jn. v., ix. (xii.)	
The departure	Matt	Mk		Jn	Pericope
The discussion as to David's son		Mk		Jn	
The answer to the Sadducees		Mk	Lk		
The forgiveness			(Lk)		QPl Pericope
Six days before the passover		(Mk)		Jn	
Simon		Mk	Lk		
The Pharisee			Lk		QPl
Alabastron of myrrh		Mk	Lk		
Anointing		Mk	Lk	Jn	QPl
Feet ... wiped with her hair			Lk	Jn	
Many sins			Lk		QPl
Disciples present	Matt			Jn	?QPl
Allusion to burial		Mk		Jn	
The midrash of S. John				Jn	QPl
The summary			Lk		Cf. Matt and Pericope
Judas and Satan			Lk	Jn	

V. The Vine and the Seed

§ 367. The influence of QPl on Papias which was illustrated in the last will be confirmed in this section and also in the next chapter.

In c. Haer. V. xxxiii. Irenæus writes: *The elders, who saw John the disciple of the Lord relate, relate that they heard from him how the Lord used to teach concerning those times (the times of the kingdom) and to say: The days will come in which vines shall grow, and on each 10,000 branches, and on each branch 10,000 twigs, and on each twig 10,000 clusters, and in each cluster 10,000 grapes, and each grape when pressed shall yield 25 measures of wine. And when any of the saints shall have taken hold of one of the clusters, another shall cry: I am a better cluster; bless the Lord through me. Likewise also a grain of wheat shall produce* 10,000 *heads, and every head shall have* 10,000 *grains, and each grain* 10 *pounds of fine flour, and the other fruits seeds and the grass shall produce in similar proportions, and all the animals . . . shall become peaceable and harmonious. . . . To these things Papias who was a hearer of John and a companion of Polycarp . . . adds his testimony in writing in the fourth of his books. . . . And he added saying: But these things are credible to them that believe. And when Judas the traitor did not believe and asked, how such growths would be accomplished by the Lord, he relates that the Lord said: They shall see who come to these times.* Another version of our passage of Papias survives in Hippol. in Dan. iv. 20: *Judas astounded by what was said by Christ said to Him, And who shall see these things? The Lord said, they shall see who have become worthy* (Zahn Forsch. vi. 128 f.).

That this matter occurred in QPl is shewn by ApPl, 22 (J, 537) where miraculous fruit grown on 10,000 branches is given to the worthy and by CEncJB, 348 f. where there are the 10,000 clusters and 10,000 grains in each ear and Christ replies to Thomas, *Blessed is everyone who shall be worthy to inherit these things.* For the derivation of these apocalypses from QPl see § 161.

There are also the following links between our matter and Leucius. (*a*) In EvT, 12 Jesus sows a core of wheat and it makes an hundred cores. The miracle of EvT is imitated by Simon in R. ii. 9, and we learn from this passage that in the original form of the Gospel fruit was multiplied as well as corn. (*b*) The millennial vine is from Baruch, and Baruch influenced QPl. In QPl *sub* LMatt, 100 there was an allusion to the nine and an half tribes, a phrase which occurs in Apoc. Bar. 78. Like Baruch (55) the apostles rest under the trees when they enter Paradise (EPl, 661) (cf. LAB, 12) as does Zosimus in NZos, 3, a context parallel with ApPl, 24. It may be suspected that Leucius derived his Baruch matter from J.

§ 368. Our discussion has probably confirmed the reader in the view which is generally held that Papias attributed to

S. John what he never said. But there is another side to the
matter. Eusebius says that Papias at any rate claimed to be
himself a hearer of S. John and Ariston. He did not, that
is, depend entirely on informants. Now after our passage
Irenæus describes Papias as a hearer of John and says that
he added his testimony. He had himself heard the matter
which Leucius used in QP1. Further, Leucius on our view
was acquainted with the Lycus valley and may have heard
S. John preach there, and it has been shewn that he was
acquainted with S. John's oral teaching. Our problem,
therefore, is acute and it is no more than reduced by the
fact that Papias copied QP1 and did not give his own
recollections of the sermon : indeed they may have been
quite vague.

Our problem is solved if we adopt the very natural
hypothesis that Leucius expanded S. John's text and
abbreviated the sermon. Now the sermon survives.
Jn. xii. 4 preserves teaching of John in which he represents
Christ as transmuting the Baruch apocalyptic in words
which seem to be based on Christ's: *Except a corn of wheat
fall into the ground and die, it abideth alone; but, if it die, it
bringeth forth much fruit*, and in xv. 4 he uses the phrase
much fruit in connection with the vine. Christ who said,
He that hath ears to hear let him hear (Matt. xi. 13) may also
have said, He that hath eyes to see shall see. Papias was
right in his impression that John's sermon was based on
Christ's words.

§ 369. Leucius spiritualised the apocalyptic of Baruch
and Cerinthus on the same lines as S. John. Though
he described the apostolic eucharist as celebrated with bread
and water he made the apostles *eat and drink with Him
at the table of His kingdom* when they were caught up to
heaven at the time of supposed Crucifixion (§ 102). So in
Rev. ii. 7, 17 Christ is the tree of life and the manna of the
heavenly banquet. That S. John's midrashim underlie
Rev. ii., iii. is shewn by iii. 21, a verse which is as certainly a
fragment of S. John's teaching as anything in the Fourth
Gospel.

The identification of Christ with the cross which we have attributed to QPl postulates as Johannine the equation Christ = vine = tree of life = cross (J, 165). This equation underlies CBRB (Lacau: J, 182) where Christ when supposed to be dead embraces Ananias and calls him *the firstfruits of the immortal fruit*. So Andrew in MA, II (J, 359) says, *O cross planted in the earth and bearing fruit in the heavens . . . thou that . . . didst bear the thief as a fruit*, and in Or. Sib. v. 257 we read, *the Man from the sky stretched out His hands on a very fruitful vine*. The same usage occurs in Ign. Sm. 1 where Ignatius is probably influenced by QPl *of which fruits are ye, that is of His . . . passion* and in Trall. 11, *branches of the cross, and their fruit imperishable*.

The identification of the cross with the vine which bore much fruit would clearly be in a line with S. John's thought and in his manner. Moreover, there is the positive evidence of Rev. ii. 7 where the partaking of the tree of life promised to the Ephesian victor is parallel with donation of the manna to the Pergamene (ii. 17; Jn. vi. 48).

VI. The Dates of the Second and Third Gospels

§ 371. While most of our larger reconstructions do not depend on the strength of one or two keystones, in the actual work of reconstruction one or two clues have been of crucial importance and among them the allusion of R. i. 43 to the return of the apostles for the seventh passover, a passage which enabled us to date the Crucifixion in A.D. 30 and which accounted for the Armenian tradition that Mark wrote in the eighth year. In view of the importance of these dates I will complete in this volume what I have to say about the evidence as to the date of Mk and Lk and about the chronology of Heg.

It is our fundamental position that apart from the citations of Papias in HE, III. xxxix., an allusion of Origen to the place of the writing of Matt and an important AJ narrative of the writing of Jn, all the notices of the Gospels derive ultimately from Heg, who had read Papias and made investigations of his own in the course of his journey. His purpose was to defend the apostolic tradition as it had been maintained by Polycarp against Marcion and other heretics, and he was as much concerned with documents as with the episcopal successions. He held that both lines of investigation led the enquirer to the same result (HE, IV. xxiv. 3).

The evidence of Heg as to Mk is ultimately that of KP, and of the highest value. PsMark, or, possibly, his informant had visited Jerusalem and Cæsarea and collected traditions about the evangelist. He had no motive for falsifying history at this point, and no fictitious matter can be attributed to his Cæsarea narrative. PsMark was a younger contemporary of S. Mark and Theophilus, and the evidence which brings Mark to Cæsarea is Markan.

§ 372. I. On our view the evidence of Heg was best preserved by Hippolytus in his Heads against Gaius, and in § 287 this evidence was shewn to underlie the Armenian colophons which according to Conybeare date from the fifth century (Expositor, V. ii. 419: § 287). They state that

Matt. was written in Jerusalem in Hebrew in the eighth year of the Ascension at the request of the church.

Mk. was written at Alexandria in Egyptian in the fifteenth year at the command of Peter.

Lk. was written at Antioch in Syria at the command of Paul in the seventeenth year.

Jn. was written in the fifty-third year at the request of the church.

§ 373. Further, according to Conybeare it was the normal Armenian tradition that Lk and Mk were written in Syriac (*i.e.* in Syria). But Conybeare, to whom I am indebted for my acquaintance with Vartan's Solutiones, failed to observe that it contains both the Armenian traditions as to the origin of Mk. Vartan says that according to some Mark wrote in the eighth year and according to others in the fifteenth.

Our attribution of this matter to the Heads against Gaius is confirmed when we turn to a context of Epiphanius which was influenced by that work (§ 287). In Haer. li. 11 we find three important contacts with it. (i) Mark is said to have written immediately after Matt, *i.e.* in the eighth year but at Rome, *i.e.* in the fifteenth year. The blunder is probably due to Epiphanius, but we shall attribute the same combination of the two traditions to Clement. (ii) The statement that after writing it Mark was sent to Egypt explains that of the colophons that he wrote there. (iii) As in the colophons Mark writes at the apostle's bidding.

My next point is that Hippolytus used Heg. (*a*) The fifteenth year is Heg's date for Peter's departure from Rome. (*b*) The eighth year was Heg's date for the departure of Matthew from Jerusalem (§ 181 D) and the return of Peter from Cæsarea. (*c*) *Antioch in Syria* in view of the immense importance of the city is a strange phrase. We have found that Heg used it (§ 224 (5)). (*d*) We have concluded that Heg identified S. Luke with the Leucius of Acts xiii. (*e*) We have already concluded that Hippolytus intended to date Jn as Heg did (§ 287). (*f*) We shall conclude that Hippolytus *sub* Epiph. li. had other contacts with Heg.

II. Cadbury cites from Conybeare (III. 416) Ephrem Syrus (cent. iv.) for the following comment on Ac. xii. 25, xiii. 1: *Saul and Barnabas . . . returned with John who was called Mark and so did Luke of Cyrene. But both these are evangelists and wrote before the (i.e.* their) *discipleship of Paul, and therefore he used to repeat everywhere from their Gospel.* The Abgar Acts and AT shew that there was a copy of Heg at Edessa.

§ 374. III. Origen who may be dependent upon Hippolytus provides the following evidence:

A. In HE, VI. xxv. he says that Matt was prepared for converts from Judaism and published in Hebrew, that Mark wrote in accordance with Peter's instructions, that Luke whose praise is in his Gospel wrote for Paul's converts and that Jn was the last to be written.

B. In Hist. Patr. i. 172 he writes: The books of the N.T.

are these: *the Gospel of Matt which he wrote in Hebrew on a roll when he was in Cæsarea in the house of a man whose descendants preserve it from generation to generation and was translated into Greek and rendered into all languages by the power of the Lord Christ* (does the editor paraphrase a sentence based on the statement of Papias that everyone interpreted as he was able?); *then the Gospel of Mark which he wrote in Greek, while Peter the chief of the apostles was with them and which was read in the assembly of princes; then the Gospel of Luke, the disciple of Paul, which he wrote in Greek at Antioch; then the Gospel of John the son of Zebedee whom his disciples after he had grown old frequently solicited at Ephesus.*

The notice of Matt shews that our fragment was written after Origen's arrival at Cæsarea. It confirms our view that Matthew resided for a time at Cæsarea and, inasmuch as Origen must have examined the MS., that EvH was a recension of our Matt. Mk is the only Gospel the destination of which is not given. We may suspect that like Hippolytus Origen was acquainted with both traditions. The "assembly of princes," however, must be the gathering of magistrates to whom the apostle preached in the various recensions of the Cæsarea narrative (*e.g.* in LJasZ, 33). Origen's notice of Lk agrees with the colophons and Ephrem. The statement that John wrote when he was old is parallel with Epiph. li. 12.

§ 375. IV. It was shewn in § 333 that though Clement states that Mark wrote at Rome his narrative of the writing of The Gospel is Cæsarean. It may be added that his phrase *in the presence of certain Cæsarian* (imperial) *knights* is parallel with the Arabic paraphrase of Origen. Inasmuch as the introduction to the narrative dates Peter's journey to Rome under Claudius it would appear that Clement like Epiphanius combines the alternative destinations. His narrative survives in HE, II. xiv. f., VI. xiv. and the Latin abbreviation. They may be combined thus:
A. II. *in the reign of Claudius . . . Peter preached at Rome.*
B. (Lat.) *in the presence of certain Cæsarian knights adducing*

many testimonies to Christ. C. II. *His hearers were not content to hear him just once and with the unwritten preaching . . . but with all kinds of entreaties besought Mark.* D. VI. *as one who had followed him for a long time and remembered what was spoken to leave a record. . . .* E. II. *Now it is said that when the apostle by a revelation of the Spirit learnt what was done he was pleased with their zeal* (F) *and authorised the book for publication in the churches. . . .* G. VI. *When the matter came to Peter's knowledge he neither strictly forbad it or urged it forward.* H. Eus. *Clement has given this story in Hytyp.* VI. J. *and Papias adds his testimony.* K. *And* (it is said) *that* (the Mark and Babylon of 1 Peter were the evangelist and Rome).

Inasmuch as the allusion to Papias may refer merely to parallels occurring in III. xxxix. it carries us no further. But G, a sentence which has no parallel and must be contrasted with F, has received far too little attention. In view of the fact that KP made Peter responsible for the writing of the Gospel and that there was from the time of Papias onwards a tendency to connect the Gospels as closely as possible with the apostles, the statement that Peter had nothing to do with the matter may be safely regarded as S. John's correction of KP. We learn from it that Mk was not written after S. Peter's death. We also infer that he had left the city where S. Mark wrote and gone to some other place at no great distance and did not return for several months. The statement tallies precisely with the probabilities if Cæsarea was the destination of Mk. E looks like an attempt of Heg to reconcile F with G. A point remains to be added about B. The word *certain* suggests that Clement had information as to knights which he does not give. If the narrative was originally Cæsarean they were Marcellus Cornelius and their friends, but if it were Roman Clement refers to an incident which must have interested the apocryphists who quarried from Heg and other writers and of which no trace remains in Christian literature. VP, 23, 24 must not be adduced.

Except in his allusion to Papias Eusebius probably bases his narrative on Clement throughout xiv., xv., xvii. 2. He elsewhere begins to use an author before he cites him and continues to use him after the citation. The fact that the Latin shews that Clement was commenting on 1 Pet. v. 13 shews that Eusebius resumes the use of Clement in K. Clement then like Hippolytus stated both the Claudian date and S. Mark's journey to Egypt. Both writers presumably used Heg *sub* Hist. Patr. i. 131 f., where S. Mark goes to Egypt in the 15th year.

§ 376. V. Papias tells us that Mark who had become (or had been) Peter's interpreter wrote accurately all that he recalled. . . . The point is that Mark remembered accurately what he had heard and interpreted in the past. If the fact of the interpretation is recorded merely for its own sake and has no connection in the mind of Papias with the fact that Mark wrote accurately, either thirty years or thirty days may have elapsed before Mark wrote what he had heard. But this view of the passage may be safely dismissed. Papias who is citing the elder at second- or third-hand does not give us the context of the elder's remark and uses his words to shew what they do not shew, that Mark *kept a single aim in view, not to omit anything of what he heard, nor to state anything inaccurately.* Nothing can be clearer than that the statement that Mark was (*or* had been) Peter's interpreter is connected with the statement that he wrote accurately. Now it is probable that Papias gave a wider application to the elder's words than he was justified in doing, but there is no reason to suppose that he was intentionally misleading his readers, and he would be seriously misleading them if he knew that Mark wrote after an interval of twenty or even ten years. We learn then from Papias that Mark wrote at a time when Peter could not preach in Greek. Peter was an able man who had been brought up in a bilingual district. Probably some of the men who bought his fish could only speak Greek. He is likely to have had a smattering of Greek before he became a disciple. At Jerusalem many of his friends could speak Greek. The baptism of gentiles at Cæsarea must have led him to feel that he ought to increase his knowledge of the language, and the rapid progress of the faith in Syria would be another motive. It is highly improbable that he could not preach in Greek when he made his journey of the twelfth year. Our interpretation of Papias involves the Cæsarean destination of Mk. It must be added that in such a context as that with which we are concerned it is natural to translate "Mark who had become Peter's interpreter." On this view the view which I have urged is almost self-evident. Lastly in §§ 209, 334 f. we concluded that Leucius and psClement independently connected the tradition that Mark interpreted Peter with the apostle's preaching at Cæsarea.

§ 377. It remains that we should examine two small splinters which may be interpreted to mean that S. Mark wrote after S. Peter's death and that we should if possible account for the view that he wrote in the fifteenth year. The former date conflicts with the whole of the evidence which we have examined, and the latter is obviously unhistorical.

VI. Irenæus writes: *Matthew published a written gospel among the Hebrews in their own dialect, Peter and Paul preaching at Rome and laying the foundations of the church. After their departure Mark also, the disciple and companion of Peter, has also himself handed down in writing the things preached by Peter. And Luke, the follower of Paul, embodied in a book the gospel preached by that apostle. Then John. . . . (III. i. 1.)*

Irenæus is not in the least concerned with our problem but only with the fact that two apostles wrote their own preaching and that two competent disciples had preserved the preaching of Peter and Paul. The passage is the beginning of a context which is based on Heg whose matter Irenæus abbreviates so clumsily that, when using the tradition that Matthew wrote before his departure from Jerusalem,[1] he actually makes him write at the time when Peter and Paul were founding the church of Rome. If Irenæus is read apart from the other evidence it is natural to interpret "departures" as meaning "deaths" and, if the sentence is pressed in a manner in which it clearly ought not to be pressed, Irenæus may be understood to affirm that

[1] See *e.g.* LM, 110 (an Acts based throughout on Heg). *Matthew (in) . . . Jerusalem wrote . . . in Hebrew . . ., and he went to Parthica.*

Mark wrote after Peter's decease. But if that was the intention why did Irenæus add *and Paul*? If it was because he had Lk in view we must infer that, just as Irenæus only affirmed that Paul's preaching survived, so he only affirmed the survival of Peter's. He was no more concerned with the dates of Mk and Lk than with that of Matt. The statement that Jn wrote last is almost invariable in the notices which derive from Heg.

VII. The old Latin *argumentum*, which is best studied in Rév. Bénéd., 1928, 196, runs: *Mark the stump-fingered was the interpreter of Peter. He wrote after the apostle's departure in the parts of Italy.* "Stump-fingered" occurs in Hipp. Ref. vii. 30 and shews that the *argumentum* derives from Hippolytus, who may have merely reproduced our passage of Irenæus. It definitely implies that Mark did not write at Rome and suggests that he wrote somewhere else in Italy after the apostle's departure from Rome, the word *exitus* being chosen because ἐξόδους occurred in the source.

§ 378. It is entirely impermissible to set the obscure evidence of Irenæus and the *argumentum* against the rest of the evidence, and moreover if a very plausible account of its origin is accepted, it is of no value. The parallels which are printed below seem to prove that Hegesippus *sub* Iren. III. 1.1 was using a writer who said that after the departures (deaths) of Peter and Paul Mark wrote at Rome the work referred to in 2 Pet. i. 15, *i.e.* K.P. Heg, who knew that S. Mark wrote before the death of S. Peter, *sub* Iren. III. iii. 3, interpreted " departure " as referring to the apostle's departure from Rome after he had founded the church of Rome in the fifteenth year (§ 207 B). He may have been using Justin's Syntagma. Justin made large use of KP, and there are possible traces of his Syntagma in Iren. III. Praef. and HE, II. xiii. 6 f. Irenæus speaks of *the refutation of all the heretics*, a task which he did not undertake, and the phrase is likely to have been suggested by the title of Justin's work (Ap. i. 26).

All matter in the parallels which is assigned to KP is italicised. It will be observed that our KP matter contains parallels with LEMk.

1 Clem. 42	Arist.	Just. Apol. i.
The apostles are from Christ . . . through the Resurrection.	He ascended	50. They when they had seen him ascending . . . *received power*
[with full assurance of the Holy Ghost]		
They ordained their firstfruits		
	The twelve *went forth into the . . . world*	45. *They went forth . . . preaching everywhere.* (Cf. 50.)
confirmed in the word . . . with full assurance of the Holy Ghost 44. having received complete foreknowledge.	(Arm.? Arist.) *miracles* accompanying them.	
		2 Pet. i. 15. That ye may be able *after my decease to call these things to remembrance.*

Tert. de Praescr. 20 f.	Iren. III. i. 1	Lact. iv. 23
They obtained the *power of the Holy Ghost* for the gift of *miracles* (Cf. Mk. xvi. 18.)	After our Lord rose from the dead the apostles were invested with *power* from on high. (So Dem. 41.)	Epit. 47. Having arranged for the preaching He *breathed on them* the Holy Spirit and gave them *the power of working miracles*. iv. 23. *A cloud* suddenly *surrounded Him* and carried Him up into heaven. . . . At His departure He endued them with *power*. De M. Pers. 7. *A cloud* enveloped Him and caught Him up.
After first witnessing throughout Judæa and founding churches there *they went forth into the world*.	(Dem. 41. They established churches.) *They departed* to the ends of the earth. (Dem. Were sent into all the world.)	They being dispersed through the provinces *everywhere* laid the foundation of the church, (So de M. Pers. 2.) *doing miracles by which their . . . new doctrine might be confirmed*. He also opened all things which were about to happen.
They *founded* other churches.	*Peter and Paul preaching at Rome and laying the foundation* of the church. Mark has handed down *in writing after their decease*, the things *preached* by Peter.	*Peter and Paul preached at Rome*. Cf. above " *laid the foundation*." This *preaching was written* for the sake of *remembrance after their decease*.

We conclude that in a passage which underlay Heg *sub* Iren. III. i. and which must have occurred in his preface the writer of KP, using Mk and claiming to be Mark said that the apostles received at the Ascension the power of the Holy Ghost by which after founding Churches in Judæa they went forth and preached everywhere, the preaching being confirmed by miracles, and that in order that Peter's preaching might be kept in remembrance after his decease the apostle bade him write it. PsMark then cited the letter which contained the injunction (§ 244).

§ 378*a*. VIII. The elder of Papias and QP *sub* Clement (§ 333 D) agreed in the statement that Mark recorded Peter's preaching. Now, unless the sermons of Acts, the epistles and the subapostolic writers completely mislead us, it is very improbable that more than a tithe of the incidents recorded in Mk found their way into the preaching of the apostles. It is true that on our view Gospels were read at Ephesus at the end of the first century and S. John discoursed on X, but this fact does not reduce the extreme improbability of the position that Mk or any other Gospel was based on preaching. Indeed, if our criticism is justified, Jn confirms our position, for it only contains a single reminiscence, the correction of Mk at a very vital point, the visit of the apostles to the Sepulchre. S. Luke did not write to help the memory of Theophilus but to confirm his faith. There is no evidence which is of any value that S. Peter preached at Rome, a fact which is in itself of interest, and, if he did preach there, it is in the highest degree improbable that Mk preserves his sermons. The whole of the evidence indicates that the apostles did not tell their hearers stories of the Ministry.

We only know of one occasion on which an apostle is said to have narrated Christ's career, and that is the only occasion on which it is likely to have been narrated at any length. Marcellus was not only a man who was weighing Christ's claims upon his discipleship, he was a procurator who was being asked to discredit a verdict of his predecessor's and was hearing evidence. Moreover Pilate's condemnation of

Jesus was one of the few incidents which had occurred in his
tenure of office which had won the approval of the leaders
of the Jews.   Again, Marcellus must have known from what
Tobias and others told him that Jesus had been associated
with John, whom Antipas had beheaded as a dangerous and
seditious demagogue.   Peter therefore, as we learn from
Ac. x. and xiii., gave an account of the preaching of John.
In the conversations which followed the sermon the procurator must have asked the apostle to tell him the whole
story, and it was obviously important that he should have it in
written form.   Mark therefore, who had heard the sermon,
did not summarise it, as he did in I Ac. Mc., but wrote a
recension of X, a work which was largely based on S. Peter's
reminiscences.   He omitted much matter which was obviously
irrelevant from the point of view of a procurator, preserved
no discourse and devoted a third of his space to the last days.

Our reconstruction accounts for the traditions as to the
origin of Mk, and it is difficult to imagine any other circumstances under which the apostle could have preached which
would have given rise to the tradition.

We conclude that according to Heg Mk was written in
the eighth year (A.D. 37) or in the fifteenth and that the
latter date rests upon a misunderstanding of an earlier
writer who referred to the writing of KP.   Cf. p. 144.

§ 379. The priorities of Mk are as follows :

(i) Mk on our view was prior to JMk, JMk to GMk; and
GMk was used by S. Luke according to Hippolytus in
A.D. 47, a date which we shall confirm from the internal
evidence of Lk.

(ii) Mk and I Ac. Mc. overlapped but were virtually the
first and second volumes of a single work.   The latter was
a constructive apology for S. Peter's missionary activities
and must have been published immediately after the last
event which it recorded, the meeting of the church which
followed S. Peter's return from Cæsarea, just as the publication of II Ac. Mc. must have immediately followed the
apostolic council.

(iii) Before I argue that Mk influences 1 Corinthians and

Romans, two epistles which were written about the same
time and throw light on each other, something must be said
as to the antecedent probabilities. (a) We have already
found some ground for thinking that the Corinthians were
acquainted with I Ac. Mc., a position which will be confirmed. Now if this is the case they are likely to have
known the companion volume. (b) Hawkins, a most
cautious writer, held that there were numerous instances
in which the Gospels influenced the epistles (Hor. Syn. 196).
He has no discussion of the matter, but he finds almost
certain allusions to LLk. vi. 28 in 1 Cor. iv. 12 and Rom.
xii. 14 and to LLk. x. 39 f. in 1 Cor. vii. 35. Inasmuch as
the incident of Mary and Martha in our view occurred
both in X and protoLk the position of Hawkins has no
direct bearing on the date of Mk. It affects however the
antecedent probabilities with which we are now concerned,
and it is worth while to state the case. In 25 S. Paul says
that he cannot support his position from Christ's sayings,
but in 35 he refers to the fact that Mary sat at Christ's feet
but Martha was encumbered by serving. S. Paul says
that the unmarried woman cares for the things of the
Lord and her position may be that of one who sits at His
feet without encumbrance. Ευπάρεδρον may have been
coined by the apostle and απερισπάστως is rare.

§ 380. (a) In 1 Cor. xi. 23 f. He writes *I delivered unto you
that which I on my part received*, the phrase which he uses in
xv. 3 before giving the list of Appearances which we attributed
to a document. His parallelism with Mk is as follows:

He took bread;	Mk. xiv. 22. *He took bread,*
and when he had given thanks,	*and when he had blessed it,*
he brake it	*he brake it,*
	and gave to them.
And he said, This is my body	*And he said, This is my body.*
which is in your behalf.	
This do in remembrance of me.	
In like manner also the cup	*And he took a cup and when*
	he had given thanks. . . .
after supper	
This cup is the new covenant	*This is my blood of the covenant.*
in my blood.	

The parallelism cannot be explained away as due to a liturgical tradition. Moreover the later use may be due to S. Paul and 1 Cor., an epistle which had great influence from the first. Further, the words *in the night that he was being betrayed* are more likely to recall the historical tradition than the rite.

(*b*) In Rom. xiii. 1–7 S. Paul concludes his argument for loyalty to Cæsar with words which recall Mk. xii. 17,

7. *Render to all their dues: tribute to whom tribute is due. . . .*	Mk. xii. 17. *Render unto Cæsar the things that are Cæsar's, and unto God the things that are God's.*
6. *They are ministers of God. . . .*	
He that loveth his neighbour hath fulfilled the law. For this, thou shalt not commit adultery, etc.	31 *Thou shalt love thy neighbour as thyself. There is none other commandment greater than these.*

(*c*) Feine has argued for the influence of the Question of the Sadducees (Mk. xii. 18 f.) on 1 Cor. xv. I cite Simpson (*Res. and Mod. Thought*, 337): " If our Lord says, ' ye therefore greatly err ' S. Paul says, ' be not deceived.' If Mk speaks of ' Sadducees which say that there is no resurrection ' S. Paul says, ' how say some among you that there is no resurrection ? ' If our Lord says, ' ye know not . . . the power of God ' S. Paul says, ' some have not the knowledge of God.' ' We shall bear the image of the heavenly ' is parallel with ' they are as angels in heaven.' "

If these three groups of parallels with Christ's teaching derive from a Gospel, they must be presumed to derive from the same Gospel, and if so from Mk, for the question of the lawyer is misplaced in Mk in § 346.

(*d*) With *Abba Father* (Rom. viii. 15) cf. Mk. xiv. 36.

(*e*) Lightfoot says that the coincidences of Col. ii. 22. with Mk. vii. 1 f. suggest the influence of the Gospel (*a*) Both argue against the vexatious ordinances from the imperishableness of meats. (*b*) Both insist that such things are indifferent in themselves. (*c*) Both connect such ordinances with the practices condemned by Isaiah.

§ 381. The internal evidence is as follows :

(i) Mk was written for a Greek-speaking church which had been visited by S. Peter, S. Mark and Alexander and Rufus (Mk. xv. 21). It has been shewn that in a passage which must have been historical KP brought all four disciples to Cæsarea shortly before the writing of the Gospel. S. Mark heard the sermon which S. Peter preached on the career of Jesus, and we have found traces of it in his Gospel.

(ii) A parallel argument may be based on our explanation of S. Mark's eulogy of the Anointer.

(iii) Apart from the interpolated glosses the Gospel gives the impression of being written for Palestinian readers. This is especially noticeable in connection with names. Bartimæus the son of Timæus (xi. 46), " the man known as Barabbas " (xv. 7) and Salome (xv. 40) are also supposed to be known. In view of the part that Pilate (xv. 1) was to play it was important that the reader should know that Pilate was the procurator. Yet he is not told. Contrast Matt. xxvii. 2.

§ 382. The internal evidence confirms the date which Heg assigned to Lk and therefore his date for Mk, for it shews that the Gospel was written before his journey to Palestine.

(i) Lk. v. 19 introduces an allusion to tiles into Mk. ii. 4. When S. Luke visited Palestine he must have noticed that the houses were seldom or never tiled. He altered Mk just because the question of the structure of the roof interested him. If he had visited Palestine the correction would have been impossible.

(ii) There is no tradition anywhere of any other scene of the Ascension than Olivet, and Olivet was the scene in 1 Ac. Mc. *Right up to Bethany in* xxiv. 50 must be due to the fact that X and L stated that Christ led the disciples towards or a sabbath day's journey (Acts i. 12) towards Bethany. Luke remembering that Christ in L twice visited that village mistranslated πρός and with some pride in his acumen added ἕως. He could not have done this after his visit to Jerusalem. The traditional site is a sabbath day's journey from the city *towards* Bethany.

(iii) If, as the linguistic evidence of the Pericope Adulteræ and the arguments of Taylor and Streeter shew is the case, L was the work of Lk, the saying *Father forgive* has the following history. (*a*) It occurred in X. (*b*) Lk preserved it in pLk. (iii) He omitted it in Lk. (iv) He interpolated it into the Markan narrative of Stephen.

I must now assume a later proof that Stephen's speech was strongly antiJudaic and ended with denunciations and the statement that he saw or, more probably, that his hearers would see Jesus descending as Messiah in judgment. The apocryphal evidence is at this point very strong. Further, in Mk. xiv. 62 S. Mark Stephenises X *sub* Lk. xxii. 69, converting a mystical saying into a threat by the additions *ye shall see . . ., coming with clouds*. Now in Acts vii. Lk not only edits out the menacing close of the Markan speech but introduces seven fragments from the pLk Passion and, among them, *Father forgive*.

We are here concerned with the fact that S. Luke in Lk edits in the reverse direction. He not only omits *Father forgive* but adds to the Husbandmen matter from Stephen's speech (xx. 9). Harris (i. 96) rightly points out that the passage derives from his antiJudaic source. Now on other grounds this source must be the Stephen of I and II Ac. Mc. Among these grounds is the fact that the block of testimonies which underlies Lk. xx. 9 underlay KP *sub* VP, 24. Nothing could be more bitterly antiJudaic than the cited words . . . *on whomsoever it* (the stone: *i.e.* Christ) *shall fall, it will scatter him as dust*. In the same spirit in xxi. 20 S. Luke repeats Christ's forecast of the destruction of Jerusalem by Roman armies (xix. 42).

§ 383. On our hypothesis all these facts are intelligible.

(*a*) PLk was probably written at Antioch, and though the first persecution was a recent memory the man who instigated it had become a disciple.

(*b*) If Lk was written on the morrow of the Herodian persecution he would regard Christ's prayer as raising a difficult problem. (*a*) I am about to shew that the disciples

connected Herod's death with the persecution and they
would regard the hierarchy as having even more certainly
deserving of punishment. (β) S. Luke in xxi. 24 used
matter which proves his conviction that the destruction of
Jerusalem foretold by Christ was only delayed by the death
of Gaius.

(c) Shortly before he wrote Acts S. Luke had been long
in S. Paul's company, and we shall find that he made large
use of S. Mark's narratives of Stephen in his account of
the apostle's last visit to Jerusalem. The martyr therefore
was much in his mind. Now Harris (ii. 31) observes that
S. Paul modifies his antiJudaic source, holding that its
statement of the divine anger against Israel was too extreme
for him to endorse. Under the apostle's influence he compensated for the introduction of the Markan Stephen into
Lk by making his Stephen narrative conform to the pLk
Passion, and he also overemphasised the fact that the apostle
was a loyal Jew. S. Luke could not have edited in Lk as he
does if he had written the Gospel after his association with
S. Paul.

(iv) The positive case for the early date of Acts has been
strengthened, and the negative argument against that date
which is based on the priority of Mk has been destroyed.

(v) The dates of Lk and Acts may be connected with the
movements of Theophilus. We have concluded that
Claudius made him a senator, and we have identified him
with the stratopedarch of the western gloss at Acts xxviii. 16.
He had returned to Syria in A.D. 41 and probably remained
there some years before he received his promotion. Presumably S. Luke wrote his Gospel during the first period
in which he was in contact with him and Acts during the
second. Apart from this consideration Theophilus was
procurator in A.D. 37, and this fact makes the late date for
Acts very improbable.

VII. The Date of the Markan Apocalypse

§ 384. In the next volume I shall maintain that the Markan Apocalypse was based on the Ascension narrative of M and that this narrative influenced independently Matt. x., xxiv., Lk. xxi., KP, Rev. vi.-viii. (§ 160). JMark has edited M in Mk. xvi. 14-17. GMark wrote either 5 or 21 f. and 32.

The following data are evidence for the time and place of composition.

A. Nothing more definite can be inferred from Mk. xiii. 7-8, 14-20, 24-26 than that the Messianic woes were supposed to be at hand. Cf. Charles, *Eschatology*, 382.

B. 9-13 shew that a persecution was imminent or had just begun in Palestine.

C. The statement that the preaching of the Gospel to all nations would precede the end (10) shews that there had been a previous period of rapid expansion. It is not suggested that this period was yet complete but that what had been achieved encouraged the hope that the delay would not be long. GMark corrects M *sub* MMatt. x. 23.

D. *The abomination of desolation standing where he ought not* (14) should be paraphrased "another Antiochus" or "another Gaius."

E. *Let them that are in Judæa flee to the mountains* (14). The prophet had advised the church to follow the example set by the sons of Matathias in the days of Antiochus (1 Macc. ii. 28). The sentence confirms our paraphrase of D.

F. *Pray ye that your flight be not in winter* (18) is suggested by the fear lest the flooded wadis would be dangerous to the fugitives. The rains were at hand or the winter ending. Two or three weeks should make all the difference. The practical details had been discussed.

G. The fact that the apocalypse was written in Greek and addressed to the inhabitants of Judæa (14) suggests that the writer lived in a Greek-speaking city on the borders of western Judæa. Cf. Stanton (Gosp. Hist. Doc. ii. 120).

§ 385. B and E suggest that the apocalypse was occasioned by the Herodian persecution. No other known persecution is possible, and we have already concluded that during this persecution five thousand disciples fled to the neighbourhood of Jericho, where if necessary it would be possible to cross the fords of Jordan and to be safe from Herod. Presumably they had followed the prophet's advice. The Herodian persecution broke out at Cæsarea not very long before the passover, *i.e.* before the end of the rainy season. The writer was thinking of a very concrete situation and not of Antichrist. Cf. B.

D is a phrase which the writer retains from the earlier apocalypse. On our hypothesis the second Gaius must have been Herod whose attack on the church would be an attack on the temple of God, a conception which is implicit in the citation of Amos ix. 11 f. by James (Ac. xv. 16 f.) [1] and which was rooted in Christ's teaching (Jn. ii. 19). Our view is supported by the fact that at the date at which the apocalypse was written a story was current among the disciples that like Gaius Herod had been struck down at the very moment that he had accepted divine honours (II Ac. Mc. *sub* Ac. xii. 22 f.), and the story gives added force to S. Paul's words, *whoso destroyeth the temple of God him shall God destroy* (1 Cor. iii. 17). The writer did not of course imply that the phrase applied literally to Herod as it did to Gaius. He retained a convenient and telling cryptogram which the reader would explain.

As regards C it is probably true to say that the expansion of the church during the septennium which followed the death of Stephen was more astonishing than anything which happened later. Almost anything must have seemed possible. We know that ten years later there was an important Christian community at Rome and the fact that S. Paul was contemplating a journey to Spain is evidence that he had grounds for believing that there was an open door there.

[1] This position has just been confirmed in a reconstruction of primitive testimony teaching by Plooj (Studies in the Testimony Book, 14 f.).